CW00924499

THE GARDENS OF MARS

MADAGASCAR, AN ISLAND STORY

THE GARDENS OF MARS
MADAGASCAR, AN ISLAND STORY

JOHN GIMLETTE

An Apollo Book

This is an Apollo book, first published in the UK
in 2021 by Head of Zeus Ltd

Copyright © John Gimlette, 2021

The moral right of John Gimlette to be identified as the author
of this work has been asserted in accordance with the Copyright,
Designs and Patents Act of 1988.

All rights reserved. No part of this publication may be reproduced,
stored in a retrieval system, or transmitted in any form or by any means,
electronic, mechanical, photocopying, recording, or otherwise, without
the prior permission of both the copyright owner and the above
publisher of this book.

9 7 5 3 1 2 4 6 8

A catalogue record for this book is available from the British Library.

ISBN (HB): 9781788544726
ISBN (E): 9781788544719

Typeset and designed by Heather Bowen
Maps by Jeff Edwards

Printed and bound in Spain by Graficas Estella

Head of Zeus Ltd
First Floor East
5–8 Hardwick Street
London EC1R 4RG
WWW.HEADOFZEUS.COM

To Mireille Rabenoro of the Malagasy human rights commission, la Commission Nationale Indépendante des Droits de l'Homme (CNIDH), with thanks for her wise advice, and in recognition of her remarkable courage.

Contents

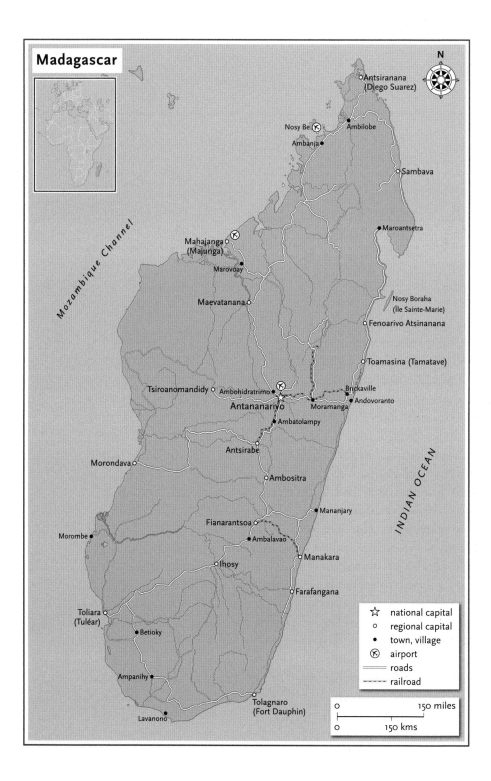

Madagascar

N

Antsiranana
(Diego Suarez)

Nosy Be ✈
Ambilobe

Ambanja

Sambava

Maroantsetra

Mahajanga ✈
(Majunga)

Marovoay

Maevatanana

Nosy Boraha
(Île Sainte-Marie)

Fenoarivo Atsinanana

Toamasina (Tamatave)

Tsiroanomandidy   Ambohidratrimo   Brickaville

Antananarivo   Moramanga   Andovoranto

Ambatolampy

Antsirabe

Morondava

Ambositra

Mananjary

Fianarantsoa

Morombe   Ambalavao

Manakara

Ihosy

Farafangana

Toliara
(Tuléar)

Betioky

Ampanihy

Tolagnaro
(Fort Dauphin)

Lavanono

Mozambique Channel

INDIAN OCEAN

☆   national capital
○   regional capital
●   town, village
✈   airport
━━━   roads
┄┄┄   railroad

○   150 miles
○   150 kms

Author's Note

ALTHOUGH MALAGASY IS A FINE and complex language, it's devoid of plurals. This may look odd in the text, and takes some getting used to. Thus, for example, it doesn't matter whether you have one *dahalo* (bandit) or several hundred *dahalo*, it or they still look singular.

The language has, however, recently been shorn of accents. These sprouted in profusion during the French colonial period (1895–1960) but have since been lost. Except where I am quoting directly, I've therefore used the modern spelling. Place names, however, are more complicated, because colonial names and new names often exist in tandem. Where the context is historical, I've tended to use the older, colonial name simply to make things less confusing. The prime examples are Fort Dauphin (now Tolagnaro), Île Sainte-Marie (Nosy Boraha), Tuléar (Toliara), Tamatave (Toamasina), Diego Suarez (Antsiranana), and Majunga (Mahajanga).

A few characters that appear in these pages have been renamed and their personalities disguised. Sometimes this was necessary for their safety or because they requested anonymity. But, at other times, I felt it was needed in order to protect their privacy (perhaps they had family problems or addiction issues). I've tried to keep these changes to a minimum. However, it was necessary in the case of Rahanta Rakoto; Camille the Lebanese; my driver-guides, Faustin, Gaspar, Justin and Achille; Alix the Peace Corps volunteer, and Big Johnny. All are based on real characters, and I hope I've done enough to give them the anonymity they want or need.

Finally, the journeys described in these pages didn't necessarily take place in the order in which they're set out here. In some instances, I've had to reorder them in order to convey Madagascar's history in a chronological – and therefore hopefully more coherent – way.

Introduction

Cherries refuse to grow on Madagascar.

<small>ARTHUR STRATTON</small>
The Great Red Island, 1965

*Madagascar is an island lying about 1,000 miles
south of Socotra… [its] gryphon birds are so huge
and bulky that one of them can pounce on an elephant
and carry it up to a great height in the air.*

<small>MARCO POLO</small>
c. 1298

*I shall not go back to Madagascar with its blood-red
earth and its creeping shadows. The whole experience
will remain isolated, an island as it were in my life
as its scene was an island in the Indian Ocean. I shall
not catch spies again or watch a firing squad, shoot
crocodiles or be a Chef de Poste…*

<small>RUPERT CROFT-COOKE</small>
The Blood-Red Island, 1953

THESE DAYS, NOT MUCH NEWS SEEPS OUT of the Repoblikan'I Madagasikara (motto: '*Amour, Patrie, Progrès*'). There are occasional articles about its ecology, usually cast in apocalyptic terms. Otherwise, the stories that filter through are often curiously picaresque: 'Captain Kidd's treasure found', or 'Welsh adventurer to traverse Madagascar on foot for lemurs'. During a lull in 2018, some papers even ran with the improbable tale of Hourcine Arfa, a French-Algerian boxer. He'd arrived on the island the previous year, to train the Presidential Guard. Finding himself in jail on unspecific charges, he managed to break out, and fled through the wilds before sailing away on a small open boat, a *kwassa-kwassa*. As a yarn, it was just too good to be true, and rapidly petered out.

Even the government news is tinged with oddity. There are around 200 political parties, and Malagasy elections are among the most expensive in the world, fought with elaborate cunning and millions of T-shirts. Recent presidents have included a disc jockey and a yoghurt magnate, and every now and then the hotels close and there's a military coup. Only a few years ago, Madagascar sprouted a rival capital city, which – for seven months – traded insults with Antananarivo. Standstills, it seems, have become a way of life.

The outside world hardly notices any of this. The truth is, few outsiders have any real idea where Madagascar is. Although it's the fourth biggest island in the world (after Greenland, New Guinea and Borneo), it's also strangely invisible. Search for it on the internet, and you're just as likely to find a cartoon. Malagasies may resent the caricatures and the talking lemurs, but that's often all Westerners see. What happens in Madagascar has little impact elsewhere, and – with the Suez Canal – it's no longer on the way to anywhere else. An old diplomat once tried to explain to me how strategically inert the island is. 'If Madagascar were to disappear,' he said, 'no one would notice.'

It's always intrigued me, this unnoticed country. As a child I was brought up on Durrell and Attenborough, and was fascinated by the outlandish animals they caught. But the Malagasy people were harder to gauge. Did they tell jokes, and have an army? Was it too hot for clothes? And what were the spears for? As the years passed, Madagascar became ever more obscure, and yet I remained curious. What happens when 20 million people are left entirely to their own devices? Would it be like the Middle Ages? In 1992, shortly after university, I tried to get out there. However, by then, only Aeroflot were offering flights. Oddly, they could promise an outward leg but not the return. This was too curious even for me, and so another twelve years went by.

By that stage, I was writing travel pieces for the *Daily Telegraph*, and Madagascar came up. I was now married and so Jayne came with me. It's a mark of how little we knew that she travelled out four months pregnant. Even today, Madagascar's medical services are skinny (with no neurosurgeons, for example, and few CT scanners), but, back then, they were skeletal. Happily, however, there were no antenatal adventures, and we were wafted around from lodge to lodge. Delightful creatures would come gambolling through the gardens, and I remember the fluffiest of towels and the whitest of beaches. Only occasionally were we aware of people, living under mud brick and reeds. Their jollity confused me, and I assumed their smiles said it all. We flew everywhere, and I returned home realising how little I'd understood.

In the years that followed, a new journey began to take shape. This time, I'd read whatever I could, and burrow deep into this island's story. Books started coming in from all over the place, including bundles of Indian reprints, done up with twine. It was tempting to linger over the detail. Who knew, for example, that widows who remarried were once stoned to death (on suspicion of sorcery)? Or that the Bara tribespeople celebrated death with eager displays of sex? Among all this literature there was violence, love, repetition and even – thanks to Marco Polo – a little absurdity (he'd chronicled lions and leopards, and birds big enough to scoop up an elephant). Eventually, however, I began to see things fitting together. By April 2018, I was ready to join the narrative, and to set off on what I now thought of as my 'walk-through' history.

L EAFING THROUGH ITS STORY, I HAD A tantalising glimpse of the Madagascar to come. I soon realised that it was like nowhere else, and that it's often been regarded as its own little continent. Malagasies, too, may struggle with their history (there's nothing written before the twelfth century) but at least they know they're unique – and perhaps alone. Traditionally, they even referred to their island as *izao rehetra izao*, or 'This is all'. For Malagasy historians, like Solofo Randrianja, it's a recurring theme. We're different, he says, thanks to remoteness, size and sparsity of loot.

But I also began to realise that, in many ways, Man has yet to make an impression on this land. True, he's burnt off much of the forest, but even this feels like only a beginning. No one knows how long humans have been here but it's no more than a few thousand years. People have never filled the landscape, and the colonisation of the hinterlands has been so tentative that, as late as the 1500s, there were great, archaic herbivores – lumpen and edible – wandering the woods. Even now, there are creatures here, like lemurs and tenrecs, that exist elsewhere only as fossils.

Man is so new here that he's still the person he was the day he arrived. There's been no time for new languages or a great flowering of diversity. Across an area three times the size of Great Britain, there are accents and dialects but only a single language (the rest of Africa, by contrast, has over 1,500). Likewise, outsiders have historically identified eighteen different tribes, but the differences between them were often more geographical than cultural. It's almost easier to divide Malagasies into two groups: those on the coast with predominantly African genes, and those in the highlands, who came from Asia. They were like that from the start, and time has yet to change them.

Later, other settlers arrived but they did nothing to make Madagascar feel more inhabited. The first were the Arabs, but they seldom ventured inland. They did, however, put the island on the map, although it was left to Marco Polo to establish the name (having muddled it up with 'Mogadishu'). Next came the Portuguese in 1500, leaving nothing but graves and a few failed forts. Other European powers – like the English and the French – were more obstinate but equally unsuccessful. The first Englishmen, settling in the 1640s, initially thought they'd found some earthly paradise or the Garden of God, but within a few years they were nearly all dead.

Madagascar has continued to defy humankind even in more recent times. Only in the sixteenth century did the Malagasies begin to penetrate the hot, dry south, and even today there are pockets of the island that have never been truly explored. Meanwhile, a French map from about 1600 depicts almost the entire interior as a dazzling blank. The Europeans simply couldn't cope with the heat and the spears. Only a couple of offshore colonies survived. The rest would end in either a massacre or malaria. The Malagasies joke that, apart from themselves, the island is defended by two great generals, *Fazo* and *Tazo*, or 'forest' and 'fever'.

Then, in the mid-nineteenth century, the outside world became aware of a new Malagasy: assertive, astute and technologically adept. Just for a moment, it seemed that a gigantic kingdom was in the making, under the Merina tribe. To outsiders, Madagascar seemed fleetingly fabulous; a land of palaces, heathens and magnificent queens. But it didn't last because, in 1895, France invaded.

Once again, the world assumed that a transformation was imminent. But in 1960, the French left, having made only a light impression on the landscape. Sixty-five years was never enough *pour franciser* – 'to Frenchify' – this island. These days, there are traces of France in the language and in the cities, but otherwise she's vanished. As the great Madagascar historian, Sir Mervyn Brown, put it, one day the colonial period will seem but 'a brief interlude' in the island's story.

Remote and defiant, Madagascar has sometimes occupied a sinister spot in the European imagination. It's often been proposed as a repository for things no one wants, like penal settlements and rocket pads. But one idea has proved unpleasantly persistent: a super-ghetto for Europe's Jews. The concept was first proposed by a German scholar, Paul de Lagarde, in 1885 but – over the next sixty years – it would pop up again and again in Britain, France and Poland. Hitler's 'Jewish Desk' even had a name for it: *der Madagaskar-Plan*. Under the scheme (devised by that cold monster of bureaucracy, Adolf Eichmann), 4 million Jews would be shipped east, in an operation financed by their stolen assets. Then, once on the island, the exiles would build their own little Israel, governed by the Waffen SS. At its height, in 1940, the plan was explained to Warsaw's Jews, but after that it faltered, and Madagascar was soon forgotten in the ruins of war.

WITH MY RUCKSACK STUFFED WITH NOTES, I prepared to leave. Three months of travels lay ahead, a prospect that now seemed slightly daunting. Madagascar is 1,600 kilometres long, which means that, laid out across Europe, it would stretch from London to Algiers.

Poring over the map, I could see a thicket of names – some as long as alphabets – but not many roads and only a few little sprigs of railway.

There'd be some difficult journeys. These days, barely 15 per cent of Madagascar's roads are paved, and the entire network is no greater than Jamaica's (although it's fifty-three times the size). Until 1895, Madagascar had no roads at all, and since then it's been a battle with the mud. Every year, rains of biblical ferocity visit much of the land, and for five months they rinse it of roads. Only the asphalt survives this brutal wash. The rest turns to goo, as the hinterlands churn to a halt. Already, my journey was feeling like a ride across Western Europe, using only cart tracks.

But as well as dirt, other more exotic hazards lay ahead. The literature of Madagascar is rich in disaster. Earlier travellers warn that, even when the sun shines, whole regions can be shut down by locusts, bandits, pestilence or coups. Even as I was preparing to leave, Malagasy soldiers were fighting a low-grade war somewhere out in the bush. It was hard to know how this tiny army was getting on, except that, in 2017, it had appointed another fifty-eight generals.

Elsewhere, it seemed, the obstacles I faced might be spiritual. People warned of inauspicious full moons grounding all the planes and wiping out the schedules. Worse still were the solar eclipses, which would bring on a collective anxiety, and empty the streets. At such times, oxen are sacrificed; mothers cover their children's eyes, and everyone hides indoors. Such strangeness wasn't new. Back in the 1930s, outsiders like the Polish writer Arkady Fiedler were inclined to see it all as a variant of madness. 'Hidden lunacy,' he decided, 'has always been smouldering at the bottom of Malagasy existence.'

Nowadays, perhaps, we demand less and expect anything. I realised that ahead lay a remarkable culture and perhaps the most beautiful country in the world. I realised too that it wouldn't be judged by its ability to function. Adventurer Christina Dodwell has known this for years. 'One of Madagascar's downsides', she wrote, 'is that few things work.'

CHAPTER I

Buckets of Beauty, or Antananarivo

*...and there I saw Tananarive, a city on a knoll...
there is no human habitation in the world more
agreeable to come upon.*

ARTHUR STRATTON
The Great Red Island, 1965

*At Malagasy parties, copious quantities
of home-brewed rum are consumed, and helpless
drunkenness is entirely expected*

The Lonely Planet Guide, 2004

*The innate Malagasy dignity makes Tana
seem truly civilised, whatever may be the state
of the drains.*

DERVLA MURPHY
Muddling Through in Madagascar, 1985

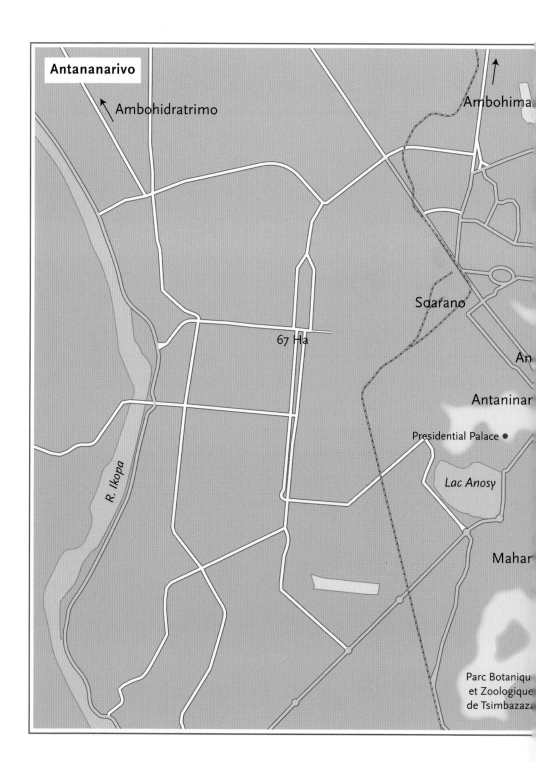

Antananarivo

↗ Ambohidratrimo

Ambohima

Soarano

67 Ha

An

Antaninar

Presidential Palace ●

Lac Anosy

Mahar

R. Ikopa

Parc Botaniqu
et Zoologique
de Tsimbazaza

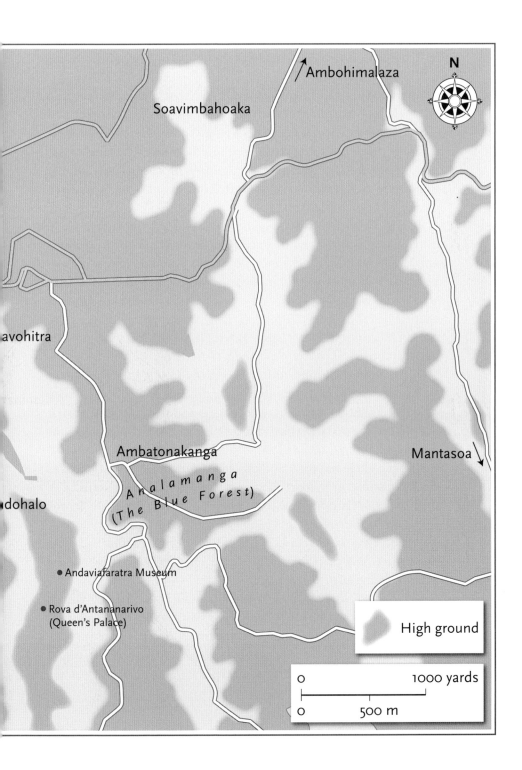

N

Ambohimalaza

Soavimbahoaka

avohitra

Ambatonakanga

Analamanga
(The Blue Forest)

Mantasoa

dohalo

● Andaviafaratra Museum

● Rova d'Antananarivo
(Queen's Palace)

High ground

| 0 | 1000 yards |

| 0 | 500 m |

NOTHING BRINGS OUT THE STRANGENESS of a city quite like the plague.

I'd arrived in Antananarivo to find it plastered in posters of rats and fleas. Although the epidemic was over, people still looked watchful and pasty. I'd half-expected a little lingering psychosis; an outbreak of the occult, perhaps, or Pepysian lust. But, as I now know, *les Tananariviens* do things differently, and make a habit of obscurity. Only in their stories were they like Boccaccio's Florentines, and it never took much to trigger a torrent of drama.

To begin with, they were suitably apocalyptic. During my first week, people had often told me they thought they'd die. They'd described how it all began, eight months earlier, with a minibus coming in from the country. Within days, four of the passengers were dead. The next victim was a basketball coach, on a visit from Seychelles, and then *la peste* reached the prisons. After that, there was no stopping it. As one medical journal puts it, Malagasy jails replicate the conditions of 'the European medieval city' and are perfect for the plague.

At that stage, everyone I met seemed to be reeling from the fallout. For months, they told me, nothing had happened: no school; no public meetings; no tourists; no cockfights and no church. A lecturer from the university described the stillness of the campus, and how even neighbours became a threat. Then, as the bubonic plague turned pneumonic, there was panic-buying, and the pharmacies were emptied of *cache-bouches*, or masks. The rich began gulping down antibiotics, while the poor had their spells. But still the disease persisted. In one area alone, Analamanga, 1,408 people developed the deadly symptoms. Eventually, even the government reacted, setting up roadblocks, taking temperatures, and cancelling doctors' leave. '*On est en guerre*,' announced the president grimly.

But even as I listened, these stories began subtly to change. Within weeks of my arrival, the plague had become little more than a seasonal nuisance. We always have it, said the taxi drivers, and people always die. Sure, more people fell sick this year, but even the final death toll – 202 – was nothing special. It's just what happens, they said, in *la saison pesteuse*.

Tana may be home to 2 million but it can still look small, French and provincial.

Months on, and the attitude changed again. People would seldom mention the plague. It had somehow transformed itself into an issue of trickery and greed. Even among my friends, a new truth had emerged. Europeans, as every Malagasy knows, have a deep-rooted fear of *la peste* and will pay anything to smother it. Aid was soon gushing in. The government had made millions from their overblown epidemic. It was all a ploy, even the *barrages sanitaires*. Nobody died, said my guide one day, and there was never any plague at all.

T ANA (AS THE CITY IS KNOWN) WAS ALWAYS doing this, throwing me into confusion. At any given time, I could never quite decide whether I was in a small, provincial French town or an Asian slum. Deep inside, it's cobbled and shuttered, and its narrow streets zigzag steeply upwards through the hills. But from the outside, it looks like a series of islands, sprawling outwards across the rice. Amid such great expanses of water, it's easy to forget that you're already in the highlands, at over 4,000 feet. In the right light, the distant city has something of the Shangri-La about it, and you can't see the rust and the kilns and

the silky black canals. Few places in the world can be so magnificent in panorama, and so squalid in close-up.

Only out here in the rice does Tana truly feel like a city. Closer in, it seems somehow to shrink. Tana may be home to over two million people and yet it has all the swagger of a village, or perhaps hundreds of villages, compacted together. Although it has only twenty-two embassies, there are over five thousand churches. Often the houses look like farms, and the roads like rivers. There are cliffs where there should be suburbs, blacksmiths, crows, old cars full of meat, and shops open to the street and lit with candles. People wash in the puddles and pee in the bushes, and there's laundry laid out wherever it's flat. If there was ever a sewerage system, it's been long since overwhelmed, and nor are there metros, buses or functioning trains. Everywhere, the air tingles with chicken, and is scented with charcoal. Tana is now often considered the third dirtiest place in the world (after Baku and Dhaka), and yet not even that makes it a city.

A Peace Corps volunteer once told me that although you never get used to the poverty, you do eventually see beyond it. It took me a while

Half of Tana's children are under-nourished, and many live on the street.

to reach that point. For some time, all I could think about were the bare feet, the trash-pickers, the tapping at my elbow, and the papery, Asiatic faces. With nine out of ten Malagasies living on less than $2 a day, almost everyone was a saver or a sifter. If Tana has no graffiti, it's only because no one has money to buy the paint. A low point was when, one night, I came across half a dozen children, huddled up like kittens, in the window of a bank. I wondered if I'd ever get used to scenes like that, but the people I met were more phlegmatic. Our poverty, they said, does not define us.

Eventually I developed a sense of normality, although I was always pleased to be back, out in the rice. I particularly liked that moment when the traffic slowed as it re-entered the city. If it was early in the morning, there might be another million people out on the dykes, heading for town: farmers, broom-makers, bottle-washers, hawkers, rock-breakers, sorcerers and clerks. With them came rickshaws and ducks and bundles of foam as high as a house. It was almost as if someone had pulled a distant plug, sucking everything into the centre.

But if it was later in the day, little moved, out in the paddy. We might sit for hours in the traffic, gazing up at the twelve hills of Tana, or out across the tiny, mud-red villages adrift in their own reflections. I wasn't the only person who liked it out here. A few wealthy merchants had built mansions in the paddy, ridiculous confections of raspberry and chrome. More surprising was the new American Embassy, safely bedded down, miles from anything that mattered. Perhaps there was no place for such a vast, glossy complex up in the hills. Or perhaps the Americans had merely wanted to experience Tana as the ancient Malagasies had: *Vohitsara*, 'the City of Beauty'.

THE MALAGASIES MAY BE POOR BUT they're never shabby. Here, only the mad get by without combs and brushes. If people ever look grungy, they're probably *vazaha* – or foreigners – working in aid.

On my first day, I took a taxi up to the mid-levels, *la ville moyenne*, and thought I'd arrived in the hairdressing quarter. In some streets, there were barbers clustered together four in a row, along with beauticians, chiropodists and nail bars. But then I realised that the pampering was everywhere, and that it spread down the hill, across the market stalls of

Analakely, and up the other side. Those who couldn't afford a salon had an old Citroën van, usually painted pink and fitted out with mirrors and sinks and revolving chairs. Even the destitute could be *esthéticiennes*, doling out beauty from an old metal bucket.

Everyone looked coiffed and trim, from the president down to the beggars. The fashion never varied, and all anyone wanted was to look oriental. Hair was parted and straightened, and any hint of curliness shorn away. Some men clearly had their heads shaved almost every day, and so being a buzz-cutter was always good business. The worst of them, I discovered, operated out of little hutches down by Lake Anosy. A taxi driver once told me I should never use them. They shave half your hair off, he said, and then start demanding money and phones.

'Can't someone tell the *gendarmes*?' I asked.

'The *police*?' he laughed. 'They're almost as bad as the barbers!'

When it came to clothes, people were equally fastidious. While eight out of ten Malagasies were going to bed hungry, they never looked worn or drab. In former times, everyone wore the *lamba*, a great white shawl that reached the ankles (and in Victorian photographs, *les Tananariviens* look like Roman senators, in Stetsons). Now, however, there were bright Chinese colours, mock-Nikes, pink straw hats, and all the nearly new outfits from Europe. This bounty – most of it jackets and Polish suits – would arrive in bales, and was distributed through a network of hawkers. Everyone loved the bleached denim and the leather, and, for the working woman, there were heels and a clutch.

But, suspicious and readily coy, people were seldom outrageous. A man in diamanté could still stop the traffic, and there was no concept of outré, bohemian or gay. I remember once seeing a man riding around on a very old Harley-Davidson, its back wheel plundered from a car. He was dressed as the Easy Rider, and as he passed I could see the crowds shrink back in horror. Even the rich wore their wealth only modestly. Exuberance, it seemed, was the sole preserve of Protestant pastors, who dressed in cream suits and pink satin ties. Where I come from, that's the outfit of an aging TV presenter, with a show about antiques.

It was mostly pedlars who served the city's aspirations.

There were shops but they were only for those with lots of money.

The biggest of these places – like Shoprite and Jumbo Score – were well guarded, out of town and foreign. They sold everything from South African socks to Batman suits. But closer in, up in the hills, the shops had a more haunted feel. Once, having lost all my luggage en route from Paris, I visited some of the cheerless boutiques on Rue Ranavalona III. Among the flannel and co-respondent shoes, there was a particularly luminous shirt. It seemed like a bargain – until the day I tried to wash it in my hotel, and the colours ran, turning my bathroom cornflower blue.

Clearly, *Tananariviens* preferred to shop among the pedlars. *Les marchands ambulantes* were everywhere. With no state benefits and almost one in ten Malagasies now living in Tana, perhaps half a million people were peddling. Across town, every spare inch was spread with fruit, telephones, peanuts and pants. The pavements had long since vanished, and the streets had become little more than capillaries wriggling through the stalls. There was nothing these hawkers wouldn't sell or do; they sharpened knives, mixed paint, told fortunes, retuned engines and delivered milk by the pail. One of the southern tribesmen even had a photocopier attached to a battery, while another rented out his bathroom scales. Occasionally, the police would appear in trucks, and the vendors would quickly gather up their lives and scatter through the alleys.

Many of the pedlars owed their survival to the city's congestion. Several times a day, the traffic would bring Tana to a hazy, clanking halt. I once met a diplomat who, without any obvious irony, described these traffic jams as 'life-changing'. Only the French word, *embouteillage*, does justice to this bottling-up of urban life. Some streets would come to a standstill for hours, packed in by a teeming micro-economy of pedlars. This happened even on the airport road, as we moved – almost imperceptibly – through the rice. Out there, it always surprised me, the things we were offered: hubcaps, hinges, catapults, kites and bottles of Guerlain de Paris. One pedlar even had garden shears, which came snapping through the window like some greedy, mechanical fish.

Of course, not everyone had things to sell. Many people just waited, and every street had its bystanders, unruffled and mute. I'd never seen such patience before, and found it menacing at first. But for many Malagasies, it wasn't unusual, doing nothing. 'We're all waiting,' they'd say, 'it's not this world that matters.'

My HOTEL, IN THOSE FIRST WEEKS, was both a love nest and a House of Curiosities. Its strange exhibits now make perfect sense. The Sakamanga, or 'Blue Cat', was always popular with new visitors, and here, in its home-made guns and copulating statues, was a hint of what lay beyond. Throughout its creaking warren of corridors, there were spears and crocodile skulls, old metal helmets, enormous banknotes, portraits of the great queens and shoals of silvery knives. One cabinet contained everything the Victorian warrior would ever need for war, including his cleaver and a pouch of salt. Another held magic charms, mostly cow horns stuffed with hair, dung, copper coins and human teeth.

I once asked if this was Tana's only museum.

'No,' said the receptionist, a little unsure.

'But it must be the best?'

'Maybe,' she said. 'All the others were robbed by our politicians.'

The lovers were harder to explain. A few were obviously professionals, dropping their ID on reception as they skittered up to the rooms (even in the better hotels, like this, there was only one injunction: *NON À LA PROSTITUTION DES MINEURS*). Other couples were more difficult to place, even though the girls were local, and the men were old and French. At first, I was a bit sniffy about them but then, seeing their contentment, I began to have doubts. Each evening, they'd sit down neatly to dinner, him with tattoos, and her in new boots. They never seemed to notice anyone else, and the old Romeos – or *vozongo* – could be conspicuously gallant.

Eventually, I got used to the lovers, and they became as much a part of the scenery as the crocodiles and guns. Later, a friend would explain how all this looks from the Malagasy perspective: 'They both get something they need. At home he's nothing but here he's rich and gets a girl who's pretty and loyal. Meanwhile, she gets a lifestyle, and the chance of escape. She may even have white children, whose life will be better than hers…'

But not everyone saw it so simply. A local barman told me that the girls used magic. 'She has very powerful charms, and she *traps* the *vozongo*! He can never leave, even when she's got his pension.'

After a few days of Tana, even the Sakamanga began to feel strangely normal. Each morning, I swam in a tiny black pool, which was patrolled by a very ferocious pheasant. There was also a rare black parrot out in the courtyard. It lived on stolen Coca-Cola, and had a call like a rusty hinge. By day, however, the place was mysteriously calm, and one could almost forget that Tana was there. Then, at night, I'd lie in bed, listening to the murmurs that came up through the plumbing. This is what it must be like for a cat, I thought, hearing dozens of voices all around.

For the staff, of course, the only oddity was me. They'd always remember who I was, even much later, after weeks away. My favourite receptionist was called Veronique. She was often trying to place me, among the complex array of Lotharios and lovers ('Are you single?' she'd probe. 'Then you must be divorced? OK, so where is your wife?'). We were on safer ground, discussing my journey. She loved the fact that I was here to write about people.

'Usually, *vazaha* just ask about lemurs. "You're Malagasy," they say, "you must know. What are they like, the lemurs? Are they big or small? And can you pick them up?" Well, how would I know? I've never even seen one.'

E ACH DAY, I SET OUT INTO THE CITY. Getting lost ought to have been easy. On a map, Tana looks like scribble mixed with hills. It wasn't much easier on the ground. River-like roads would plunge through the contours before losing themselves in a cataract of vowels. Some of these places would eventually make sense, like Antaninandro ('Out of full sunlight') and Ambatonakanga ('Guinea Fowl Rock'). But most remained defiantly bewildering, to be mumbled at best. Even the Malagasies will sometimes look at a place name and wonder how it's said.

If I never actually got lost, it was only thanks to the *Rova*. Perched high above the city, this great burnt-out palace was never out of sight. It was visible even 15 miles away, out in the rice, and at night it glowed bright orange as if – once again – it was on fire. Freakish and pseudo-European, no one was really sure whether they liked it but the Rova was at least a landmark. However perplexing Tana could be, I only had to glance upwards to know exactly where I was.

From the very beginning, however, I was lost in the language. Malagasy was once described as 'the Italian of the Southern Hemisphere',

and there are moments when it can be joyously onomatopoeic (*kakakaka*, for example, means 'laughter' and *mibobobobo* is 'to make a bubbling noise'). But beautiful though it may sound, it's also well defended against its students. There are no plurals, no genders, and many of the words are tortuously long. Even 'little things' here are *kanonkanona*, and 'a bite' is an *ambilombazana*.

As I walked around, I tried a few phrases, but people only looked puzzled. Even when I called out '*Veloma*' or 'Goodbye' (literally, 'May you live!'), all the girls would titter. Malagasy was clearly not spoken as it was written. At times, I wondered how the words now swirling around me had ever been captured in writing. Gerald Durrell had obviously had similar moments, during his visit of 1990. 'Malagasy,' he wrote, 'is a fine rackity-clackity, ringing language, which sounds not unlike someone carelessly emptying a barrel of glass marbles down a stone staircase.'

The Rova, a great burnt-out palace, re-fitted in 1869, dominates Tana's skyline.

Most of the time, the best I could hope for was an outbreak of French. But I never quite gave up on Malagasy. As I plodded through the hills, I'd write things down, for unravelling later. There were always lots of jokes and jibes hidden away in the names of streets. One particularly steep alleyway was called Tsiofakantitra, or 'The Old Can't Make It'. But my favourite of all was Isorakaka, or 'Out of Breath'.

From the *Rova*, Tana descends hundreds of feet, through tiers of ever-diminishing gentility. Around the summit there are mansions and ministries, and at least two cathedrals. It was the *haute ville* in every sense, and I sometimes climbed up here for breakfast. Everything was grand, and covered in shutters and tiles and clumps of acanthus. Even the potholes seemed bigger here (and there was one by the *lycée,* just the right size for a little car). Only the rich were missing. The traffic and the kidnappers had driven them off, into the outlying hills. I sometimes wondered if they'd ever come back to reclaim their villas. But these were no longer roads for their fancy Cayennes.

A little lower down were the professional classes. As well as the beauticians, here were the physicians, apothecaries, astrologers and bankers. There was also a street of Indian jewellers, and a tiny outcrop of art deco, where the surgeons lived. Then, dangling over the city, were the leafy gardens of Antaninarenina, where the preachers used to gather. It was also the best place for socks and Bibles and bags of old stamps. Rather harder to explain were the oyster-sellers up here, and the little naval base (complete with a crew of brawny *matelots*). While I always enjoyed *la ville moyenne*, it often felt like a bit of old Marseille that had somehow got lost.

From the mid-levels, several enormous stone staircases descended into the lower town. Heading down, the changes weren't obvious at first, and there was still a semblance of order. Here were courtrooms and barracks; old cinemas (now gospel halls); circumcision parties; poinsettias as big as a car and lavish displays of sausages and meat. Here too were the last public toilets, with signs not for men and women but *PIPI* and *KAKA*, or 'pee' and 'poo'. It was even possible to find the daily papers, all pegged out for everyone to read. Meanwhile, somewhere among all this was the Sakamanga and a gallery that sold nothing but erotic sculptures and petrified dinosaur dung. Even the *makorelina* (or prostitutes) here were as respectable as any, working the cobbles in their fake Ferragamo and kitten heels.

There was only one last patch of calm before *la ville basse*. The Avenue d'Indépendance was originally bulldozed through by the French in the 1930s. In such a compacted, upended city, it still felt like a runway. Around the edges, its colonnades had also survived (with the occasional burnt-out shop). But it was a constant battle, keeping the avenue clear. Every morning, the *gendarmes* would sweep it of vagrants, and a street cleaner would scoop up the waifs asleep in the drains. No sooner had the nightlife departed than the snake charmers appeared, along with the drummers, the quacks, the magicians and the maimed. One tribesman was particularly memorable. Proud and legless, he looked like someone wading slowly through the asphalt.

Before heading further, I asked Veronique what she thought.

Although proud and dignified, 90% of Malagasies live on less than $2 a day.

'Don't!' she said. '*Anything* could happen.'

With that, she took out a map, and began crossing out the areas she thought unsafe. As her pen moved through the *arrondissements*, obliterating vast tracts of the city, I realised how anxious she was. The *Rova* and *la ville basse* were swiftly deleted, along with much of the mid-levels. By the time she'd finished, all that remained were a few streets around the Sakamanga. Then, just for a moment, her avenging nib hovered over the Avenue d'Indépendance before that too was gone.

'Never walk anywhere,' she said. 'Never take anything with you, and never carry money. Never go into *la ville basse,* or any of the markets. Avoid going out in the dark, and never speak to anyone.'

After such graphic warnings, it still surprises me, my survival. Although I often wandered out through the Lower Town, I was never robbed, and was usually ignored. This was particularly puzzling, given that these were some of the poorest communities in the world. Across much of Tana, people get by on less than a euro a day. The poor even have their own version of the Horsemen of the Apocalypse, who are known as *Les Quatre Mis*. They are *miloka, mifoka, misotro* and *mijangajanga* (or gambling, drugs, drinking and wenching).

I never had to go far before I was in among the tarpaulins and the rust. At one end of the Avenue was a sort of Frenchified souk, known as the *Zoma* or 'Friday'. It was once thought to be the largest market in the world, and in 1895 a correspondent from the London *Times* had called by, taking great delight in all he found: 'native ironmongery, hats, dried locusts and sweetmeats'. Since then, not much had changed, although these days you might also find a toaster or a holster or a wedding dress. Only the treatment of pickpockets was different. Nowadays, they were famously blatant, whereas back then anyone found stealing was instantly wrestled to the ground and stoned to death.

Just beyond the Avenue was a vast flat area, known simply as *Lalamby*, or 'Railway'. It began with old marshalling yards, but soon became a crush of stalls and workshops and people living in boxes. There were a few factories here, making knickers and socks for export, but they didn't have jobs for everyone. So, for most people, it was just a question of peddling or waiting. Some had their entire world gathered up under a single umbrella. I must have made an exotic sight in my coat and boots, hurrying along.

Beyond Lalam-by, life became even simpler still. A dense weft of shanties – now without drains or names or second storeys – sprawled off into the rice. One of the most primeval areas was known simply as '67 ha', and I only ever went there once, by taxi. Even then, the driver locked all the doors, and shrivelled in his seat. Suddenly, there were eyes everywhere, and skinny fingers on the glass. Out here, the concept of ownership no longer meant much. Only one in three people would ever pay for their electricity, while all the others simply clipped themselves to the national grid. 'Everything's stolen,' said the driver. 'They come into the city at night, and take whatever they can, even the concrete paving.'

It seems I'd arrived at the bottom of the heap. Lots of cities merge hills and hierarchy, but perhaps nowhere more than Tana. Over the next few weeks, it often felt as if poverty was merely a matter of altitude, and that everyone's status was as old as the rocks. Maybe this would be true of all Malagasies? Even in their proverbs, there was always the sense that you are what you are, and that nothing will change. 'Delight is not for the poor,' they say. 'Only in sleep do we resemble the rich.'

ODDLY, THE RICH THEMSELVES HAD BECOME invisible. Even though I looked in all the obvious places – hilltops, pinnacles and eyries – they were nowhere to be seen. Sure, there were a few unexplained walls and impregnable communes (with names like 'The Bird Park') and there were the colourful follies out in the rice. There was also *le quartier chic*, a cluster of fortified condos out at Ivandry. But I'd been expecting more: mock-Tudor, perhaps, or a little Versailles. These people were, after all, fabulously moneyed. A mere sixty families owned most of the country, including mines and forests and all the fuel. How had they managed to disappear?

Everyone had their own ideas.

'I heard they're all in Mauritius…'

'…or the States, if they're smart…'

'No, Paris! They like the shopping.'

But not all the millionaires had gone. Across the city, there were always traces of conspicuous wealth. It might be a private army of black-clad guards or a caravan of Range Rovers snaking through the centre. Once, I came across a shop that sold tiny electric BMWs for children. Often, too, their riches would rub off on the politicians. On one occasion, the president's wife appeared in a dress worth $8,000, and Tana united in a howl of derision.

The rich may not have been visible or popular but they did provide an endless fund of stories. In the popular imagination, they were mostly *Karana*, or Indo-Pakistanis, and they rigged everything from the general elections to the price of rice. They also bankrolled all the ministers, hoarded all the gold, stole the vanilla and kidnapped each other. There was always a certain silliness about the rich. Often, they spent so much on ramparts and razor wire that they had nothing left for the mansion inside. Across Tana, this was a common explanation for unfinished walls.

'And why would they *kidnap* each other?' I asked.

The answer was always the same: easy money. I often wondered about all this, and which bits were true. Everyone loved their kidnapping stories, which they larded with dismay. In one tale, the kidnappers bought their victim a PlayStation 4, to keep the little brat quiet. But in other stories, the gangsters were politicians or rustlers or, like Rambo unleashed, dripping in grenades. Every week, the newspapers ran stories of a shoot-out with the SAG, or *le Service Anti-Gang*, and in their spattered portraits, the dead were always abductors, out harvesting the rich. One of the most famous corpses was that of Zahid Raza, who'd run into a squall of bullets in August 2017. The *Karana* had long suspected him of kidnap, even though he himself was not just wealthy but the Malaysian Honorary Consul.

Lucky Tana – its paupers may not have had much to enliven their lives, but they did at least have the antics of the rich.

I N THIS GREAT ANT HEAP OF A CITY, making friends was never going to be easy. Before setting out for Madagascar, I'd spent months putting together a little network of contacts. Gathering the names wasn't difficult and eventually I had a book full of doctors, politicians, academics, beach bums, chancers, anthropologists and drunks. It had all seemed so easy, and I had no idea then that most of these people were already dead, missing or living in France.

There were, however, clear signs of the complexity to come. In London, people who'd known Madagascar well warned of a society that was almost impenetrable to those from outside. Don't expect to make friends, they said, or to understand your hosts. Malagasies never say what they mean. They will be charming but distant. Never ask penetrating questions or demand their opinion. Never be dogmatic, and always smile, and seek the middle ground. It is polite to be uncertain (and they will be excessively polite). As a foreigner, you're automatically rich, loud, arrogant, blunt and outspoken. You will never know when you have offended them, and the insult will fester for years. If it all gets too much, just keep smiling. There will be moments when you feel betrayed. Never lose your temper, or you'll suddenly find they're all against you.

Although there was a lot to remember, my first meetings in Tana were gratifyingly bland. At first, I couldn't find anyone, or the phone would be answered with a gabble of panic and a click. But eventually, two ladies from the university's English literature department agreed to meet me for tea. They arrived half an hour early, and were effusive in their gratitude and greetings. One of them was local but the other, Gladys, was half-Sakalava. She told me she'd learnt her English off the BBC, and she spoke it with a delicate, antique accent, just like one of the Archers.

'Is there much call,' I asked, 'for English literature?'

'Oh yes,' said Gladys, 'I run a Jane Austen course.'

With that, Madagascar was forgotten, and there we were in a tropical Hampshire. Even the tea was half-English, with chocolate gateau and *sambos*, or samosas. Our small talk sustained us through another pot of Earl Grey, a plate of madeleines and two strawberry milkshakes, and we never really returned to the subject in hand. It was almost as if there was something brutal and crass about mentioning the thing we'd all met to discuss.

It was much the same with my next lot of visitors. Often, these meetings had taken weeks to arrange, and then – after the rituals of peanuts and tea – my guests would suddenly announce they had to go. Of course, I was doing something wrong, but I never knew what. One of my most spectacular disappointments was Professor Michel Razafiarivony, the rector at the *Faculté de Théologie*, who arrived one evening, all clad in black leather. Although aged sixty-five, he was very tall and athletic, and reminded me of one of the great American sprinters. Sadly, however, we never got much beyond the topic of his cold, which we treated with a large tumbler of Scotch. He then said his goodbyes, climbed back on his moped, and spluttered off into the night, and I never saw him again.

Even my friendly journalist would be mysteriously shy. Although Rahanta Rakoto had once been a stringer for the BBC, she was now semi-retired and managed a small TV station. As she wouldn't be coaxed into town, I had to travel out to her studios, deep in the rice. But I knew immediately that our meeting had already ended. While Rahanta was genteel and sweet-natured, she had about her a powerful aura of reticence. Her interesting life was clearly not to be shared, and she left me with a single thought, that society was collapsing and that everything was wrong. On my way out, I asked her if she still reported crime.

'No,' she said, 'there's too much of it. It's everywhere now.'

I had more luck with the aristocracy. *Tananariviens* can be readily divided into those who are nobles and those who aren't. I never had much difficulty spotting the difference. Although the aristocrats were almost as poor as everyone else, their sense of entitlement somehow lent them an air of exuberance. They also tended to announce themselves, either in titles or with a sliver of history. 'If we still had a monarchy,' one of them once told me, 'my wife would be queen.'

Of all my contacts, perhaps the most blue-blooded was Mireille Rabenoro. She worked in the old American Embassy, in a room slightly overfilled with squeaky black plastic sofas. But despite the squeaks, she cut an elegant figure: a *patricienne* who'd spent her life in revolt, and who now looked magnificent in flowing charcoal and mother-of-pearl. The Rabenoros have always been leaders, and Mireille's mother was a Supreme Court judge, while her father, Césaire, ran the Académie Malgache. But Mireille had always chosen to lead from the barricades, and for almost fifty years she'd fought the police, the misogynists, the army and the rich. As a reward for her courage, she'd ended up as the government's Commissioner of Human Rights.

'There are,' she said, 'some very evil people out there.'

'Doesn't it frighten you, your job?'

'Yes,' she admitted. 'But then we have to do it, don't we?'

I became fond of Mireille, if slightly in awe. We met up a few times and once she even came down to the Sakamanga, where we sat, rather incongruously, among the lovers. Her stories were usually horrifying, and at least one ended with a village in flames. She'd teach me that whatever version of Malagasy history you like, there's always another. She'd also describe the country's curious vortex of indecision, and how all the big issues would spiral upwards through the hierarchy before being finally lost. Malagasies, she said, are particularly skilled at losing papers.

There were two other aristocrats I came to think of as friends. One was Manitra Andriamialisoa. He told me his mother still lived in the same semi-derelict fort that his family had owned for hundreds of years. But Manitra had somehow managed to step outside the feudal cycle, and had gone to the States as a Fulbright Scholar. The experience had left him chronically loquacious, but what he said was often funny and occasionally brilliant. He was also one of the few people I met who wasn't afraid of the city at night. Despite the evangelism now leaking into his family, he was happy to join me in the search for bars. In our big glasses, we must have looked like a pair of owls, out on the town.

'Did you know,' he'd say, 'we have no words for "What's the time?"'

The other kindred spirit was Aro Rakontondrabao, who had a small estate on the edge of town. There have been Rakontondrabaos at every great moment in Madagascar's story. They'd given the country its first gynaecologist, its first female doctor, and its first private car. Aro himself was a palaeontologist and was sympathetically reverent and pale. But it was a cruel vocation for a man with so much rice and so little money. He'd never seen the caves he was supposed to be studying, and often he didn't even have the change for a taxi home.

'I think,' he once said, 'we're the original Hebrews.'

I must have looked surprised.

'It's true,' he insisted. 'Come out tomorrow, and you'll see what I mean.'

Few foreigners have ever truly understood what Malagasies believe, so there wasn't much hope for my little day trip. Part of the difficulty, I realised, was that Malagasies were notoriously coy in matters of faith. But there was also the problem of syncretism:

so many beliefs stitched together, and then with other ones bolted on. If Madagascar's religion could be compared to a building, it would be a tottering edifice of belfries, minarets, erotic sculpture, magic stones and sacristies, most of it underground.

For the majority of people, the common theme was Christianity. But it was preached in all its different variants, and was often mixed with Islam and the occult. It also varied in depth, from the profoundly evangelical to a flimsy veneer. Then, beneath all that, there was something else, a much older deity, Zanahary. He himself would sometimes emerge as the Christians' God, but those around him were not so easily reassigned. To Malagasies, they were all the dead they'd ever known: the *razana*, or ancestors.

The ancestors made almost everyone anxious. People told me they appeared in dreams, and that they were in the rocks and the rivers and up in the hills. It didn't matter who they'd been – whether ancient kings or the people next door – they'd never truly died. They were always out there, orchestrating illnesses, killing off cattle and manipulating fate. Together, they were like the Court of God, and could be wanton and vicious. But they might also intercede on behalf of the living, arranging lovers, loans, fertility and babies. In return, all they needed was undivided adoration.

Everywhere, the dead were in charge, or so it seemed. *Tananariviens* were always consulting them, and leaving out offerings of blood and rice. Even the politicians would pay a visit to the ancient tombs before an election. But the only sure way of keeping the Ancestors happy was by living life exactly as they'd done. Any change was dangerous. It didn't matter how useful an innovation was, if it wasn't *fomba* – or customary – people would reject it, and so would parliament. The risk of ancestral vengeance, said Aro, was just too great.

'Isn't that stultifying, hindering change?'

'Of course,' he replied, 'but we only need to survive this life.'

THEOLOGICALLY, MY DAY IN THE COUNTRY was thrillingly strange. I kept thinking about Aro's words, as I edged out of town. My taxi took hours to extract itself from the stalls and the charcoal sellers, and the bundles of fodder. At some stage, we passed a *briqueterie*, its basins of mud teeming with tiny figures like Giacomettis. As we drove by, they all turned and waved. This is how life had looked for the dead, and how it would look for all the unborn.

Eventually, we reached the outer hills and began to climb. It was a cool, wet day, and the eucalyptus hung like mops in the valley walls. In places there were small terraces of rice, which gathered themselves into gigantic staircases, disappearing off into the mountains above. Then there were little villages of ochre and thatch, and I began to feel the centuries peeling away. Had Umbria looked like this in 1370s? Perhaps, but I never decided because we'd arrived in Ambohimalaza, and there was Aro, waiting by the church.

'Remember what I told you about the Hebrews?'

At that moment a priest appeared, a great ram of a man in a thick white sweater. Through Aro, he explained that Ambohimalaza was in the throes of a schism. It was the Protestants' fault; they'd refused to accept that the nobles buried here were the original Israelites. The town had split on the issue. So now it had a brand-new church, a new layer of dogma, and a new congregation, 2,000 strong.

'But how do you know they're the Israelites?' I asked.

'It says in Leviticus!' huffed the priest. 'They never touch their dead.'

From the church, we drove out to the family estate. It was a pretty place, if not exactly the Promised Land. A long drive curled upwards through the terraces to a rise mounted with fruit trees and a great orange tower. This looked like any other mansion, except stretched upwards, as if the stone was miraculously tensile. The windows were now high in the walls, and tightly shuttered. These days, only Aro's cousin lived here, along with his wife. They were very small and Asiatic, and lived in a darkened jumble of old gilt and chandeliers. The cousin had once been an eminent chemist but had long since reverted to twigs and bark. There were leaves scattered over every surface, soon to become his magical balm.

'And is it true,' I asked, 'about the corpses?'

'Yes,' said the cousin, 'we never touch them.'

'But our neighbours do…' said Aro.

The cousin nodded. 'Yes, and we're all invited to their *famadihana*.'

'An exhumation,' explained Aro. 'They're walking the dead.'

THE NEIGHBOURS' TOMB WAS A LITTLE further up the valley. It was a sort of spiritual bunker, squat and white, and fitted with frosted windows and a heavy steel door. Inside, there were thirty tenants, each neatly labelled, wrapped in silk, and arranged around the shelves.

Aro told me that, across the highlands, every good family had a place like this. Like so many Malagasies, it horrified him, the way the rest of the world went to their graves alone and neglected. Why did Europeans spend so much on their homes, and so little on eternity? People often told me they were saving for the afterlife. 'A house is but a voyage,' they'd say, 'while a tomb is forever.' For some, it was only the end that mattered. 'Never ask someone where they're from,' I was once advised. 'The real question is: *Where's your family tomb?* Our birthplace means nothing. All that counts is where we're buried.'

I never got the sense that death was somewhere remote. To those around me, the Ancestors were so immediate that the mausoleum was merely a portal between their differing states ('Death isn't an end,' said Aro, 'merely a change'). The *famadihana* was the day the dead – or at least their bones – briefly returned to the land of the living, to be shown off and feted. It was a last hurrah, on the threshold of ancestry.

All of this made the family tomb – squat and indestructible – a sort of theological bolthole. As everyone knew, those who didn't make

it would drift the uplands forever, vapid and forgotten. Throughout Malagasy history, to be banished from the tomb was always a far worse punishment than death. Even now, the families of those who'd died abroad would do anything to get the remnants home, safely tucked up in *ny tanindrazana*, or ancestral soil. But the worst fate of all, said Aro, was to have no tomb at all. 'It probably means your family were slaves.'

By the time we arrived, the exhumation was in full swing. Gathered round the tomb were the cousins (all in matching primrose-yellow outfits), a jazz band, a rum stall, and around five hundred guests. They'd all be expected to make a little contribution to the day. One of the cousins had an old exercise book, in which each offering was noted. The guests all paid up, because – as everyone knew – those that didn't would soon be lepers.

The bones had already been exhumed and paraded.

'*Désolé, Aro,*' said the cousins, '*mais nous ne pouvons pas être en retard…*'

The start time had been fixed by the *mpanandro*, or astrologer.

'A propitious time,' explained Aro. 'You can't run late.'

Now the bones were being returned to their shelves, wrapped in fresh silk, and a great party was getting under way. The musicians thrashed and trilled, and several enormous pans – each the size of a bathtub – were brought to the boil. Soon a monumental lunch was spreading out across the hill, comprising 200 kilos of rice, a hundred chickens and a pig. Then there was dancing, more rum, and a few appeals to absent *razana*. Everyone went a little wild that afternoon, including, I noticed, one of the waiters from the Sakamanga. It was like a wedding, with only the happy couple missing.

'IT's A BIG DEAL HERE, BEING DEAD. People think about it even more than sex.'

Across the table, I could sense another horrible confession forming. Camille wasn't smiling and a fifth whisky was now settled in his meaty hand. I'd often seen him around, and had assumed he was French and just another of the Sakamanga's lovers. But then I began to notice that

A family gathers, in matching outfits, to 'walk the dead'.

the girls were always different, and then, one night, I found myself sitting near him at dinner. 'No, I'm Lebanese,' he said, and it turned out he was a mining engineer. 'They send me to trouble spots. You know, piss-poor, civil war, that sort of thing. That's how I ended up here, right? But I've been everywhere, I guess. Liberia, Congo… the worst was PNG, where they cut my driver up and sent him back in pieces…'

The tumblers of Scotch had no effect. It was almost as if nothing ever reached his soul, even whisky. After two decades of geology, bar girls and deserts, his face was curiously colourless and his eyes inert. Perhaps the key to it all was his reference to a much earlier age, and his seventeen years with the Christian Phalange. The things he told me still make me blanch (although I imagine he won't be the only veteran whose moral compass no longer functions). But it puzzled me, the way Camille unburdened himself of his unlovable life. I even wondered if he hoped that none of it was real, and that this was him testing it on others. The trouble was, it was all far too confessional to be anything but true.

I asked him about his girls.

'I can always find a woman here.' He shrugged.

'They're very poor.'

'No, these aren't whores, just girls I meet. You see, people are pretty relaxed here. Adultery isn't a big deal, like it is in the West. They even have an expression: "What happens on market day doesn't count." I've known girls who've got themselves knocked up while the husband is overseas, and – you know what? – he just comes back and accepts the kid as his own. Why? Because he's doing just the same. "You're no longer a husband," he says, "when you leave the house." All these guys have mistresses, and they call them the *deuxième bureau*, or the "second office". And if the men are doing it, so are the women. So, yes, I can always find a girl.'

AFTER THAT, THE SAKAMANGA NEVER had quite the same appeal. It wasn't only the lovers that were beginning to grate, but also the sheer lovelessness of travel. After weeks of hotel life, I was suddenly craving a home, even someone else's. It was friends in Australia who helped me out. Go and find the Andrianarivony family, said their email.

I still laugh when I think about the first time we met. I'd asked Lydia and Avana over for dinner and they turned up looking very formal and slightly overwhelmed. Lydia worked for a bank, and in her black suit was conspicuously angular and elegant. But she soon warmed to the sound of English. Although she spoke it every day at work, it was only ever the language of figures and Forex. Now, she was finding everything funny, or at least amazing. 'Oh my God,' she said, 'you eat rice! Just like we do!'

Her husband, Avana, was more rounded and less Asian, but equally intrigued. Although he spoke French and a little English, neither gave him the voice he needed. Avana was never sure what to say, and over the next few months I'd come to appreciate him as much for his silence as for his hard-won words. But in his own introverted way, he was painfully generous, even though me and my world were utterly alien. It was a surprise that he never somehow managed to disguise. '*Regardez ce menu!*' he blurted. '*C'est si cher!* We never eat foods so expensive!'

That night, Avana lost himself in food. He had foie gras, a steak, a strawberry smoothie and half my spaghetti, before ordering a large pot of rice. He explained that he couldn't sleep without rice, and that it was a bit of a national obsession. Did I know that the Malagasies eat more rice per head that anyone else? Avana could even reel off all the different words for rice, and said that it was only rice that mattered, and that everything else was known as *laoka*. Then, finally, when he'd finished both rice and plaudits, he pushed back his chair and smiled happily. 'And yes,' he said, 'you must come out to stay.'

The Andrianarivonys lived in the more fragrant part of Soavimbahoaka. A few miles north of the city, it was a small suburb, scattered untidily over the hills. As usual, the poor occupied the lower reaches, where the roads had crumbled away. They lived in shacks made of flattened oil drums, and queued at the public tap, and – like 60 per cent of all *Tananariviens* – used a communal latrine. But the sounds wafting up the valley weren't necessarily unhappy, just the throaty rumble of gospel and trumpets. I once wandered down there, and, like the Pied Piper, re-emerged with my own entourage of children.

Lydia and Avana lived higher up, and had a well of their own. Like all the other houses up here, theirs also had a little rectangle of banana trees and bougainvillea, all boxed in with walls and wire. Across the yard, there were a couple of concrete stalls for the maids, and an outhouse for a country cousin who'd come up to work. There was also a Peugeot under an awning but never the money – said Lydia – to get it running.

The house itself was big and decked, and looked like an old grey ferry, moored to the hill. Inside, a narrow staircase led up between several enormous spaces, each the size of a ballroom. Amid such dizzying dimensions, neither children nor furniture made much impression, and even the paintwork had spread itself thin. Every now and then the pipework would burst into song, and whenever anyone opened the fridge, all the lights would dim. Only the kitchen was built to human scale, but it was all dark blue, like the bottom of the sea. At times, I felt I was living in a film set, designed by people who'd never actually seen a house, just heard one described.

There were two children. They'd seldom met any Westerners, and eagerly vied to become friends of the monster. As soon as I arrived, Jimmy, aged twelve, took to the piano, and gave a long and doleful rendition of 'Auld Lang Syne'. His younger sister, Gloria, sought a more protracted encounter, and made me read her a chapter of *Les Filles de Malory School*. These children, I realised, were going to need all the Enid Blyton they could get. In their lifetime, the country's population could easily reach 130 million. Already, almost every other person was under fifteen, and of those, only half could read. In the brave new Madagascar, only the Blyton kids were likely to thrive.

None of this bothered us much in those happy few days. The maids sang as they cooked, and whenever the power went off, they'd squeal 'Blackout! Blackout!', as if it was something joyful, like Christmas. In the afternoon, there'd be a thunderstorm, rinsing everything pink, and then a carnival of frogs. Nothing was entirely familiar – the whooping birdsong, my old straw mattress, the cinnamon tea and prawn cakes for breakfast, the bells of a distant nunnery and the hymns that drifted up out of the rust. Only Avana bridled at the healthiness of it all and would often sneak off to the *gargote* for a plate of wobbling fat or for his *mofo menakely*, a magnificent doughnut shimmering with sugar.

On my third day I announced that, sadly, it was time to leave.

'You still heading out west?' asked Avana.

'*Eugh*,' said Lydia, 'nothing there but bandits.'

I SPENT MY LAST WEEKEND WITH THE Andrianarivonys, wondering what to do. Although Avana saw no particular virtue in work, his free time sat heavy on his hands. During the week, he was a clerk at the town hall, but as *les fonctionnaires* were often on strike, his days off could sometimes go on for weeks on end. In those moments, he'd just sit and smoke and think. Malagasies even have a word for this state, *mipetraka*, which is the human equivalent of Power Save. At least Lydia had her church and her *TV- novellas*. But otherwise, there was little else for her and the children to do. Everything is so expensive, she'd say.

'And what would you do,' I asked, 'if you had the money?'

'Fix the car and buy a microwave oven.'

It was different for the poor, who had their cockfighting, their dominoes and their violent bouts of rugby. None of this held much appeal for the Andrianarivonys. Nor did they want to be seen at any of the big city concerts, which were far too indelicate and raunchy. But the masses loved them, conceded Lydia. A big singer – like Dama – might even find himself elected to parliament.

So, that weekend, our only outing was to a charity lunch for Vulnerable Young Women. The journey there was harrowing enough. We had to clamber down into the village and find a *taxi-be*, or minibus. Because these never stopped, we then had to run alongside, and hurl ourselves in through the open doors. After that, it was a half-hour ride into town, squashed together with twenty others. Every day, over 700,000 *Tananariviens* have journeys like this, arriving dusty and deflated.

But our vulnerable guests had a nice day out. They all had ponytails and wore neat little cardigans and skirts. Most of them had been plucked from prostitution. When lunch arrived, they sang 'Onward Christian Soldiers' in Malagasy, and then ploughed through a mound of rice. Afterwards, we all formed up for a photograph. Looking back at those pictures, I realise now how inured I'd become to the wily ways of Tana. Few of the girls were more than fourteen.

B EFORE LEAVING TANA, I ASKED MANITRA to take me on one last foray into the night. Everyone had told me how dangerous it was. Veronique the receptionist said the robbers would take everything, even my shoes. But, somehow, I suspected that it was never as bad as people hoped. *Tananariviens* loved misadventure, and thrived on anxiety. Perhaps it was because they had no real idea how bad things could get in the twenty-first century, with skunk and drill and *gangstas* on wheels. Tana was probably no more dangerous than New York or London, even at night. But it was still brave of Manitra, agreeing to come. He was probably more worried than he cared to admit, but he wanted to show me how the city changes.

The transformation began almost as soon as the darkness came leaking through the streets. The vendors would roll up their bundles and take down their stalls, and hurry away. Suddenly, everyone was gone. The city that was megaphonic one minute was a murmur the next. The most immediate hazard was the uncovered drains, now like mantraps in the dark. But that night we took a taxi, riding down into the sodium glow. It all felt like a *film noir* (or *orange*, perhaps): the cobbled lanes; the louvres shut tight; the figures darting out of the light and the dogs, grazing in the shadows. Manitra explained that the Malagasy night wasn't divided into hours but tiny snatches of poetry. It was now late, or *misafo helika ny kary*, 'the time when the wild cat washes itself'.

A cortège of glossy black Land Cruisers passed.

'Politicians,' said Manitra, 'off to the casino.'

We ended up at The Glacier. It was a bit of a literary pit stop for me because all the great writers had been there, from Dervla Murphy to Gerald Durrell. It was just as they'd described, shabby and fun and packed with old whores. I half-expected to find Camille here, but perhaps it just wasn't quite sinister enough. The girls even seemed rather apologetic with their offers, and soon drifted away. That night, there was a band in, and they looked more African than any I'd seen before. The music was different too, more thunderous and proud than the scratchy tinkling of Tana. I asked Manitra where they were from.

'You're going there tomorrow,' he said. 'They're Sakalava.'

'And what are they singing about?'

Manitra listened for a moment.

'Usual stuff. Girls, guns and cattle. You'll see.'

The Gardens of Mars

*While the sheer size of Madagascar has caused people
to gather together for sustenance and self-protection,
its wide open spaces have also facilitated escape.*

SOLOFO RANDRIANJA AND STEPHEN ELLIS
Madagascar: A Short History, 2009

*I had a sense – which never truly left me in
Madagascar – of being in a place scarcely earthly…
melancholy, lush, secretive.*

RUPERT CROFT-COOKE
The Blood-Red Island, 1953

*The Sakalavas were… until recently, born brigands
and cattle-lifters, and their women have the reputation
of being the most stately in Madagascar.*

ARKADY FIEDLER
The Madagascar I Love, 1946

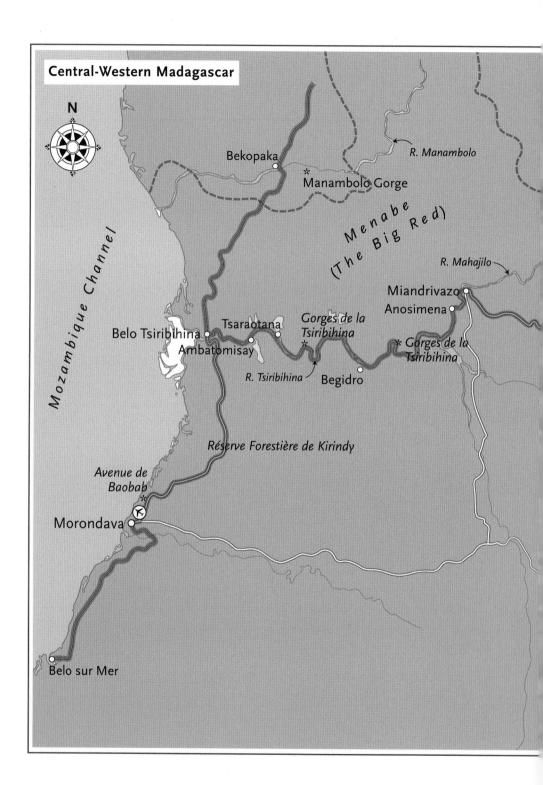

Central-Western Madagascar

N

Mozambique Channel

Bekopaka

* Manambolo Gorge

R. Manambolo

Menabe
(The Big Red)

R. Mahajilo

Miandrivazo

Anosimena

Belo Tsiribihina

Tsaraotana

Gorges de la
Tsiribihina
*

Ambatomisay

* Gorges de la
Tsiribihina

R. Tsiribihina

Begidro

Réserve Forestière de Kirindy

Avenue de
Baobab
*

Morondava

Belo sur Mer

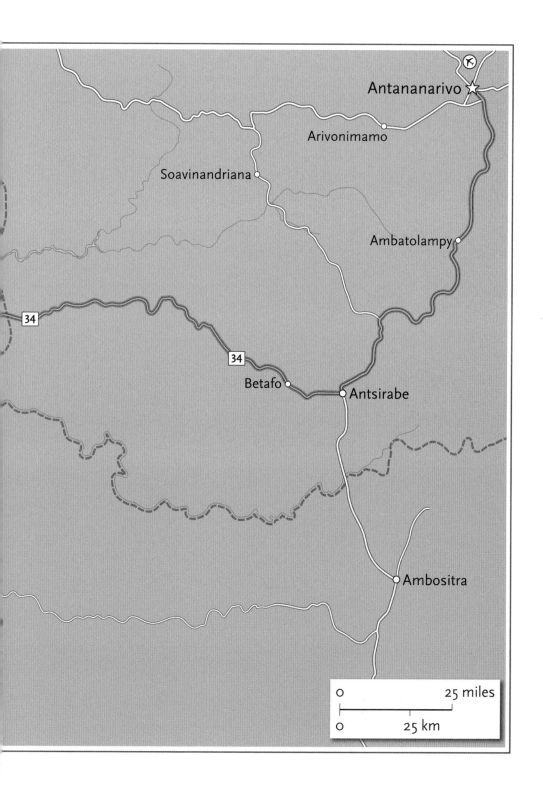

To the people of Tana, the Mid-West was still another world. The paths coming in from the west had never brought anything but trouble. Even now there was only one road – the RN34 – and no railways or buses, or proper towns along the way. The newspapers never mentioned *le moyen ouest* and nor did the government, and so – for most people – it was simply space on the map, usually empty and brown. Of course, my new friends knew all about it, and its dinosaurs and sorcery, but this didn't make it *accessible*. During the rainy season, most of it could only be reached by sea, and so for much of the year it was as remote as, say, France or the Moon. But it was dry now, and I'd found a Land Cruiser with a driver called Faustin. With him, I'd do the first 300 kilometres, and then go on by river. Manitra was envious. Out there, he said, everything was different: hotter, wilder and emptier. The place was known as Menabe, or 'the Big Red', something I'd soon understand. It wasn't just that the earth and all the rivers were red. It was also a state of mind.

'If you think this place is seventeenth century, out there it's the twelfth.'

A s MANITRA HAD PREDICTED, IT WAS an unforgettable journey. After Tana, we passed through the rice, and then what seemed like Tuscany, Borneo, the world of Hieronymus Bosch and Middle Earth. At some stage during this drive, I would fall asleep and then wake up, utterly lost.

But even from the beginning, I remember thinking how random things had become. The memories of those first few hours are fabulously disjointed: the punts, the *petanque* and the brickmakers' wives; a taxi full of goslings; the concrete Virgins; the hilltop villages, daubed in ochre and floating on water; the fishermen casting their nets and the car wrecks, still limping along; an ancient policeman wearing a *kepi*; the strawberry stalls, the pines, the ox-carts and a beautiful girl breaking rocks with a hammer.

Faustin was a thoughtful companion, and knew all the place names and tombs and magic pools. But he was different from the people out in the paddy, with his heavy limbs and his head all shaved and shiny. His forebears weren't from the *hauts plateaux*, he said, and they'd never got used to the dogs and the cold. Even though Faustin was born up here, he still found the houses strange. The typical dwelling, or *trano gasy*, looked like a thatched loaf, two storeys high, with sky-blue shutters. 'Everyone here sleeps *upstairs*,' he explained, 'and only the cattle and children sleep down below…'

After a few hours we passed Ambatolampy, where we stopped at the foundries. This is where Madagascar's hubcaps are melted down and turned into saucepans and spoons. Inside its blackened workshops, a prickly burnt-aluminium smell caught in the throat. The moulding teams worked fast, reshaping the hot sand with their hands and bare feet. They also had a special kind of bamboo piston for firing up their kilns. It's said that these bellows are found nowhere else in the world except Kalimantan. But Faustin said we shouldn't hang around. 'See how young these men are? The fumes make you sick.'

Beyond the town, the hills began to empty. For a while the rice terraces continued to collect in the gullies. But then, after four hours, there was nothing but grass and brittle tufts of *Philippia* and *Helichrysum*.

Treeless, burnt and empty, parts of the Mid-West can look like a newborn planet.

There were no trees or houses now, just the endless, borderless, waterless savannah. In places, the hillsides had collapsed, leaving great crimson wounds the size of amphitheatres. It's thought that, once, this whole area was covered in forest, but then came the humans and their tribal wars. After a particularly bloody clash, in 1821, the grasslands were all but abandoned. For hundreds of miles to the north and south, the savannah was stripped of life. Even now, it's referred to as the *efitra*, or 'partition', a beautiful no man's land that separates Madagascar's Asian highlands from the Sakalava.

The hills were now turning mauve, and Faustin drove faster.

'You worried?' I asked.

'We have to go quickly, there are many bandits and ghosts.'

'Oh. Are we going to be robbed?'

The *levaka* or eroded gullies of no man's land.

'It should be OK. We have a big car. They'll think we have guns.'
'And what about the ghosts?'
'*Vazimba*. They're everywhere here, in the hills.'

Tʜʀᴏᴜɢʜᴏᴜᴛ ᴛʜᴇ ᴛᴀʟᴇ ᴏꜰ Mᴀᴅᴀɢᴀꜱᴄᴀʀ, the Vazimba have always been there, flitting around between history and myth. Everyone agrees that they belong in the past but what's not decided is where they are now. Back in Tana, I'd often heard them mentioned. Once, a watchman stopped me in the street with his sacrificial chicken. Did I want to see him kill it? He pointed to a long slab of rock. '*C'est là que les Vazimba tuaient leurs poules!*'

To people like the *gardien* – and Faustin – the Vazimba are Super-Ancestors, peculiarly spiteful and cruel. In the popular imagination, they're small, grotesque, wide-mouthed and fanged, barely human and yet not quite beast. Every country has its trolls and goblins, but nowhere are the Little People as insistent as here. The Vazimba are in every dark corner and every lonely place, just waiting for revenge. It's said that they were the original inhabitants of this island, and that the *faha vazimba* – or the Age of the Vazimba – only ended with the arrival of Man. Armed with clay-tipped spears, these elfin natives were no match for the invaders, and fled into the wilds. Nowadays, their haunts – usually waterfalls and crags – were visited only by the desperate and the sick, with offerings of honey. But these were also dangerous places, and so were the graves. Faustin showed me several that day, now just mounds in the turf. He told me we should never point at them or go too close.

'But why are the Vazimba so angry?' I asked.

It was simple. 'They've no descendants. No one tends their tombs.'

Oddly, there was always more to these stories than age-old myth. Anthropologists now think that there really were beings like the Vazimba, and that they have their origins in science. They may not have been bestial or pixie-like, but they were this island's first inhabitants. It's also likely that they were technologically primitive, and that they were easily overrun. Perhaps this is when their name first appeared, derived from the word *simba* (those 'broken' or 'spoilt'). They may even have lived for a while in the wilds before their kind either became extinct or merged with their invaders. But what's really strange about these Proto-Malagasies is that they themselves were newcomers, and that they'd travelled over 3,700 miles, only arriving in recent times.

I still can't quite absorb all this, and the idea that until a few thousand years ago, this gigantic island was uninhabited. For perhaps 80 million years, it had remained pristine and untouched, and then, in around 8000 BC, someone arrived and began chipping rocks and sawing up bones. This makes Madagascar one of the last great land masses to be discovered and peopled, long after Australia and the Arctic. By the time Madagascar got its first permanent settlers, mankind was already busy building cities and writing history, and several great civilisations – like the Minoans and the Mesopotamians – were either already over or on their way out.

Even more bewildering is the fact that these first permanent settlers weren't from continental Africa – 240 miles away – but the other side of the Indian Ocean. Everyone agrees that they came from Borneo. It was a Jesuit missionary, Luis Mariano, who'd first noticed, in 1613, that the language here was like Malay. Ever since then, linguists have been pulling the words apart, and have discovered that over 90 per cent of them are of Austronesian origin. Many words are identical, like *mati* (the dead) or *anak* (a child). Even better, the linguists have been able to pinpoint the language to a particular valley in Kalimantan, known as Barito. Quite why these Indonesians left and set off for Africa is still a mystery. The historian Herbert Deschamps once described it as '*la plus belle enigme du monde*'.

Beautiful is a good word for a puzzle like this. It's a mystery so tantalising it seems almost crafted. Nobody even knows when the first Indonesians arrived. They might have been the chippers and sawyers of 8000 BC, but if they were, they were probably only the first wave, and would leave little of themselves behind. After that, there came successive waves, including perhaps the Vazimba and those that displaced them. But it was the Asians who arrived at around the time of Christ that left the most enduring impression. We can time their arrival quite precisely because they brought iron but not Hinduism. This means they must have left Kalimantan after smelting started (the second century BC) and before the new religion arrived (the first century AD). But there were probably more waves even after that. The great Norwegian linguist and missionary Christian Dahl, who worked in Madagascar for three decades from the late 1920s, concluded that modern Malagasies speak the language of Borneo, circa AD 400.

My friend Aro the palaeontologist had, however, disputed all this.

'It's a lie,' he'd said, 'started by the French.'

'And why would they lie?' I'd asked.

'It suited them to say we were uninhabited, then Asian, then African and now European. None of it's true. We're from Ethiopia. We even *look* Ethiopian, don't we?'

Although I had to admit to some similarities, I still preferred the Borneo theory. It wasn't just the faces and the language; up here on the *hautes terres*, Asia was everywhere, and explained so much about my journey: the terraces of rice, the foundries and the bellows, the silk, the astrology, the baskets, the ancestor worship and the everlasting tombs. One of my new friends had even gone so far as to suggest that all Malagasies were oriental at heart, 'kowtowing and submissive'. But most people weren't even sure where Borneo was. This only made it seem even more remarkable that their ancestors had made it across the ocean. Even now, nobody really knows how. Did they sail across, or float on the currents? Or did they travel round the edge, via India and Oman and then down the African coast?

'See?' said Aro, with a glint of triumph. '*None* of it makes sense.'

A S THE GRASS DARKENED, WE PASSED through a gap and Africa appeared. In that light, it felt like the Scottish glens, but way below I could sense heat and colour, brilliant reds and clumps of green. As we descended the great *escarpement occidental*, the road turned to crumbs. Faustin called the big potholes 'cow baths' and the little ones '*nids-de-poule*', or chicken-nests. For a while we got stuck behind an ox-cart, which was struggling on the steep, loose stones. To slow itself down, it was towing a sort of human brake: an old tyre, mounted with a boy in rags. As we passed, he waved, almost lost his balance, and laughed.

Everything would be different from here: the huts, the hats, the braids and the magnificent gold teeth. Even the grass had changed, and was now bobbing with cattle. These weren't the dewy-eyed creatures of the highlands, but *zebus*, those knobbly hunchbacks with a loose-fitting hide and the horns of a giant. Each one was attended by its own personal heron who was there to pick ticks and was known as the *pique-boeuf*. It was funny to think of this loyal relationship, patiently repeated across the country, eleven million times. Until recently, Madagascar had more *zebu* than people, and, even now, two out of three of them live out here, in the west. But not everyone likes the meat. During the First World War, *zebu* kept the French army going, and was known to the soldiers as *singe*, or 'monkey'.

Faustin laughed when I told him this.

'Tell that to these guys,' he said, 'and they'll probably kill you!'

Out here, he said, cattle matter and are never a joke. A man is only as good as his herd, and his wealth is measured in horns. The more *omby* he has, the more wives he deserves. The cattle world even has its own language, with over eighty words to describe what's good and bad. In fact, across the Big Red there's almost nothing to do but herding, and there's even a *zebu* in the Menabe flag.

For our last few hours, we were in the dark. Faustin drove as fast as he could, and wouldn't even stop to pee. 'No time,' he said, 'for *bushy-bushy*.'

As we descended, I could feel the air folding around us like hot, black wool. After a while, I could no longer remember the chills of the highlands, and the dust and heat began to feel normal. Our last town was called Miandrivazo, said to be the hottest place in Madagascar. That night it was all in darkness, but in the headlights we could make out the wreckage of a market, all black and charred. It was the *dahalo*, or bandits, said Faustin. A few weeks earlier they'd come into town and torched all the stalls.

We stayed on the edge of Miandrivazo, in a newly built place that looked a bit like a ranch. It was run by a very ancient Frenchman and his Malagasy girl. It was said that he came down here about every three months, to warm up his bones.

I WOKE THE NEXT MORNING TO A WIDE African sky and a broad flat basin, shot with splinters of glittering river. Although the distant horizon was like a thin brocade of terracotta, the valley here was lettuce-green and squealing with life.

Faustin had only one last task, to drive me through the meanders to Anosimena, where I'd meet my boat. It was a treeless ride, up over the ridges of straw and dust. The views went on forever, with huge dry watercourses tumbling through the rocks. Everything was red here: the riverbanks, the water, the sand, the earth, and everyone's clothes. When Arab traders first saw this land, they called it *Gezirat al-Komr*, or the Island of the Moon. But if only they'd ventured inland and seen all this redness, they'd have called it the Gardens of Mars.

Our path was slowed by crowds of tribesmen. Faustin was excited to be among the Sakalava, if slightly overawed. All he'd say was that they were different, that they never took advice or orders, and that the great gold teeth were a sign of fidelity and wealth. Of all the island's eighteen tribes, they were the most African, the most unpredictable and the most impressive. 'They love fighting,' he said, 'even the women.'

After about ten miles, we reached Anosimena. It had something of the frontier about it, perhaps because it was the end of the road and the beginning of the river. A hard-baked track led down through the stalls to the water. Here the Sakalava could buy whatever they'd need for a life on the river: catapults, hair extensions (both blonde and crimson), coloured felt trilbies, rare barks (for the treatment of evil) and huge silver bangles as thick as a finger. I bought a knife made out of car parts, if only to tempt a reaction from one of the vendors. They were all women, beautifully sculptural and still. The knife-woman also wore a magnificent edifice of braids, more topiary than hair. I asked her about the white powders she also sold, and got a gold-capped smile.

'*Calcium*,' she leered, '*pour la virilité*.'

Quite when Madagascar acquired its first Africans is just another of the island's mysteries. Most historians agree that they arrived long after the Asians, perhaps around the eleventh century, and that's why they speak the Asians' language, which was already established. But no one knows why they came, or how. One idea is that they were already half-African, half-Indonesian, living on the African coast, and that they were forced offshore by one of the great Bantu expansions, around the year 1000. The only problem with that is there's little evidence of any Indonesian settlement in Africa. Another possibility is that they didn't come willingly at all, and there's a hint of this in an old Arabic word: *Saqaliba*, or slave. People would be traded here for over five centuries, until 1896.

But whatever their origins, they brought Africa with them. Nowadays Malagasies are – in crude genetic terms – almost half African and half Asian. But it wasn't just genes they brought. They also gave Madagascar new music, new poisons, a new cattle culture, new spirits and new words. These days, Malagasies speak more Bantu than they realise, especially when they are out with the *omby*, *ondry* and *akoho* (or the cows, the sheep and the chickens). Even the cat is African (*saka*), although the crocodile has somehow retained a foot in each world and is either a *voay* or a *mamba*.

While the Sakalava may have started out as slaves, they were soon the slavers. By 1610, they were the most powerful grouping in Madagascar. Although never truly Islamic, they'd adopted Arab names, Arab habits, and an Arab monarchy with Arab rules. They'd also become handy with guns, and, with a little tutelage from English pirates, they became adept bandits, regularly raiding the highlands for slaves. With the slave-money came more muskets, more powder and shot, and more swords ('the Wives of Guns'). By 1650, the Sakalava king, Andrianda-hifotsy, was able to field an army of 12,000 warriors armed with flint-locks. After that, there was no stopping them, and the Sakalava empire would engulf almost all of western Madagascar from top to toe, only petering out in the 1750s. But, even then, the Sakalava weren't beaten, and continued to harass their neighbours – and then the French – well into the twentieth century.

Throughout its existence, this great pirate-powered pseudo-caliphate remained almost unknown to the outside world. Even the highlanders kept well away, and were known as the *amboa-lambo*, or 'dog-pigs' (thanks to their disgusting habit of keeping hounds). Of course, there were Europeans on the coast, trading slaves, but few ever ventured inland. Some of the first to do so were Anglican missionaries, beginning in 1875. But even they travelled with huge retinues of up to seventy warriors. One of the earliest visitors was the Reverend William Pickersgill, who described his mission as 'a guerrilla band, bristling with guns and spears'.

But probably the most muscular of all these Christians was the Reverend Edward McMahon. He also happened to be the great-grand-father of the Australian friends who'd introduced me to Lydia and Avana, and they'd once sent me a picture of their forebear, looking disarmingly suave. Between 1880 and 1892, he ran several expeditions into Sakalava country, or modern-day Menabe, going further than any other Westerner had ever been before. On his first trip, the food ran out after a week, and his followers were forced to eat their shoes. Being 'dog-pigs', his servants were often murdered, usually at night with a spear through the tent. 'The Sakalaves,' wrote McMahon, 'were painted savages, all armed and very rowdy.' His second expedition was so long and arduous that by the time he got back to the highlands, not even his wife knew who he was.

McMahon's last expedition in 1891 found the Sakalava in a sorry state. Their king, Toéra, was locked in a Brobdingnagian civil war with his brother, Ingréza (or 'the Englishman'), who'd set up a rival kingdom of bandits and rustlers. McMahon had gone out in search of Toéra, and had hoped to win him over with gifts, including handkerchiefs, gilt buttons, beads, gunpowder and a clockwork music box. But not even this was enough to tempt Toéra, and so the two never met. After thirteen futile months, McMahon headed home and the brothers resumed their low-grade war.

Within a few years, Toéra would have a new enemy: the French. With an army of 10,000 warriors, he marched out to meet them, and on 30 August 1897 they clashed right here at Anosimena. Today, it's just a place to buy wigs and potions, but back then the scene was set for a bloodily asymmetric encounter. The French released blizzard after blizzard of bullets, ripping through the warriors until nothing moved. It was the end for Toéra too, the man who nearly had a music box – and a chance of survival – and who is remembered instead as the last of the Sakalava kings.

A PICARESQUE VOYAGE WAS SOON TAKING SHAPE. After saying goodbye to Faustin, I found my boat, the *Hasina 3*, which was moored some way out in a channel through the sand. Small, top-heavy and brightly painted, it was the kind of barge a fairy queen would have used for making stately rides downriver. Up aloft was a sort of throne deck, and the one below was scattered with cushions. As the only passenger, I usually had the decks all to myself. Out in the stern was a tiny housing where the crew lived, along with two chickens and a duck.

Even the crew had something elfin about them. Only the skipper, Dada, was a Sakalava, and he'd sit above the wheezy old engine, steering with his toes. The other crewmen were highlanders, and were quick, light-footed and seldom seen. There were two deckhands called Rifé and Sambatra, and a cook, who was very slight and sinewy and known as 'Bobola', or Fatty. Every evening, he'd conjure something remarkable out of not very much, a salad perhaps, or a platter of seafood.

Then, presiding over all of this was a Puck-like figure, known as Nat. Although he looked about fifteen, he insisted that he was married and had children of his own. But he knew the Sakalava and the rivers well because his father had been a mechanic here, working for the French. He also had a way of announcing things as if it were magic. 'Tonight, we make a new itinerary! *Tout a changé!* Our first village has just burnt down!'

As soon as we were ready, the boys began to punt us out through the narrow channel. Although the Mahajilo river was only waist-deep, it was cluttered with boats – mostly tobacco barges, or *chalands*, and dugouts laden with lemons. But it soon broadened out, and after half an hour we entered a much bigger, redder waterway, the Tsiribihina. From here, said Nat, we had another 160 kilometres to go.

It was mesmerising, being out in the currents. Although the river here was barely deeper, it had opened out to the horizon, and was like a desert of churning liquefied mirror. In order to get through the shoals, one of the boys would have to dangle off the prow, shouting directions. Then, whenever we grounded in the sand, they'd all jump off and heave us free.

For a while, we saw little of the banks, just a slim, attenuated trim of ochre, dog-toothed with mauve. But then, by about noon, the river started to narrow again, and the land around us began to rise, thinly bristled in scrub. The scrawny woodland, known as *savoka*, was all that was left of a much grander forest, now all burnt away. But as the banks folded in around us, the trees darkened and began to billow up like great thunderclouds of green. We were entering the Gorge of Tsiribihina.

The Tsiribihina river now took a dreamy, unhurried course between the cliffs. The walls of the gorge were too steep here for mankind, and so a much older forest had survived. Out of this dense, whistling broccoli of colour rose magnificent, lanky trees. Some were perhaps six storeys high and as white and knobbly as stone. Their canopy looked like another woodland, floating high above, and pouring creepers and orchids. Then, even higher still, and way above the forest, were the well-rounded hills of the savannah, like giant eggs covered in lawn.

Nat joined me at the rail, and I asked how the river got its name.

'It means "No diving here"…'

'Because it's too shallow?'

'No,' he laughed, 'the crocodiles!'

The boatmen knew every click and squeal, and every flash of feathers. Over the next few days, they'd point out all manner of birds, from the brilliantly coiffed to the vaguely annoying. They also spotted several different types of lemur, a glorious repertory of frogs, two boas, and half a dozen chameleons, all different and all equally improbable. This is to say nothing of the river's outlandish botany: its primitive cycads, spiky palms and Jurassic-looking ferns. Everything seemed either alien or prehistoric, and that's hardly surprising. Some 90 per cent of

Madagascar's plants and animals are found nowhere else in the world. In terms of plants alone, there are 14,000 species here – compared to say, Britain, with a mere 3,800.

Bobbing along the river, it was easy to get a bit fanciful. I began to think of Madagascar as a laboratory, turning our prototypes that had long been forgotten. It wasn't a new idea. In 1771, the French naturalist Joseph Philibert Commerson had said this of the island: 'Here, nature seems to have withdrawn into a private sanctuary in order to work on designs different to those elsewhere. At every step you are met by bizarre and wonderful forms…'

But brilliant as he was, Commerson hadn't reckoned with plate tectonics. Madagascar isn't so much a new world as the relic of an old one. To understand its wonder, you need to go back about 150 million years, to the break-up of the supercontinent Gondwana. At that point, what's now Madagascar was sandwiched between the African continent, Antarctica and India. As they split up in the mid-Jurassic period, Madagascar and India floated away on the Earth's fluid-like crust. After another 50 million years, Madagascar neared its present position, and

A militiamen with his pet chameleon. There are 62 species of chameleon here, or two-thirds of the world's total.

India began to tear itself off and drift towards Asia. With that, the last vestiges of a land bridge failed, and Madagascar became separated from its mother-continent by a deep trench of ocean (now known as the Mozambique Channel). For the last 80 million years, it's been almost a continent all of its own.

As a free-floating fragment of Gondwana, Madagascar became something of a last resort. Jurassic life forms, which have vanished elsewhere, have survived here, particularly among the plants. Meanwhile, the only new creatures to arrive were those that could float. This meant that – apart from pygmy hippos and crocodiles – none of Africa's big names made it, and so there are no lions and elephants and roaming ungulates. Left to themselves, the floaters and swimmers have therefore thrived, and now, very often, they're all that remains of their kind. This is particularly so of Madagascar's 170 mammals, of which only the bats can be found elsewhere.

But the island's creatures haven't just thrived, they've also diversified. An example of this is the tenrec, a sort of multi-nippled, rapidly reproducing hedgehog. It's possible that Madagascar's population began with a single castaway – pregnant, obviously – and yet now there are some thirty species. The same is true of lemurs. Across 107 species, there are some the size of a toddler, and others no bigger than a hen's egg; some, like the aye-aye, are amusingly ugly, while others, like some of the sifakas, wear cream pyjamas and maroon velvet gloves. The chameleons too seem to be in fancy dress, their ninety-two species wearing everything from Fabergé to mud. No wonder Commerson had sensed artistry at work, and some great agency churning out species just for fun.

Most of the time, life on the banks could seem startlingly lovely. In places, the forest would part, and there'd be waterfalls and banana groves, and luminous strips of rice. Once, we spotted a gang of charcoal burners asleep under a mango tree, and as we passed they all got up and grinned, shouting out for bottles. But mostly it was only the herons attending our progress, looking like butlers in their tatty green tails. Then, as the sun cooled, the great herds would come rumbling down to the water, under clouds of swirling rust.

Even the crocodiles had a certain charm as, with a lash and a smack, they vanished in the shallows. Malagasies once thought, quite reasonably, that the crocodiles mated with the waterbirds and that's why they laid eggs. But there was always fear too, and the idea that these beasts were ancestors who'd come back to haunt them. An account from 1670 describes the role of crocodiles in criminal trials, with the accused being forced to wade a river to determine his guilt. Even in Victorian times, they represented the greatest obstacle to travel, and were always picking off soldiers and cattle. As McMahon put it, rather grimly: 'There is nothing dangerous in Madagascar except crocodiles, which abound in the rivers.'

We only saw a few that day, and they didn't stop us swimming.

'The Sakalava now kill them,' said Nat, 'as a cure for asthma.'

It will be a sad day when the crocodiles finally disappear. They are all that remains of Madagascar's megafauna, and when they're gone there'll be no wild animals weighing more than 11 kilos.

The other Big Beasts were all faintly ridiculous and never stood a chance. Among them was a jumping aardvark, and the *tsyomby-omby*, or pygmy hippo, which just looked like pork for everyone else. Slightly more imposing was the *archaeolemur*, which – judging by its skeleton – was the superhero of the lemur world, with the body of the Incredible Hulk and head of a warthog. Even bigger was the elephant bird, which was 10 feet tall but, with a brain no bigger than a peach, it was flightless, gormless and ultimately hopeless. None of these lumpen giants would survive the arrival of humans, and by around AD 1200, they were probably all gone.

One day, the crocodile too will vanish, leaving us with nothing but bones and a few pairs of shoes.

WE CAMPED OVERNIGHT ON THE RIVERBANK, with two families from the forest. They were all nomadic farmers, and because the gorge was still narrow here, they had to plant their rice in the shoals. Between them, they had few clothes, just shorts and trilbies. The first family lived in a shallow cave, furnished only with a meagre scattering of pans. Their children, I noticed, were all armed with catapults.

'They do the hunting,' said Nat, 'every day.'

The other family lived in a shelter made of leaves and branches, out on the sand. They were about to boil up a kingfisher, which one of their boys had killed. Although they had chickens, these were only for selling to passing boats. I offered the children a tin of Marks & Spencer's sardines if they could beat me in catapult contest. I was confident of my chances until the six-year-old stepped forward and pinged off three direct hits. He'd never seen a tin before, and couldn't believe it contained a fish. I like to think that, thanks to that fish, there's now one more kingfisher out on the river.

'And what about lemurs? Will they eat them too?'

'Sure,' said Nat, 'it's the best meat of all.'

For a while, we all sat around munching wild honeycomb, which was deliciously scented and waxy. Then a local militia arrived, sent by the village. They made an incongruous sight with the football shirts, axes and shotguns. Hadn't McMahon travelled with a bunch like this, in 1890? Nat said that they'd been sent to protect us against *dahalo*, or bandits, and to take us to some waterfalls to swim. At first, they looked merely warlike and surly, but they soon lightened up when we got under way. One of the gunmen had a gold tooth, and although I never knew his name, I came to think of him as 'Goldie'. He also had a large bag of cartridges and a homemade *kabosy*, or banjo, which made a noise like barbed wire on glass. But it was nothing compared to his own pain, and I noticed him wince.

'Toothache,' said Nat, translating.

I found some paracetamol. 'Take two every four hours.'

'What's an hour?' said Goldie.

I tried to explain but it was not good. 'What's a watch?' he said.

Goldie didn't even know how old he was, although he took a guess at twenty. He said he wasn't frightened of anything because he had good magic. His *ody gasy*, or charms, would protect him against everything: snakes, spears, ghosts, storms, madness, leprosy and locusts. A bit of toothache wouldn't worry him either. Eating cures everything, doesn't it?

'OK,' I said to Nat, 'then let's ask him to supper.'

Goldie brightened at first but then scowled when he saw the pork. Pig was *fady*, he said. It was taboo to eat it.

Overleaf: The nomadic hunters who live on the banks of the Tsiribihina.

We found him some biscuits, and soon our friendship was back on track. Goldie then nestled down among the cushions on deck, and there he stayed all night. I preferred to sleep out on the sand, between the two families. It was a hot, still night, and in the gorge everything sounded loud and close: the hunters coughing; someone peeing in the river; an owl, and the mewling of the lemurs.

By dawn, the sand felt cool and clammy. I got up and went to the waterfall. Our *gardiens* were already there, wrapped in shawls. They'd found proper food, and were roasting a large *goadrano*, or black-crowned heron.

T HAT MORNING, WE LEFT AT ABOUT TEN – or, as the Sakalava call it, 'gunfire'. A few miles downstream, I noticed that up in the hills, parts of the savannah were now black and charred.

'*Dahalo bediabe*,' said the cook. Lots of outlaws.

'Yes,' said Nat, 'they're covering their tracks...'

I must have looked surprised, but he just smiled.

'They've gone. These guys only attack in the afternoon, so they can escape in the dark. And this *feu de brousse* is probably a few days old, so maybe now they'll be far away, even with their cattle. But, you know, there are a lot of them round here. We call this the *zone rouge*. It sounds like a war zone, doesn't it? Well, I suppose it is, kind of...'

'And who are these people, the *dahalo*?'

'It's a bit complicated,' said Nat, settling himself at our little table.

Outlaws have often loomed large in the economics of Menabe. After centuries of slaving and stripping down the hinterlands, the lawlessness seemed natural. With the demise of the Sakalava empire, a dystopia emerged. Plunder became a means of survival and only the best thieves survived. By 1875, all that remained was a society of bandits. Pickersgill reported that everything was stolen, even the women. His Norwegian colleague Arne Walen declared that 'a more thievish people than the Sakalava can hardly be found anywhere'. Athletic and hard-drinking, they were brutal by instinct. Twenty years later, another missionary, George Smith, described 'a floating population of robbers on the lookout for plunder'. Women and luggage bearers were still targeted, but the big prize was cattle.

Rustling became an art form, and even the children were encouraged to steal. In the Sakalava tradition, no boy was considered fit to marry unless he'd snaffled a few of his neighbour's beasts. It was like a game at first, and no one got killed. If the boy was caught, the most he could expect was to be enslaved, at least for a month or two. But then, in the 1920s, the meat-packing plants appeared. Stolen cattle could now be made to disappear, and reappear as money. The raids got more ambitious, and the gangs got bigger and took up guns. Even the French could never completely manage the *dahalo*, and so the bands are still out there, up to eighty strong.

'And who are they?' I asked. 'Kids, young men, mostly.'

'What, they use *children* on these raids?'

'Yes, they want people who can run! The kids are sent by their parents, to get some quick money. It's big business, right? These *dahalo* can get like 100,000 ariary for one *zebu*. That's *twenty-five* euros! And it's not just cattle they're after. They sometimes raid shops for food or maybe some money. They've even been robbing the gold prospectors – so now there are *gendarmes* protecting them. But, you know, the *dahalo* aren't scared! They just run in the forest, and, hey, no one wants to chase them in there. They got simple guns, and some of the gangs are, you know, a little bit crazy…'

'Do they ever stop the boat?'

'Sometimes. They just want some rice, and so we give it.'

'But don't they want to rob the foreigners?'

'No, they're frightened of *vazaha*.'

This time, I smiled, but Nat insisted.

'They've all seen *Rambo*,' he said, 'and all those dead people.'

Over the next few hours, we passed several deserted tobacco warehouses and a few abandoned villages. Nat said that the lawlessness had become too much for them. We did, however, stop at one of the surviving settlements, called *Begidro* or 'Many Lemurs'. From the river, the only sign of life was the naked women bathing in the shallows. As we pulled in, they looked up at me sullenly and without moving at all. At that moment, I wasn't sure whether I was relieved to be Rambo or deeply ashamed. Nat shouted out our names, and a village elder appeared, wearing only shorts. He was a slight, stringy man, part Asian, mostly

African. His voice sounded rapid and scratchy.

'Something's wrong,' said Nat, 'some *zebu* are missing.'

Already, spearmen were setting out along the river. Across the village there was an air of resolve, as if something inevitable needed to happen. The elder led us up through lanes of thatch and bright-red daub until we came to an open area of flat, hard earth. There were many more armed men here, perhaps a hundred. Some had shotguns but most were armed with long knives called *coup-coups* or short stabbing spears. In their Barcelona and Manchester United shirts, they looked like Goldie's militia, except more inanimate and dangerous. Nat called them the *kalony*, or village column.

'No photos,' he warned.

The men didn't move all morning. They were the rearguard, ready in case the *dahalo* attacked while the trackers were out. I asked Nat what the *kalony* would do if they caught an outlaw.

'Kill him.'

'So no police involved?'

'Never. If you call the *gendarmes*, they're just going to lock the guys up, and then the *dahalo* pay a bribe, and they go free and come and kill you! So you make sure you kill them. Tie them up, spear them, and then a bit of petrol and – *whoosh* – it's all over. The guy's disappeared, and no one knows nothing.'

THE ELDER WAS CURIOUS AS TO WHY I'd called by, and so I explained that I'd come to see the sorcerer. This was a perfectly sensible thing for a traveller to do, and the old man nodded solemnly.

Around here, the Sakalava never did anything without a spell. Consulting the *ombiasy*, or 'Man of Much Virtue', was like going for a spiritual check-up. He would read your fortune, clear out old curses, neutralise any *gris-gris* (or evil spells) and top you up with a dose of luck. He might even confound your enemies, or perform a little *mosavy*, or black magic. The Sakalava have always believed in the supercharged effect of lethal hoodoo. During the time of the kings, it was the custom to have someone buried alive in the foundations of a royal village. Even as late as 1914 there's a report of an *ombiasy* killing a child and spreading his entrails across the fields to ward off locusts. Infants were obviously particularly potent, and, according to McMahon, were always being abandoned or killed. Even today, there are categories of children vulnerable to magic, particularly albinos and twins.

'We have two *ombiasy*,' said the elder, 'but one is old.'

The younger sorcerer lived in an untidy structure of mud and branches, a bit like a nest. Inside, we arranged ourselves around him, on tiny stools two inches high. He was more Asian-looking than the rest of the tribe, and set out before him were several home-made charts covered in symbols. Nat said he already knew everything about me, and the *ombiasy* smiled.

A Victorian depiction of the Malagasy sorcerer.

'You have a daughter who is kind,' he said.

'Yes.'

'And you saw crocodiles yesterday.'

'Yes, also true.'

'And you were recently wounded with a knife…?'

In the darkness, I could hear Nat snigger, so I changed the subject.

'I wonder if you have anything to make me bulletproof…?'

Nat said the *ombiasy* didn't usually sell amulets to *vazaha* but he could show me how to make one. With that, the sorcerer produced a cow's horn and all the magical things that went inside: a hank of human hair, a needle, some dung, a scorpion's tail and a crocodile tooth. He called it a *mohira*, and said that, with this, I could shoot him and he'd be fine. We laughed about this, but then he was suddenly serious. 'Never eat melons or pork,' he said, 'or your *mohira* loses its power, and then you're dead.'

Before leaving, the *ombiasy* offered to tell my fortune. For this, he used an old Arab technique, with *sikidy* beads. First, he spread them out on the mat in front of me, and then he spat on his hands and consulted his charts. After a long and earnest discussion among the Malagasies, it was Nat who spoke. 'You should be OK,' he said. 'Nothing will happen.'

S UDDENLY, FROM THE NEXT SHACK, there were howls of pain. It wasn't one voice but the sound of many women. For a terrible moment, I thought the *dahalo* were back.

'They're mourners,' said Nat 'The neighbour died.'

The *ombiasy* knew the full story. It was a tale of truly Jacobean villainy, with a slightly incongruous local ending. The gist of it revolved around two brothers who'd argued over a piece of land. The older sibling had resolved the issue with an axe, splitting a chunk off his brother's head. The dead man, who was aged eighteen, was now being attended by his wife and the women of the village. In the old days, they'd have placed him in the sun, and drained him of fluids. Things were simpler now, and a bit more chemical. From here, the body would be carried to his father's house, where it would be injected with formalin and kept for a month while a tomb was built. Throughout that time, the wife would have to stay with the corpse, her head always covered.

'And what will happen to the brother, the killer?'

The sorcerer frowned, as if he'd not thought of this before.

'He'll pay five cows to the wife, and then he must marry her.'

Like all Malagasies, the people of Begidro believe that those who've died are never quite dead. But, unlike the highlanders, they won't be raising their ancestors in years to come and parading them around. This is partly because the dead are always there, moving among them, and to see them, all that's needed is a trance or *tromba*. But it's not just relatives who appear in these moments. The Sakalava believe that there's a whole world out there in this fourth dimension: movie stars, cowboys, *dahalo*, good-time girls and everyone else who's already died.

As if their spiritual ether wasn't already crowded enough, there was then a cast of improbable creatures. Perhaps the deeper you go into the *brousse*, the more surreal you become. Out here, the Sakalava imagination is richly infested with oddities and monsters. Nat knew some of these beasts, and the crew the rest. One was a blood-sucking ox called the *songaomby*, who was very fat and fast. Another was the *tokantongotra*, a sort of shaggy sheep with only one useful foot and another growing out of its chest. How had such a fabulous ogre ever come to be? It particularly hated dogs, and was always sucking out their eyes.

Perhaps slightly more endearing were the *kalanoro*. Unlike the Vazimba, they were animals, not people, and they had long fingernails and eyes that glowed like coals. But, according to the cook, they weren't hostile to humans, and were often drawn in by the smell of food.

'They like *frites*,' he said, 'and chocolate pudding.'

After Begidro, the sides of the valley flattened, and the savannah came rolling down to the river. All day we watched, as the *kalony* fanned out along the banks and up into the grass. Our worlds seemed to be separated by so much more than water. While I sat leafing through Smith and McMahon, they were out there with spears, hunting men.

Overleaf: Arriving in Tsaraotana or 'Good Village', a haven of tranquillity in the lawless Mid-West.

THE GARDENS OF MARS

We seemed to have arrived at this point from different centuries, thousands of miles apart. At one stage, our boat pulled over to deliver some rice to a distant outpost, and the militiamen came scrambling over the dunes to meet us. I noticed that this particular posse all had shotguns, painted up like modern art. What a way to go, I thought, blasted away by a Rothko or de Kooning.

Fortunately, the sorcerer was right, and nothing happened that day. Although there were little patches of burning grass, it was only ever *tavy*, or farmers' fires. In places the river widened, and the water swirled and bubbled over the shoals, but then it narrowed again, and life resumed its sleepy hum. Once, we passed under a great red cliff, densely festooned in flying foxes. The bats were the same colour as the rock, and I remember thinking how like our own foxes they looked, except with enormous wings like plastic macs. Sadly, the river-people here see them only as lunch, a couple of pounds of easy meat.

Towards the end of the afternoon, we stopped at Tsaraotana, or 'Good Village'. When George Smith called by in 1891, he'd found that many of the women were slaves captured in the highlands and co-opted as wives. It seems that, over the decades, their progeny have prospered, and now the village had a school, five *gendarmes*, several hundred *zebu* and a fearsome militia.

'The *dahalo* never come here,' said Nat. 'They're too scared.'

As we wandered through the huts, an ordinary day on the savannah was drawing to a close. The cattle were being driven out of the grass into corrals, and the villagers were returning home with baskets of crayfish and cassava. A bloom of red dust rose off the football pitch as two teams of bloodied girls slogged it out. One of the *gendarmes* was acting as referee, and trotted among them, his Kalashnikov slung across his back.

'And this is the school,' said Nat, arriving at a shed.

It may not have looked much but it was progress of sorts. Traditionally, Sakalava children have never had it easy. The girls were considered worthless, and the boys would be bullied into adulthood, kicked and shot, and circumcised with axes. It's said that they weren't punished for stealing, only getting caught. Writing in the 1960s, the American traveller Arthur Stratton had concluded that the Sakalava were committing tribal suicide, due to their refusal to adapt. 'They have opted for death', he wrote, 'not a watered-down life.' Well, now, here they were, half a century later, with their own little school. While it may not have had pencils or furniture, or even books, there was at least a teacher with a piece of chalk.

I WAS SORRY TO BE LEAVING THE RIVER. For all its woes, there was magic everywhere, in the people and the hills.

On our last night, we camped on a sandbank at Ambatomisay. The river was much wider now, but just as shallow and red. Along the south bank was a baobab forest, and a small village built of reeds. Although the baobabs were tall and solid, and looked like watchtowers, they'd offered little protection against the *dahalo*. Two years earlier, the huts had been burnt to the ground, and so now, every night, the villagers paddled out into the shoals and slept on the sand.

Before long, an impromptu community was taking shape on our little islet. Among the villagers was Monsieur Levelo with his eight children. The oldest of them, called Zelma, looked about fifteen, but because they'd never been to school, none of them knew their age.

The women of Tsaraotana, descended from slaves captured in the Highlands.

THE GARDENS OF MARS   77

Aurelia thought she was seven, although she looked about five, and they all liked the boat and the light that it brought. Although they never asked for anything, there was always an air of expectation, as if their show was about to begin.

Eventually, when the river was nothing but a gurgle of glassy moonlight, Monsieur Levelo lit a huge fire. Suddenly, the family seemed to fill the place with their flames and their songs and their wild music, which sounded more like a band than a simple *kabosy*. Then, with their father's voice booming out across the water and through the forest, the children began to dance. It was always anticlockwise around the fire,

The shoals of Ambatomisay, a refuge from bandits.

and always compelling. Despite the uncertainties of their world, they moved with flawless precision. Perhaps I'd simply become accustomed to the chaos and spontaneity of the grasslands, and now here was this: the perfect synthesis of geometry and sound.

T HE SEA WAS NEAR AND ALONG THE BANKS I could now see bicycles draped with fish. On the afternoon of our third day we reached Belo sur Tsiribihina, and I disembarked. The crew ran this gauntlet all the time, so I tried not to sound too momentous. Nat was already thinking about the journey back. Because they were battling against the current, it was a harder journey, and so they never stopped.

'It's not good,' he said, 'the river at night.'

There was no great welcome at Belo, just an old Toyota and a drunk called Gaspar. My heart sank when I first saw him, puffy-faced and swigging water from an antifreeze can. Worse, he spoke little French, and so – for the next fortnight – we'd have to get by on a few Gallic grunts. But Gaspar never registered much and, sleepless and parched, he'd soon come to regard me with unalloyed disinterest. I realised, of course, that this wasn't personal, and that he looked like a boxer because everything beat him. But he was at least Sakalava, and for that I'd be grateful. It meant he knew the bush and the potholes and all the spectral people who inhabited the roads.

We didn't linger in Belo. It seemed to be at the end of an era, or perhaps the beginning of another. Everything was dusted in pink, like a faded film. There were several old churches, all abandoned to the breeze, and several new ones going up. I remember a wheelwright too, hacking out spokes from a stump of wood. In 1976, Belo had been down to its last few inhabitants, but then came the zoologists and a new lease of life. These days, the town even had its own fancy restaurant, where everything was served on stiff white linen. It had become a sort of culinary frontier, one last taste of shrimps and *crème caramel*, before plunging into the bush. All those lemurs and the Tsingy de Bemaraha were still another hundred miles away, off to the north.

It was an unsettling drive, perhaps the worst in the western savannahs.

Between the rivers Tsiribihina and Manambolo, there was nothing but dust and desiccated forest. In places, the *piste*, or track, felt like a tunnel through the twigs. Gaspar called it the *andalandahalo*, or the Bandits' Road. There were very few people out here but whenever they appeared, they always seemed desperate. From nowhere, they'd run at our truck, begging for biscuits or bottles or just some water. They all had axes or spears, and some were militiamen with painted guns. I had a feeling that, for many of these people, this was all there was to it, and that the road was their home.

Wherever there were hollows, there were children, cooling in the mud. Most looked small or misshapen, or distended with disease. A doctor once told me that, in rural areas like this, every sixth child was suffering bilharzia. It would kill them eventually, after years of toying with the bladder and wrecking the liver. This made no sense to the doctor. 'It can all be cured!' she said. 'With a single pill!'

The road-dwellers had nothing to offer, except a little extortion. This was easy, among so many potholes. They'd simply fill one in with bits of debris, and then demand a fee from anyone passing. These could be ugly exchanges, and I'd feel Gaspar tense with each new roadblock. It was like being repeatedly robbed, a few pence each mile. One of these days, I thought, the tollmen will abandon their niceties, and just strip down the car. It happened sooner than I could have imagined. Six weeks later, a van full of Germans was stopped near here and enthusiastically ransacked. Even now, I can almost picture the men who did it: a gang of highway robbers, slung with amulets and catapults, and wearing camouflage shorts.

The reward for all this was the *tsingy* itself. Poetically, if not geologically, it's a vast collection of cathedrals, thousands of spires crushed together into a few square miles. Of all the world's great natural wonders, few look so unnatural. Everything about it seems Gothic and sculpted. There isn't a single pinnacle that hasn't been bevelled and shaped, or artfully scalloped, and yet some of these works are over 100 metres high. But it's not just a skyline. Descending into limestone, there are cloisters and corridors, tiny atria of captive forests, secret gardens with palmeries and orchids, and pools full of frogs. Sometimes it's hard to believe that all you're seeing is a block of seabed, heaved from the depths during some great tectonic refurbishment, and then gnawed by the wind.

I spent the day climbing up through the jungle and into the stone. With me was a local guide, who led me from chamber to chamber and down through the grikes. Gigantic roots groped their way along the corridors, and at some stage we slithered down into a little chapel full of bats. The zoologists have always known how important the *tsingy* is, and new species are often tumbling out of the dark. In recent years these have included a miniature lemur, a brand-new bat, and a curiously dandyish frog.

Eventually, a network of ladders led us upwards into the spires. Nowadays, lots of people climb up here, just because they can. But for the Sakalava, it's still the holiest of places. Although their world has no centre, or even a heart, this is probably as close as anywhere gets. Once, to be entombed up here was the equivalent of landing in heaven. Few of

the tombs, however, had survived the visitors and the noise of the West, although my guide knew of one. It was tucked away in a shallow cave, a bundle of bones wrapped in bark. The dead man, said the guide, had lived in the Time of the Kings (so, deep in the nineteenth century). I tried to picture him with his slaves and his flintlocks and his beaten-up sons, and I wondered what he'd have made of the modern era. An age of magnificent machines, perhaps. Or the descent into chaos.

THE LEMURS WERE IN FESTIVE MOOD, as we came down through the woods. You never forget your first lemur (or your first kangaroo). Everything about them is faintly absurd: the teddy-bear bodies, the man-like hands, the furry pyjamas, and the expression of surprise. I suddenly thought this all over again, as I watched them in close-up. They were all different. Some had ears like ping-pong bats, and others were spectacled or gingery. Of Madagascar's 107 species, at least eleven hang around the *tsingy*. Their lives, it seemed, were just a game.

Europeans have always gone soft at the mention of lemurs. They were given their name by Carl Linnaeus, the Swedish naturalist, who'd never even seen one (he thought they sounded like Virgil's spooks that crept around at night). But the very first description was provided by William Keeling, captain of the East India Company's *Red Dragon*, in 1608. He'd seen an adorable creature with a 'long tail like a Fox garled with white and blacke, the furre very fine'. It was the beginning of a little obsession that would eventually lead to movies and ads.

But Keeling had also recognised that the lemur wasn't a monkey – and that's the key to its survival. Nowadays it's thought of as a pre-monkey, or *prosimian*, an earlier version of what was to come: slower, less dextrous and appreciably dimmer. It would never have competed in the monkeys' world but then – in Madagascar – it would never need to. Washed ashore 40 million years ago, the island's lemurs would long predate the modern ape. The monkeys couldn't even follow them out here, because within a few million years the currents changed, making the crossing more impossible than ever. The creatures now bouncing

The Tsingy de Bemaraha, a strangely Gothic world, sculpted from limestone.

round the *tsingy* are therefore a cute reminder of the Cenozoic age.

The Malagasies have always been a little more ambivalent about their distant cousins. It was once thought lemurs could speak (but that they refused to do so in case someone made them work). Even now, they're sometimes regarded as ancestors, although they're more often eaten or turned into pets. It's estimated that some 28,000 of them now live in chains and cages.

'And do they make good pets?' I asked the guide.

'No,' he said, 'they never learn. So your house is a toilet.'

I SPENT MY LAST DAY ON THE WESTERN savannahs at Bekopaka, by the river. Perhaps in the years to come, Menabe will have many more hotels like the Soleil du Tsingy, with its fresh croissants for breakfast, an infinity pool and all those sinks of petrified wood. Someone had even hauled a few tons of marble up the hill and built a sun deck for nudists. Maybe one day the Sakalava will appreciate a place like this but, for now, it must seem utterly mysterious, like something dropped from Space.

Most of the staff were from the highlands, and were equally puzzled by the Sakalava. The manager and his wife were new, and were horrified to find themselves so deeply immersed in cavemen and hunters. 'And they've got such big *cocks*!' he whispered. 'I think they must be more African than us...'

Some of the cleaners, however, were Sakalava, and offered to take me to a festival of fighting, called *moraingy*.

'Everyone will be going,' said the manager, 'even the *dahalo*.'

Gaspar drove us down to the village, and then sloped off to find some hooch. My new friends were called Noce and 'Johnny the Vazimba'. Although we had no common language, I could tell they were excited, and a little scared. A large crowd had already gathered on the dusty red field in the middle of the village. Among them was a ringmaster, a bare-chested boy armed with a bullwhip. There were squeals as he started driving people back to the edge of the arena, cracking the whip over their heads. But then the crowd surged forward again, as the fighters appeared. They made an impressive sight, all torso and muscle, ebony-hard and taut with sinews. It was impossible to tell which were the farmers and which were bandits. They all had gangster haircuts and a ready sneer. Next to me, Johnny gasped, and I could feel the crowd edging back.

There were more snaps and screams, and the fighting began. I've never seen sport played with such ferocity and malice. Each bout only lasted a few seconds, and was soon a blur of intertwined limbs and flailing fists. The object, it seemed, was simply to overwhelm one's opponent with a surge of fury. On one occasion, this violence outlasted the round and spilt out into the crowd, which fell back in terror, upsetting stalls and scattering peanuts and chickens. In the stampede, I lost my friends and never saw them again. But the fighting didn't stop, and I was instantly swept up by the peppery mob, and back into the arena. Gusts of hot, rich fear now rose off the crowd.

The athletes fought on into the twilight. Sometimes it was the women fighting, and they'd grab a handful of plaits before pummelling the face. No one ever seemed to win. All that mattered was to look undefeated

Moraingy fighters, offering a few seconds of overwhelming violence.

and to appear unhurt. It was a beautifully Sakalava evening: gutsy, irrational and wild. But, eventually, it was too dark to see anything, and so I extracted myself, and set out for the drinking dens in search of Gaspar. The next day, we had a big drive ahead, back down through the *zone rouge*, and out to the sea.

B EFORE US LAY A GREAT, BURNT-OUT FOREST, over 50 miles deep. For hours, there was a light stubble of tree trunks across the horizon, all wispy and white. After retracing our steps, and rafting across the Tsiribihina, we'd taken the road for Kirindy. It was like driving through the mind of Paul Nash, a lustrous landscape of stumps and bone. In a few places, the fires were still burning, but elsewhere lawns had appeared, in brilliant shoots of succulent green. This is what the cattlemen want – 'the green bite' – and so, every year, they set the scenery alight, and burn off everything indigestible and woody. The old forest can only take so much of this, and will eventually turn into desert. Even now, there were occasional tracts of roasted earth, bristling with bunch grass.

Man may only have been here for a few thousand years, but he's made quite an impression. All over Madagascar, there are scenes like this, as human beings possess the terrain and make it their own. Of course, not all of it had been forest, and there's plenty of evidence of grass from the start. But it's estimated that, by the sixteenth century, the central highlands had been almost entirely cleared of woods. Now, across the island, only 10 per cent of the original forest remains. The worst period was between 1960 and 1990, when almost half the trees were lost. At one point, some 275,000 acres were being cleared every twelve months. That's like plundering a different English county each year, and then setting fire to whatever remains.

All of this appals outsiders. Some commentators see Madagascar as the precursor of our fate, a doomed ecosystem bowling along down the path to extinction. Even in the most respectable papers, it's been described as 'seared', 'lifeless' and 'four-fifths barren'. The science isn't always particularly scientific. Often, it's claimed that a third of the island is burnt each year, but this can't possibly be true. Another writer has even suggested that – at the present rates of erosion – the island will be completely washed away over the next 3 million years.

But perhaps the most colourful of all these claims is the idea that, from Space, Madagascar looks as if it's bleeding to death. That's not what the photos show, but perhaps *someone* has seen it? Maybe, but it sounds a bit lyrical for an astronaut.

At Kirindy the forest momentarily recovered, and we stopped for the night. Near our roadhouse was a research station, and that evening I visited the scientists. They said that their little reserve was an island of life. Even in torchlight I could make out a carnival of beasts, with crested couas and sickle-billed vangas, and a very excitable lemur the length of my thumb. Among the revellers, I also came across my first fossa (or *Cryptoprocta ferox*), a skulking dog-like creature with the manners of a mongoose. It's unusual to find them at a party because they eat all the chickens and kill the lemurs, and nobody likes them. This particular one had adapted to the loss of his forest by hanging round the kitchens.

As I was leaving, I thanked the scientists, and wished them luck.

'*Merci,*' they said, 'we'll need it. Just one fire, and we're finished.'

The next morning, two of the biologists came to the roadhouse and asked for a lift. Chery and Haja were only students, but they were passionate about science, and talked all the way to Morondava. They said that people here were very poor, and that they faced a choice: either they burnt the trees for their cattle or they joined the *dahalo*. Chery said he'd once found some locals roasting lemurs. 'Why do you do it?' he'd asked, and they told him they'd rather kill lemurs than people.

'And what about the future,' I said, 'what do they say?'

Chery smiled wearily, and it was Haja that answered.

'*Aleo maty rahampitso toy izay maty androany.*'

(It's better to die tomorrow than today.)

Just beyond the roadhouse, the forest fell away again, and we were back among stumps. Only one plant has survived this arboreal holocaust: that knobbly old watchtower, the baobab. Not everyone likes them. The American Arthur Stratton thought they were 'an evil growth, an outrage against nature, self-indulgent, a shocking tree'. Even the Malagasies believe they're cursed, and that they were planted upside down as a punishment for vanity. But they also respect them, and sometimes they're holy. Just beyond the roadhouse was a small grove of *baobabs sacrées*, which were dressed in *lamba*, and fed on blood. Every year, a prize *zebu* would be killed here, and ritually drained over the roots.

Soon, there were so many baobabs, they were almost a forest. They survived, said Chery, because they weren't a tree but a succulent, and weren't made of wood. If you were to construct one, you'd have to start with a gigantic column of sponge, and then encase it in stone. The Sakalava would sometimes smash their way in to steal the water. Some of these great vegetables contain over 200 gallons, but they don't seem to mind being fenestrated. A thick scab of masonry forms over the portal, leaving the baobab more castle-like than ever.

Just outside Morondava, we came across a parade of towers known as the Avenue des Baobabs. These are the poster boys of the tourist trade, and yet some of them are over eight hundred years old. It was funny to think that, when these were seedlings, Madagascar was completely unknown to the outside world.

'Yes,' said Chery, 'and the Sakalava people didn't even exist.'

S EX CAN BE A GREAT SPECTACLE FOR THE Sakalava, especially in death. For a people so deadpan in their deeds, they can be surprisingly torrid in their thoughts. Over the last century or so, art thieves have scoured this countryside, stripping down the graves. The statues they're after are only carved out of wood, and are often rotten and infested with termites. But the bigger the breasts, the better the booty. There's also a market for blow jobs and enormous members, although the real money lies in copulating couples. These days, in New York, you can expect to pay over $100,000 for a pair of Sakalava, doing it doggy-fashion.

The biologists told me there were few graves left, and that they were all secret. But they did know of one on the Morondava road. It was set back deep in the trees, and from a distance it looked like a tumbledown four-poster bed. An old *gardien* appeared, crackling and wheezing, and took us on a tour of his wooden lovers. On each post there was a standing couple, pneumatically endowed and intimately merged. Anthropologists say that they symbolise regeneration, and that through conception, the dead find rebirth. 'Is that true?' I asked the old man. 'Is that what the Sakalava think?'

Sakalava funerary art. Much of it has been stolen, ending up in New York and London.

Chery translated this, and there was a wheezy laugh.
'No, he says, we just like sex.'

A T LAST, THE SEA APPEARED, LIGHTLY SPECKLED in canoes and
schooners. I'd like to have stopped and gaped, but we still had
another four hours of driving. At Morondava, the biologists left us.
They said I'd like the coast and the people there. Although they were
still Sakalava, the Vezo were very different from their cousins inland.
'They hate violence,' said Chery, 'they never carry guns or anything,
and, whenever there's trouble, they just run away...'

The road too was different now: no longer dappled and eerie, but a
long white drench of sand. Sometimes, the track disappeared altogether,
and we were out on the flats or nosing through rivers. Occasionally, the
water would swirl round the windows, and Gaspar would start sweating
hooch as we became perceptibly buoyant. But then we'd be back in the
swamps, or swooping along through a shoulder-high furze, known as
spiny forest. It always fascinated me, this garden of cranks. Everything was
armed and barbed, and some of the trees looked like trolls. But easily the
most freakish was the *Didierea*, a sort of armoured asparagus, sprouting
10 feet higher than anything else. They seemed to love the salt and the
excoriating sunlight, and were always clustered thickly along the lagoons.

It was a while before we encountered any Vezo. For the first few hours,
the only people we saw were the tollmen, still lazily threatening and
demanding coins. But then pigs appeared, and Gaspar scowled. Only
the Vezo were uncouth enough to put up with porkers. This wasn't the
only thing the Sakalava despised: the Vezo were nomadic, half-Christian,
ungovernable and filthy. For the rest of the week, Gaspar went into
a sulk, his mood only intermittently brightened with a litre of rum.

At dusk, we splashed through the last lagoons, and into Belo-sur-Mer.
Even in the half-light, it was an alluring place with its palm trees and
sandy inlets and a pool full of schooners. For six months a year, these
boats were the only link to the outside world, as the roads disappeared
under the rains and mud. This made Belo an island, at least in the mind
of its 8,000 souls. I'd be staying a little way out, in the dunes, with a
novelist known rather neatly as Madame Ink.

Laurence Ink had spent almost all her life extracting meaning from the ends of the Earth. Lean and resourceful, her great knot of hair was now flecked with grey. She once told me she knew it was harmful, the isolation, but that it worked for her novels. Although born in France, for years she'd shut herself off in the wilds of Quebec. But then, in 2000, her books began to demand something new, and she came out to Belo. By this time she had a husband, and together they'd built a little wooden library and a fleet of cabins. But then her husband died and, in her grief, the wandering stopped. 'So this,' she said, 'is where I stay.'

But there was no real danger of it feeling like home, or civilisation. Laurence said that although she loved the Vezo, they lived their lives on a different plane. When she opened 'Entremer' to guests, she found it almost impossible to get any staff. While the Vezo were congenitally friendly, they'd never quite come to terms with the twenty-first century. 'They don't go to school,' she said, 'and so they've never learnt how to *learn*. They're brilliant at what they do, but they really struggle with anything new. I have to repeat everything, time after time. The simplest things! Like filling bottles and making beds. And then, at the end of the season, they forget it all, and so, the following year, we have to start all over again…'

T HE VEZO'S WORLD BEGAN JUST BEYOND my cabin, and spread out for miles along the dunes. Laurence called them the *Vezo de sud* because, every December, they'd load up their boats and head off south. She said that there were little migrations like this all along the west coast, from Nosy Be down to Faux Cap. 'One morning, I'll suddenly wake up, and find them all gone.'

But nothing moved during those few days. The Vezo had their entire lives sprawled across the sand, including pigs and dried barracudas, babies and canoes. Everything seemed to shimmer in the heat, and there was no shade except their tiny tents, woven from reeds. The women had daubed their faces in *masonjoany*, a lumpy sunblock that became cracked and flaky, and made them look like slightly comical cadavers. Water was brought up in oil drums, and the dunes were thinly scattered in little grey turds. Around each shelter there was also a rich litter of bones, old shoes, palm leaves, bottles and tortoiseshell. It was always hard to know what the Vezo still owned and what they'd discarded. By December, they'd have to strip themselves down to a few essentials. A Vezo family owns nothing more than can be stashed in a canoe.

In every sense, they travel light. It's said the Vezo carry with them almost no culture: no education, no art, no land, no view of the future and no thought of the past. As one anthropologist, Dr Rita Astuti, put it: 'The Veso can be described as transparent people because they lack the residues deposited by the passage of time.' Perhaps it was a good thing, I thought, to be so readily ephemeral, and to leave nothing behind? Not even death worries the Vezo. 'When you're dead, you're dead,' they say. A funeral is merely an occasion for reclaiming gold teeth, and for throwing a wake, with lots of drink and hymns, and plenty of sex. They say that only one thing ever troubles the Vezo, and that, of course, is fish.

There may be a clue here, as to how the first Malagasies came to be. The arrival of Indonesians will probably never be explained. The great American historian Jared Diamond has described it as 'the single most astonishing fact of human geography'. It's not just the distances involved (3,700 miles), there's also that great wet obstacle, the Indian Ocean. As my friend Aro had said, nothing makes sense, whether plunging through the middle or slipping round the edge. But, in the search for origins, it's just possible that the Vezo – unwittingly – hold the answer. Although they have no idea why, they've even described themselves as the *vahoaka ntaolo*, 'the ancient people of the canoe'.

I often watched them building their boats, down on the beach. Every *lakana* starts out as a tree trunk before it's pecked into shape by little axes and awls. Eventually, after six weeks of chipping, a vessel appears, elegantly smooth and jet-like. There are no nails involved, and even the mast and the outrigger are only lashed in place. It will then have a name like *Toujours Courage*, and a sail made of sacks. These pirogues may not look like clippers but they're the best boats in the country, and the Vezo are always making them for everyone else. Even more surprising, they're Asian, say the experts: the African dugout is nothing like this.

I once went out in a pirogue, with a couple of Vezo. It was like a log at first, until we caught the wind and the rice sacks bellied. Suddenly, we were slicing along, across the lagoon and out to the reef. The owner,

Relatsa, thought nothing of this, and was still on his phone as he swung round the mast. He told me that they often sailed out, way beyond the reef, and might be away for weeks. Sometimes, they even took their families, and would sleep on the sandbanks, wrapped in their sails. It was dangerous work because the sea was *masiake*, a watery version of 'violent'. But the pickings were good. As well as fish, there were sea cucumbers for Chinese, and shells for the tourists.

'And are they good, the sea cucumbers?' I asked.

Relatsa looked at me in horror.

'*Non, dégoûtants!*' he protested. 'You'd have to be a savage to eat them.'

So did the Proto-Malagasy come bobbing over the ocean on these flying logs? The theory is not without its problems, particularly in terms of navigation. Out mid-ocean, there were no booming reefs to guide you home. And how did the sailors reach Madagascar, without bumping into Mauritius or Réunion on their way?

But it could still have happened. After all, the Austronesians had made longer journeys, out to Hawaii and the Easter Islands. In the Indian Ocean, they'd also have found some useful currents. Indonesian flotsam was always washing up on Madagascar's shores. In the past, this has included pumice from Krakatoa, and a wartime sailor, shipwrecked off Java. More recently, the tide has brought with it large chunks of MH370, the Malaysian plane that mysteriously vanished in 2014. So, ocean-hopping is possible, and the Vezo have shown what man can endure, and what their boats can do.

A CROSS THE INLET WERE THE NEW VEZO, or at least a Victorian version of those on the dunes. The story goes that, in about 1870, Napoleon III had sent the Malagasies two carpenters, to help them build ships. The carpenters were brothers, called Ludovic and Albert Joachim, and in Belo they found a sheltered inlet and plenty of wood. Being Breton, they knew of two types of schooner: the two-masted *goélette* and its little sister, the *boutre*. In the short time left to them, they taught the Vezo everything they knew about shipbuilding, and then they died. Ludovic was the first to go, in 1902, and he's buried at the edge of the village, in a little blue grave shaped like a ship.

One morning, at low tide, I waded out across the inlet and into the shipyards. It was all just as the brothers had envisaged: a row of ships laid out on the beach. With their great grey ribs, they looked like gigantic carcasses, bleached by the sun. Some had obviously lain like this for years, perhaps the buyer dead or builder gone. But others were more gingery and wriggling with shipwrights. No one used measurements or plans. Everyone, it seemed, had Breton *goélette* inside his head. Having been trimmed down, the great limbs of wood would then be slotted together, sheathed in planks, drenched in shark oil and caulked with hemp. I once asked one of the master builders what it took to build a schooner. Four hundred planks, he said, 300 kilos of nails and 14 kilometres of hemp. The finished boat weighs over 30 tonnes.

'That doesn't sound very mobile,' I said.

'Everyone helps, carrying it down to the sea,' replied the master builder.

I'd heard that, recently, one of the launches had toppled over.

'It's true,' he said. 'Every so often, we lose a few people.'

All morning, the inlet echoed to the tap and smack of chisels and adzes. Belo, it seemed, had become deeply enmired in the nineteenth century. Immediately beyond the schooners, there were shebeens and prostitutes and great black barrels of molten tar. But, elsewhere, everything was prim, each alleyway delicately woven out of reeds like a suburb of baskets. I even came across a small iron church with a statue of Christ, toying with an axe. People here lived such precise shipwrights' lives they'd almost forgotten they were Vezo, like the gypsies in the dunes. Laurence Ink said that the two groups no longer intermarried, and that the *Vezo de sud* were accused of killing dolphins and begging and offending the gods. To her, all this nagged away at something much deeper, and I think I know what she meant.

Civilisation can be surprisingly callous (and a bit overrated).

On my last evening, I took a walk among the older Vezo. The dunes looked gloriously orange in the fading light, the dramas of the day now a sleepy chatter. After a mile or so, I found a turtle carapace, about the size of a bathtub, and nestled in flip-flops. It was a cruel fate after such a long life. Then, suddenly, there was someone at my side. It was Gaspar. He'd run out of money and had nothing to drink. I think he thought that I'd got lost and that, unless he found me, he'd be stuck out here forever.

THE REST OF THAT WEEK FELT MAGNIFICENTLY Indian, or perhaps even Persian. Maybe this shouldn't have surprised me. For almost 1,200 years, traders from across the Middle East have had their eyes on this coast. It was the Arabs who first brought back stories of a moon-like island, but it was only during a more Persian period that settlers arrived. While the fifth caliph, Harun 'the Upright' al-Rashid, was enjoying a golden age (AD 786 to 809), his little outposts were appearing, down here in Menabe. At first, all the merchants wanted was turtle-shell, honey, soapstone and beeswax, and it was only later they started purchasing people.

A working *goélette*, built to a Breton design, unchanged since the 1870s.

For the next 800 years, these little Baghdads seemed to thrive. But then, under the Sakalava kings, they disappeared, and with them almost all trace of Islam (all that survived were the astrologers and diviners and a revulsion for pigs). Only in the language did the mini-caliphs linger on. 'Music' was still Arabic (*musiqa*), and so was 'writing' and 'paper' and all the days of the week. It may not have seemed much, but it was the nucleus of something. When, in the nineteenth century, a new wave of Muslims appeared – this time from India – the west coast suddenly seemed like their natural home. Soon, all the old entrepôts were flourishing again, including Tuléar, Majunga and Morondava. Even the Persians were back, or at least their *imams*, building gigantic mosques with Tehran's money.

Of all these places, Morondava was probably the most Indian or Pakistani. It was said that the *Karana* owned half the businesses and all the schooners out in the bay. Without them, the entire west coast would have closed or starved (or gone without beer). It didn't matter how shallow the estuary or silted the river, their flat-bottomed boats would find the market. Back in Tana, people had always resented this. They'd said the worst time was the rainy season, when places like Morondava were cut off for months. That's when the Indians would start flying in tyres and toilet paper, all marked up by 40 per cent.

But if the Sakalava resented any of this, they didn't show it. Morondava seemed to be caught in a state of perpetual party. Everyone was out making money, noise, love or merry. Suddenly, there was sound everywhere, and booming colours. All the taxis were a flaming orange, and the town's police car was pea-green (and missing a wheel). I remember singing fishwives too, and a *gendarme*, looking resplendent in his costume jewels. Then, all along the waterfront, there were posters for 'Miss Menabe', and even the pizza shops were throbbing. No one seemed to mind that the sea was chomping through the streets at the rate of a metre a year, or that the harbour lay scattered on the beach like the ruins of lunch. This was Africa's Asia: raucous, unbridled and slightly raffish.

Only the *Karana* were holding back. They had about them the air of hosts, stuck with guests who refused to leave. All day, they stood in their doorways, looking watchful and wan. Their shops were magnificent: *bijouteries* cascading with trinkets, and *quincailleries*, stacked to the ceiling with shovels and lanterns and rolls of barbed wire. It sometimes seemed as if – Alice-like – I'd fallen down some Asian rabbit hole and ended up in Rawalpindi. The merchants came in all different shapes and sizes: robed, turbaned, bushy-bearded, dodo-plump and flamingo-thin, or sallow and suited, and scribbling in Urdu. The great Harun the Upright would have been almost at home here, if a little perplexed by all the phones.

The big jewellers never walked anywhere, but were always trotted around in rickshaws, or *pousse-pousses*. One of them had an old coin I fancied, and so we spent all afternoon sitting round his ashtray, haggling and chatting. He had a sister in London. Maybe I knew her? She was sixty-eight and lived in Wembley. But there was nowhere better than Morondava, and he'd lived here all his life. Tana was all right but too dangerous now, for Indians. His father was from Gujarat, and had come for the gems. You don't find these coins any more. People melt them down for *vonga-vonga*, or bangles. There was a wife once, but she walked out in 1997. Now he had this new girl, and two fine little babies. Life is full of surprises.

He paused and lit another cigarette.

'But, yes,' he said, 'I do worry. Things change. We may have to leave. But where else can I live? I'm Malagasy! I tried India once, and flew up there to stay with some friends. But after two weeks, you know what they said? You may *look* an Indian but you think like a Malagasy, and you're an African inside…'

The *Karana* won't be the last wave of Asians on this coast. There was now much talk of the Chinese, and, back in the forest, I'd often seen their road-trains, hauling out peanuts and timber. But the Chinese themselves were still a mystery in Morondava. The old jeweller told me that Beijing was now busy buying up passports and exporting people. Others told me that they were all triads, expelled from Hong Kong. The biologists even had a story about some Chinese who'd come out to Kirindy to make a porn film among the baobabs. 'They're obsessed with baobabs,' said Chery. 'It's the only thing they ever want to see. Sometimes, we try to show them the lemurs, but all they say is: Can you eat them, and what are they like?'

The new Asians, it seemed, still had much to learn. A few years back, the Chinese had bought up the old sugar refinery on the edge of town. The first thing they did was to reduce the monthly wages, with no one getting more than $37. But the Sakalava can only take so much of slavery, and so they'd risen up, killed the security guards, burnt down the offices and sent the new mandarins packing.

'So people aren't worried,' I asked, 'about the Chinese?'

The biologists looked at each other and shook their heads.

'No, they're not scary like *vazaha*. They just look like people from Tana.'

F LYING OUT OF MENABE WAS LIKE REWINDING the story and playing it all backwards. First the Asians disappeared, and then the Sakalava and the cattle, and then all the other remnants of life. Before long, we were at 30,000 feet and back at the beginning. Below, I could make out tiny threads of forest, like purple veins, and great red rivers of sand. But then, for an hour, there was nothing but the glowing rock, and Madagascar now looking orange and crumpled, like a newborn planet.

CHAPTER 3

The Happiest People in the World

*A Paradox proving that the inhabitants of the
isle called Madagascar are the happiest people
in the World*

Pamphlet published by Walter Hamond, *c.* 1644

*Everywhere beneath the placid surface of
Tuléar's dusty streets a sort of Wild West
desperation dwells.*

The New York Times, February 1997

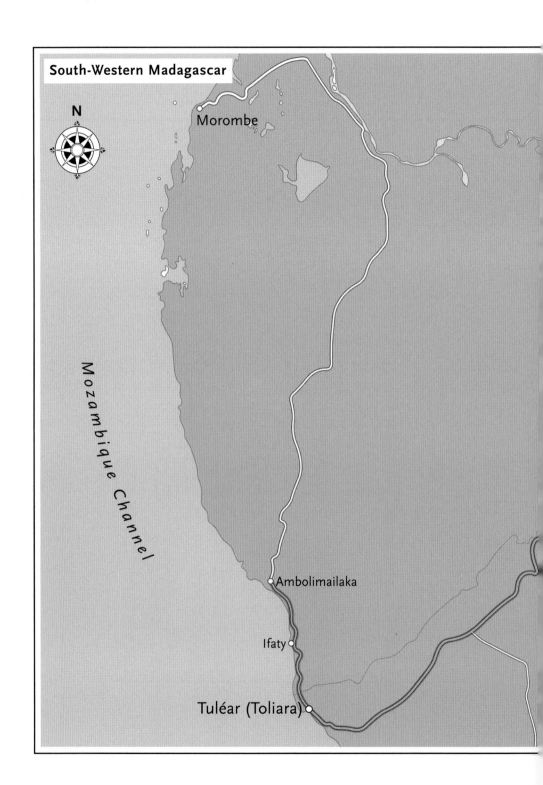

South-Western Madagascar

N

Morombe

Mozambique Channel

Ambolimailaka

Ifaty

Tuléar (Toliara)

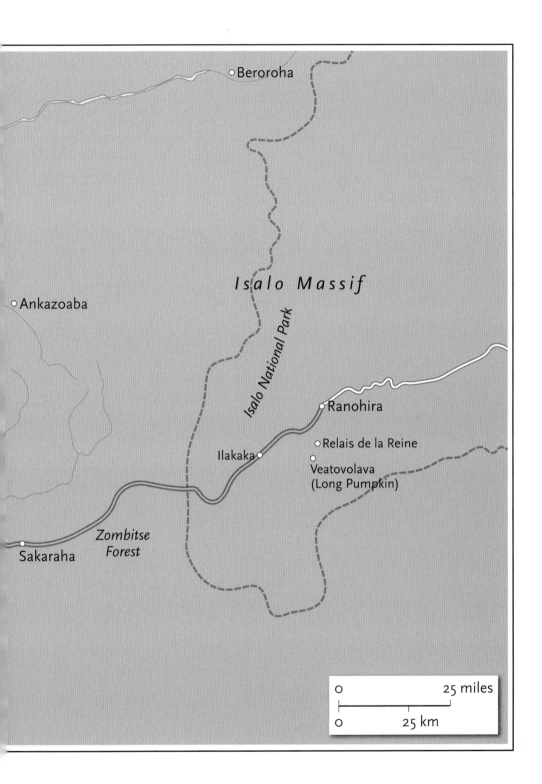

Beroroha

Ankazoaba

Isalo Massif

Isalo National Park

Ranohira

Ilakaka

Relais de la Reine

Veatovolava
(Long Pumpkin)

Zombitse
Forest

Sakaraha

0   25 miles

0   25 km

Every new world has its Wild West. While Madagascar's ungovernable quarters cover most of the island, there's one that's particularly feral. Looking back through its history, the south-west was hardly ever occupied, and only ever plundered. It's had no great kings or empires, and – until the twentieth century – control ranged backwards and forwards between three warring tribes. Everyone warned me about it, this land emptied of life. Between Morondava and the southernmost point of the island, a distance of over 720 kilometres, the coastline is almost bare. There's only one town of any size, Toliara or Tuléar (population: 156,710), and only one main road ever reaches the sea. It's no better inland, the map just a tangle of riverbeds, all thinly sprinkled in scrub and caves.

Everything here works against man: the spiky grasses, the droughts, the scorpions, the locusts and termites. But of all its plagues, easily the worst was the Europeans. It was inevitable that they'd find the south-west sooner or later, as they came sailing round the Cape. To begin with, however, it had seemed they weren't interested, and that Madagascar had escaped. The first to land were the Portuguese, on 10 August 1500, the feast of St Lawrence. They found the Arabs, of course, and smashed up their forts. But otherwise, they assumed that *São Lourenço* – as they called it – was a desert island, and left it alone.

Their ships, however, were often blundering into the reefs, and spilling themselves all over this coast. Over a period of eleven years, three great vessels floundered, including the *Conceiçiao* in 1527. More than 800 castaways clambered ashore, and they're often considered Madagascar's first community of Europeans. But almost all of them were speared or clubbed in the opening encounters with the western tribes. A few, however, fought on, and are remembered in the names of caves (like 'la Grotte des Portugais') and some tiny forts. The last four survivors were rescued by a passing ship in 1531. Their experience would set the tone for the next 300 years.

Back in Tana, I hadn't met anyone who'd been out here.

It's too far, people said, too poor too hot and too wild.

In the story of this coast, there's one place name that often recurs. St Augustine's Bay is no cosy inlet, but a great scoop of ocean,

25 kilometres across. From the air, it's hard to believe that this was once a gateway to Europe. Nowadays, there's nothing there but dunes and sandbars and little pink islands, all delicately frilled with a lace of surf. Everywhere, the sea glows and the shallows are turquoise, smudged with orange where the larger rivers enter the bay. I'd seldom seen a place so beautifully desolate. Then, right out in the mouth, the last of the settlements appeared, now the miniature city of Toliara.

In 1595, a Dutch expedition had appeared in the bay. Its commander, Cornelis van Houtman, was a salty patriot, always eager to gather up an empire from whatever had been left by the Portuguese. Until then, his greatest discovery had been the Falkland Islands, but in Madagascar he'd hoped to find somewhere a little less stark.

The signs weren't good. The Portuguese had never seen the Ilha de São Lourenço as anything other than a stopover on the way to the East. Several French explorers had tried their luck but with no success. In 1527 – the same year as the *Conceiçiao* disaster – Jean Parmentier had called by, in the hope of trade. But all he'd acquired was a couple of goats (in exchange for a hat). Worse, on his second day, one of his crewmen, a Scot called 'James', was speared to death on the beach (thereby achieving the dubious honour of being the first Briton to land – and die – in Madagascar). Twenty years later, another Frenchman, Jean Fonteneau, had run into similar problems. 'The people there,' he wrote, 'are negroes and valiant. But they are wicked and do not want to trade merchandise with any strangers.'

For some reason, van Houtman thought he'd be luckier. But things were soon going wrong. Around the bay, the Dutch found little of interest. Whenever their men went inland, they never returned. Meanwhile, on the beaches, the trade was often horrible: the Vezo offered van Houtman a ten-year-old girl in exchange for a pewter spoon. Then the food began to run out, and the Dutch lost 122 men to sickness and native attacks. Van Houtman couldn't cope with this, and was vicious in response, hacking up the locals and displaying their remains. People would remember his barbarity for decades to come.

Van Houtman would return to the bay four years later, in 1599. This time, unsurprisingly, all the natives ran away. After five weeks, the Dutch had nothing to show for their trading but a cow and some milk.

St Augustine's became known as the 'Bay of Hunger', and over the next forty years it absorbed several more Dutch expeditions and hundreds of lives. However lovely and turquoise it looked, the bay was useless, concluded van Houtman, and so was Madagascar. It was merely the *coemiterium Batavorum*, 'the cemetery of the Dutch'.

With the Dutch gone, it was then the turn of the English. They'd been slow to explore the Indian Ocean (the first English ship to enter it was Sir Francis Drake's *Golden Hind* in 1580, approaching from the East). As usual, they had their disasters, and a landing up north, in 1601, was aborted by scurvy. But within a few years English fleets were regularly stopping in St Augustine's Bay. For some reason, they developed a good rapport with the Sakalava, who they regarded as virile and strong ('They affect copulation very early,' noted one of the sea captains, with no discernible distaste). Soon, a little trade was developing: brass wire swapped for sheep, and seven glass beads in exchange for a cow.

By 1630, the English were ready to settle. To begin with, they only stayed for the winter months, and so never experienced the withering, eyeball-searing heat of summer. Some of the colonists even enjoyed themselves, and tried to encourage others to invest. Madagascar, wrote their leader, Richard Boothby, 'is the chiefest paradise this day upon Earth'. The settlement's surgeon, Walter Hamond, was even more light-headed in his praise. This, he said, was 'the Richest and Most Fruitfull Island in the World' and its people were 'the Happiest'. Certainly, the king, Charles I, was taken in, and appointed his nephew, Prince Rupert, as viceroy. Fortunately, a big fund-raising scheme collapsed but the craze survived. Madagascar even appeared in Anthony van Dyck's portrait of the viceroy's successor, the Earl of Arundel. Painted in 1636, it captures the island at a rare moment, sumptuously nestled in fantasy and velvet.

Nowadays, there's no trace of the English settlements. But their loyal subjects had survived, and I still expected to find them – as Happie as Ever – down in Toliara.

THE TOWNSPEOPLE WERE ALMOST as chirpy as the surgeon had said. This may have been partly because it was winter, and there'd be no more rain for the next six months. Everyone seemed to be out shopping or dancing or doing handstands on the beach. This was the place to buy a pink straw bonnet or a tortoiseshell guitar, and the joy was infectious. No one slept. At night, everyone was out, groping through the dark, dressed in sequins. Then, each morning, yet more schooners appeared, and a caravan of ox-carts would wade out to meet them.

There was no obvious trace of Englishness. Just over a century ago, the French had remodelled the whole town as 'Tuléar', a clean white grid of boulevards and squares. To David Attenborough, it was reminiscent of a chic resort on the Côte d'Azur – but then that was 1960. Since then, a luxuriant black mould had established itself, and much of the plaster had crumbled away. It sometimes seemed as though a much older port were re-emerging: swashbuckling, loud and tentatively bawdy. All the *cyclo-pousses* had names like 'Mad Max' or 'Girlfriend', and their riders would clank around as if they were pirates on wheels. Meanwhile, one of the hotels even looked like a ship, complete with a prow and funnels and a seedy grog shop down in the hold.

Whenever I thought things couldn't get more burlesque, they usually did. The sea, it seemed, was always throwing up oddities. People even claimed that the city's famous show dog, the *Coton de Tuléar*, was salvaged from a shipwreck (half-Scottie, half-fluff, it's thought to have washed ashore in the nineteenth century). Stranger still were the coelacanths. Ever since 1995, they've been turning up in the locals' nets, after millions of years grazing the sea bed. The university now had a little collection of these monsters, all laid out in pickling tanks. As dinosaurs go, they may be tiddlers but – at 5 feet long – they're like prehistoric halibut, dressed in suits of armour. What chutzpah, I thought: to have spent so long in obscurity, and then to reappear in fancy dress.

There was little hint of what lay ahead. I did, however, spot a mask in the archaeological museum. It was hidden away among some weapons that looked like giant surgical instruments, now furry with rust. What struck me about the mask was the mouth – not the smile so much, but the human teeth.

Despite all this merriment, the optimism of the English hadn't lasted.

Overleaf: At Toliara, the French had built a fancy new town (Tuléar) over an old English settlement.

In August 1644, a huge expedition set out, under the command of John Smart. With the civil war still rumbling on, he'd found no shortage of volunteers. After seven months at sea, they arrived in St Augustine's Bay. There, they began the long and uncomfortable process of starving to death. Of the 140 men and women who signed up, only 12 would ever make it home. First the cattle died, and then the crops. Within three months, two out of three of the adventurers were sick, and after a year, those that survived were eating hides ('Very good meat,' noted Smart bravely, 'if well dressed').

This time, the Sakalava weren't so friendly. They were annoyed that the English had forgotten to bring the carnelian beads they'd promised. Smart, too, was tetchy, and accused the natives of being 'base and false'. But they weren't half as irritating as the women he'd brought. They were just 'she cattle', he wrote, and a waste of supplies. By May 1646, the experiment was over, and the last of the settlers set fire to their homes and sailed away. Most of them, including Smart, died at sea. But one of the survivors did at least provide the colony with an epitaph, pleading that, in future, God divert all good men from the terrible fate that is Madagascar.

This was not, however, the end of the English on this coast (although it was probably the end of their good intentions).

Like the early English, I enjoyed this coast at first, and stayed for a few days up at Ifaty. Beyond the salt pans, the sea was the colour of amethysts, and the beach would arc off into the distance like a sliver of silver. At times, all I could hear was the hiss of pines and the mumble of the reef. My hotel was set on a tiny promontory, and often it was just me and the waiters. 'Sometimes,' they said, 'it doesn't rain for a year.'

Occasionally, outriggers would appear and I'd watch them move almost imperceptibly across my view. I realised that these were the same Vezo as I'd seen up north, and that this is where they came on their retreat from Menabe. Already there were several thousand of them, assembled in the dunes a few miles to the north. Just as before, they'd created a basket-like settlement, although this time bigger and far more pungent. It was said that the Vezo could smell Ambolimailaka – with its crush of people and pig pens – even far out at sea.

Despite the sea, I was never entirely happy in Ifaty. The real problem was that here I was, among so many people just like myself. Along the beach, there were more hotels like mine, and more Europeans. There was nothing wrong with them, of course. Most were simply seeking out a variant of home, with bluer skies and warmer water. But they had a powerful effect on the Vezo. A people who'd survived for thousands of years without cash were now selling everything: fish, massages, plaits and sex. Perhaps this troubled me more than it should have done. The Vezo were entitled to modernise, but was this their future – a life spent servicing the whims and urges of others?

There was also something else bothering me. I soon recognised it as the nasty aftertaste of history. Europeans had a poor record on this coast for arriving in numbers, helping themselves, and then leaving it all, emptied of people.

The trade in humans had begun only gently but by 1700 it was out of control.

To start with, the Arabs had sought only boys, to be used as ornaments at court. But during the twelfth century, Malagasy slaves began appearing in souks across the Middle East. In 1178, the Chinese historian Chou Ch'ü-fei reported having spotted some in the market in Zanzibar. He called them 'Malays at the end of the earth in the country of the blacks' or *K'un-lun-Ts'ong-chi*. They'd been acquired at no great cost – some beads, perhaps, or a few bolts of cloth. But then, over the next few hundred years, a little light barter turned into a business. The Sakalava, having been harvested themselves, now became the captors, and grew rich in guns. By the time the Portuguese arrived, Swahili merchants were exporting between two and three thousand slaves a year, mostly to Oman and Arabia.

All this changed again in the plantation era. By 1640, the demands of the Dutch East India Company were almost insatiable, and soon others followed. All the great slaving powers have left a bit of themselves in the language of this coast: Swahili, Arabic, Portuguese, English, Dutch and French. But it was the Europeans who became unstoppable, thanks to their powerful guns and copious silver. The Sakalava had long since lost interest in beads. By the mid-seventeenth century, all that mattered was muskets and Mexican *reales*. Even today, 'pieces of eight', or *ocho reales*, still haunt the currency, although they're now known as *ariary*.

The new industry would suck the life out of first this coast, and then the hinterlands. From St Augustine's, the human exports were dispersed across the globe. Many were destined for Cape Town, St Helena, Réunion and Mauritius. But others were sent much further afield. By 1680, they were all over the Americas. Almost half of the 32,473 slaves on Barbados were from Madagascar. It was the same story in the Bahamas, Jamaica and Peru (where, even now, there are 7,000 people living in Morropón who are known as the *Malgaches*). Within a few years, they'd also be turning up in Boston, New Jersey and Manhattan. Of the 20,000 or so bodies interred in New York's African Burial Ground, at least 3 per cent are Malagasy.

These days, people never mention their losses. But they're proud of their 'Americans', and are always finding new Malagasies among the great names. It's an impressive list of lost souls, with everyone there from Aretha Franklin to General Colin Powell.

APART FROM THE VEZO, WAS THERE anything left of the Happiest People in the World? And what had become of them, after the hunt? On my map, I could see a great corridor leading inland, and I assumed this was the route the slavers took. There was nothing for about 200 kilometres, but then, about halfway across the country, a great massif appeared, known as Isalo. Even on paper it looked like a fortress, with its sheer walls, 3,000 feet high, and a lumpy plateau. That, I decided, had to be a focus of survivors, and all I'd need was a brilliant driver. Fortunately, at that moment, my fixer in Tana came up with Toky.

A Mahafaly distiller making bootleg. The tribe have never liked officialdom, Christianity or rules.

At first, it felt odd teaming up with a Highlander again. I'd forgotten how formal the people of Tana could be. Toky was no exception. Ponderous and prematurely middle-aged, he was tortuously polite. Every word was carefully selected and polished, like a piece of fine cutlery, just right for job. Although he could be generous and wise, there was always the sense that he was in attendance. It was like having my own Jeeves, someone to make everything work, to save the day, and then quietly vanish. During our weeks together, I'd try everything to break through the layers of decorum – dinners, beer, family snapshots – but he wouldn't have it. Toky was a model of restraint, even deep in the wilds.

'When you're ready, sir,' he'd say, 'we'll leave.'

For the first few hours, we drove up through the spiny forest. It was a good road, so we didn't really need our large white *quatre-quatre* (four-wheel drive). But it was good to be high up, soaring through the scrub. Within an hour, all the rivers had turned to sand, and there was nothing but silvery thorn. Everything looked warlike out here, either covered in daggers and studs or weeping poison. I was surprised how cruel the plants could be. Toky said that *famata*, one of the euphorbias, had a sap so noxious that the tiniest speck would leave you blind.

During those first hours, there were few signs of life. At some stage we passed a bus, piled high with bicycles, sacks, chairs and goats. Perhaps the whole village was on the move? The only other vehicle we

passed was an old van, so smacked out of shape it now looked like a rhombus. But then a waterhole appeared, and a tiny distillery, making moonshine. Amid the mud and smoke, I could make out three sinewy figures, almost naked and matted with soot. As soon as they saw us, they scowled and started shouting for money.

'They're Mahafaly,' said Toky. 'We're now in their territory.'
Of all the Malagasy tribes, there's none so anarchic as the Mahafaly. No one knows when they first appeared, but they've always fought. For centuries the slavers were their enemy, but now it's the government. They've never liked officialdom, Christianity or rules, and were always rebelling. Their last great revolt was in 1971, when they seized the police post at Ampanihy. Although the Mahafaly were only armed with catapults and spears, the *gendarmes* responded in truly Victorian style. As the locals charged, the police opened fire, and over a thousand warriors were killed. It was not an experience any government wanted to repeat. So, said Toky, if they wanted to make their hooch, there was no one to stop them.

'And what would happen,' I asked, 'if anyone tried?'
'OK, they'd probably set fire to the savannah, and destroy it all.'
After that, we didn't see much of the Mahafaly. Only occasionally did they appear at the roadside: men with spears, women breaking rocks and children carting water. Soon after the distillery, the spiny forest fell back and the grasslands unfurled. Sometimes we'd see no one for miles, and then just a child, tending a goat. At one point, a straggly pot-bellied youth stepped out of the straw and tried to sell us a lizard. 'In the dry season, it can get very dangerous here,' said Toky, 'as people start to starve.'

'And does it always look like this,' I asked, 'so *uninhabited*?'
'Well, yes... although there are 150,000 Mahafaly.'
'Perhaps they're hiding...'
Toky smiled. 'Yes, maybe. Hiding, and watching every move...'
We only passed a few villages, their walls as red as the earth, and thatched in grass. But however shy they were in life, the Mahafaly could be magnificently theatrical in death. Out on the savannah, we saw more and more of their tombs. Around Sakaraha, almost every knoll seemed to be crowned with enormous white mausoleums. It was hard to connect these great pedestals with the stringy wraiths living out in the grass. Some were the size of mansions, sheared off at shoulder

height, and mounted with baobabs and horns and gardens of bone. One of them was even shaped like a battleship, and decorated with anchors and life-sized cannons.

'Are they always so far from the village?' I asked.

'Yes,' said Toky. 'To prevent the dead returning by mistake.'

He described some spectacular funerals. These were legendary occasions, and I'd often read about them. No expense was spared in despatching the dead. While the tomb was being built, the deceased would be packed in charcoal and stored in the village. Then, when the bones were dry and clean, the festivities would begin. There'd be days of drinking and war dances, and a parade of wailers and virgins. As elsewhere, sex was an important part of bereavement, and so was the killing of cattle. The family would almost destroy themselves with a pageant like this, and by the end they'd be left with only a fraction of their wealth. For the deceased, it was like being reborn, and he or she would even acquire a new name for the journey ahead.

Toky pulled over among a cluster of gigantic tombs.

'We can't stop long. Don't get out. It's *fady* to visit these places.'

Across every surface, there were paintings. Among them, there was always a portrait of the deceased, usually an abstract rendering of an ID photo. But the other pictures were harder to gauge: warriors on charging horses; Bruce Lee, kicking his way through the crowds; a scene from *Titanic*, and lots of movie stars, armed with machine guns. Perhaps here were the Mahafaly as they hoped to be: sexy, implacable and armed.

No one should be surprised by any of this. The Mahafaly were bound to be a little reclusive after hundreds of years of being hunted down. Unlike the Sakalava, they hadn't emerged from slavery with their own mini-empire. Instead, they'd been consistently dystopic, forever defending themselves against civilisation. By the eighteenth century, the Europeans had developed a truly industrial appetite for slaves. Between 1729 and 1830, they'd export 113,400 people from Madagascar. For an island with a population of between one and one-and-a-half million, that was a devastating loss. But for the Mahafaly, even more telling is the fact that 60,732 of those slaves were from the central highlands. This suggests that the slavers had already scoured the west coast and were now pressing deep inland.

Had I been here three centuries ago, I'd probably have seen the slavers coming through. A Dutch merchant, writing in 1719, describes a Sakalava party setting out on behalf of their Western clients. There would be up to two hundred of them, all adept in the handling of guns. As they worked their way inland, their captives would be sent back down the line in great caravans of cattle and humans. Often, the slavers would simply be buying up the spoils of intertribal wars. As one English witness, Robert Drury, put it: 'The epidemical evil of this island is their frequent quarrels with one another, and the very cause so many of them are sold to Europeans for slaves.'

Looking back, it might have been the other way round: slavery fuelling war. These were often strange little conflicts, more like sport than homicide. Drury describes how each battle was preceded by an exchange of insults and songs. The fighting itself would be vicious but short-lived. The Sakalavas were famously fazed by the sight of their dead companions, and would assume that the gods were against them. At other times, the confrontation might be called off due to a plague of locusts, or at the insistence of the women. Both armies wept whenever great warriors were killed, but – for the winning side – there was human booty.

Back on the coast, the Europeans were ready with their money. Negotiations often began with an orgy of drinking. This didn't always go well, and on one occasion the Sakalava king, Lahifoty (or 'Light-foot'), drank so much he died. His subjects immediately assumed he'd been poisoned and turned on the Europeans, slaughtering them all. But things simplified as the century wore on. By 1817, there was a set price for a human life. A slave was worth 2½ lb of gunpowder or fifteen silver dollars.

A HINT OF THESE OLD WARS STILL lingers on, across the savannahs. Several hours down the road, we passed through a small tuft of forest known as Zombitse. Toky said it was all that remained of the vast woodland that once covered these plains. But I'd barely got used to the shadows before it was over, and we were out on the savannah again. In places, the straw had been burnt away by cattlemen but mostly it was golden: a glorious seething pelt of yellow, rippling off in all directions.

Along the horizon, I could now make out the mesas, tiny hummocks of pale blue.

By this stage, we'd also passed into new territory. The tribe here has always worried other Malagasies. The Bara (or 'People of the Interior') are still thought of as the island's dancers, athletes, thieves and fighters. Even the Bradt Guide – usually the epitome of tact – describes them as 'nomadic cattle rustlers'. Legend has it that the Bara are so battle-ready they only wash one side of their face at a time, the better to keep an eye out for trouble. There are five times as many of them as the Mahafaly, and they'd continued to make sport of warfare long after everyone else. Even in the mid-1890s, they were running massive raids against their neighbours. During one of these raids, witnessed by *The Times* correspondent Edward Knight, they stole over 500 cattle and 300 people. 'No captive of the Bara,' he wrote, 'ever returns to his home.'

I read this out to Toky, as we drove along.

'It still happens,' he said, 'these little wars.'

'And what are they fighting about?'

'Cattle mostly. Sometimes whole villages are destroyed. You'll see.'

After an hour, we came to a small settlement, nestled deep in the grass. Toky slowed down but didn't stop. He said the place had no name, and that only women and children lived here. But they were very fierce, and didn't want visitors. Originally, their village had been much further north but then, two years ago, all the men were killed in a raid. After the killing, the women moved south, and settled here, by the road. The journey had taken them two months, and now they had nothing. A few of them worked in the mines.

'So who was it?' I gasped. 'Who did all this?'

'The *malaso*,' he said. 'They're a bit like *dahalo*, only worse.'

Like the bandits up north, the *malaso* always start with children. Every Bara is a rustler at birth, born into the game of pinching cattle. But the *malaso* have somehow made an industry of this, driving the boys into enormous gangs, perhaps eighty strong. Famously filthy, they're known as 'the Yellows', and can cover the country like a human plague. Often, however, they're well-armed, with old AKs or bits of hardware from the Second World War. Often, too, they think they're invincible and that, thanks to their amulets, the bullets won't touch them. There's

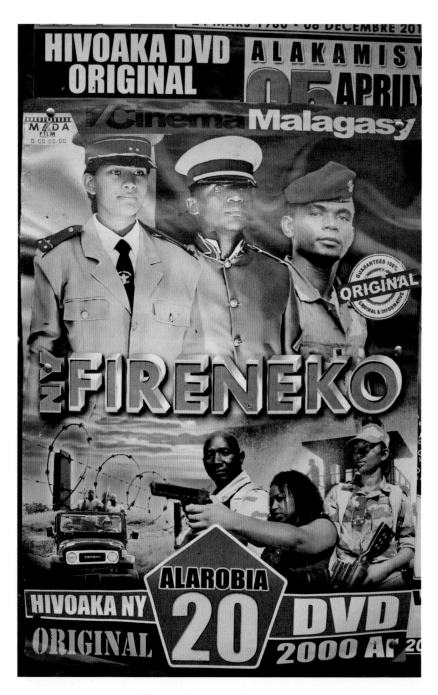

A Malagasy movie poster. Unlike real life, the baddies or *malaso* are always roundly beaten.

also plenty of ganja to make it all fun, and to anaesthetise reality. Time and again, the *malaso* are preceded by tales of *gris-gris*, and eyes prised out for their magic powers.

Malagasies often talked about the leaders of these psychotic little armies. Everyone knew who they were, and yet they were seldom caught. In their *noms de guerre*, there was the full range of madness, from the chillingly cute (like 'Bad Lemur' and *Zaza Mola*, or 'Crazy Baby') to the coldly bland. Two of the more recent *malaso* bosses called themselves 'Eric' and 'Derek'. But not all of them had fancy names or endless luck. Only a few months earlier, another warlord, called Revato, had run into an ambush. After a life spent killing *gendarmes*, he'd discovered at last how mortal he was.

During my time on the massif, I'd meet several people who'd been robbed by *malaso*. One man – a cook – told me his parents had lost everything in a single night. One moment they were cattle farmers and the next they were nothing. There'd been no help from the *gendarmes*, who were too remote, too under-powered and too corrupt. It might even have been them, said the cook, supporting the raid. Everyone knew that they made a bit of extra, renting out guns.

'What about the army?' I asked. 'Are they any better?'

No one seemed to think so. Like the *gendarmerie*, the army was a skeletal outfit. At best, it could muster 13,000 men (and twelve old tanks). But, as the highlanders were reluctant recruits, the ranks had been filled with southern tribesmen, all eager for guns and indifferent to rules. Only in the movies were they truly heroic. These films appeared everywhere, and I'd often watched them. The story was always the same. An officer, exquisitely coiffed and Asian, spends 109 minutes blasting his way through the *malaso*, and then, right at the end, he gets the girl.

Out on the savannahs, it was a different story. Usually, the army had nothing left to fight with but terror. My friend Mireille Rabenoro, the human rights commissioner, had often talked about the burning huts. Every year, it seems, Madagascar has its own My Lai or Bloody Sunday. During one operation in 2012, the army had killed forty rustlers, and then set fire to ninety-five homes. Then, three years later, they'd killed 161 people in a single sortie. But still the little wars have rumbled on (and in 2018, almost eight hundred 'bandits' were killed). Only twelve months before my visit, the military had launched its

most destructive raid of all, torching 480 homes up in Antsakabary. Everyone was traumatised by this grassy carnage. I once met a wildlife guide who was still haunted by his years in the army. 'I had to kill so many people,' he told me. 'I don't like to. They were Malagasy. But they had guns just like ours.'

Sometimes, these little conflicts were fought without any soldiers at all. As in Menabe, the villages of the south would often form their own militias. If they planned things well, they could exact a colourful revenge. Everyone remembered Fenoevo, in 2012. The photographs are still out there, splashed all over the web: ninety thieves, trussed up like pigs and speared to death. No good ever comes of these atrocities but

The Isalo massif, a great prehistoric sandpit, turned inside out.

perhaps they give the *malaso* pause for thought. Even a pause, however, wasn't enough for the people out here, in the Village of the Widows.

S OON, THE GREAT MASSIF WAS LOOMING out of the horizon, and surrounding us with rock. However formidable it had seemed on the map, Isalo now looked like some fabulous intergalactic fortress, with its giant buttresses, and portals half a mile wide. Way up in the battlements I could make out forests and more little mountains, spilling off into the distance. Even the geologists struggle to explain all this without sounding absurd. It's said that Isalo is the sandy sediment of a great karoo, or pit, about a hundred miles wide. Over millions of years, this sludge hardened, and then, during some flexing of the planet's plates, the whole thing popped out, like an enormous cake. Ever since then, the rains have been trying to sculpt it into shapes – or *runiformes* – and now it's gargoyled in ogres and dragons and other improbable creatures.

Even the outworks were monumental. They reminded me of stacks of silver coins, each as thick as a factory, and piled twenty high. The savannah seemed to sweep in among them like some gorgeous golden carpet. Somewhere in here was the Relais de la Reine, a little hotel embedded in the rock. It had been founded by an old French paratrooper, who'd originally come out here '*pour nomadiser*', to toughen up and go a bit native. But the massif had left him enchanted, and in the 1990s he'd come back and settled. Somehow, over the years, he'd managed to insert nursery gardens in among the monoliths, along with orchards and secret lawns, and his rocky hotel. Almost immediately, I understood his enchantment, and could have stayed for weeks.

Each morning, I'd scramble up into the columns and follow the path through a little network of canyons. There were more gargoyles up here, perhaps chickens and goats, carved by the wind. But if I walked far

Les crêtes, the outer rim of a plateau, and the beginning of a strange hidden world.

enough, there was something else too. High in the cliffs I could make out tiny caves, like bubbles of gas that had long since burst. Some of these, usually hundreds of feet above the ground, were tightly packed with slabs of stones. These, I discovered, were the graves of the Bara. Death is not the end but the beginning of a long, hard climb.

There were no Bara living in the gorges, but they did have a village out on the savannah. Toky discovered that one of the gardeners, called Fusée (or 'Rocket'), lived there, and that he'd be happy to take us. It was an unforgettable walk, under the mango trees, along the stream and out through a canyon. Fusée explained that they'd once had crocodiles in their little lake but now they'd all been eaten.

I asked if there was anything in particular they wouldn't eat.

Yes, lemurs, said Fusée. They're too bony, and pigs are *fady*.

Soon, we were out in the grass, and walking through hills. Fusée was proud of his people, and thought they'd been here over a hundred years. Before that, this was Sakalava country, but they'd all run away. Now it was theirs and they had thousands of *zebu*. But the Bara were always moving, especially when people died. This was their second village out here. The first was unlucky so they'd burnt it down.

'The dead are dangerous, you know. We should stay far away.'

Suddenly, over a hill, the new village appeared, all mud and thatch.

'Voatavolava,' announced Fusée. We'd arrived in Long Pumpkin.

A crowd immediately appeared, but Fusée took us straight to the chief and then shrank back. Although Monsieur Bahidy was only about forty, he carried a spear, and had a bright pink *lamba*, which he wore like a toga. While he never smiled, it was obvious he was curious to talk, and we were beckoned inside his small red hut. His only possessions were his bed, his suitcase and his weapons, and so we sat on the bed while he held court. He described a life that was both lawless and perfect. A man could be rich here, with over 2,000 cattle and eight wives. There were good fowl too (although ammunition was expensive). The *malaso* didn't worry him. At night, his men slept with the cattle.

And you've got guns, I noted.

'A few,' he said, 'but we're good with spears, and the men are strong.'

With that, he growled a few orders, and ushered us outside. A few moments later a boy appeared with a huge snorting bull. In the brief squall of dust and limbs that followed, the great beast was wrestled to the ground. Monsieur Bahidy said nothing but waved the boys back to work, and I somehow felt that I'd been warned.

E VERY WEEK, THERE WAS A love market in the local town. Most of the time not much happened in Ranohira, and it all felt sleepily French. According to one story, a poor white couple had arrived here in 1924, on honeymoon, and had accidentally stayed. It seems they'd spent the rest of their lives trying to make it like home, with a square and a café and a tiny hotel. Here, they'd served hors d'oeuvres and rosé, and had gradually withered away as the world forgot them. By the time the Irish writer Dervla Murphy arrived, in 1983, they'd been dead for a decade, and there was no trace of them or their gingham or their ten Siamese cats. 'No one', she wrote, 'would voluntarily linger in Ranohira.'

Obviously, she'd not been here on a dating day. Toky and I took our seats at the café and settled down to watch. It was like a prom for rustlers. All the boys were in town, dressed in sparkly jackets, striped shorts and floppy hats. Here were Isalo's very own rhinestone cowboys, missing nothing but horses. The girls were even bolder. They were jaunty, magnificent young women, slinkily dressed in pinks and orange, and festooned in silver and bangles. They all wore bonnets too, usually an outrageous turquoise or trimmed with ribbons. It was hard to imagine how any man could marry three or four of these girls at once, when just one would overfill your life.

'And expensive too,' said Toky.

'Let me guess. Twenty *zebu*, maybe thirty…?'

'Exactly, and you'd better pay up, or the family will find you.'

But there'd be no supplementary wife for me that day. I did, however, find a mountain guide, who called himself 'Coco'. Come back tomorrow, he said, and I'll take you up, onto the plateau.

The walls of the massif began just north of the town. In the cool of the morning, we climbed one of the gullies, and then, after a mile or

The weekly dating festival in Ranohira.

In the Mid-West, even the trees look armed and dangerous.

so, scrambled up through a portal onto the summit. We were now on
a plain of colossal rocks, all baked red and gnawed by the wind. They
no longer looked like animals, but hulks and shipwrecks, and great
spouts of rust. The trees up here had crocodile skin, and the grass was
coppery and sharp. Coco described these Jurassic pastures as *bozaka*,
and said that, until 1962, there were people living here. But then they'd
all been expelled, and it became a park. Nowadays, the only buildings
on the plateau were the great square tombs of the Sakalava, abandoned
in the eighteenth century.

All morning, we walked along *les crêtes*, or the rim of the escarpment.
Coco knew every beast and all the flora. Along the way, he introduced
me to a sand snake, some chameleons, a troupe of troglodytic lemurs,
a plant like an elephant's foot (*Pachypodium*) and a psychedelic freak
called a rainbow milkweed locust (*Phymateus saxosus*). The toxin it
secretes is the novichok of the natural world. 'Just one lick,' said Coco,
'and you'd be dead in minutes.'

Eventually, we descended into a gorge and ate by a pool of evil spirits. Coco didn't mind me swimming but couldn't bear to watch. There were lost souls everywhere, he said, and whenever you yelled, you'd hear them shout back. Although the massif had always been a refuge for the Bara, it was also an uncertain place, infested with ghosts. For someone like Coco, deep, black water was the perfect spot for the worst of these ghouls.

'And what about the plateau,' I asked, 'do people still visit?'

'All the time' – he nodded – 'to ask for babies, and to bury our dead.'

At first, I hadn't noticed the tombs, they were so high up. As before, each one was packed into a tiny cavity, sometimes hundreds of feet above the ground. The Bara don't see tombs as the other tribes do. They're not magnificent places, but remote and dangerous. 'At our funerals,' said Coco, 'people are often killed.'

Before leaving the massif, we scrambled in among the columns, peering up at the graves above. I asked Coco about the funerals, and he explained it like this: when you die, you're buried here at the bottom of the cliffs. Then, when your bones are dry, they're carried back to the village and scraped clean. Next, the astrologer will find an auspicious day, and the funeral will be announced over the radio. People come from all over the savannahs and there's a lot of drink. You're then packed into a coffin of palissandre, and there's a big procession up here, into the rocks. After more *toaka gasy*, or home-made rum, your relatives will then shin up the cliffs to the perfect cave. The greater you are, the higher they'll climb. Occasionally, they'll fall. Last year, a man fell 40 metres, and was instantly killed.

'So did you continue with the funeral?' I asked.

'Of course, we had to! We came back for him later…'

That's how it always works, said Coco. With every fall, there's more rum, more climbing and more little coffins. But eventually, you'll be properly dead, enjoying eternity from the top of the world.

'And does anyone ever visit the grave again?'

Coco shook his head. The Bara will never revisit their ancestors but will never leave them either. They can never go anywhere, and they can

Overleaf: At one point, Ilakaka was producing a third of the world's sapphires.

never change. They need to be here, watching and being watched, and will be here forever, the dutiful sextons of these remarkable mountains.

Like all Wild Wests, Isalo has its Klondike. Only a few miles from the massif, there was a great, rusty boomtown known as Ilakaka. Everything was orange here: the tin, the camps, the river, the washing and the streets. Toky and I drove through these slums several times, and on our last morning we stopped and hired a miner to take us out to the pits. Haja had been here twenty years, since the beginning.

'I came with my brother,' he told us, 'we'd hoped to get rich.'

We drove out along the main drag, past the casinos and money shops, and then off through the shacks. Until 1998, there'd been almost nothing here, and then word got out of the sapphires in the subsoil. Suddenly, men appeared from all over the island, and overnight a town took shape, complete with bars and brothels and shops selling handbags and shovels. Within a year, there were 100,000 desperadoes living here, and Ilakaka was producing over a third of the world's sapphires. It's said that just 20 kilos of these stones would have paid off the country's debts, and yet, somehow, the money always vanished. Most of the time, the business was managed by old hands from the Middle East, Sri Lanka and India, and there were still a few around. Among the names above the doors, I could see Nasars and Singhs, 'Iqbal's Gems', and the 'New Sahara'. Occasionally, I even spotted the dealers themselves, riding around with a posse of thugs, or carrying a briefcase chained to the wrist.

And what about Haja, asked Toky, had he struck lucky?

No, he said, he was still waiting for that big stone.

Across the camps, there were still thousands of others, waiting for luck. No one wanted to tempt the idea that this was forever, and so there was no sanitation and most people lived in old boxes and scrap. We passed a tiny church with an armoured door, and a hut full of slot machines, called *Les Jokers*. Then we were out on a bright orange moonscape, pocked with pits. Some of these holes were 30 metres deep, and many were abandoned. But, in others, there were huge teams of miners, working barefoot and passing the spoil – shovel to shovel – up out of the ground. It was a gruelling sight: Malagasies once again working in human chains.

The companies' pits, announced Haja. This was 'Swiss Bank'.

Elsewhere, the miners made their own pits, burrowing tunnels through the dust. The gems were harder to find now, and so most of the diggers had gone. Those that remained were desperate men, lizard-rough and weeping dirt. The tunnels were always collapsing, and so hundreds had died. They never get the bodies out, said Haja, and so they're all still down there, under our feet. One of them was his brother. 'We were orphans,' he said, 'and we came here together. He was all I ever had. But I'll never leave him, and I'll always be here.'

The old violence of the savannahs still flared up in Ilakaka. People said it was the most dangerous place in Madagascar, and everyone had stories. In some versions, it had a murder rate up there with New York, and all the soldiers were gangsters. But, of all these tales, one stood out, and it went like this.

A few years back, an imponderable character had appeared here, on the sapphire fields. His name was Muhammed Jamal Khalifa, and he was a well-practised outlaw from Saudi Arabia. During the 1980s, he and his brother-in-law, Osama Bin Laden, had fought in Afghanistan against the Soviets. But then, in 1986, the two *jihadists* had fallen out, and Khalifa had ended up in the Philippines, conspicuously close to another revolt. There were lots of adventures in the years that followed: he was sentenced to death in Jordan, and then turned up in California, with a bomb-makers' handbook. But, as always, he wriggled out of trouble, and ended up with a fish shop in Jeddah.

Quite why he dumped the shop and came out here is a mystery. Was he gathering a war chest, or had he abandoned fish and taken up gems? No one seemed to know. But then one fine day in 2007, thirty gunmen had appeared at his mine, all clad in black, and killed the Saudi. They despatched him so swiftly and neatly that people began to wonder who they were. When the government in Riyadh sent an airliner to pick up the body, tongues were soon wagging. Was that the CIA who'd just called by? Or *al-Qaeda*, out for revenge?

'Neither,' said Toky. 'Just the *malaso*, doing what they've always done.'

It's a terrible thing, history, never quite going away.

Toky and I drove back to the coast, across the savannah and down through the spiny forest. Had we been travelling this way in the spring of 1711, we might have seen another curious figure crossing our path. He had long, filthy hair and a wild beard, and was all dressed in skins. In his mid-twenties and as tough as rawhide, he'd have made a daunting sight, even without his spears. The Sakalava had just captured him in battle, and were now marching him north. But although he was got up in the manner of a local warrior, he looked different to everyone else around him. Beneath the stink and the skins, there was a Londoner. He was Robert Drury of Cheapside, son of the landlord at The King's Head.

Toky was intrigued. 'You sound as if you know him.'

'Well, yes,' I said, 'he's a bit like a neighbour.'

'And how did he end up *here*?'

'It's a long story. He was shipwrecked off Faux Cap…'

Toky whistled. False Cape was hundreds of miles to the south, the other side of the *pays des épineux*, or the Land of Thorns. Everyone knew that the struggle down there had never been about cattle or slaves, but water. These days, bandits made it almost unreachable by road, and the only way in was by plane. It was even worse at the turn of the eighteenth century. You arrived by shipwreck, and then had to fight your way out.

'So that's why you're going,' said Toky, 'because of Mr Drury?'

'Yes. I just hope it's not true, all the things he wrote.'

CHAPTER 4

The People of the Thorns

There are no dentists in the south.

ARTHUR STRATTON
The Great Red Island, 1965

*The Antandroy are an independent and restless
race. They loathe any form of comfort, as they
do clothes…*

CECIL WEBB
The Odyssey of an Animal Collector, 1954

*The people, though wild-looking, seemed to be the
mildest robbers that ever cut throat.*

EDWARD F. KNIGHT
Madagascar in War Time, 1896

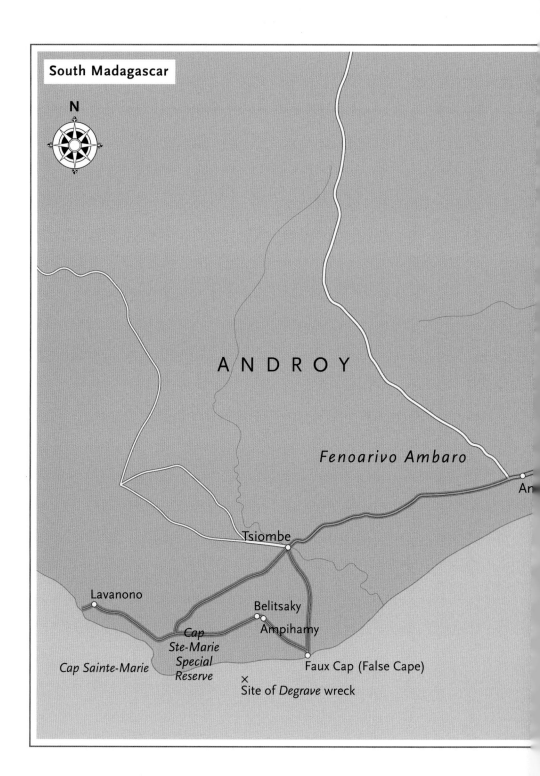

South Madagascar

N

A N D R O Y

Fenoarivo Ambaro

An

Tsiombe

Lavanono

Belitsaky
Ampihamy

Cap
Ste-Marie
Special
Reserve

Faux Cap (False Cape)

Cap Sainte-Marie

×
Site of *Degrave* wreck

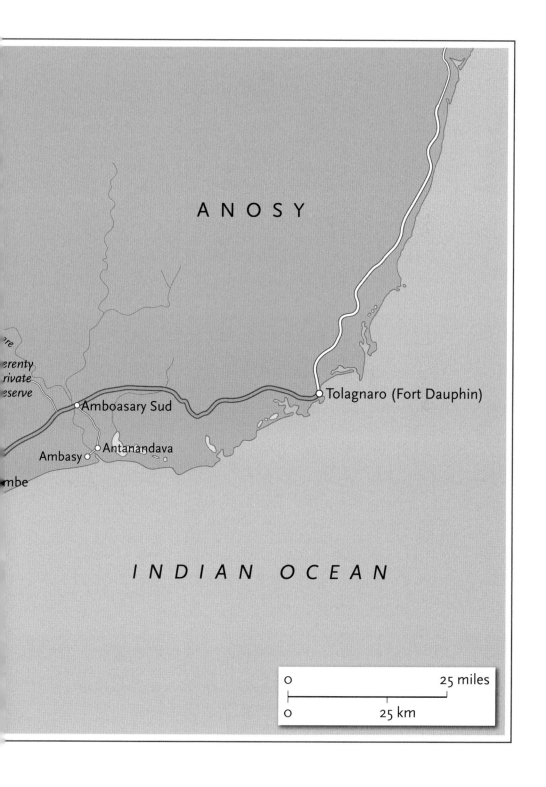

ANOSY

 serenty
rivate
eserve

Amboasary Sud

Antanandava

Ambasy

mbe

Tolagnaro (Fort Dauphin)

INDIAN OCEAN

| 0 | 25 miles |
| 0 | 25 km |

THE LAST MORTAL CRUMBS OF Robert Drury are now buried deep beneath the London School of Economics. Like me, he'd spent much of his life around legal London. After his Malagasy adventures, he'd settled in a house on Lincoln's Inn Fields, and his local church was St Clement Danes. It was here, in the church's boneyard, that he'd finally ended up, in March 1733, and he now has a library built on his grave. He'd died at the grand old age of forty-five.

Returning to London, it hadn't been easy, finding jobs. Drury was last heard of working as a porter at East India House, on Leadenhall Street, and hanging out at Old Tom's Coffee House on Birchin Lane. It was here that people first heard his extraordinary story. The other customers had never heard anything like it before. Drury would tell them about a queen so fat she could hardly walk; about how the savage Mahafaly fought great battles high on hemp; about the last of the Vazimba, who had flat heads (and were excellent cooks); about castrations, and captured girls, and the practice of licking your leader's feet. Drury would spare them nothing, even his moments of atrocity and funk. Among those listening was the novelist Daniel Defoe, and it's now thought that he not only absorbed the stories but ghosted a book. *The Pleasant and Surprising Adventures of Mr. Robert Drury, During his Fifteen Years Captivity on the Island of Madagascar* was published in 1729, and was such a success it would go through six editions.

But the book fared badly in the years to come. The critics began to see it as more Defoe than diary. Certainly, the novelist had filled out the text with bits of his own and snippets of history. There are also moments of literary bluster, although Drury is very different to Defoe's other heroes (like Robinson Crusoe and Colonel Jack), and is always weeping and snivelling and licking people's feet. Perhaps the main problem for the book was that readers simply couldn't imagine a world as cruel as the Land of Thorns. Between 1717, when Drury was rescued, and the beginning of the twentieth century, very few Europeans would visit the region (and survive). Even the unstoppable explorer Grandidier had only ventured a few kilometres inland, in 1866. When the French finally got round to pacifying the region forty years later, they'd have to flood it with Senegalese troops, and would capture over 16,000 muskets. It's hardly surprising that Androy – as it's known – had become somewhat forgotten.

It's still difficult, getting in and out. While there are now a few roads sidling in through the thorn, they're not to be trusted. As in Drury's time, there's only one sure landing, and that's at Fort Dauphin (Tolagnaro). But, while I'd be approaching it comfortably, on wings, he'd be out in a 52-gun merchantman, now shipping water and about to sink.

M OST PEOPLE WONDER WHAT ALL THE fuss is about when they first see Fort Dauphin. Flying down Tuléar, the colours of the south suddenly change in the last few minutes. Gone are the livid reds, to be replaced by succulent greens. Then the plane banks through one last, jagged line of mountains, and water appears: turquoise rollers, tiny emerald coves and gorgeous panels of glowing paddy. Amid all this is the fort, like a little paw, brown and splayed and reaching out into the sea. From it, a delicate bow of gold and surf sweeps off into the blue, meeting the horizon where the mountains end. Visitors have often wondered why this isn't a Côte d'Azur, and then they remember that Tana is nearly 700 miles to the north, that this is where the rain ends and – only a few hours to the west – Androy begins.

On the ground, Fort Dauphin still feels like a gateway to the great unknown. At the airport, there are two ancient anti-aircraft guns, suggesting that – even now – they're expecting trouble from all directions. The fort has spent much of its history under siege and there's still a sense that beyond the walls, the wilds begin. This is partly because, around the promontory, there's always a rumble of surf, and out in the bay the beach is littered with wrecks. But even in town, life has a certain intensity, and everything's imported. I remember seeing great hand-painted billboards for air freshener, American school buses, a squad of soldiers dressed in Barcelona shirts, and a Norwegian cemetery full of missionaries, all tucked up in snowy-white marble.

The best time was the evening, when even the colours seemed borrowed. There was usually a Mediterranean moment, around about dusk. Sometimes, I'd wander over to the Baie des Galions and sit in a little bar that was itself a bit like a galleon, moored in the cliffs. At other times, I'd peer down into the harbour and watch the canoes come in. I was never tempted to climb down and meet the *piroguiers*. They were all Tanosy tribesmen, and fought a lot. Sometimes I'd see blades

flashing, and at that point the fishwives would pile into the fray and drag the protagonists clear. It seems the Tanosy have always alarmed outsiders. 'Noisy coast savages,' noted *The Times* correspondent in 1895, 'with hideous Papuan mops of hair... often repulsively ugly.'

Across the neck of the promontory were the old ramparts. Most of the bastions had crumbled away, and the bits that remained were like gigantic lumps of cake. The undergrowth was now so thick it was hard to make out a plan, but there was still a prison among the crumbs. Malagasy jails are famously unhealthy (with men packed in fifty to a room, and the women casually exploited), but this one looked strangely picturesque. One of the warders was sitting up in the brickwork in his jeans and flip-flops. He told me they'd got 250 prisoners inside, and that they sometimes let them out, to look for food.

Further out, on its own little spur of rock, was the citadel. It was still an army camp, although the guards let me in. This time, a grand scheme opened out before me, and it was like being back in the seventeenth century. I could make out batteries and pepperpots, a small *residence* for the governor, and a network of embrasures and revetments. This may not have been the first stronghold on this coast (both the French and the Portuguese had tried little forts way out beyond the shipwrecks), but it was certainly the most ambitious. Even the current soldiery was dwarfed by its structures, and looked vaguely nomadic among the ruins. Like their predecessors, they kept goats and played ball games, and the only sign of the last 300 years was an old Land Rover, which a couple of troopers were prising apart.

Scattered through the pine needles were half a dozen cannon. The Société Française de l'Orient had put everything into this venture, and spent over 10 million *livres*, sending out ships and guns and even priests. But the venture would fail catastrophically, leaving some four thousand Frenchmen curled up in the sand. By the time Robert Drury sailed by in 1703, Fort Dauphin was already a ruin, and had lain abandoned for almost thirty years. The scattered guns were all that remained of a hasty retreat.

Fishing canoes in Fort Dauphin, belonging to the Tanosy, a tribe that has always alarmed outsiders.

In the origins of the fort, there's a cautionary tale for both venturers and virgins.

Things had begun well, with a generous grant from Cardinal Richelieu in 1642. The following year, the foundations of the fort were laid out on the promontory, a site known to the Tanosy as *Taolagnaro*, or 'the Place of Bones'. It wasn't an auspicious name, but then nor was the French one. Even before the colonists had stepped ashore, the *dauphin* in question had become a king – Louis XIV – thanks to the sudden death of his father. Misnamed from the start, the fort would never be lucky.

Only for a moment was Madagascar the brightest jewel in the Sun King's crown. Wax, honey and hides all made their way home. To begin with, the soldiers of the Société had easily dominated the outlying tribes, with a mixture of murder and marriage. The Tanosy were terrified of their red faces and thunderous weapons. But then the colonists started bedding the native girls, who they called *marmites* (because they were like little cooking pots, blackened by fire). Even the governor, Sieur Jacques de Pronis, acquired a chieftain's niece, and installed her in the little *résidence*, along with her parents and all her brothers and sisters.

It was at this point that things started to go wrong. The other colonists resented the expense of their new royal family, and hated Pronis because he was Protestant. After a brisk revolt, Pronis would spend the next six months in chains before being rescued by a passing ship. He emerged in no mood for compromise. First, he had the rebels banished to Île de Bourbon (which is now Réunion, but was then uninhabited). That done, he killed off the Tanosy who'd been sleeping with his princess, and had another seventy-three enslaved and shipped abroad. Never again would the French be loved – or trusted.

There was then a brief interlude of genius. For the next five years, until 1654, Fort Dauphin was governed by a scholar called Étienne de Flacourt. No foreigner had ever understood this island better, and his great opus, *Histoire de la Grande Île Madagascar*, would be the standard reference book for the next 200 years. There was nothing that escaped his scrutiny, whether it was warring tribes, a killer chameleon or some primitive transvestites. Who knows how differently things might have worked out if he'd survived his return to the island in 1660. Instead, his ship was intercepted by Barbary corsairs off Madeira, peppered with gunfire, and then suddenly exploded. In Fort Dauphin, all that remained of him was a tree called *Flacourtia* and a stone tablet, which he'd had carved with this warning: 'O ADVENA LEGE MONITA NOSTRA TIBI TVIS VITAQUE TVAE PROFITVRA CAVE AB INCOLIS VALE' ('Oh newcomer, read our advice. It will be useful to you, yours and your life. Beware of the inhabitants. Farewell').

His successors would have done well to heed his words. From now on, the Tanosy and the Antandroy would be constantly pouring over the walls. The venturers would learn that they could never replace themselves quickly enough, and that for every native they killed, there was always another, more angry than ever. By 1670, there were only 200 colonists left, and this great cake of a fortress was already falling apart.

As for the virgins, they shouldn't have been here at all, and shouldn't have stayed. There were sixteen girls altogether, all orphans from the Hospice de la Salpêtrière in Paris. They'd been on their way to the Île de Bourbon to serve as wives for the settlers. But when their ship, the *Dunkuerquoise*, snagged itself on Fort Dauphin's reef, the girls begged to stay. This suited the colonists well, and they abandoned their local wives and arranged a mass marriage. Furious, the Tanosy were once again over the walls, and speared almost everyone to death. Only one of the girls and twenty settlers survived. A few days later, on 6 September 1674, they set fire to their stores, spiked the guns, and sailed away.

Before leaving the fort, I dropped in on the *résidence*. It seemed a small place for so much history: a single room with whitewashed walls. I tried to imagine Flacourt, sitting here with his specimens, or Pronis, packed in tight with his relatives and in-laws. Along one wall was a glass case, full of charms and love potions. Tanosy women, noted the sign, were well-known for their *qualité amoureuse*, and, until recently, they'd had their faces tattooed as a mark of sexual success.

As I was studying the old photographs, there was a giggle at my elbow. It was the doorkeeper, a gingery, full-figured girl, perhaps twenty-five and perceptibly Caucasian. She spoke a slow, sultry French, and told me she'd once had an English boyfriend. I assumed that, in saying this, she wasn't suggesting anything in particular but was merely displaying her credentials. But, just in case, I moved away from the potions, and into the safer territory of slings and spears. She followed, distractedly gazing into the cases. At what point, I wondered, had her ancestors merged their fortunes with the Tanosy? Perhaps she was Norwegian? Or a Pronis princess? Or perhaps she belonged to a more ribald era, when all the rules lapsed, and anything went.

With the departure of the French, Fort Dauphin had become a bolthole for pirates. Chief among them was Abraham Samuel, a runaway slave, who'd shipped out of Boston in 1695. Over the next two years, he'd taken to piracy and assumed command of his ship, the *John and Rebecca*, which he then ran aground off the Fort Dauphin. There, an elderly matriarch of the Tanosy told him he was her long-lost son, and had him crowned king. With his band of forty-five men, he then moved into the fort, where they enjoyed a life of girls and plunder. Any ship that came too close was enveloped in canoes and charged £100 in 'harbour fees'. It was well known that King Samuel thought nothing of slaughter, and that at least one crew had been cut to bits.

This is how things were the day Robert Drury first clapped eyes on Fort Dauphin, in April 1703. He was well aware of the reputation of King Samuel and his men ('revengeful and bloody murderers'), as were his shipmates aboard the *Degrave*. By now, the hold was flooded, and the powder magazine under 4 feet of water. But, despite this, the captain decided not to take his chances with the pirates, and so the ship lurched on towards the southern capes, and certain disaster.

UNTIL THIS MOMENT, THE LIFE OF Robert Drury, while a little unusual, had all gone to plan. Two years earlier, his father had sent him, aged thirteen, to India, to make his fortune. The young Robert was to sail out on the *Degrave* with £100 worth of goods, and spend a year or so trading before sailing home. It took six months to reach Calcutta, but they eventually arrived in August 1701. Many of the crew wouldn't survive their time in Bengal, and even the captain died, to be replaced by his son, Nicholas Young, aged twenty-five. The trading, however, was brisk, and Robert thrived. On 18 November 1702, the *Degrave* set out for home, laden with 130 bales of cloth, 50 tons of paper and 100 tons of saltpetre.

The first hint of trouble came as they were sailing down the Hugli, and the *Degrave* hit a shoal. At that stage, the leak didn't seem important, and Captain Young carried on. The problem got worse, however, and so, three months later, they called in on Mauritius, which was then uninhabited. There, they spent several weeks, trying to plug the hole. They also picked up some Indian sailors – or Lascars – who'd been marooned there by pirates. Now heavier than ever, the *Degrave* would set out again, still leaking badly.

Off the coast of Madagascar, the crew dumped the saltpetre and a few of the cannon. It was enough to get them past Fort Dauphin, but still the *Degrave* was shipping water. Young had hoped to limp round the coast to St Augustine's Bay, but it was still another 400 miles to go. As he neared the southernmost point of the country, he realised the situation was hopeless, and looked for a beach on which to land. Sailing past False Cape, he spotted a long stretch of sand about 12 miles short of Cap Sainte-Marie. Immediately, the crew began throwing the rest of the cargo overboard and cutting down the mast. The plan was to impale the *Degrave* on the reef, and then get everyone ashore before she broke up. It almost worked, and only a few were drowned. One hundred and seventy made it ashore, including Captain Young, with his father's heart in a bottle. He'd promised the old man that, whatever happened, he'd get it home, and bury it in Dover.

All this drama hadn't gone unnoticed. The local tribesmen had never seen so much cloth washing ashore, or so many whites. Hundreds of warriors assembled on the sand, ready to meet the new arrivals. They were the Antandroy, or 'the People of the Thorn'. At that time, the tribe was almost unknown to Europeans – or at least, few had survived to tell the tale. Standing there, wet and exhausted, Robert Drury must have realised that his life was about to enter an uncertain chapter.

For the journey out to the capes, I hired another *quatre-quatre* and two Tanosy. They were both brave, enthusiastic, drink-addled and in ruinous health. The driver, Justin, was the broader of the two, his face mottled and puffy, and as black as carobs. He'd spend all day furrowed in concentration but then, as soon as we stopped, he'd find himself a litre of gut-rot and swill it down, glass after glass. Sometimes, I could almost feel the click as the tension released, and his eyes moistened and flickered out of focus. I often wondered what horrors he saw, out in the cactus.

The guide, Achille, was more engaging and a well-seasoned wreck. Half his upper teeth were missing, and those that remained were little black pegs. He was constantly ingesting chemicals, just to feel normal: Coca-Cola and nicotine by day, and rum by night. As he didn't have the money for any of this, he was often asking me for small advances. These didn't make him grateful or genial, and throughout our time together he remained subtly aloof. But he was always eager to find what I needed, even if it meant travelling in the dark or marching for miles out through the dunes. Only his English faltered. He'd never formally learnt it, but this didn't stop him embarking on long speeches that made no sense at all, and which, by the end of the day, were little more than a scattering of words.

İT WAS 180 KILOMETRES OUT TO THE CAPES, and it took us two days. On the first morning, we drove out through the lush green coastal strip. To begin with, it was like travelling through an old Flemish land-scape, a brilliant tableau of work, now drenched in colour. Everyone was out sawing, chopping, clipping, picking, ploughing, hauling wood, or waddling along under a yoke of milk. But then the road began to rise, and the trees gave way to cacti and scrub. Everything had a rattle now: the leaves, the cicadas and the grass. A new shrub also made its appearance – the euphorbia, like a bouquet of thorns.

'Soon now,' said Achille, 'and we are in Androy.'

A little way on, we passed over a ridge, and – way below – a great natural frontier appeared. The banks of the Mandrare river had been planted with sisal, perhaps 5 miles deep on either side. It made the valley look as though it had been carpeted in spears. As we descended, everything flared: the temperature, the redness and the light. The people here were no longer carting logs and milk but water. Achille said that, in the dry season, the Antandroy would travel up to 40 kilometres, just to find water. As they hauled their little wooden trolleys up into the hills, he'd stare at them intently, as if he'd never seen them before. They're like us, he'd say, but different.

'Twins, yes, but not the same. Old enemies but also our brothers.'

There were now small groups of Antandroy, marching through the

During the dry season, each of Androy's three rivers disappear.

sisal. They always walked at a brisk pace, and were lightly dressed – just a loincloth, sandals, a felt trilby and a shawl. Usually they were armed too, with either a spear or a slingshot, or perhaps a little *anakamboa miheake*, or tomahawk. The Antandroy have always lived on the edge: nearly fighting, nearly starving and almost out of water. Many thousands had already left Androy, to work as navvies or guards. Over the coming weeks I'd see them all over the country, always looking Gandhi-like and vaguely dangerous. I was surprised how much they worried Achille. He told me they said whatever they liked and did whatever they wanted.

'And they get angry, right? Very quickly. We have to pay attention.'

We spent our first night on an old French plantation, deep in the sisal. At the heart of Berenty is a last tussock of the forest that once covered this valley floor. Spread out along the riverbanks are all the eccentrics that once thrived across the south: silver-bellied baobabs, spiky euphorbias, tamarinds and the lanky *Didierea*, known down here as the octopus tree. The same French dynasty – the de Heaulme family – still ran it all, and around the farm was almost a century of junk, including a traction engine and an ancient hangar containing a de Havilland Chipmunk. This was an impressive collection, considering

that the first de Heaulme had arrived on a motorbike in 1928, with his family in the sidecar.

Naturally, everything has sought sanctuary in here, and although there were only 500 acres of woodland, there were over two thousand lemurs. It seemed that almost everywhere I looked there were rivulets of fur, pouring out of the trees. Although the Antandroy consider *makis* nothing more than a ring-tailed lunch, I couldn't help thinking how human they looked. They even had a way of punishing intruders, and that night they'd be up on my tin roof, dancing till dawn. Then, when breakfast appeared, they rushed my table and stole all the bread.

The Antandroy will walk huge distances for water, sometimes 40 km a day.

At eight, Achille appeared, looking bloodshot and spent.

'Better go,' he said. 'The road is very bad. Just mud, like a river.'
After the Mandrare, there was never water where it ought to be. It
hadn't rained for eight weeks, and none was expected for another eight
months. Everywhere, children were out in the heat, carting barrels and
shouting for bottles. People here still talk about the great droughts of
the twentieth century, and, in particular, 1942. While the rest of the
world was absorbed in war, the Antandroy were selling their pans and
their clothes, and begging for water. It's said that the final humiliation
was to become Christian, to ensure a decent burial.

'We call it *maro taola*,' said Achille, 'the Time of Bones.'

All around us, a new dry season was taking shape. There are only
three rivers in Androy and they all eventually disappear. The smaller

gullies had already dried up, with the cattle gathering unhappily in the last sticky hollows. From now on, they'd have to get by on *raketa*, or Barbary fig.

Raketa has an interesting history for such a bat-eared weed. Originally Mexican, it was introduced by the French as a sort of natural barbed wire around their fort. Conditions were much to its liking, and from 1769 onwards it spread out and engulfed the south like a botanical bush fire. For Androy, this turned out to be a godsend: the region now had shade, and its cattle had prickly pears. But then, in 1928, the Mexican cochineal beetle caught up with its Mexican cactus, and that was the end of not only the prickly forest but also 300,000 cattle. The raketa would eventually recover, but not Androy. Thousands left and never came home.

Ahead of us, there were children swimming in the road. As Achille had predicted, it was still a mud bath, despite the desiccation all around. In places, the water was deep enough for a scarlet dip, but mostly it was just a well-churned mousse, bubbling up past the windows. Occasionally we'd come across a truck, completely becalmed, and up to its axles in sludge. Whenever this happened, a team of Antandroy would emerge from the cargo and scamper around with shovels and planks. The worst stretches of road were those where stumps of asphalt had survived. They were now like little table mountains, just the right height to rip off a wheel.

All day, we rode along like this, on a conveyor belt of gloop. Around us, the plains were a magnificent silvery-blue haze of thorn, and remained defiantly featureless, mile after mile. I started making a note of all the things that stood out, but it's not much of a list: an ox-cart laden with pots and pans; an old fertiliser factory, picked clean like a carcass; some boys with catapults, loosing off big round stones at their cattle; three women with their faces painted orange and their plaits woven like baskets. They all froze as we passed, as if they'd seen a ghost.

'Ee, *vazaha*!' squealed Achille. 'They never seen a white man!'

We stopped only once, for a bowl of offal in Ambovombe. The sand lay in drifts in the street, and there was a large market, selling mostly sausages and rope. But there was also a clothes stall with hundreds of old suits dangling on strings (they looked like a crowd, I thought, with only the people missing). The place where we ate, called the Hotel Gasy, was obviously the haunt of the local gentry, and they sat around in conical hats watching an old television. At one point a chicken salesman appeared at the door, wearing a huge feathery coat of squawks. When no one took any interest, he tried a bit of begging. '*Kado! Cadeau!*' he pleaded, and when that had no effect he stumped off, muttering and clucking. Achille watched him go and took a deep swig of Coke.

'No one never invade Androy,' he said. 'They have nothing to steal.'

We arrived at the capes long after dark. In the headlights, I could make out a steep track down the cliffs, and then the milky white outline of dunes. Eventually we reached Lavanono, and Achille found us some huts along the beach. I couldn't see the ocean, but I could hear it booming, out on the reef. My hut was made of *Didierea* logs and lined with old bedspreads. There was whalebone everywhere, and I could now make out voices, out in the rock pools. The owner of the huts cooked me a gigantic glittery fish, and provided liquor for the boys. I was suddenly very happy to be here, wherever I was. All I knew was that I'd reached the very end of Madagascar (although, right at that moment, it felt like the end of the Earth).

A lemur, as depicted on an Androy tomb.

Cap Sainte-Marie has never raised much hope in the hearts of mariners. There's always been a sense that if you find yourself here, you've probably had it. The explorer Jean Parmentier may have had this coast in mind when, in 1529, he wrote of *la mer sans raison*, 'the unreasoning sea'. Throughout history, these great colourless, wind-scoured bluffs have worked well with the ocean in grinding up ships and snuffing out life. When the *Koning David* foundered here in 1639, its hull split open, spilling over four hundred sailors into the sea, and yet only one would ever make it back to Holland. In the years that followed, hundreds of others would find a frothy grave around the capes. Among them was the Scottish poet William Falconer, who was drowned in 1770, and Robert Pitcairn, after whom the islands are named. They all perished here, in the unreasoning surf. The cape, it seems, was only ever a saint in name.

After Lavanono, we drove back along the cliffs and out to the headland. It was a gloriously untenanted hinterland of spines and greyish-gold rock and tiny, knobbly shrubs, bent double in the blast. In the bright white light, everything looked seared or shrivelled or brilliantly stark. Out in the sand, there was no sign of life other than the radiated tortoises (which were like big yellow starbursts, painted on helmets). Whenever we came across one, we'd stop, and Achille would jump out and lift it gently off the track. It was a moment of uncharacteristic tenderness. Perhaps he felt that he and the tortoises had much in common, on the brink of extinction. There was once a time when a driver could wait for hours while thousands of tortoises crossed the road. Not any more. Up north, it's a Christmas delicacy, and on the New York black market, a miserable expatriate will fetch over $10,000.

Nearer the edge of the great blue abyss, everything shrank back. Even the gnarliest of shrubs now ventured only ankle-deep across the rubble. Humankind, however, had been less sensible, and during the madcap eighties a tiny military base had appeared up here (apparently, Tana's Marxists had worried that the South Africans would find the Cape, and come scrambling up, and into the spiny forest). All of it now lay abandoned, and the old barracks were being slowly whittled away by the wind. I also found a life-sized statue of Mary herself, looking equally battered. Someone, it seemed, had smashed his way in, through her chest.

'Local people,' tutted Achille, 'they think she has gold inside.'

For a long time, we sat on the cliff edge. Below us, the ocean sucked and heaved, detonating great, feathery explosions of surf. The *Degrave* was lucky to have missed all this, and to have found its beach. Not even the nine-lived Drury would have survived such fury.

'Where do he land, your white man?' asked Achille.

'About 15 kilometres that way,' I said, pointing east.

Achille whistled. 'No road. Only sand. We have to walk.'

T HE *DEGRAVE* HAD COME ASHORE near the village of Belitsaky, which, upon hearing the news, had immediately emptied. While the women fled into the spiny forest, the men had set out for the beach in the hope of plunder. They did a thorough job of tidying up, and in the years to come there'd be little trace of the wreckage. For a long time, the only evidence of any catastrophe was a chunk of broken bell that some local divers had found (and which now sits, dusty and dysphonic, in Tana's museum). But then, about twenty years ago, an archaeologist from Sheffield University, called Mike Parker Pearson, found two 8-foot cannons out near the reef. They were Swedish finbankers, he concluded, of exactly the type used by the East India Company. Because neither he nor the looters of 1703 had the means to lift them out of the shallows, there they remain.

It took us a while to find Belitsaky, even on wheels. There were now lots of tiny villages out in the thorn, and they all looked similar: a stand of acacia, and a few small huts made of branches, lashed together with strips of bark. Life here was lived with whatever came to hand, and I saw people washing in puddles and roasting cicadas over the embers of fires. No one had windows or furniture or even latrines. At night, the Antandroy would simply take to their mats; if they had possessions, these would be locked in a suitcase and stored up in the rafters. Such sparsity has often puzzled outsiders. As one UN report put it: 'We find it extremely difficult to introduce improvements because the Antandroy seem to be happy…'

Overleaf: The Antandroy, or People of the Thorn.

The wreck of the *Degrave*, 1703. Almost 170 souls got ashore, most to be slaughtered.

I remarked on this to Achille.

'They don't like *things*,' he said, 'and when they die, they burn it all'.

Eventually we reached Belitsaky, and when Achille told them we were looking for a shipwreck, a large crowd gathered. For an hour, we all sat under a tamarind while he told the whole story, beginning with London and ending with loot. Throughout it all, no one dared look at me, and there was no sound but scratching and suckling and crackly chests. I was surprised how sweet the crowd smelt, a mixture of woodsmoke and earth. The villagers obviously never did laundry – a waste of water – and their clothes were shiny and brown, like shreds of oilskin. Only the chief wore something recognisable: an old Chinese police shirt, complete with silver buttons. A long tradition of recycling had clearly survived.

When Achille had finished, there was silence.

'Can you ask them if they'll take me to the cannons?'

'They don't know what cannons are,' said Achille.

I drew a finbanker in the dust.

'OK, a long metal pipe,' said Achille, and turned to the chief.

They spoke for ages. 'Sorry,' said Achille, 'they never heard this story.'

We drove on as far as we could, towards the sea. The track ended at Ampihamy, where Achille repeated the story all over again. This time, the chief nodded thoughtfully, and said I'd need some herders to show me the way. It was still another 7 kilometres to the sea, so I'd need two guides, said Achille, because they were scared of the dark. With that, two boys appeared, in their best shirts and flip-flops. Neither had water.

'Are they going to be all right like that,' I asked, 'out in the *brousse*?'

'Sure,' said Achille, 'they're Antandroy.'

'And why are they unhappy, being out after dark?'

'That's the *jiny*. It's like a zombie.'

Although the dashboard thermometer still read thirty-five, we set off at pace. The boys didn't seem to notice the cactus round their feet, or the little snakes slithering away in all directions. For the first hour, we crossed a deep, flat plain of agave and spikes, before entering into a system of ridges, and the beginning of the dunes. At that point we were joined by a child, who'd run all the way from the village in the hope of my plastic bottle, and who refused to leave until it was his. The

boys, on the other hand, took no interest in me until the sun cream appeared. Attracted by the smell, they took great dollops of it, which they worked into their hair, and then we were friends.

As the sun began to cool, we met a woman wearing a fish, as if it were a hat. My legs were now beginning to burn after so long wading through sand. But then the sea appeared, and a long, misty beach, with a queue of cows. The herders had brought them here for the well, perhaps the only sweet water for miles around. Way off down the shore, I could make out more herds trudging this way. There were also canoes out on the sand, and when the fishermen heard I was there, they came

The beach near Belitsaky. Wreckage from the *Degrave* still turns up here.

running up the dunes, dressed in only shorts and goggles. Just for a moment, we all stopped and stared, fleetingly uncertain where the encounter was going. Maybe Robert Drury had felt something similar, except for hours – or years – instead of seconds?

Achille reappeared next to me.

'This men say the guns were here. But now the sea took them away.'

The survivors of the *Degrave* had soon realised they weren't to be eaten. While the natives weren't obviously hostile, it wasn't easy to watch them, making merry with the cargo. The survivors, between them, had lost over £63,000 worth of goods, the equivalent today of almost £15 million. But the Antandroy did at least kill a cow for them, and roasted the pieces still covered in hair and skin. Perhaps the English had been

A descendant of the Antandroy villagers who'd greeted the shipwrecked Europeans in 1703.

lucky after all. Up to that point, only three of them had perished, and 170 had made it ashore.

That night, they slept up in the dunes, wrapped in lengths of calico and silk. Later the next day, a boy called Sam appeared out of the scrub, and told them he was also English, and that he'd been marooned here by pirates. He and his companions were now the guests of a one-eyed king called Andriankirindra. The king said he wanted the new arrivals to come to his capital, and he lived about 50 miles inland. He would treat them well, said Sam, but they must come now.

The survivors prepared to leave. In writing about the beach many years later, Robert Drury would remember almost everything – the reef, the cows, the sand and the herders. Only one detail was missing: the enormous fragments of prehistoric eggshell, scattered through the dunes.

THAT NIGHT, WE STAYED NEARBY, deep in the eggshell.

It had taken several hours to walk back through the cooling sand, and it was dark when we reached the village. But Achille had said he knew somewhere we might find rooms, out at Faux Cap. It was very dirty, he warned, and was called the Cactus Hotel. Although we only had to do another 12 miles, it would be a gruelling drive. In the glare of the headlights, the track looked like a ravine, and the scrub had turned into freaks. Justin now had his face pressed up against the windscreen, and spoke only in whispers. *Kokolampo*, said Achille. It was a bad time for spirits.

After that, reality struggled to reassert itself. The Cactus was like Old Mother Hubbard's lair, out on False Cape. The owner, Maria, had several old crumbling cottages up in the cliffs, and she lived in the largest of these with her fourteen children and all their babies. One of the daughters gave me a candle and a pail of water, and took me out to my shack. When we opened the door, there was a scuttling of feet as things ran for the thatch. I preferred to spend the evening nestled down among the babies, in the glow of their new TV. Also with us was a gigantic egg, about the size of one of the tots. It all felt like a quiet night in with Humpty Dumpty.

Sunrise brought more eggs, or at least a trail of shell down the dunes and along the shore. For a while, I followed the fragments, some as big as my hand and the thickness of a saucer. Had I wanted to, I could have followed the debris all the way back to the shipwreck, past Cap Sainte-Marie, and on up the coast to Tuléar. This vast complex of dunes was once the roost of that giant dolt the elephant bird, or *Aepyornis*.

It still surprises me, how completely this gigantic creature has disappeared. Not only was the *Aepyornis* once numerous, it was also unmissable. In its day, it was the biggest bird in the world, weighing in at almost half a ton. Even the eggs were monstrous, each one big enough to make 150 omelettes. While unbroken specimens are rare (one recently sold at auction for over £66,000), the Antandroy now run a brisk trade in gluing the fragments together – like Maria's. Meanwhile, few skeletons have ever been found, although there is one in Tana, at the ethnographic museum. I remember it towering over me, like some strange articulated crane with tiny wings and legs like tree trunks. The head was minute, hardly big enough to think, and that perhaps was the problem. For thousands of years, the elephant bird had occupied an Eden-like land, unmolested by predators, growing ever more vulnerable and stupid. It would be no match for hungry humans, or their greedy fires.

A depiction of the *Aepyornis*, or elephant bird, from 1594.

But even in the culture of Madagascar, the *Aepyornis* has vanished. No descriptions or depictions have survived, and among all the island's mythical monsters there are none with wings and chunky thighs. Only through the Arabs do we get a glimpse of it. A *roc* (as they called it) appears in *The Seven Voyages of Sinbad the Sailor*, swooping around, snatching up elephants. In the 1290s, Marco Polo even borrowed a '*rukh*' for his own great work, and for years afterwards Madagascar was synonymous with these jumbo-eating superbirds. But by the time Europeans arrived, there were none to be seen. Flacourt was told of an ostrich-like bird, living out among *les ampatois* (or the Antandroy), and in 1669 there were reports of a giant bird jumping out of the trees and eating people. Perhaps it was just a case of too much sun, or too much *rhum*.

It's possible the *Aepyornis* was still around in Drury's time, but unlikely. No European had ever seen one, and the chances are it had been extinct for over 500 years. Drury himself never mentions the *Aepyornis*, and may not have given much thought to the fragments in the sand. But on every dune, he'd have seen what I saw: an untidy scattering of eggshell, as if some great chick had just waddled off the nest.

THAT DAY, MADAGASCAR FELT DRIER and more brittle than I'd ever known it before. It took us two hours to work our way through the spiky hinterlands, back to Tsiombe and the road heading east. It was dark last time we came this way, and now everything seemed startling and raw, like clips from a film. One moment there'd be crowds of papery faces at the window, and hands tattooed with work, and then carts and oxen, and a market laid out in the bright-red powder, and then the ash-coloured scrub again, and the road like an orange ribbon, rippling off towards the sky. There were few recognisable sounds, but I found myself absorbed in the detail: the haystack houses, the petrol sold in old bottles; a game of football played on the riverbed; cattle eating cactus and the little fortresses of thorn, where they stayed at night. It was hard not to feel detached, as if none of this was now. But then something would jolt me to my senses, like a tray of tiny birds being passed through the window, all perfectly roasted and looking like miniature chickens. Just for a second, I wasn't quite sure whether I was completely enchanted or about to throw up.

In some ways, not much has changed in the last three centuries. The survivors of the *Degrave* would have seen much the same people doing much the same things. But their journey was also dangerously debilitating. For every hour we drove, they walked for a day. Some had lost their boots or shoes in the shipwreck, and now had to manage the thorns and the scalding sand in just their stockings. Even today, the wounds caused by Androy's home-grown stilettos can take weeks to heal, and are known as *les plaies malgaches*. Back in 1703, such injuries weren't well understood and could easily be fatal. For the time being, Drury and his companions carried the wounded, but it couldn't last. From Tsiombe, they still had another day's walk to King Andriankirindra's capital, at Fenoarivo.

On any other occasion, the one-eyed king would have made a magnificent sight, dressed in skins and amulets and covered in pistols. But he was already alarmingly drunk, and clearly delighted with his new acquisitions. It soon became clear he'd no intention of letting the Europeans go, but would keep them as pets. He'd already got Sam and two Scottish mariners, and now he had 170 English specimens. In a display of his greatness, they'd be paraded among the other tribes, and in the meantime they'd live in the village, in one of his thorny corrals.

But Andriankirindra had obviously underestimated his scabby captives. That night, the Scots and the English got together and planned their break-out. Remarkably, not only did they manage to escape, but on the way they also seized thirty muskets, a couple of aristocratic hostages, and the king himself, now babbling with rage.

This time, Captain Young headed straight for Fort Dauphin. Although Abraham Samuel (or 'King Samuel') was not to be trusted, there were no other ships for hundreds of miles. But even the fort was a long way off, and – unknown to them – it was the other side of a waterless desert. Between here and the Mandrare, there were no other rivers, and it would take them three days to pick their way through the *pays des épineux*. Back then, there were no roads or wells, or prickly pears, or footballers and roasted birds. This time, they'd have to abandon their wounded, and everyone – including the Gujuratis the shoeless, and a young amputee – would have to fend for themselves. Hot on their heels was an army of angry warriors, just waiting for their moment.

By the third day, the survivors were out of water, and licking up the dew. 'There is no torment,' wrote Drury, 'like the torment of thirst.' Everyone was weak now, and the crew would do anything to buy time and favour. One by one they released the hostages, starting with Andriankirindra. Drury saw him go, and watched in fascination as the king's sons gathered round him, licking his feet. Without their hostages, the Europeans were now more vulnerable than ever, and the Antandroy closed in for the kill. The first to go was the amputee. He was easily outrun by the spearmen, who tore off his wooden leg, and killed him in the sand. Now everyone was running.

Then, at a place called Ambasy, the river appeared. It was only a mile away, down through the dunes. Drury didn't hesitate. With people now dying all around, he began to run, heading straight for the water.

T HE MANDRARE STILL LOOKS AS promising as ever: a delicious curl of cool, out in the distant haze. As there was no road down the

The Antandroy always worried the French, who maintained a garrison in Tsiombe until 1946.

west bank, we drove back through the sisal, and crossed at the bridge. Here, the riverbed was still half a mile wide, and on the far side a track led out through the plantations, and into the dunes. It took us as far as Atanandava, a tiny market town huddled in the sand. There, we were directed to the mayor, who had a shed among the stalls. It was a bit like visiting royalty, with everyone gathered around his chair.

Once again, Achille told the story, ending with the killing.

We know Ambasy, said the mayor, it's only 7 kilometres away.

By now, many of the villagers were listening at the windows, and two men stepped forward, offering to take us. Despite the heat – it was still thirty-five – a lively excursion was soon under way. Loaded up with manioc and dried fish, we set out through the orchards, our new guides now singing and dancing up ahead. Everything was fortified here, and even the vegetables were walled in with cactus. But then, after an hour, we were in dunes, wading upwards through great mountains of sand. Everything out here was a dazzling white, except a single outcrop of pink. I thought nothing of it at the time, and on we went.

Antandroy women are famously demanding, and divorce is common. Adultery is punishable by a fine paid in cattle.

At first the walking seemed easy enough, but then with each ridge came another, even bigger and hotter. At one point we found ourselves in a vast space between two drifts, like a stadium of burning dust. Soon, everything was in flames – skin, muscles and curiosity – and I began to wonder if I'd have dunes forever, seared on my retinas. Fortunately, at that moment, we reached our last ridge and the river appeared, a few miles upstream of the mouth, and looking a refreshingly unlovely ox-blood brown.

No boats. *Fuck it*, I thought, the end of the road.

'No,' said Achille. 'Remove the trousers. We walk.'

I had a sudden vision of the huge crocodile I'd seen up at Berenty.

'It's OK.' Achille shrugged. 'They sleep now, where it's deep.'

With some reluctance, I stripped off, wrapped everything in a bundle, and stepped into the river. It felt luxuriously cool and silky underfoot, and even a hundred yards out the water was only up to my waist. We must have made a curious sight, wading across this watery plain, with our clothes on our heads. Way off, on the far bank, a crowd appeared, along with a herd of *zebu*. Eventually, after plunging through the deep central channel, we reached them, and clambered out onto the sand. Hundreds of eyes – female, infantile, bovine and rheumy – watched as we ate our fish. One of the children held out a hand, so I gave her a slice of manioc. This drew a snort of outrage from one of the older women, who had skin like a tortoise.

'What's the matter?' I asked Achille.

'She's angry because you feed the kid, and she's hungry too.'

The angry eyes never left me, and I was glad when the time came to go. Many of the women had brought with them 20-litre cans, and when they'd filled them, we all set off for Ambasy. It was exactly as Drury had described, on a little rise, about a mile from the river. Most of the villagers lived in tiny A-frames, not so much huts as little thatched cupboards. Only the chief had walls and tin. Dressed in shreds of greasy grey cloth, he was a kindly and solicitous man, who in another world would have been a physician or a judge. As before, he listened to the story in silence, as did the villagers. They didn't even stir when a snake slithered in among them, and out the other side. When we got to the bit about the killing, and the boy with the wooden leg, the old man nodded thoughtfully, and said something to Achille.

'He says he wants to show you something. Up the hill.'

Everyone came with us, including the herders, the water carriers and all the children. A few minutes on, our procession reached the rim of a sandy escarpment, with views right out across the Mandrare. This is the place, said the chief. We now call it *Vohibasia*, or Gun Hill.

From here, Drury had run pell-mell for the river. Behind him were the Antandroy, 'like so many greyhounds', picking off the stragglers. To run even faster, Drury tore off first his coat and then his waistcoat, leaving them behind in the Ambasy dust. Next to him was a woman he knew, and together they almost reached the river. 'But,' he later recalled, 'as I looked back at the pop of a gun, I saw the woman fall, and the Negroes sticking their lances into her sides...'

Ducking a second shot, he plunged into the silky brown water. After three days in the desert, it was almost too much. Despite the shots now raining down, he stopped three times during those few hundred yards, to fill his hat and drink. But then he was running again, and he carried on running up the far bank, and through the great white dunes. These he'd remember as 'a sandy open place we could see no end of', but where the sand turned pink, the crew made their stand. With 'an army of two or three thousand' now closing in, it was a forlorn encounter, and the Europeans were soon out of shot. 'Our people who had money made slugs out of it,' recalls Drury, 'and when that was done, they took the middle screw out of their guns and charged their pieces with them...'

All afternoon, they 'played' the enemy, until they had nothing left to fire. Remarkably, that night – 9 May 1703 – there were still 130 survivors, assembled in the dunes. Even then, they knew they could expect little mercy, and only three of them would ever make it home. One of them was John Benbow, son of the famous admiral (who has a pub named after him, in *Treasure Island*). That night, he and twenty-nine others made a break for it, and five days later they reached Fort Dauphin. Apart from Benbow, they'd all perish in the journeys to come. It took Benbow three years to get back to London, only to die in 1708, at the age of twenty-six. He's buried in St Nicholas' churchyard, in Deptford.

The king was furious when he heard of the escape, and ordered a massacre. Captain Young was the first to die, with a spear in his throat. I half-wondered whether he'd still had his father's bottled heart, and whether it was still here, somewhere in the dunes. But the Antandroy were assiduous scavengers. Almost everyone was butchered and stripped (and then – for some reason – had their bowels cut out). Nowadays, said the chief, there was no trace of a massacre, and all the stories had been forgotten. But the little pink outcrop had at least got a name: *Ampitifirambazaha*, or 'the Place of Shooting the Foreigners'.

Only three boys were spared: Drury, Sam and another midshipman. None of them was older than sixteen, and they'd be perfect as slaves.

AFTER SO LONG IN THE THORNS, Fort Dauphin now felt like a proper city. I was looking forward to being back in the present, and to some of the quirkier features of modern times: cobbled streets, croissants, ramparts, 'The Freedom Bar', sunken barges and oysters, sold by the basket.

But I'd miss Achille. Despite his detachment, he'd proved surreptitiously loyal, and in a different life we'd have surely been friends. In that perfect world, I'd have taken him and Justin out on the town, and we'd have made merry in the bars. But in reality, I knew they thought differently about drinking, and I worried where we'd end up on the oblivion scale. Besides, they were already looking clammy and gaunt, and, once I'd paid them, they made their excuses and disappeared.

'We will leave nothing for the archaeologists,' Achille once told me, 'our lives are still only sticks.'

With a day to spare, I asked around about Abraham Samuel. But no one had ever heard of the slave-king, and there was no royal tomb. It seems that ships had eventually stopped calling at Fort Dauphin, and that King Samuel had died, splendidly forgotten, in 1708.

But historians now think he wasn't as bad as people imagined. According to Sir Mervyn Brown, when Benbow turned up at the fort, and described the events in the dunes, King Samuel sent out a rescue party of over two thousand warriors. They were too late, of course, to

Overleaf: Ambasy village, the Mandrare River, and – beyond – the dunes where the massacre took place in 1703.

prevent the slaughter, and the Antandroy had long since fled. But the mission does say something about the king's reputation. If only Captain Young had trusted him more, and if only the *Degrave* had stopped at the fort, then the whole disaster would never have happened.

ROBERT DRURY WOULD EVENTUALLY make it to Fort Dauphin. but only after his long captivity and another journey halfway round the globe.

He was still only fifteen when he became a slave, in 1703. For the first nine years, he was the property of the Antandroy royal family, and at first he was little more than a pet. His master's wife, who was also a slave and about the same age, treated him well. He learnt how to gather wild honey, and roast the local hedgehogs, known as tenrecs ('Their skin,' he'd recall, 'is as brown and crisp as a pig's'). In this bucolic tale of ordinary royals, all the names become quaintly phonetic, and sometimes Drury reads like Swift. Along the way, we meet *Woozington* (King Hositany), *Deann Mevarrow* (Andrianamiavaro) and those irrepressible oiks, the *Merfaughla*, or Mahafaly.

Later, Drury was put to work, first as cowherd, and then as a hunter and warrior. There were lots of wars. Sometimes it was the royal family fighting each other, cutting off testicles and stealing cattle. But at other times, the fighting ranged over many months and hundreds of miles of spiny forest. Often the enemy was the Mahafaly, and it wouldn't take much to start a fight. One of the most catastrophic conflicts was sparked by an insult, when the Mahafaly king named his dog after a neighbouring chief. In the ensuing war, more than six thousand men poured into Mahafaly territory, sacking everything in sight. Narcotics often fuelled the fighting, with most of the warriors heading into battle off their heads. Only Drury refused to get 'giddy', and was always on the lookout for booty or a chance of escape. During one of these wars, he even managed to capture a wife. She was 'extremely handsome, of a middle stature, very straight and exactly shaped', and would be the only girl he ever loved.

Eventually, in 1712, Drury finally saw his chance, and slipped away. For a month he trekked north, only to be caught up in another war and captured by the Sakalava. This time, slavery was more Vaudevillian, if not outright strange. The Sakalava king was an octogenarian, festooned in jewellery, and his wife's breasts were so large they came down to her waist. Drury's first owner was the king's grandson, a great sexual adventurer, who was said to be six foot eight. Drury's job was to keep other gallants off the royal wives, and he became 'Captain of the Guard'. His next master, *Rer Moume* (Remony), was a paraplegic, with twelve wives and a hundred muskets. This time, Drury was put in charge of the guns and given his own cattle, living a life of 'Affluence and Ease'.

Drury's travels might have ended there if an English ship, the *Drake*, hadn't anchored offshore in October 1716. By now, there was a rumour circulating the London taverns that Drury was still alive, and the captain had been asked to keep an eye out. He also had with him a letter from Drury's father, addressed simply to 'Robert Drury, on the Island of Madagascar'. The crew could barely believe their eyes when a wild creature appeared – ragged, mop-haired and barely intelligible – and introduced himself as the long-lost son. As always, the Sakalava were happy to do business, and so Drury was exchanged for a brand-new musket. The *Drake* set sail on 17 January 1717, and – after dropping some slaves in Barbados and Jamaica – was back in Gravesend nine months later. Drury had been away for over sixteen years.

He found it hard to settle. His home had been sold, his father had died, and England was different (a new parliament, a new German king, and an additional Scotland). No one had work for a man who'd spent half his life turning feral. For a while, Drury did a stint as a clerk, but then, in September 1718, he signed up with the slave-ship *Mercury*. The following year, the vessel reached Madagascar, and he finally made it to Fort Dauphin. Drury was happy to be back, and immediately shed his European garb in favour of a *lamba* and spears. The Tanosy had never seen anything like it, a *vazaha* so fluent in their language and so adept with the 'javelin'. Seven months later, the *Mercury* set sail with its hold full of slaves.

There was only one last stop, in Morondava. There, he met up with his old master, Remony, who – despite his paraplegia – was now the king. Although Drury had made the full transition from slave to slaver, he wastes little time on reflection. But he was surprised to find all his cows, just as he'd left them. We kept them, said Remony, just in case you ever came back.

T HIS PART OF MY JOURNEY HAD come to an end. Fort Dauphin would take me into the eighteenth century, but no further. The French had never recovered from the humiliation of 1674, and after that the promontory was only ever an outpost, usually short-lived. Although twelve years later the Sun King had declared sovereignty over Madagascar, it was an empty gesture. France had no one out there, and was the mistress of nothing.

The next four decades would be about anarchy. No one tribe was dominant, and up on the Île Sainte-Marie, a tiny criminal state was taking shape. Between about 1680 and 1720, it would be a hideaway for some of the world's most outrageous gangsters. Now, however, it's just a plane ride away, and so I booked my ticket, and headed out for the airport.

CHAPTER 5

The Anti-world of St Mary's Island

*The vast riches of the Red Sea and Madagascar
are such a lure to seamen that there's almost no
withholding them from turning pirates.*

LORD BELLOMONT, GOVERNOR OF NEW YORK,
1699

*The modern visitor has some difficulty in believing
that St Mary's island was at one time the greatest
pirate stronghold in the world and that this idyllic
tranquil spot once reverberated with the violence
and debauchery of pirate crews returning from
successful expeditions.*

MERVYN BROWN
Madagascar Rediscovered, 1978

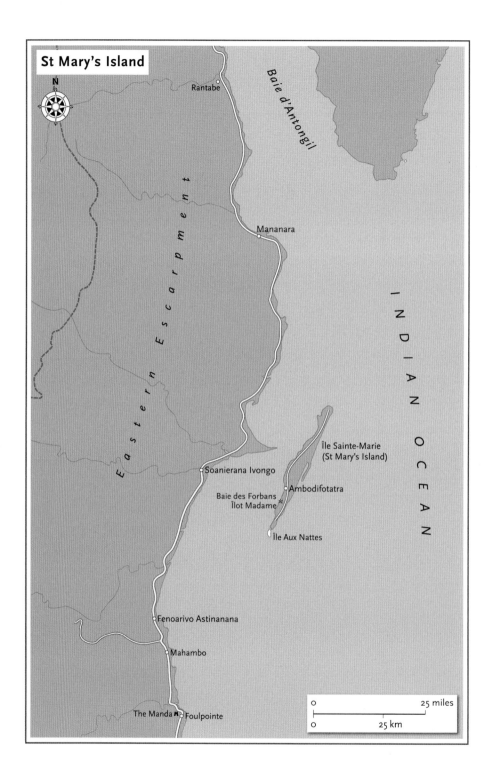

St Mary's Island

N

Rantabe

Baie d'Antongil

Mananara

E a s t e r n   E s c a r p m e n t

I N D I A N   O C E A N

Île Sainte-Marie
(St Mary's Island)

Soanierana Ivongo

Ambodifotatra

Baie des Forbans
Îlot Madame

Île Aux Nattes

Fenoarivo Astinanana

Mahambo

The Manda Foulpointe

0   25 miles

0   25 km

HISTORY IS LITTERED WITH SANCTUARIES for the wicked, like Tortuga, Kowloon Walled City and London's Alsatia. But St Mary's (or Île Sainte-Marie) isn't like any of these places. From the air, it's a picture of innocence: deep royal blues, and a long, thin spindle of sand, tufted with jungle. There's no obvious place to hide: no caves or slums or complex of creeks. A delicate frill of reef runs round it all, and the rest of Madagascar looks dreamily distant, through 10 miles of haze.

Nowadays, there's no reason to come here, except to do nothing. Every week, hundreds of Europeans make the journey, and then sit on the sand until it's time to go home. Perhaps that's all the pirates ever wanted. They were often described like tourists, in their 'speckled shirts' and fancy stockings. It's even been suggested that most of them were gay, and that the bond known as *matelotage* was about much more than being a 'mate'. But they can't all have been gay, or doing nothing, because every Sainte-Marien claims to be of good pirate stock. I sometimes wondered if the islanders had noticed a difference, and that the latest arrivals weren't like those who'd come before. Perhaps not: after all, this place is what it's always been, the *Île des Vazahas*, or the Isle of Whites.

MY PLANE HAD BEEN CARRYING SEVERAL large wooden boxes of money, and so as soon as we landed, we were surrounded by guns. This was normal for Sainte-Marie, said my *tuk-tuk* driver, and so were all the giant clams, and the sheets of tin, caught in the trees. This year, he told me, the cyclones had carried off his neighbour's house and most of the local boats, but this was normal too. In fact, he said, '*cette année était plus normale que la plupart*' (this year was more normal than most).

It took me a while to get used to the new normality. Everything now was wet and warm, and most of the paddy fields were only the size of a room. But things grew faster here, and bigger. Even the papayas looked like little wrestlers on steroids. By contrast, my first hotelier was very blonde and shrivelled, as if he'd been drained of everything but yellow. He was annoyed that I'd interrupted his breakfast – a large glass of white – and left me to his wife, who was Malagasy (and who, I noticed, wore the same uniform as the cleaner and the girl in the kitchen). He later told me that he was from Dieppe, where he'd never had to put up with madness like this. It had taken him a week to nail everything back into place, and now he had no clients. The couple did, however, have a lemur, which let out great angry sobs, like a teenager, every time I passed her cage. It was all I could do to stop myself flipping the latch and setting her free.

After that, things got better, even faintly idyllic. The next day, I moved across the island, to a place on the beach. The people here had no time for uniforms, and did everything with a swagger. As well as hammocks and tortoises, there was a thatched billiard room and a jetty made of driftwood. On the owner's desk was a stash of jetsam, including old bottles and munitions, all crusted in shell. Every evening, there'd be a band, with home-made lutes and drums, banging out their salty songs. Then, each morning, a girl would appear in the shallows, hunting for octopus with a tiny spear. Even the name over the door belonged to an earlier age: 'Libertalia', or the Land of the Free.

Daniel Defoe would have been surprised to find that his little utopia had become a hotel. Although there are still those who insist that Libertalia really existed, and that it was here in St Mary's, none of it's true. This time the story was pure Defoe. There was never a Captain Misson or a parliament of pirates. Everything was invented: the white flag, the fine buildings, the democracy and even the motto ('God and Liberty'). Defoe had carefully inserted this perfect society into his great book on villainy, *A General History of the Pyrates*, published in 1724. Surrounded by fact, it developed a life of its own.

But Libertalia wasn't meant to mislead, only inspire. In this little corner of Madagascar – radical, dissenting and colour-blind – Defoe had created a blueprint for his ideal England. There'd be no kings, no bosses, no boundaries and no money. These were popular ideas at the time, and Libertalia was there to show how it worked. Defoe even described how the savages appeared, and destroyed his society. His words were written with such conviction that, even now, people search for the ruins.

THESE DAYS, NOT MUCH REMAINS OF St Mary's robbers, except their genes and their bottles. Although there was plenty of piracy in the

Between 1680 and 1720, St Mary's Island was a bolt-hole for pirates. At its height, it was home to over a thousand gangsters and criminals.

local names – like the Baie des Forbans and Buccaneer Island – I never found much when I visited these places (except mud and mangrove and giant clams). But I enjoyed my walks among the Sainte-Mariens. Everyone had a smallholding and was living on mango and jackfruit. A lot of people had stories too, some taller than others. One man told me that almost everyone here had a funny blood group, perhaps European. Another said he was sure he was foreign, and that all his ancestors had come from *Anglisa*.

'And what about the graveyard?' I asked.

On the map, I could see a place marked '*Cimetière des Pirates*'.

'I know it,' said an old man who had a crackly laugh like breaking sticks. For a little fee, he agreed to take me there, and off we went, around the bay. As we clambered over the roots, and up a grassy knoll, he told me all about his life in heaven. His name was Roland Razafy, and he was mostly Malagasy, and a quarter pirate. He'd done every job there was, and was now a watchman. Once, he'd helped an American find Captain Kidd's treasure but then the president came along and said it was just a bit of old lead, and took it away. Still, he didn't mind not being rich. They had everything here: the biggest mangoes, the purest water and the easiest girls. *Mamy ny aina*, he said, with a rattly grin: life is sweet.

After that, I didn't hold much hope for the graves. Roland, however, insisted they were all pirates, and had a tale for each of the tombs. But while some of the headstones were decorated with skulls and bones (or real cannonballs), they were all too recent. To have been a sea-robber, Monsieur le Chartier of Ducey would have had to be at least 130 when his *flûte* finally sank in 1836. I also doubted whether Mademoiselle Verges would have made much of a pirate at the age of four. Still, the stories were fun, and worth a few pounds. Roland too was happy, and after pocketing his booty, cackled all the way home.

By 1712, there were over four hundred pirates living on St Mary's. At its most dystopic, there may even have been more, perhaps a thousand. For many, this was as near to heaven as they'd ever get. Most were American, French or English, scabby rascals, scooped off the streets or snatched from taverns. A few were former slaves who'd find a curious form of democracy among the riff-raff. None of them had ever expected to end up here, with a shack of their own, a couple of girls, and a glut of fruit. They even had their own shop, supplied by Mr Frederick Philips of New York. It was wickedly expensive but here was everything a pirate would ever need: rum, Madeira, hens, Bibles, slaves, whipsaws, gunpowder, speckled shirts and trinkets for their molls. The girls of St Mary's would soon have the reputation of being the easiest and brassiest on the Indian Ocean.

But it wasn't all low life. The leading figures – like William Kidd and John Bowen – had often been respectable captains. The temptations, however, had been just too great. When Captain Taylor returned to St Mary's in 1721, after a raid on Malabar, he had with him a haul of diamonds worth 4 million dollars. At today's prices, the payout – *for each member of his crew* – was worth over £950,000. With money like that, the robber-captains would become some of the most powerful gangsters in the world: the Escobars of the early eighteenth century, or the Al Capones. They'd enjoy influence, immunity, retirement homes (Cuba, in Taylor's case) and even private education for their half-caste children. For the time being, they were safe here too: the navies of the world never seemed to make it down to St Mary's.

If there's any booty left, it's probably out in the Baie des Forbans. In the mouth of the inlet was a little island called the Îlot Madame, which was now linked to the shore by a system of bridges. Roland had told me that the best treasure was about halfway across, and so, one morning, I set out over the causeway, and dutifully peered down into the shallows.

It's thought that if anyone was ever to drain the *baie*, they'd find it cluttered with wrecks. A Belgian diver called Pierre van den Boogaerde once listed them. Some – like the *Mocha*, the *Soldado* and the *Dolphin* – had been scuttled by the pirates in 1699, to block off the entrance. Others had contracted a bad case of worm, and had settled more gently into the mud. One of them, HMS *Serapis*, had quite literally died of drink. Captured by American rebels off the coast of Yorkshire in 1779, she'd been given to the French, who fitted her out for the Indian Ocean. Her sailing days ended when her liquor store ignited, and in the ensuing fire she was blown to bits.

'Yes, but the best wreck,' said Roland, 'is Captain Kidd's.'

If there was anything there, I couldn't see it: just lumps of concrete, some beer cans, a few sea urchins and a little pink arm, torn off a doll.

The *Adventure Galley* has been ruining careers for over three hundred years. The first to fall was its commander, William Kidd, when he re-nounced his commission and became a thief. Next to go were the Indian traders who, in 1698, surrendered the *Quedagh Merchant* – along with a cargo worth, today, over £18 million. At this point, Kidd ought to have stayed on St Mary's and enjoyed his retirement. But he couldn't resist just one more trip to Massachusetts. It was a move that cost him not only his livelihood but also his neck. Arrested, he was sent for trial at the Old Bailey, and hanged in 1701. His body was painted with tar, and for many years hung from a gibbet on the banks of the Thames. It was a reminder that the life of a pirate is short and merry, but mostly short.

The *Adventure Galley* still hadn't finished dishing out misfortune. Fate had reserved particular scorn for those who'd come out looking for treasure. One such was Roland's old boss, the underwater explorer Barry Clifford. His chances of finding anything were always slim. Kidd himself had described stripping out his old flagship and setting it on fire. Clifford, however, had staked everything on his search, and in 2015 he emerged from the sediment with 50 kilos of shiny metal. It wasn't just the president who declared it was lead, so did UNESCO. What's more, they said, it wasn't a shipwreck that Mr Clifford had found but a builder's tip. 'They've destroyed me,' announced the treasure-hunter, and that was the end of the *Adventure* venture.

Like their ships, most of the pirates met a torrid end. Drink and worm got some of them, and malaria others. Few of the big names died glamorously. Captain Nathaniel North was murdered in his bed, and Bowen was carried off by the dreaded 'dry belly ache'. As for Thomas Howard ('a morose ill-natur'd fellow'), he'd taken to abusing his Malabari wife, which didn't sit well with her relatives, who got together and had him skewered. By 1722, the drunken republic was all but over.

That same year, the Royal Navy sent a squadron down from Madras to finish it off. The sight that met their eyes wasn't pretty. There were only a few outlaws left. One was a well-addled Jamaican, known as the 'King of Ranter Bay', and the other was a Scot called James Adair, who was now living 'a very profane and debauch'd life'. Everywhere, there was junk: broken china, bottles, discarded spices and burnt-out ships. It was almost as if a great, wild party had been suddenly interrupted, and all the revellers had fled, leaving behind only their brats and the clearing up.

D EBRIS IS STILL THE MOST MEMORABLE feature of the Îlot Madame. Although it's only small, and has been absorbed by the causeway, the island is stacked with trash. Among the fridges and shipwrecks I even spotted a tiny gunboat, and a miniature pavilion with louvred shutters. Some of the boats were now being cut up with lamps and saws. Others just sat, waiting for worms that can eat through metal.

Although it doesn't look royal, this was once the home of a pirate-princess. As memorials go, she probably deserves better than this, an outcrop of scrap with a scurrilous name. Princess Betia was no madame or Pompadour. She and her family would transform eastern Madagascar, politically at least. It is, however, a long and tortuous tale, and – to be fair – at the heart of it all there's a lot of sex. The gist of it goes like this…

It all begins with Thomas White, an English thief. After years of harvesting the Indian fleets, he and his men retire to the Malagasy coast. Here, they take up girls, and, in a feat of Olympian miscegenation, produce hundreds of children. One of Tom's favourite half-castes is Ratsimilaho, who's born around 1694. As soon as the boy is old enough, he's sent to England, where he learns about Latin and brutality. His father dies while he's away, but by 1712 Ratsimilaho is back in Madagascar, and looking for trouble. Soon, he has an army of half-castes, 200 strong, and they set about conquering their neighbours. Over the next thirty years, they acquire over 400 miles of coastline and form a new tribe: the Betsimisaraka. In time, it will be the second-biggest tribe in Madagascar, and many of its people will always think of themselves as *zana-malata*, or the 'Sons of the Half-Castes'.

In 1750, Ratsimilaho dies, leaving a daughter, Betia. She lives out on St Mary's, and when the royal court implodes, she seeks the protection of France. Not everyone is happy, and the first French officials are all speared to death. But then Princess Betia marries a corporal from Gascony, and things settle down. Later, the French will joke that the Gascon is impressively endowed (he's always been known as *La Bigorne*, or 'The Anvil'), and that Betia had signed away everything just for the sex. It's a sordid joke but it will make good history. By 1818, the French have a permanent presence on the island – now called the *Île Sainte-Marie* – and will build its first fortress on a nearby hill.

They will also happily bed themselves down on 'Madame's Islet'. It acquires a tiny port and a governor's house. Although the name will always make them smirk, this is the beginning of French Madagascar.

S AINTE-MARIENS ARE STILL GRATEFUL for the water between themselves and the mainland. Although it sometimes swallows ferries, and is an unhealthy medium for sharks, it's also a boundary. Over there, life isn't quite so sweet, and, besides, the islanders have never felt entirely Malagasy. The French have always known this, and at independence in 1960 would offer them all homes in France. But the Sainte-Mariens had no need for a refuge: they have their channel.

Before leaving the island, I joined a small boat out on the water. The crew were mostly biologists, and until that morning I'd never re-

alised that their submarine world could be so riotous. To begin with, everything was quiet. Ahead of us, the mainland began swelling up, almost imperceptibly at first, and still a far-off iceberg-blue. But then spouts of vapour appeared in the distance, and off to our left, a creature – twice the size of a bus – burst out of the water and landed in a blast of sound and spray, a bit like a bomb. It was the *baleines à bosse*, said the scientists: humpbacks, back here to breed. Even their newborns are gigantic, weighing in at over a ton.

'And how many are there?' I gasped, during a moment of calm.

'Hundreds,' said the skipper, 'maybe thousands.'

The calf of a humpback whale, born off Île aux Nattes.

That morning, the whales did everything they could to get themselves noticed. They huffed, puffed, leapt, slapped, clapped and launched more of their bombs. Sometimes, whole pods would appear around us, like little archipelagos of snorting black islands. It's probably absurd to describe any animal as happy, but these were ecstatic. They'd just swum over 5,000 miles up from the Antarctic. Now, here they were, at what can only be described as a giant cetaceous orgy. One of the biologists had an underwater microphone and asked if I'd like to listen. The device would pick up every male voice over several kilometres. '*Ils sont très excités,*' she warned.

From the speaker came a din like a mob, trying to get in. The sound wasn't so much angry as frenzied and shrill. I hope the Sainte-Mariens never get to hear it, or perhaps, this time, they really will be up and gone.

A FEW WEEKS LATER, I WAS ON the opposite shore, buying drinks for the local ghosts.

Foulpointe was once a place as nefarious as Sainte-Marie, and has never quite shed its pirate name ('Hopeful Point'). These days, it's where Malagasies go on holiday, and its loveliness begins way down the coast. It took my *taxi-brousse* all morning to pick its way along the sandy berms, through the coconut groves and over several great rivers. If anything, the loveliness faltered slightly as Foulpointe appeared. Most of the hotels seemed to have their own little frizz of razor wire, and some looked like penitentiaries painted by children. But then, suddenly, we were on the beach, another dreamy sweep of silver and palms.

I'm not sure when old Fidèle appeared, or how we hooked up. One minute I was eating a roasted crab, and the next we were off to see the dead. He told me that, for seven generations, his family had been looking after the town's history, as well as its fort and all the ghosts. He'd talk about the spirits as if they were friends. They all had their likes and dislikes, and their different moods. His favourite was Dr Couillaudeau de la Touche, who'd passed away in seventeen-something. But there were lots of others, including the *kalamoro*, or forest sprites, and a couple of *zazavavy an-drano*, or mermaids, who sounded suspiciously English. Among all these otherworldly beings, Fidèle was obviously popular, and it wasn't hard to see why. With his bony head and his knobbly joints, he was almost there himself.

On the way to the graveyard, we stopped to buy rum and cigarettes. 'I don't smoke or drink,' said Fidèle, 'I just do it for *them*.'

The rest of the day continued like this, never quite returning to normal. For a while, we sat with the doctor, drinking rum. Fidèle also smoked the two cigarettes, and introduced me to his other friends, some of whose names had been washed away. Then we walked out to the point. At times, England appeared, or so it seemed. We'd pass streams and small stone buildings, and great spreading trees would close over the track. Perhaps a little piracy had rubbed off on the landscape?

But then we arrived on the promontory and an unmistakably tropical strand. It has an odd place in Madagascar's story. Of all its characters, easily the most improbable landed here, in 1785. These days, in Foulpointe, he's remembered only by Fidèle (and they often drank together, and smoked cigarettes). But elsewhere – in Poland, Slovakia and Hungary – he's still a national hero, and has starred in films and novels and at least two operas. He is, after all, the only Polish king this island has ever had. There's even a street named after him in Tana, with its own little plaque: *Rue Benyowski, Homme d'Aventures.*

Like all great adventurers, Count Maurice Benyowski could tell a good tale, and was everywhere at once. Born to Polish parents in a Hungarian town (that's now Slovakian), nobody is sure which he was. But by 1762 he'd taken a commission in the Habsburg army, and ended up in Poland.

The fighting was all very much to his liking until 1770, when he was captured by the Russians. This time, he was sent into exile, and ended up over 5,000 miles away, on the far side of Asia. But the bogs and bears of Kamchatka held little appeal, and so the count escaped. It was the beginning of a rollicking adventure that would eventually take him to Madagascar – via the Aleutian Islands, Alaska, Japan,

A shrine at Foulpointe. The biros were planted by students seeking good luck in their exams.

Formosa, Macau and Mauritius. His description of this odyssey would later be translated into eight different languages, and yet not everyone believed it. 'Sheer invention,' reads the English introduction. Even his biographers had their doubts. According to one of them, Benyowski was nothing more than 'a hare-brained braggadocio […] a prototype of Baron Munchausen himself'.

But that's not how the French felt. Louis XV was impressed by the Count's plans for Madagascar, and in 1773 agreed to fund an expedition and a great new city, called Louisbourg. To begin with, it seemed to exceed expectations. Benyowski reported that he'd subjugated the entire island and that Louisbourg was now a thriving metropolis. But then, in 1776, he announced that the Betsimisaraka had elected him as their *ampanjakabe*, or king. At this point, the new king, Louis XVI, smelt a rat, and sent out a commission of inquiry. The investigators discovered that most of the settlers were dead, and that Louisbourg wasn't a city but a couple of huts. Benyowski immediately resigned.

The fort, or manda, at Foulpointe, built around 1820, and armed by the British.

It was eight years before he got the funding for another kingdom. In the meantime, he toured Europe and the American colonies with his magnificent prospectus. At one point, he fought the British at the Battle of Savannah, and then, a few years later, he was over in London, asking for money. But no one fell for it. 'A boasting braggart,' wrote one of his critics, 'all of whose geese were swans.' Eventually, however, he did find sponsors, out in Baltimore. They're probably best remembered for their improbable names (Messrs Messonier, Zollikofer and John Hyacinth de Magellan) but they did provide a ship, called *Intrepid*. A year later, it was moored off Foulpointe, and Benyowski was charging up the beach.

The conquest of Foulpointe was probably the high point of King Maurice's rule. Although he did start another city – this time called Mauritania – it's never been found. It hadn't lasted long. Unamused by the loss of his trading post, Louis XVI had despatched a few troops from Pondicherry. At the end of May 1786, they finally located Benyowski up north, and he died when a boule smashed through his chest. It's said that he was buried by two comrades who'd been with him since Kamchatka. Now, however, even the grave has disappeared, and all that remains of the king is a small hill near Antongil ('*Mt Beniowski*'), and, of course, his wandering spirit.

'NEXT,' SAID FIDÈLE, 'WE MUST GO TO the *manda*, to speak to the gods.'

A few miles up the road, a huge shape appeared among the trees. At first, I could hardly believe what I was seeing. It was like some vast extra-terrestrial doughnut, complete with gun ports and vast metal doors. Originally, they say, it had been disguised to look like a hill. But now the earth had gone, washed away by almost two centuries of rain, leaving only this torus of mortar. Modern designers often struggle to achieve this sort of symmetry and simplicity, and yet this was also a *manda* – or fort – over 70 metres in diameter. Even empty, it was formidable. It's small wonder that people still saw it as a home of the gods. Near the entrance was a little shrine, heaped with money and cow skulls and hundreds of biros.

'Why all the pens?' I asked.

'Students,' said Fidèle. 'Asking for luck, in their exams.'

Inside, there was more ingenuity. A tunnel, 7 metres long, led in through the wall, opening out onto a large circle of grass. From here, steps led up to the gun decks, which were set deep inside the ramparts and ran all the way round, in two narrow tiers. Despite the under-growth, it was still possible to creep through them. Dark and musty, this was just as I imagined life on a Georgian warship. Even now, there were twenty-three heavy guns in place, all British and of Napoleonic vintage. But they worried Fidèle. He said it was only a matter of time before the Chinese stole them and melted them down. He loved his fort, and was always embellishing it with stories and secret tunnels. He even had his own idea who'd built it.

'Queen Victoria,' he insisted, 'she didn't like the Portuguese.'

'The *Portuguese?*'

'Yes, they make a lot of slaves here. And she loved the black people.'

But it was never Britons manning these guns. The clue was in the masonry, a peculiar blend of coral, slaked lime and egg white. By 1820, over 150,000 eggs had been applied to the fort. It was the work of a shrewd and dangerous people, now pouring out of the highlands. Although they couldn't write, and had never seen a horse or the sea, they'd soon learn. Within a few years, almost all of Madagascar would be theirs. They were the island's first true conquerors, and were known as the Merina.

'Terrible people,' said Fidèle, 'always making trouble.'

CHAPTER 6

Royal Tana, and the All-conquering Merina

*Among all my friends and acquaintances who either
accompanied me or visited Madagascar… only two or
three have survived.*

CAPTAIN LOCKE LEWIS
'An Account of the Ovahs', 1835

*That sort of shoddy Clapham, dreary, puritanical
hypocritical Antananarivo.*

EDWARD F. KNIGHT
Madagascar in War Time, 1896

*If wealthy Malagasy families still own slaves today, even
when they are living in the centre of Paris, it is because
it is a durable feature of Malagasy civilisation.*

SOLOFO RANDRIANJA AND STEPHEN ELLIS
Madagascar: A short history, 2009

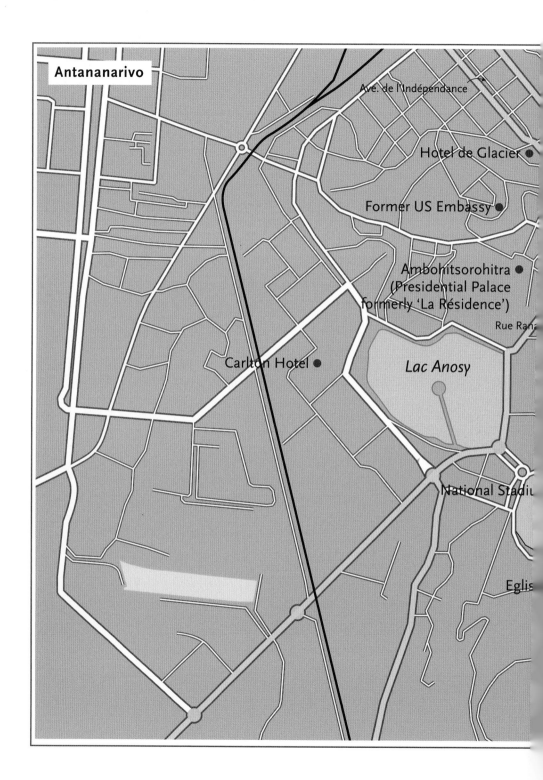

Antananarivo

Ave. de l'Indépendance

Hotel de Glacier ●

Former US Embassy ●

Ambohitsorohitra ●
(Presidential Palace
formerly 'La Résidence')

Rue Ran

Carlton Hotel ●

Lac Anosy

National Stadi

Eglis

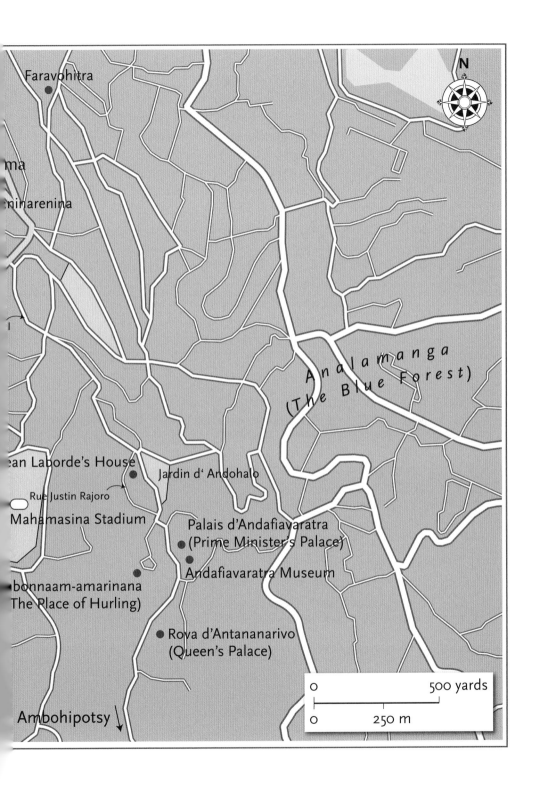

Faravohitra

ma

ninarenina

Analamanga
(The Blue Forest)

an Laborde's House

Jardin d' Andohalo

Rue Justin Rajoro

Mahamasina Stadium

Palais d'Andafiavaratra
(Prime Minister's Palace)

Andafiavaratra Museum

bonnaam-amarinana
The Place of Hurling)

Rova d'Antananarivo
(Queen's Palace)

Ambohipotsy

| 0 | | 500 yards |
| 0 | | 250 m |

Y<small>OU'D HAVE TO BE A BIRD TO UNDERSTAND</small> the Merina. Only from above does their empire make sense. I'd never really appreciated this until I flew in from the east, returning to Tana. No sooner had the plane left the coast than a great jungly wall appeared, known as *le faille*, or 'the fault'. This escarpment runs almost the length of the country and rises to a height of over 5,000 feet. It had taken the early Indonesians hundreds of years to find their way up, but by the sixteenth century they were on the top, with a fortified plateau all of their own.

Through the clouds, paddy fields appeared. Sometimes it was no more than a gulley with a trickle of green. But in other places the plateau was like a lake, speckled in islands. The Merina would have been nothing without their rice. It turned them into planners, storers, counters and strategists. Life was no longer just about today but about tomorrow too, and the next four months. It also enabled them to travel great distances, to explore, and to prey on their neighbours.

Nearer Tana, a great military landscape took shape. Everywhere there were perfect red circles, carved into the hills. On the ground, you never notice these giant ditches, or *hadivory*, and yet most are over 15 feet deep. From the air, however, they look ominous, the outward signs of a society that's extremely violent, technically canny and powered by slaves. By 1610, the new domain had acquired its first firearm – an arquebus – and a sinister name: *Imerina*, or 'Distant Views'. The new chief, Andrianjaka, would soon begin wiping out the last of the Vazimba, who were no match for these upstarts with metal.

Beyond the forts, the modern city of Tana appeared. I could now make out the shanty towns in the cliffs, and laundry on the riverbanks. In among the rust and the churches, there are twelve sacred hills. Back then, at the start, this was all there was of Imerina. But its people were ambitious, and always keen to take on the world. 'Our rice shall extend to the sea,' they declared. This hilly chiefdom would be the beginning of an empire, and only the birds would know how tiny it was.

P<small>EOPLE WERE STILL FRIGHTENED OF THE</small> twelve hills, perhaps more than ever. These were dangerous places, and although most of them still functioned as forts, only the ancestors lived there now. Each hill had its own underclass of *gardiens* and sweepers, and every day they'd clear out the ditches and sweep the tombs. But these weren't places to linger. Everyone knew that ruins were vindictive, especially when the dead felt neglected. So, most of the time, the hilltops were empty, and I'd have them all to myself, or just me and the kings and a few hundred tombs.

Of all the forts, easily the most eerie was Ambohimalaza. This time, I didn't go alone but was joined by Aro, the palaeontologist. He explained that this was *la nécropole royale*, home to some of the earliest kings and some of the greatest Merina. Densely packed within the earthworks, there was now a little circular town just for the dead. On every street were miniature mansions, one-storey palaces and Romanesque villas. Here were the *andriana* – or nobility – at their most flamboyant and detached. Nobody else could be buried here, explained Aro. The freemen, or *hovas*, had their own cemeteries, and so did the *andevo*, or underclass.

'And is your uncle here?' I asked. 'The gynaecologist?'

'Yes,' said Aro modestly. 'All my family. Except the babies.'

'Oh. Why not the babies?'

'They can't be ancestors. So they're buried outside.'

On one of the other hills, all the tombs had been destroyed by fire. Although it sat almost at the end of Tana's runway, Ambohidratrimo was one of my favourite redoubts. Conical and covered in pines, it had a narrow path spiralling up the outside, and was mounted with a whorl of ditches and boulders.

Until a great fire destroyed everything in 2017, there'd been several kings and nobles up here, laid out in wooden hutches. Now it looked much as it had in Vazimba times, a great bald summit of sacrificial rock. People still came up here to kill their chicken, and spill a bit of honey and rum. Sitting among the feathers was an old caretaker, dressed in her socks and three old skirts, despite the heat. She spoke some French, and so we chatted for a while about some of the big shots who'd lived up here. You can't just become a noble, she said, you are what you are. Often, they'd had names like 'Healthy Dog' (because you don't want to make the spirits jealous). The last king to rule from this rock had died

Overleaf: The *hadivory*, or fortifications of old Imerina are best seen from the air.

in 1710. They'd all ended up in the little 'cold houses', or *tranomanara*. The wives of the *andriana* could only join them if they were noble too. It's still like that. The *andriana* run everything here.

I asked how you could tell if someone was noble, and she paused. *'Juste, ils savent. Et ils ont les bons cheveux raides.'*
(They just know. And they've got nice straight hair.)

Across the city is the holiest hill of all: Ambohimanga, or 'the Blue Mountain'. But unlike the others, it's not just a cemetery or a repository for kings. To the Merina, this is the nucleus of their *fanjakana*, or empire – as well their Narnia, their Swiss Cottage and their Camelot. Until 1896, no foreigner was allowed inside, and every night a great disc of stone, weighing over 12 tons, was rolled across the entrance. Even now, there's a whole list of things you can't take in, including alcohol, umbrellas, onions, pigs, pumpkins and hedgehogs.

Twice I went out to Ambohimanga, and both times came back feeling slightly bewitched. Was that real, what I'd just seen, or a bit of make-believe? The ramparts and the disc were familiar enough, but the castle itself seemed to have slipped from the pages of C. S. Lewis. It was very small and pretty and was said to have been made with 16 million eggs. The guides also showed me a giant royal bathtub, and a plumbing system that had been serviced by virgins. Then, in the middle of it all was a large Victorian pavilion, so feather-light and delicately fretted it might easily have floated away. Inside, there were deep red brocades, Japanese wallpaper, and tiny gilt palm trees down the dining-room table. Here, the last queens of Madagascar had whiled away the monarchy, just like the English queen in her little Swiss cabin. Victoria had even provided some of the fittings, including a large gold mirror and a London clock, made by 'Parnell of Bow'. It all felt like another elaborate royal fantasy, steeped in red dust, and over 5,000 miles from the Isle of Wight.

Across the courtyard was a much darker structure. Although the roof was steep and tall – almost Thai or Khmer – the rest was made of logs, like a barn. This wasn't what I'd expected of a conqueror's house but then, in the gloom, I spotted tridents, a bed with 8-foot legs (to deter assassins, apparently), and a little box in the corner for the twelve royal wives. There was even a portrait of the great man himself, looking athletic and Asian. Only one contemporary description of him survives, from 1808. By then, he was over sixty, and 'very ugly, with straight hair, having the appearance of a Malay'. In my notes, I'd come to think of him as 'APM'. But this doesn't do justice to a warrior whose name had once emptied the countryside, and now fills the page. He was Andrianampoinimerinandriantsimitoviaminandriampanjaka (a name that is often shortened to Andrianampoinimerina).

His rule had begun almost accidentally, with a spate of murders. In 1787, his uncle, the king, had sent men up here to kill him, and had ended up dead himself. APM then killed off the other four pretenders – all stabbed (or forked) – and proclaimed himself king. After that, he was unstoppable. His spearmen secured the twelve hills first, and then set out into the *hauts plateaux*. These were messy encounters, involving both rhetoric and spears. Often the bodies of the dead were sold back to their relatives, enthusiastically dismembered. APM usually led from the front, invoking magic. His message was simple: either you join me or you become my slaves. He had no qualms about selling off his subjects to foreigners. By the time of his death, in 1810, over 49,000 souls had been shipped to Mauritius and Réunion. The highlands have never recovered from this sale of humans, and people still talk about its landscape of ghosts.

For those that remained there was tyranny, with all the usual benefits. APM devised councils, a standing army and a network of canals. He was, in the eyes of one American commentator, a 'savage of genius'. The punishment for theft was instant death, and the lazy were beaten, and smokers enslaved. He also encouraged colonies, although he warned the settlers that if they ever returned to Tana, they too would be slaves, along with all their children. An anxious empire began to take shape.

Pilgrims still cringe before his grave, crawling forward with their sweets and rum. It doesn't matter that the grave is empty (the French had considered the corpse far too subversive, and removed it from Ambohimanga). Nor does it matter that the king has now been dead for over two hundred years. 'Our ancestors are everywhere', say the guides, 'even in the trees.'

IT'S ONLY 8 MILES BACK TO ROYAL TANA. The journey probably hasn't changed much over the last two centuries, or so it seemed at first: the same cockfights, the same little open-air operas and the same ox-carts and mud brick. But then, on the outskirts of the mountain-city, cars began to crowd in, and everything turned to concrete.

It seemed to take my taxi hours to climb 'the Blue Forest', or Analamanga. About halfway up, we came to a lumpy football pitch, called Andohalo. That afternoon, there were three games playing, all swirling together like Brownian motion, and not quite touching. I recognised the pitch from old sepia prints. This is where the queens were crowned, and where the citizens would meet, sometimes 15,000 at once. Analamanga was the perfect hill for a capital city. In 1794, APM had moved his court here, and had renamed its village after his scraggy troops: Antananarivo, or the 'City of a Thousand'.

The citadel he established still worries the town. Over time, turrets had been added, along with clocks and bells and a giant bronze eagle.

Looking towards the Queen's Palace, circa 1854.

Sometimes, this great confection appears – resurrected – on banknotes, stamps, postcards or sachets of sugar. At these moments, everyone sees something different: a symbol of national pride, perhaps; one of the Wonders of the World; 'an architectural freak' (as one novelist put it); a mark of progress; a display of power; or a celebration of slavery and the work of despots. But, for now, it's none of these things. It's just a ruin: that great, burnt-out shell, the *Rova*.

I had a friend who remembered the night the palace caught fire: 6 November 1995.

Simon Peers still lives up on the crest, near the ruins. It's hard to describe what he does, it all sounds so Georgian. A clothmaker, perhaps or a master weaver? He'd arrived thirty years ago with a backpack and had fallen in love with Malagasy textiles (and a beautiful local debutante). Probably his most memorable work was a shawl, woven from the silk of over a million golden orb spiders. In London, it had caused an arachnoid sensation, with its own exhibition and a TV show. For Simon, the destruction of the *Rova* and hundreds of costumes had come as a terrible blow.

'I remember it so well, and this fire out on the hillside, and the wind is blowing in from the east, and it blows it towards the palace, and then – it all happens so quickly – it reaches the surrounding buildings (you, know, the little palaces? The wooden ones?) and they go up. It's *horrible*, but then it reaches the Manjakamiadana, the Queen's Palace, and there's nothing we can do…'

'Wasn't there anyone trying to put it out?'

'Two old Soviet fire engines, but they didn't have the water pressure…'

'So what about saving the stuff inside?'

Simon sighed. 'It was unreal. There were lots of people running in and out with all kinds of things. Some of it was art but there was a lot of weird stuff too, like lamps and electric fans and filing cabinets. I remember seeing the Minister of Culture sitting there, *on a golden throne*, surrounded by objects! They say they managed to save about 1,600 pieces, but, you know, it was only a fraction of what was in there, and a lot went missing. There were so many looters that night, and I guess a lot of them were killed when it all went up…'

'What do you mean, "all went up"?'

'Well, the Manjakamiadana's like an enormous furnace, an old wooden building all clad in stone, so when the fire catches – *whoosh* – the whole thing goes up! Flames shoot out of the top! High in the sky! Everyone must have seen it, all over the city. And they're *worried*. This thing's been there forever, and now it's burning. It's like a message from the gods. The ancestors are angry. It's been a big issue for Madagascar, one of things that just won't go away.'

Two things stand out from my visit to the ruins: a eunuch and a hoard of giant guns.

I might never have noticed the eunuch if I hadn't hired my own private rogue. Fortunately, as well as ruins, the *Rova* has plenty of rogues. Every visitor has to run the gauntlet of drunks that hang around the gates, touting tours. I chose the most sober, who also happened to look the most villainous. Vincent Jany had a constantly shifting gaze, and a *zebu* tattooed across his hand. But he also spoke flawless English, which puzzled me. What misfortune had brought him to this? Perhaps he'd been a bookkeeper for the triads, or the *dahalo*'s dentist? But there was no point in asking. Vincent Jany would talk about anything – death, beef, the stupidity of government – but not himself.

'People still want to destroy us,' he'd say.

I knew where this was going, but I still asked. 'Who's *they*?'

'Everyone. From the East, the coast... all of them.'

'And so you think they set fire to this place?'

'Yes, they hate the Merina. They're still frightened.'

We were walking around the edge of the summit. In the middle was the outline of the Queen's Palace, rising five storeys out of the dust. Only its outside walls – the cladding – had survived, looking like a box of arches. It reminded me of a railway station that had somehow lost its tracks. Around the base were the plinths of much older mansions, which had also floated off on the evening air. One of them had belonged to APM, and it was here that he'd died in 1810. Someone had tried to rebuild it after the fire but had got no further than its barn-like ribs before the funds ran out.

'And this is where Radama lived,' said Vincent Jany.

King Radama I (1793–1828), displaying his penchant for British uniforms.

Near the old king's barn was that of his son. This time, the restoration had been completed, and it smelt of creosote and tree stumps. It was hard to imagine that this was ever the home of Radama I. The son of a tyrant, he was famously petulant. By the time he inherited his father's title, aged seventeen, he was already dissolute, wasted and married. But he also had his father's appetite, and – as well as another eleven wives – there were plenty of others who'd service his needs. To be summoned here and lavished with the new king's attention was considered an honour. Perhaps less welcome were the symptoms that followed.

'He had syphilis,' said Vincent Jany, 'and it made him mad.'

With that, he beckoned me aside, to meet the eunuch. Elf-sized, Ikidoka was all that remained of Radama's life. He appeared to be wearing a steward's jacket, and his hair was gathered up in a topknot. His function, said Vincent Jany, was to watch over the royal females. He was perhaps the very essence of servility: an attendant, carved from granite, and as impassive as ever after two hundred years.

The guns were easier to read. Each one was embossed with the insignia of the British crown. There were ten in all, and like those in Foulpointe, they were all big enough to punch a hole through a ship. Also, like the *manda*'s cannons, they were all junk, the leftovers of the Napoleonic wars. But they were still lethal, and, in the wrong hands, capable of transforming towns and rearranging lives. Madagascar would learn the hard way that progress usually begins with a bang.

As always with guns, they were supposed to make things better. By 1816, Madagascar was causing two problems for Britain. First, it was available to the French, and – if they ever recovered from their Napoleonic fiasco – they might start threatening the sea route to India. Second, it was still a hub of slavery (which Britain, after a long overdue attack of conscience, was committed to suppressing). As to what to do about these problems, conquest was never on the cards; the island was too big, too unruly, too unhealthy and too poor. There was, however, an alternative: to befriend the leadership, and buy their compliance.

That year, a small delegation was sent, and climbed the escarpment with a selection of presents. It was a perilous eight-day journey, up through the boulders and forest. But Radama was charmed, and a few months later a second party was sent. This time, thirty British soldiers clambered up the path in their spiffy uniforms. '*Thanaan-arive*' (as they called it) had never seen anything like it, and although most of the soldiers died, the diplomacy survived.

Within a year, a treaty was signed, involving the guns. This time, King Radama was carried down the escarpment and through the jungle. This was no mean feat for the Merina, who still referred to the east coast as *Mātētāaně*, or 'the Land of Death'. But it was worth the effort because the British had turned up with some stupendous gifts, including a chiming clock, a compass, a bedstead, a dress uniform, a map of the world and Madagascar's first horses. Although the horses promptly died, the clock was an instant success. It's said that when it chimed, the king 'danced with joy'. The British promised that there would be more presents like this, and plenty of guns. On 23 October 1817, Madagascar signed its first international treaty.

They say Malagasy politicians still talk about their treaty, and that there's always a copy in the president's office. It's only a short document – four pages of scrawl – but it conveys a sense of Madagascar's importance. Every year, she would receive 1,000 dollars in gold, 1,000 in silver, a vast cargo of muskets, 400 uniforms, 12 swords, 600 pieces of cloth, a full dress uniform for King Radama and two horses. Known as 'the Equivalent', this was considered fair recompense for the loss of a slave trade. All Radama had to do was to ban their export, which he did with enthusiasm. The punishment for exporting slaves was to be enslaved.

Soon, the great guns were being hauled up the mountain paths, across the plateau and into the *Rova*. '*Ça aurait dû être notre grand moment,*' said Vincent Jany, 'we could have been great.'

We were now sitting on the parapet, looking out across the city towards the mountains. Radama would have had this view. But instead of these paddy fields of rust, he'd have seen great sheets of rice. He'd also have seen his army mustering way below, at Mahamasima. The area where they gathered is now the national stadium, and if we listened carefully we could just hear the gusts of scorn and approval rising out of the stands. We could also hear the mumble of traffic, and somewhere a siren, honking along like an urgent goose.

Radama would have missed nothing from up here. He'd have seen his warriors swarm together for the new campaign (20,000 in 1817, and five times that three years later); he'd also have heard his new band and his weapons, and he'd have watched as the deserters were burnt alive. He'd have seen the dead, too, returning from the battlefields, slung between poles and off to the family tomb. But then the big day would come, and he'd see his army off. They had to move quickly. Each man had to carry his own rice, and if he was out in the field for more than a fortnight, he'd begin to starve.

'He was our Napoleon,' said Vincent Jany, 'simply brilliant.'

'I thought you said Radama was mad?'

'You had to be, to do what he did.'

From here, the armies ran off into the wilds. Over the next eight years, they captured Tamatave (1817) and Majunga (1824), and even reached Fort Dauphin, where they winkled out the French (1825). Despite the drink and the syphilis, Radama was a tireless campaigner. But as well as his new weapons, he also had an Irish general. James Hastie was a Quaker from Cork, and had arrived in the country as a sergeant, sent to look after the horses. But he soon got the hang of this threadbare warfare, fought at a trot. By the time he died in 1826, Hastie's warriors loved him, and at his funeral the great guns of Tana fired every fifteen minutes throughout the day. With his help, Radama had conquered almost two-thirds of the island.

In this sort of fighting, there was no time for niceties. In one battle, over three thousand Betsileo were driven over a cliff, and often the useful captives were simply castrated and all the rest killed (Ambositra, for example, is still 'the City of Eunuchs'). But even for the Merina, things could go wrong. Despite his speed, Radama usually lost half his men, and during the Menabe expedition of 1822, some 20,000 warriors were caught out and starved to death. By the end of these campaigns, Imerina was so short of labour that it would have to send out another army, to gather more slaves.

'And that's why they hate us,' said Vincent Jany, 'even now.'

These wars were always more about slaves than territory. Radama seldom established garrisons, and where he did they were no more than posts for trading slaves. Beyond them, there was no sense of government. Emptied of life, the savannahs and the spiny forest reverted to wilderness. In many of these places, only the lawless thrived, and gradually they became the dystopias that they remain today.

Apart from his cold stone eunuch, only ash remains of Radama today. Even his new-fangled palace had gone up in smoke. Tranovola, or 'the Silver House', is said to have changed the way Malagasies thought about home, and soon everyone had wanted one, with glass and verandas and upstairs rooms. Radama had also had it fitted out with mirrored walls, and hundreds of tiny silver bells. By the time he died, in 1828, he was a great conqueror, and colourfully psychotic. In a fit of pique, he'd slit his own throat. His funeral was truly Napoleonic, at least in scale. Over 20,000 *zebu* were slaughtered, and everyone was ordered to shave their head. During the mourning period, clapping was banned, together with dancing, bathing and sleeping on mattresses. Prostitutes were only permitted to trade if they handed over half their proceeds to the dead king.

Radama was interred here in the *Rova*, along with everything he'd need for the afterlife. This included 12,000 silver dollars, 80 British uniforms, 10 bulls, 12 horses and a sideboard. But it's all dust now, part of the rich subsoil of kings, quietly nourishing the weeds.

A T AROUND THIS TIME, MADAGASCAR underwent an intellectual revolution, and ended up partly Welsh. This Welshness would not only permeate the language, it would also seep through the religion and into the schools. If you were ever to trace it back to its source, you'd find yourself out in Henfynyw, knee-deep in Ceredigion's nettles. Here, somewhere in the undergrowth, are the ruins of Neuaddlwyd Academy. It may not look much – a plinth and the outline of two rooms – and yet it would become the model for thousands of schools across Imerina. None of this happened accidentally, of course. It was all down to four remarkable pupils: Jones, Bevan, Griffiths and Johns. Together, they'd see to it that Madagascar underwent a conversion. Even more remarkable, it would do so without even a hint of force. In this, the Malagasies claim, their country is unique.

The first to arrive were Jones and Bevan, in 1818. They still have a street named after them in Tamatave ('*Rue Jones et Bevan*'). Here they gave the Malagasies their first taste of Calvinism – and Welsh – and built the first church. But Madagascar still wasn't ready to give up its gods. Apart from Jones, almost every member of the mission perished in the months that followed, including Bevan, both wives and all the children. Jones, however, was made of stern stuff, and two years later the London Missionary Society sent him back to Madagascar. This time, he battled his way up the escarpment to Tana, where he was joined by Griffiths and Johns.

Immediately, the Welshmen got to work on the language. Not only did they learn it (a feat still considered impossible by many foreign missions), they also reduced it to a written form. Even now, say the linguists, there's a strong hint of Welsh in the way words appear (the letter 'o', for example, sounds like 'oo'). But Jones and his friends had only just begun. By 1826, a mere four years after their arrival, they'd translated the New Testament, or *Testamenta Vaovao*. It's all there, from the gospels (*Matio*, *Marka*, *Lioka* and *Jaona*) down to *Korintiana II* and St Paul's letter to the *Efesiana*. That same year, a printing press arrived, but the man sent to build it immediately died. Undeterred, the missionaries studied the manual and assembled it themselves, printing over three thousand Bibles. This powerful body of words would sustain the faith through the bad times to come.

It wasn't long before the Merina had a new, Welsh god. At first, Jones was worried that they were beyond redemption. The scale of fornication was Gomorrean, and everyone was grinding away, even the children. Sex was part of the street life and part of the festivals, and Jones was a source of great curiosity to the city's women (eventually, he'd marry a Mauritian to fight them off, and the new 'Mrs Jones' would be Tana's first white woman). But Jones also found unexpected levels of culture and sophistication. 'The people in this country,' he once wrote, 'is further in civilisation than numbers in Wales.' The only real obstacle the missionaries faced was King Radama. He wasn't interested in *Jesoa Kristy*, although – as a novel form of punishment – he liked the idea of crucifixion. He was also interested in upgrading his economy, and so he reached a deal with the Welsh. If they could instruct his people in skills like weaving and tanning, they could teach a bit of *Jesoa* too. By 1828, there were over half a million converts.

Andafiavaratra, one of Tana's royal palaces, and the work of a regime that no one dared call ridiculous.

The schools were now everywhere. The first one was up here in the *Rova*, in Radama's barn. But soon, every hill had its own little Neuaddlwyd Academy. Two centuries on, Malagasy education still sounds vaguely Georgian. A school is still a *sekoly*, with *kilasy* (classes) and *lesony* (lessons), and children still write with *pensily* and *penina*, and get thrashed for forgetting their *boky*. Over the years, some of these Little Britons would even adopt Welsh names like Radavison (Davison) and Raharijaona (Harry Jones), and there are still plenty of Victorias and Daisies, or Ravikitoara and Radezy. Sometimes, it's hard to believe how all this happened. Between 1818 and 1835, there were only ever twelve missionaries in Madagascar.

But this island has never been kind to its utopias. Its Cambrian Age would soon be over. Although there's still talk of an enduring 'Anglo-Malagasy Civilisation', it's only ever in academic circles. Most Malagasies have no idea where their prayers come from, or the letters on the page. With the death of Radama, the Welsh days ended, and it was time for the old gods to take their revenge.

I WALKED BACK THROUGH THE CINDERS to the Queen's Palace. Our world is full of empty spaces left by tyrants. The woman who built this place, the Manjakamiadana, was a queen of emptiness. It's estimated that during her thirty-three-year reign, almost half the population perished. First, she cleared out what was left of the western savannahs, and then turned on Imerina itself. It was almost as if she wanted to empty it of anyone that mattered: soldiers, generals, courtiers, courtesans, uncles, husbands, foreigners and everyone down to the dancers. By the time of her death in 1861, up to two and a half million people had died. Queen Ranavalona even emptied the world of herself. By 1995, all that remained of her was a palace, once the largest wooden building in the world. Then, with the great fire, that too was gone, and now all that's left is its fancy cladding, and a cube of air.

When Vincent Jany reappeared, I asked him about the new queen.

'The last great Malagasy,' he declared.

I must have looked puzzled.

'She tried to save us,' he said, 'from what we've become.'

Ranavalona makes a curious saviour, but then nothing was simple.

She was born as 'Miss Yellow', or Ramavo, in 1778. In old age, she'd be described as 'puffed up' and 'overbearing', but in her youth she was supple and well-proportioned, with feline features. At twenty-two, she was married off to the future king, Radama, who was then still a child. In later years, he'd garnish her with diseases, but then – once he'd slashed his windpipe – she'd kill off his family and seize the crown. Her allies now were the sorcerers and the Keepers of the Royal Fetishes. They'd always hated Christianity: it made humans of slaves, and replaced the afterlife with Hell. Now was their chance to save Madagascar.

The queen was soon clearing out her kingdom. To begin with, however, she was cautious. Although she repudiated the anti-slavery treaty, she let the British stay. As long as they were still churning out soap and glass, they could even keep their churches. But then, in 1832, she announced that Christianity was treasonous, and had marriage abolished and all services banned. Magic now began to take its proper place again. Every decision was made with beads, and babies born on unlucky days were instantly killed. Ranavalona also began teasing out disloyalty with the help of the gods. The ordeal she deployed – known as the *tangena* ordeal – would kill around three thousand people a year. Madagascar would be saved, or at least spared the prospect of entering the present.

In royal Tana, there were always pretty places to die or or undertake the ordeal. One of these was at Ambatondrafandrana, a little balcony of rock, just outside the *Rova*'s gates. It's still a memorable place at sunset, with the city turning pink below. In later years, a little Greek temple would be added, for the hearing of trials. But in the 1830s, justice was a more straightforward matter, and involved only a few strips of chicken skin sprinkled with *tangena*, a local poison. The principle was simple; the accused swallowed the skins, and if he then regurgitated them all, he was considered innocent. But if the skins didn't reappear, then the accused would be shorn of body parts; ears and nose first, and then arms and legs, before vanishing over the edge. The dead, who were clearly unfit for the family tomb, would then be left for the dogs and crows, and their ghosts would wander the slopes forever. As a form of celestial justice, it was obviously perfect.

The numbers must have pleased the queen. It's now thought that hundreds of thousands underwent the ordeal. Even if they survived,

the *tangena* would leave them paralysed or sterile. Among those who died were five of the queen's lovers, some courtiers (who she thought had bewitched her with gonorrhoea) and a troupe of dancing girls. The death of the dancers was witnessed by an American called Lieutenant Frederick Barnard. He noted that even though they spewed up their skins, they had their brains beaten out all the same.

THERE WERE OTHER PRETTY PLACES along the ridge, perfect for killing. One of them, called Ambohipotsy, was way over on the northern promontory. 'Never go out there,' said my friends, 'it it very dangerous. You'll be mugged.' But eventually my curiosity got the better of me, and off I went one afternoon. It's surprising the things you find, where the roads run out. At the far end of the ridge I came across an old Russian fire truck, now turning petunia-pink in the sharp mountain light. Then, out in the weeds, I stumbled on some teenagers with a bottle of Scotch. At first, we were all so shocked we didn't know who was mugging who. But then they all laughed mirthlessly, and when I pulled out my camera, they posed with their spliffs. As I slipped away, one of them called after me. Did I know what this place was called?

I said I did, but the others were laughing again.

'*La colline blanche*,' he squealed, '*à cause de tous les os!*'

This was typical of old Tana, to call a hill 'white' because of the bones. The Merina had always made a great display of their executions. This was an age when criminals were slowly dismembered until they confessed. People wouldn't forget sights like this, and that was the point. Queen Ranavalona was always looking for new ways to impress her subjects. Those who displeased her might find themselves flayed or boiled, or their testicles thoughtfully crushed. Best of all, however, were the displays of hunger. The convicts could either be sewn into buffalo hides and left to starve or fettered together with huge chains and sent out into the countryside to perish in pairs or groups of six. Soon there'd be lots of White Hills, not just Ambohipotsy.

The royal throne, a gift from the British, and the last queen, Ranavalona III.

But then, on 14 August 1837, a new kind of victim had appeared among the bones, called Rasalama. She wasn't surprised to find herself up here, stripped naked and pinned out with spears. Two years earlier, the queen had finally banned Christianity, and since then its obstinate adherents had been hunted like game. But although the missionaries would flee, it was too late to silence the hymns and secret meetings, and to burn all the texts. Rasalama would merely be the first to die. Hundreds of others would follow, singing their way up the hill and over the edge.

Most of the martyrs began their last trajectory a little further along, at Ambon'Ampamarinana, or 'the Place of Hurling'. It's only a short walk from the *Rova*, and so the queen would have heard all the wailing and all the hymns. Not that she cared. It had become obvious that Christianity was undermining her mystic powers, and by early 1849 it was time to get serious. Almost two thousand Christians were rounded up and tried. Most were fined, and around a hundred were flogged or sentenced to a life in irons. The rest were to be killed. Some were poisoned, and because it was considered taboo to spill noble blood, all the aristocrats were burnt alive. The last fourteen, however, were selected for an airborne death, and led up here to the Place of Hurling.

Nowadays, there's a small church to commemorate this moment. It's made of honey-coloured stone and looks as if it's just arrived from Oxfordshire. In fact, everything about this scene is almost perfect: the tiny gardens, the pots of geraniums and the cluster of old wooden mansions. It's like a little English village, except on the edge of an abyss. From here, the new converts fell over 200 feet, landing in what are now the slums behind the national stadium. Of course, like all martyrs they didn't entirely die, and would live on in etchings and stories and marble plaques. For the London Missionary Society, it was just what they needed, and prompted an unstoppable wave of righteous horror.

But for most Malagasies, the horror was more immediate. This period is still referred to as *Ny tany maizina*, or 'The time when the land was dark'. The sight of so many falling neophytes seems to have triggered a new sense of abandon in the royal court. There was no obvious ideology: a queen who dressed in Parisian shoes (and gowns by Worth) was being guided by magic. The persecutions were merely an expression of power, and so it went on: the sewing, boiling, flaying, pushing, crushing and crucifying. The worst year was 1857, when, in a single magnificent trial, thousands of people were convicted at once. Among them were 1,237 cattle thieves who'd have plenty of time to reflect on their past. For weeks afterwards, they could be seen in the wilderness, fettered together and dragging their dead.

*L*ES *TANANARIVIENS* NEED NO REMINDING that as the savannahs emptied, their city filled with slaves. Even now, nothing worries this city more than the idea of slavery, and the thought that 'the Lost' and 'the Forgotten' are all around or – even worse – in the family tree. It's not just about tombs and crinkly hair. The *andevo* are people without history, and therefore they barely exist. Everyone frets about this, and about just how free their ancestors were. Sometimes their name saves them, but more often than not it's about how you look. Whenever I asked someone to describe another person, they'd always begin with the tone and colour of the skin before working through to the curliness of hair. These things always matter. As the economist and traveller Nigel Heseltine once put it, 'The straight-haired brown-skinned Merina of pure Malay descent do not, in general, inter-marry with anyone showing the slightest sign of African blood…'

But it's hard for Tana, always shrinking away from what it is. If you were to rifle through the DNA of this town, you'd probably find that everyone was a little bit Lost or slightly Forgotten. They are, after all, Queen Ranavalona's people, most of them stripped of history and brought up from the coast. It's estimated that between 1820 and 1852, around a million slaves were brought to Imerina. The queen's military expeditions – like those of the kings before her – were little more than glorified hunting trips, for gathering humans. But these forays came at enormous cost. During that same period, almost 160,000 soldiers died. Of all the Merina sent to the coast, more than a quarter died of malaria, and in 1837 over 12,000 were killed in a single campaign against the Sakalava. But still the slaves came. Little by little, the Merina were replacing themselves with those they'd conquered.

The demand for slaves was never met. Many were now imported and, even today, in the language of slavery the *mojambikas* (or *les mozambiques*) are the lowest of the low. So many arrived that, despite the violence, the population actually grew. By the end of the nineteenth century, there were still half a million slaves living in Imerina. They did everything, from growing the rice to guarding the wives. This would leave the Merina almost incapable of effort, and the kingdom became almost defenceless against outside raids. Tana itself would be a city of slaves, its original Asiatic people now outnumbered two to one.

Even now, you don't have to look far to find an *mpanampy*, or 'assistant'. My friends would insist that slavery was everywhere, all over the city. They might be herders or hod carriers, but most were maids. Often they'd been sold by their parents for a few pounds a month, and would sleep in the pantry. One woman told me her neighbour had several girls living under the kitchen table. Even the rich had 'assistants', and when they went to Paris the *mpanampy* came too. 'Slavery,' laments the historian Solofo Randrianja, 'is a pillar of Malagasy civilisation.'

To see how this works, I went to see someone I knew in Faravohitra. As an orphan, Hanta Randrianarimalala had spent much of her life among those with nothing, and had been reared by the Quakers. At some stage, they'd sent her to Wales (which was a natural place to recharge her faith), and in time she'd be given her own care home, for girls who'd been lost. I'd met her on one of her fund-raising trips to London, and immediately liked her. Hanta was unassuming, motherly, small and unstoppable. She seemed to make a family of everyone she met. 'You must come and see us,' she'd said. 'The girls have had bad lives. But I can make it better.'

The house was a relic of the missionary era. Over the years, it had often threatened to collapse, but then the funds had arrived, usually from Wales. Now it stood white and tall again, in its own patch of earth. Inside, it looked much as it had in Victorian times: polished and church-like, with lunch for fifty boiling away on a bed of sticks. But despite the enormity of it all – the great black fireplaces and the fifty beds – it still felt like home. Next to each bunk was a tiny stack of clothes: the worldly possessions of a teenage girl. Hanta said most of the children had come straight here from prison.

Suddenly, there was singing, as the girls returned from school.

For a moment I watched them, puzzled.

'How did children like this end up in prison?'

'There's nowhere else for them…' said Hanta.

'But they're so *young*. Twelve, maybe? Thirteen?'

'Yes, but these are the kids that get forgotten.'

It was always the same story, she explained. 'These girls are sent up from the coast to work. You know, maids, that sort of thing. But often they don't get paid. OK, so the parents complain, and suddenly the kid is accused of theft. She took a mobile, they say, or some money. Well, then she's taken off to the prison. It's not a place for a child, and yet she may have to wait eight months for her trial, maybe more… But nobody knows what else to do, and it's like she'd not really there. People just don't see her any more, and so – *paf!* – she disappears. Across the whole of Madagascar, there's only one place that will take them, and that's us, Akany Avoko. So we do what we can. Get them to school, give them a family…'

Hanta's daughter appeared, with a large platter of sliced mango.

She told me that, one day, she wanted to be a judge.

'It seems such a safe place,' I said absently, 'and happy…'

'That's the problem,' said Hanta. 'Most of the time, they don't want to leave.'

S LAVERY IS ALWAYS USEFUL WHEN you need a new Detroit, and all your workers have vanished. That, roughly speaking, is the situation that Queen Ranavalona faced in the mid-1830s. She was desperate for metal. Not only was she fighting several different wars all at once, she'd also fallen out with the Europeans. Britain and France hadn't taken kindly to the persecution of traders (and Christians), and would soon appear offshore, blasting away at the Merina forts. The queen needed weapons. She also needed soap and crockery and sulphuric acid, and everything else that keeps a kingdom going. Twenty thousand slaves were gathered together and despatched to Mantasoa.

I discovered that the outlines of her little industrial Wonderland were still there, a few hours east of Tana. So, one weekend, I hired a driver and we set off through the foothills. Eventually this road would have reached the escarpment, but long before that we veered off into the boulders and pines of the eastern plateau. I noticed that the people here sold strawberries and smoked sausage, as if they were suddenly

Austrian or had forgotten the tropics. Then Mantasoa appeared, and a mysterious alpine lake like a scoop of blue amid the firs. My hotel, L'Ermitage, was equally confused about all this, and had been built in the style of a large Swiss chalet. During its fifty years of life, it had also been a casino, and the seat of a runaway government. The owner was from Cheshire, and served local caviar for dinner. She told me she'd never forgotten the day parliament met in her wedding suite.

'Terrifying,' she said, 'paratroopers everywhere.'

In the morning, I set off round the lake in search of the ruins. They were more formidable than I'd imagined, despite the weeds. Several great blocks of Victoriana had survived including smokestacks, kilns, loading bays and a gunpowder factory, which was now a school. But the centrepiece was the *haut-fourneau*, or blast furnace. Made from blocks of limestone, it was sepulchral and gaunt. Inside, I could still make out the *creuset*, and the deep runnels in the stone. Here the slaves had produced their first cannon in 1841, and another 150 had followed. There was even a plaque to commemorate this triumph. *RANAVALONA MANJAKE*, it read: 'Ranavalona is Queen'. I doubt the slaves had felt much euphoria as they set off for Tana, dragging their guns. It would be some years before they had their revenge, but in 1857 they rose up against the factories and smashed everything to pieces.

Out on the edge of the complex, a large wooden house had escaped the riots. It had a roof like a planter's hat, and around the outside was a loggia. I don't know what you call this style. Tropical Gothic? *Malgache nouveau*? Every gatepost was topped with a large stone penis. I was stealthily studying one of these when, all of a sudden, the caretaker appeared. 'This is where the queen lived,' she said.

I wasn't expecting this. 'Oh, right. Funny stones...'

'Yes, she was here with her lover, Jean Laborde.'

The queen's sex life was obviously complicated, and still has tongues wagging. Usually, she emerges from the gossip as an over-engined woman with a taste for brutality. Even in the most royal accounts, she gets through four husbands, including Radama, and has the second one speared to death for witchcraft (and, in some reports, he still haunts her, so she has him dug up and decapitated, replacing his head with that of a dog). But other versions of her life – which the missionaries did nothing to discourage – are far less restrained. In these tales, she travels with eight bodyguards, known as 'the Sparrowhawks', who she keeps as her harem of men. She also has a slave to trim her pubic hair, and every year she presides over a mass orgy, that begins with her bathing in front of the crowds. When her maid refuses to take part, she has the girl publicly raped by her executioner-in-chief.

In this great thicket of stories, it sometimes seems that the real queen gets lost. Perhaps there's also a little misogyny involved, and a bit of French propaganda. Ranavalona was undoubtedly despotic, but was

Jean Laborde (1805–1878), the blacksmith's son, who gave Madagascar its own short-lived industrial revolution.

The Queen's House in Mantasoa, known as 'The Black Versailles'.

she sex-mad too? And was she really having it away with her architect and armourer, Jean Laborde?

Admittedly, everything about his early life sounds like a terrible novel. Born to a local blacksmith in Gascony, Laborde runs off with the dragoons in 1817, at the age of twelve. After a few rollicking good adventures, he and his faithful African servant, 'Mr Black', end up hunting for treasure off the coast of Madagascar. There, in 1831, they're shipwrecked, and the following year Laborde is presented to the queen. She immediately realises that he's handy with a musket, and she sets him up with a workshop. He also introduces the people of Tana to hairdressing, and teaches the men how to trim their moustaches. It seems there's no end to his talents. In 1835, he builds the queen her new wooden palace, which incorporates a tree so big that it will need 10,000 slaves to drag it up from the forest.

'Yes, they were lovers,' insisted *la gardienne*.

We were now walking up the path of the ithyphallic house.

'See? The garden is like a woman's body.'

This time the symbolism eluded me, and although I didn't like to admit it, I couldn't see all the breasts and vaginas that she could see. But the caretaker still hadn't finished. Inside, there was all the evidence of a passionate tryst: coloured plates, some lustrous fruitwood furniture, a room for Laborde and another for the queen. The two of them had even produced a love child, said the caretaker with a lubricious wink. This was a popular rumour, and usually involved the country's next king, Radama II. But, reproductively speaking, it would have been quite a stunt: the queen was already fifty-three when Laborde washed ashore. But the caretaker wasn't going to let a detail like that spoil a good story.

They called this place *La Versailles noire*, she said: The Black Versailles.

In some ways, Laborde was doing something far more remarkable than pleasuring the queen. Without any formal education, and with only the skills of a smithy, he'd created an enviable factory complex. Not only had he learnt to smelt ores at 1,500°, he was also producing porcelain, dyes, tiles, muskets and cotton. It was, in every sense, a one-man industrial revolution, and how he did it remains a mystery. He'd even finish it off with his own tomb, mounted with another huge phallus of stone. This time, there's no ambivalence: it's a symbol of Merina power.

Quite why Laborde did all this is anyone's guess. Lust hardly explains it, and nor does money. He must also have known his guns might be used against Europeans, and that the queen was a volatile tyrant. But it's true, he was always keen to please her. As well as the factories, he built her a park full of antelopes, and acquired a camel from Egypt, which he then had marched across the country from Majunga. He also made a great pageant of the queen's visits, laying on fireworks, ballroom dancing, banquets and bullfights. Perhaps people have misinterpreted his loyalty. They've certainly never forgotten his greatest *faux pas*. In 1841, he'd gone before the queen to announce that her blast furnace was complete. His attempt at Malagasy caused a shudder at the time, and has had people tittering ever since.

'*Vita ny haut fourneau*,' he said. Your cunt is done.

LOYAL PEOPLE NEVER BECOME DISLOYAL – they just confer their loyalty on someone else. That, I suppose, is what happened to Laborde, although no one really knows. On my return to Tana, I walked over to his townhouse on Rue Justin Rajoro. It was only ten minutes from the *Rova*, just beneath what's now the football pitch at Andohalo. The house wasn't grand: a long, low ranch house built out of bricks. I imagine that if France had ever conquered the Wild West, she'd have covered it in buildings like this. There were still a few cannons lolling in the flower beds, and inside Laborde had managed to create a palatial effect with high double doors and a great expanse of polished parquet. Nowadays, it was home to a business selling dietary supplements. I got the feeling it had been a quiet day.

'Do they make you fatter or thinner?' I asked.

The salesman wasn't sure, and nor had he heard of Jean Laborde.

'That's his statue,' I said, 'in the garden.'

'Oh,' said the salesman, 'I thought it was Lenin.'

It's true, Laborde had got a bit goaty in middle age, but he still liked a party. In June 1857, the queen held a fancy-dress ball up at the *Rova*. It was one of the more burlesque moments of the Malagasy Terror. Most

A *kabary*, or royal gathering, at Andohalo.

of the nobles turned up as cavaliers and Spanish courtiers, which gave them a good excuse to wear tricorne hats, ostrich feathers and plenty of braid. Chief among the guests was the queen's son, Rakoto – later Radama II – who Laborde now felt was the country's best hope. The ball would be like the celebration of a revolution that hadn't yet happened.

During the dancing, one of Laborde's house guests, called Ida Pfeiffer, played the piano. She belted out a few *polonaises* and *schottisches*, then finished off with a few dainty *contredanses*. These days, Pfeiffer isn't well known outside her native Austria, but back then she was a celebrity across Europe and America, famous for her travels. She'd already been twice round the world, and written five books. Along the way, she'd done a little spying in Russia, met Borneo's cannibals and, in India, she'd travelled with everything she'd needed in a small leather pouch. Her advice to other adventurers was to carry eggs packed in coal dust, and – if they had children with them – to travel with a goat. In 1856, she'd decided that, at the age of sixty, she needed to meet Madagascar's

The trial of the European conspirators, 1857.

fabled queen, and so she set out that May from Vienna. Almost exactly a year later, she emerged at the top of the escarpment, and Laborde took her in.

She immediately realised the danger she faced. Back at his house, Laborde told her there was a plot to overthrow the queen and showed her the weapons the conspirators had gathered. It wasn't much for a cannon-maker: some swords and pistols and a few 'leather shirts'. But Laborde assured her it would be enough. Rakoto was going to arrange for the *Rova*'s gates to be left unlocked, and on the appointed night the conspirators would burst in and seize the queen. Gloomily, Pfeiffer realised that 'there was no turning back'.

What she didn't know was that the plot had already been betrayed. Some say it was Rakoto himself that gave the game away. Others blame the English (who had no interest in a plot that was both Catholic and French). Either way, the conspirators would soon find out that the game was up, and that all they could do was await their fate. There was no prospect of escaping Tana alive, and so the queen was able to string things out and play with their minds. There were several great meetings where she asked her people what they'd do: should she poison the *vazaha*? Or should it be a public execution? , and several others were dumped in the country dressed in irons. The last mock trial was held at Laborde's house, and was attended by the queen and a hundred nobles. 'I think,' wrote Pfeiffer, 'our hour has come.'

But Ranavalona hesitated. She didn't want to kill the foreigners outright and risk an invasion. They had to die in a way that didn't look as if she'd killed them. This wasn't something she excelled at, but she was a cunning queen. She told Pfeiffer and the conspirators they had an hour to pack. They were to set out immediately and leave the country forever. An armed escort would lead them down the escarpment. Although this journey normally only took eight days, it was not one they were expected to survive.

Queen Ranavalona's plan – for death by travel – worked almost perfectly. Although Laborde survived, Pfeiffer and several of the other conspirators would spend the rest of their lives dying of that journey. There was still no road down through the jungle. Even better, the guards were there to encourage the travellers to take their time. 'In the most pestiferous regions,' wrote Pfeiffer, 'we were left in wretched huts for

The Malagasy army, circa 1860, trained and equipped by the British.

one or two weeks at a time.' In one place, Beforona, they were ordered to halt for eighteen days. At other times, they were dragged from their sickbeds and forced out into the rain.

Instead of eight days, the walk took seven weeks. By the time they reached the coast, on 16 September 1857, Pfeiffer was a wreck. She was shipped first to Mauritius, where she seemed to rally. She even managed to knock out a draft of her last book, but it took all her effort. The following March, she sailed for Hamburg, and from the German coast a special train took her back to Vienna. There, in October 1858, she died from the complications of malaria – or, as she liked to call it, *Madagascar fever*.

I'D SPEND DAYS TRACKING DOWN THE queen's remains, first on paper and then on foot. It sometimes seemed that, in death, Ranavalona was almost as dangerous as she'd been in life, and that the day she died – 16 August 1861 – was only the beginning of a new kind of terror.

Initially, she'd been laid to rest at the royal fort out at Ambohi-manga. Her funeral was a lethal affair – not just for the cattle. Some 25,000 *zebu* were slaughtered, but then one of her cannons blew up, taking with it eighty spectators and a couple of tombs. To the Merina, it must have seemed as though the queen was not yet finished. For the next thirty-six years, her fury explained everything: the droughts, the cholera and the outbreaks of madness.

But then, in 1897, she was on the move again. This time it was the French, bringing her back to Tana. As with her predecessor, they were concerned that her presence was inspiring revolt. For the safety of all, she was cooped up in the *Rova*, in a small wooden hutch with another queen. This would have been fine but for the great fire of 1995, which engulfed all the tombs. At first, everyone assumed this was the end of the royal ancestors, and that they'd all been lost. But then a few days later, one of the queens turned up downtown, lying in the street. Word got out that this was Ranavalona, and for days the city shrivelled in fear. Why was she back? And what would she do? Calm was only restored when it was announced that the bones weren't hers, but those of a lesser queen.

Years on, *les Tananariviens* sleep easier. There's nothing at the *Rova* now but an empty plinth, and the Queen of Magic has vanished forever (or, at least, that's what they hope).

WITH RANAVALONA GONE, Tana suffered an attack of piety from which it has never truly recovered. Churches began to appear all across the Blue Mountain: honey-coloured, English and clanking with the bells. These are still the most insistent buildings on the hill, and still dominate the skyline and chime out the hours. Back in 1867, the Malagasies had never seen anything like them. Until then, stone was only for the dead and their tombs, and it was considered *fady* – or taboo – to use it anywhere else. Even the palace was built of wood, and the idea of living in stone was thought slightly macabre. So, the day the law changed, so did Tana. From being a town of shacks, it became a city of churches.

The man who transformed old Tana is buried at Ambatonakanga, beneath a truck-sized lump of the limestone he loved. As always with the missionaries, his vocation had emerged only accidentally. James

Cameron was originally sent out as a weaver in 1826 but somehow found himself as the city's architect and civil engineer. As well as the churches, he designed factories, the reservoir (Lac Anosy) and what would become the standard Merina home, or *trano gasy*. He was also the one who remodelled the Queen's Palace, by cladding it in stone. It was inspired by the new Murthly Castle in Perthshire, which, as a child, Cameron had watched his neighbours build. Now, with its Italian towers, bullseye windows and Byzantine arches, the newly clad palace looked ominously similar (it wasn't the happiest comparison: the new Murthly was never finished, and eventually, in 1949, the family had it blown up).

Soon the Merina were embracing their new evangelism, and even the courtiers took to wearing top hats and frock coats. Before long, there were churches everywhere. Over the next twenty years, another 1,200 were built, and Madagascar became one of the most Christian countries in the world, a position it maintains to this day. Even the *Rova* acquired a new church, built in the style of Wren but with magnificent spittoons (necessary, according to one commentator, due to the ladies' habit of taking great pecks of snuff, and then snorting it out). Bibles too did well, with over 20,000 sold in a six-year period from 1874.

But not everyone liked the new Tana. The journalist E. F. Knight thought it 'colourless and dull', and that every day was like a Sunday. Writing in *The Times*, he had nothing good to say about the missionaries. He hated the fact they were carried everywhere in palanquins ('a foolish habit'), and the way they spoke of charity while propping up the despots. He also despised the Merina for aping them, in their silly black outfits. Tana, he declared, was 'a sort of shoddy Clapham'; dreary, puritanical and sober.

ONLY THE ROYALTY WERE STRUGGLING with the new sobriety. Radama II was everything his mother wasn't: generous, weak, forgiving and drunk. He had himself crowned in the uniform of a British field marshal, and his reign would be one of the shortest and merriest in the country's history. Instead of sorcerers and wizards, he surrounded himself with a circle of drinkers known as the 'Red Eyes', or *menamaso*. They unravelled all the traditions so carefully preserved by

Queen Ranavalona, and were famously decadent. Even their drinking den offended the gods, and was known as 'The Stone House'.

During Radama's one-and-a-half-year rule, the message from the *Rova* was that anything goes, and it usually did. Once again, Tana was open to all. Within months, the missionaries had returned, along with the pigs, the Christians and Jean Laborde. Foreigners were even allowed

Prime Minister Rainilaiarivony, circa 1864.

to buy land, something considered unthinkable before. Suddenly, it seemed as if that mystical link between land and ancestry meant nothing at all. Such effrontery terrified people. At any moment, the ancestors would respond with fury and plagues.

This time, the sorcerers rose in revolt. Across Imerina, a fit of dancing broke out. During this great collective hysteria, known as the *imanenjana*, the bewitched often danced themselves to death. Emaciated, helpless and entranced, they were messengers from the afterlife, and in their death throes they expressed the anger of the ghosts. With the country now utterly unhinged, the traditionalists moved in on the royal circle. On 11 May 1863, all the Red Eyes were speared to death, and the following evening it was the turn of the king. Because it was still taboo to spill royal blood, he was throttled instead, with a length of silk cord. His body then disappeared and there'd be no funeral and he'd never have a tomb. This means that, in the Malagasy imagination, Radama hasn't truly died, and that he's still out there, tottering blearily through the ether.

A LONG THE RIDGE, THERE'S ONE LAST royal palace, as cranky as any. From a distance, Andafiavaratra looks like a great glass bosom that somehow defies everything – including gravity – and dangles upwards into the sky. But, closer in, its great stone façades are brimming with everything: a bit of Mughal, a touch of Baroque, a dash of raspberry and more than a hint of municipal theatre. It's the work of a regime that no one dares call ridiculous, that's used up its loot, and that's on the brink of collapse. Even now, the city is not sure if it likes this place. There's just enough money to plug the leaks, but most of the time it's left to thieves. What remains of its treasures were always going missing. Even the gatekeepers looked like villains.

There were four when I visited, all bloodshot, toothless and parched. 'Forty euros,' they demanded.

I offered four, in ariary, and they licked their lips and sneered assent.

As I crossed into the glass-domed hall, one of them broke away and followed, slinking along at my heels. Beneath the carapace of droppings and dust, his breath sounded unpleasantly interested. I tried to ignore him, but the room was magnificently empty. The walls – now painted in tangerine stripes and sugary prawn – rose up three storeys all around us. Up near the glass was a tiny balcony, delicately fretted, like a picture frame for people. It was once hoped that great orators would appear here, and – in its day – the walls here were papered in glittery gold. But things would never quite work out for this sumptuous folly, and by the 1890s it was merely a repository for junk.

'And what's it used for now?' I asked, turning to the *gardien*.

But he'd already gone, leaving me alone with the empty applause. The man who created all this was almost as fanciful as the palace itself. Although Rainilaiarivony was never quite a king, whenever a queen appeared, he always married her. For almost thirty years, he was a professional husband, and ruled Madagascar as if it was his. King Radama was barely dead before Rainilaiarivony – his prime minister – scooped up his widow. It didn't matter that she was fifteen years his senior or that he already had a wife and sixteen children. He abandoned them all, and appointed himself as the ruling consort. Then, when that queen died, he married the next one, even though, at fifty-nine, he was almost three times her age. While both queens, Ranavalona II and Ranavalona III, were benign and decorative, they're mostly remembered as sepia prints. In every other respect they've almost faded from view, and are known as *les reines fainéantes*.

Rainilaiarivony would not be so easily forgotten. As a baby, his parents had considered his birthday unlucky, so they'd snipped off two fingers. After that, he'd left nothing to chance, and was conspicuous in everything he did. As commander-in-chief he always dressed as a victor, in enormous top boots and braided tunics, and even as the royal consort he was there to be noticed. He never wore the black evangelical garb of Tana, but strutted around in loud check suits, silk socks and fancy neckties ('more like a bookmaker,' noted an English journalist, 'than a non-conformist statesman'). His palace was the building that went with the suit.

In different circumstances, he might have been brilliant. There were moments when Rainilaiarivony's Madagascar seemed improbably advanced. It had compulsory education two years before France, in 1880 (and only ten years after England). It also started sprouting factories again, and ports. The shops in Tana now sold suits and sewing machines, and you could buy whisky, umbrellas and jars of jam. In years to come, the French would sometimes find it hard to justify their claim that they'd come to civilise the country.

In the oratory's anterooms were cases stuffed with gifts from enemies and friends. For the Malagasies, it was often hard to tell one from the other, in the nineteenth century. France had lavished the monarchy with some splendid trinkets. In among the cabinets, I spotted sparkly medals and a set of silver fish knives, a plumed helmet and a clock that had stopped at precisely the moment Queen Ranavalona died. But the British gifts were always better. Some had been donated under the treaty of 1817, including a full-sized golden throne, and a set of *jingals*, which were a sort of super-musket, made in India and capable of knocking off heads at over a thousand yards. Even more splendid were Victoria's gifts. I noticed that she'd sent her fellow queens a pewter picnic set, six

Ranavalona III, Madagascar's last monarch, grants a rare audience to a *vazaha* journalist.

silver goblets, a gigantic wine jug decorated with hunting dogs and a miniature clockwork theatre, complete with an orchestra of monkeys, dressed in breeches and wigs. With love like that, the century was British.

The gifts, however, told only part of the story. They continued to pour in through the 1880s, and Tana even felt fleetingly English with its Anglican cathedral and a prissy new paper called the *Madagascar News*. But the British were already losing interest. With the opening of Suez in 1869, Madagascar was no longer a threat to the Indian trade routes. By 1890, it was merely a pawn in a much greater game. That year, the French agreed to recognise Zanzibar as British if the British would acknowledge that Madagascar was theirs. Immediately, the London Missionary Society tried to prevent the deal by petitioning parliament. But they were too late: the grouse season had already begun, and there was nobody there. The rest, as they say, is *histoire*.

The Zanzibar deal brought to an end a British century, and the Merina queens. Perhaps Rainilaiarivony's greatness was always more Ruritanian than real. Beneath the baroque and the fancy gilt, the kingdom was collapsing. It was now completely dependent on slavery, and only the nobles thrived. The government they ran was corrupt to the core, and, according to the London *Times*, was nothing more than 'a machine for robbing'. It was even worse in the country. Bandits from all over the island were now raiding Imerina. In the outer forts, the soldiery had nothing to fight with but rust, and by the 1890s most of the island was beyond their control.

We catch one last glimpse of Rainilaiarivony as the monarchy fails. By now, his great glass mammary is piled with jumble. The old man trusts no one, refuses all advice, and hasn't left Tana for years. His eleven sons are all drinking themselves to death, and things are piling up around him. The oratory now looks like a grand bazaar, and is heaped with baskets of dried fish, gold chairs, mouldy grain, sacks of sodium sulphate, a billiard table and a chandelier of Baccarat crystal. Scattered among the rubbish are the country's treaties, and scraps of ancient uniforms. Sometimes the old consort himself appears, now with dyed hair and dressed in a yellow silk robe and pointed crimson slippers. He still likes clothes, and when the French go through his wardrobe they'll find a cache of starched shirts from Bon Marché and over two hundred pairs of silk socks. But they have no respect for greatness like this, and one of the first things they'll do is sell it all off and turn this place into their barracks.

AROUND TANA, THERE ISN'T MUCH Britishness now, except on Sundays. Although there are Union Jacks everywhere, they're only bedspreads and stickers. Even the embassy is down to its last two staff, compared to France's sixty-five. To most Merina, Britain itself means almost nothing, except as a source of football and queens. As for English, it's just a language, essential to careers, and worn on T-shirts ('*I AM NOT PERFEOT*,' reads one, '*but I am a vimited edition*'). But despite this obscurity there's still, deep down, something spiritually perfect about the concept of 'British'. I never really appreciated this until my friends Lydia and Avana took me to church.

'It's just like England,' they insisted. 'Nothing's changed.'

Our taxi dropped us just below the prime minister's palace, at Andohalo. There was already a queue of expensive black cars squeaking over the cobbles. It was a day for godly bumper stickers ('*Proud to be an Anglican*', read one) and large straw bonnets. In all its red brick and Gothic, the church – Avaratr'Andohalo – looked uncannily London-like, if slightly austere. The choirs made up for it. There were ten in all, each a shimmering vision of lilac or strawberry or lime-coloured satin. Their delicate quavering voices rose to the rafters, only to be washed away by the booming swell of the suits and hats. Somewhere, deep in the congregation, was a deacon in a downy-white surplus, and occasionally I'd hear a sound I recognised, like *Anao ny dera*, or 'Thine Be the Glory', sung in Austronesian. It was funny to think that, for many Malagasies, this wasn't paradise but England, and that a whole generation would grow up thinking that London was like a Sunday morning that went on forever. Only the beggars at the door kept us anchored in Africa.

On the way home, I mentioned that we had beggars in London too. Lydia was outraged at first, and then disappointed. It was almost as if I'd uttered a heresy, and admitted a chilly draught of doubt. Avana, however, was more curious, and suddenly had lots of questions. Was it true that London froze every winter, and that the river turned to ice? And were there drug dealers too? And what about Prince Charles? Did he murder Diana?

WHILE THE MONARCHY WHILED AWAY its last few years in vicarage teas and displays of braid, the French prepared to land. After their humiliation in 1870 at the hands of the Prussians, they needed a conquest. They were also under pressure from the *Réunionais*, who'd outgrown their little island and were desperate for grazing. All that was required was an excuse. These were never very convincing. One involved a little shoot-out with some Arabs, and another was a row over wills. But as British interest in the island tailed off, the excuses became less and less important. By 1883, France was replete with reasons, and ready to invade.

The first Franco-Hova War still feels half-hearted. Although the French captured several ports, including Majunga and Tamatave, they never had the strength to push inland. During the campaign, their elderly commander died of 'fatigue', and even his replacement had to be replaced. Eventually, Paris ran out of patience and demanded a treaty. The document that was signed in December 1885 left everyone a loser. The French were forced to abandon all their conquests except Diego Suarez, and Madagascar was to pay 3 million francs to see them go. Tana would also be saddled with a *résident*, who'd exert a spectral influence over Malagasy affairs. But the 'phantom protectorate', as it's known, was never more than ghostly, and when in 1894 France demanded that Madagascar surrender its sovereignty, it was politely ignored.

But *la résidence* is still there, as malicious and magnificent as ever. I often stopped outside, trying to work out what it was people hated. Nowadays, Ambohitsorohitra is the seat of the president in town, and it's the place *les Tananariviens* come whenever they're angry. Over the years, scores of people have been shot out here, in front of the gates. There's even a red ribbon running around the palace perimeter so that everyone knows how far they can go before the guns open up. No one, however, has shown more contempt for Ambohitsorohitra than the historians. For them, it's a ridiculous phenomenon: an imperial tyrant in its frilliest knickers. But although it may look dainty, with its curly dormers and golden nymphs, it's also a statement of intent. The man

A large pothole in the Upper Town. It often feels as though Malagasies live in the ruins of their past.

who built it brought everything with him, dragging the windows up the escarpment. He'd never been abroad before, and nor would he need to. France was not coming as a guest but was here to rebuild the place in the image of herself.

By October 1894, Paris was ready. With the Malagasies still not taking the hint, the *résident* ordered his people out of the city. His entourage, consisting of almost three hundred civilians and soldiers, had a long walk ahead of them. They were heading for the port of Majunga, over 340 miles away across the plateau, down through the savannah, and into the dry zone. There was no road, and they'd have to follow a path sometimes no wider than a person. By any standards, it was a phenomenal journey. Eventually, after twenty-six days, the entourage arrived. At about the same time, the French National Assembly passed a resolution endorsing the invasion of Madagascar, and releasing 65 million francs in funds. Within two months, the first ships were off Majunga, and *les matelots* were splashing ashore.

I DIDN'T IMMEDIATELY FOLLOW THE entourage off to Majunga. Although there was now a road and *taxi-brousses*, there were also bandits. This time they worried me, and I began to dwell on the stories. As everyone kept telling me, the Majunga road was not what it was, and the *dahalo* were now abandoning cattle and rustling vans. One story in particular caught my eye, in a daily paper. It involved a gang who'd stopped a minibus, ordered everyone out, and then cut off their hands. No one knew why this was or what had become of the gang, but it was an unsettling thought with eleven hours of road ahead. I then remembered that my friend Aro the palaeontologist taught out in Majunga, and that he was always travelling along the RN4.

'You'll be fine. It's the most beautiful road in Madagascar.'

'OK,' I said, 'but what about the guys with *coup-coups*?'

'That was unlucky. There are lots of vans.'

'And how do I stay lucky?'

'Go early. Travel in convoy. And keep a few euros to give the robbers.'

Luckily, I never needed the euros, but I did everything else. And that's how, two days later, I ended up in Majunga, numb and pummelled but complete with hands.

CHAPTER 7

A Road Through the Bones

The French, I said to myself, have an island
worth fighting for.

Edward F. Knight
Madagascar in War Time, 1896

May those who come here find Madagascar kinder
and more hospitable than I did! May they not know
the anxieties and sorrows that are fading from
my memory like a bad dream…

Édouard Hocquard
L'Expédition de Madagascar, 1897

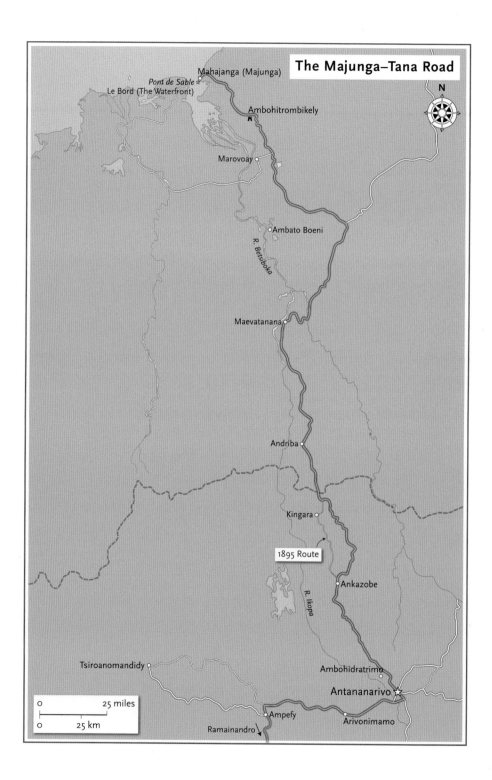

ONE DAY, I SUPPOSE, THE SLUDGE WILL get the better of Majunga. For centuries, nature has been doing everything it can to clog up the city. In places, there's so much sand in the streets that dunes appear, and people play *boules* in the drifts. But this is nothing compared to the sediments, which are borne in great billowing red clouds down the Betsiboka River. Every day, thousands of tons of watery clay come glooping down the estuary, silting the harbour and filling the docks. In the first half of the twentieth century, a whole new promontory appeared, the consistency of mousse. Nowadays, the bigger ships never reach the waterfront but have to wait out at sea, to be unloaded by barge. Only the sailing boats ever come to the quay, and at low tide the *port aux boutres* is like a car park for schooners. Eventually, perhaps, even the sea will stop coming, and there'll be nothing here but a village of boats.

But *les majunguites* show no signs of giving up yet. Everyone was working – hauling, sluicing, knotting and touting. It was the sort of waterfront Conrad would have loved, in all its brawny detail: the rough gangplanks; the spindly barefoot sailors; the lines of stevedores, powdered in cement and spices; the rickshaws piled with bricks and the prostitute, unbuttoning her breasts and snorting with scorn. I also remember a bar in a shipping container, and an old Ismaili, dressed in long white robes, cooking a curry for a thousand guests. He told me that weddings here were always like that, which is why his pot was the size of a bath.

Only at midday did everything stop, as people fled the glare and the searing white sand. Majunga wasn't only the oldest port in Madagascar, it was also the hottest. Sometimes it seemed as though I hadn't simply dropped from the highlands and crossed the dry zone; Majunga was almost East African, like one of those great cities – Mombasa, perhaps, or Dar – that feel as if they're both at the edge of the ocean and in the middle of the desert.

Beyond the quayside was the Arab quarter, a lively sprawl of white-wash and lanes. Although it's many years since the Arabs held sway, there were still a few Zanzibar doors, looking like armoured cupboards, and everyone was Muslim. But they were all different – Kohodjas, Ismailis and Daoudi Bohras – and had arrived from different empires, and had their own different mosques. Only the Comorians were missing, having tired of riots and fled the country in 1976. The Bohras, on the

The schooner harbour in Majunga. Conrad would have loved it here, amongst the rickshaws and the prostitutes.

other hand, were prospering as usual, and were even building a new concrete mosque in the manner of a mall. It was a strangely featureless lump for a people so temperamentally ornate.

They may also have owned my hotel, the Akbar. The upper floors were scattered with armchairs where the men came to talk. My room was wired a bit like the city, and throughout the night it fizzed and crackled, and then – just before dawn – in one last great flash of blue, it all fell silent. After that, things were quiet for a while until the rumbling began in the street below. It was the *pousse-pousse* boys, plunging through the sand, off to greet the morning sludge.

ON THE HILL ABOVE THE PORT, the Merina were about to learn what the rest of the world had long suspected: that war is dirty, expensive and mostly unfair. Until then, Madagascar had only ever been punished or battered at the edges. Now here was a force trying to smash its way through. Although the little hilltop fort, or *rova*, may once have looked daunting, by January 1895 it was almost a century out of date. It was certainly no match for iron ships, melanite and mortars. These days all that remains of it is a fancy gatehouse, and a rampart about as formidable as a garden wall. From here, the Merina would have had an uninterrupted view of their future, as the French put up a squall of shells and then sent their sailors to silence the fort.

Back in Tana, preparations had not gone well. The Merina had known for years they'd need to fight. Finding the weapons was the easy part. Several British officers were hired and sent to London to do the shopping. They were all veterans of the Anglo-Zulu War and believed that, with the right equipment, a native army could prove lethal. Colonel Digby Willoughby even set up an office at 12 Pall Mall and started calling himself 'ambassador' (and it was only when he spent £300 on a splendid uniform that Tana sensed *folie de grandeur* and had him fired). More successful was Colonel Shervington, who managed to purchase an enormous consignment of Winchester rifles and Gardner machine guns. These things still turn up from time to time. I once spotted a stash at the police barracks in Moramanga, where even now they're referred to as *armes de guerre repeating*.

But finding arms was easy compared to finding an army. In theory, the Merina had over 45,000 men at their disposal. But their ranks were never impressive. For every four men conscripted, three bribed their way out. The rich, of course, never fought, and nor did royalty, slaves, politicians and nobles. Even when an army could be mustered, only a fifth of it ever reached the front. Most of the time, the soldiers simply ran out of rice, and wandered home. Or perhaps they were southerners and couldn't care less what became of Tana. Although deserters were still burnt at the stake, this never stopped the army draining away. By the end, there were so many convicts they ran out of logs.

So, what happened in Majunga on 14 January 1895 is no great surprise. As the French climbed the hill, the last of the Merina merely abandoned their guns, and melted away.

L OOK CAREFULLY AND THERE'S STILL an invading army hidden away at the back of Majunga. It's there in the street names – France, République and Liberté – and in the grid of avenues around the hill, all laid out like rows of tents. It's also there in the city's habits: in the way, every morning, the platoons run through the streets in full song; and in the elaborate hearings at the Tribunal, where the prisoners still arrive draped in chains. Across town there are even a few captured cannons scattered about, as well as several monuments *aux soldats de l'expédition de 1895* ('*MORTS POUR LA FRANCE*'). Out on the coast road, Marianne herself appears, now Goliath-sized and painted silver. With her 5-foot sword, she manages to look both lissom and dangerous (always a confusing combination to those who aren't French). Majunga, however, now largely ignores her.

But the city still draws in old French soldiers. It's always been a little Toulon or a La Rochelle (even as independence approached, in 1958, there were 2,500 Frenchmen living here, many of them veterans). The old boys were still coming, to blow their pensions and find a girl. They often met up in the little bistro opposite my hotel, known as Parad'Ice. It all felt like something dreamed up by Marcel Pagnol, or made from the offcuts of *Manon des Sources*. The walls were bare and dusty, the floor looked like an old concrete map, and there was always a skinny girl behind the bar, distributing disdain. An ancient refrigerated cabinet sat in the corner, whirring and dimly luminescent, and from the kitchen came *saucisses* and crabs and a succulent hash of herbs and *crevettes*. Despite the decay all around him, the *patron* was always stately and Gallic, although I was never quite sure if the girl was his lover, or just one of his daughters. He once told me that France used to be just like this.

'*Ou peut-être,*' he added, '*c'est comme ça que je m'en souviens.*'

(Or maybe that's just the way I remember it.)

Perhaps all this shouldn't have surprised me. Maybe it's just what happens when an army – over 20,000 strong – descends on a town, covers it in camps, and then marches off, much of it to die. The landings hadn't gone well from the start. On 25 February 1895, six weeks after the capture of the *rova*, the expedition's advance party arrived. Most splashed ashore at the Point de Sable. But because the town's wharf wasn't long enough, the unloading took days, and eventually the horses and mules had to be thrown overboard, to swim ashore. Then the soldiers built their camp across the hill, and before long it was beginning to fester under a 'putrid haze'.

But in the photographs of that time, there's no hint of the squalor and the bacteria to come. Officers dressed in stiffly pressed white drill are posing around the base of the city's famous baobab. Planted by the Arabs over seven hundred years earlier, it had become magnificently gnarly and ugly. Until then, it had been a place of execution, but it'll now become a place to carve your name and pose for pictures. Standing next to this great pot-bellied ogre, over 21 metres in girth, the soldiers look small and edible.

Majunga's colonial police in the 1890s.

There are more of them down on *le bord*, or the waterfront. Most are wearing pith helmets, but some are in turbans and embroidered waistcoats or enormous ballooning breeches. By April, 14,773 soldiers will have come ashore, together with 7,000 North African porters. They'd be supported by two cruisers, twelve gunboats, six steam launches, seventeen batteries of artillery and forty-two river barges. Among

French officers beneath the famous baobab, circa 1895. The tree looks much the same today.

the troops were fourteen battalions of conscripts and six of colonial troops, including Dahomeyans, Zanzibaris, Hausas from West Africa, Congolese, Algerian *tirailleurs* and around a thousand Sakalava, out for revenge. Last to arrive was the Foreign Legion: over eight hundred troops of the *Régiment d'Algérie*. Not all were Algerian. At least one was English ('very agreeable', according to the doctor), and claimed to be a descendant of Charles I. They were all armed with the latest in homicidal hardware, including Lebel's 'repeating rifles' and smokeless bullets. It was like an army of Babel, in red, white and blue.

The waterfront's still there, and the hideous tree. One of the old French boys told me I'd still find names from 1895, carved in the bark. But if they were there, I never saw them, among the thick new folds of dinosaur flesh.

Every evening the Arab Quarter would empty, and we'd all head down to *le bord* to catch the breeze. Sometimes, people would light little fires on the breakwater, and hawkers would appear with barrows full of coconuts. Then, as the sun slithered rosily into the sea, we'd be suddenly enveloped in darkness. But still people stayed, strutting around by the light of their phone, showing off outfits and eyeing up talent. It was, I suppose, the Sakalava equivalent of the Italian *passeggiata*, except louder and wilder (and lighter on mink).

One evening, I met up with Aro, and we sat in the glow of a tiny funfair. As the chair-o-planes whirred emptily overhead, someone brought us bottles of beer and chicken *brochettes*. That night, almost everyone around us was Merina, on holiday. For them, the big draw was the pedal cars. These could be hired and filled with children, and then, for a few ariary, the local boys would push them – screaming and blaring – down the front towards the Point de Sable. Aro watched them go, and smiled. Although Merina himself, he'd become fond of the Sakalava. They are so much less complicated than us, he'd say, and so much easier to live with.

And what did they do, I wondered, when the French invaded?

'Nothing,' said Aro. 'They were glad to be rid of us.'

Overleaf: The Point de Sable, where the French invaders waded ashore in February 1895.

THE GARDENS OF MARS

France's colourful army comes ashore, February 1895. The Senegalese troops were probably the most effective.

EVERY GREAT JOURNEY ENDS IN BRAVADO, and begins with doubt. The great French army of April 1895 had done it the other way round, and set off in triumph. The bands played as the columns moved out, and the *tirailleurs* sang as if they'd already won. In their minds, Tana was just over there, through the hills, and they'd all be home in a matter of months. It was a glorious start to the catastrophe ahead.

I took a more conventional approach, hunched up with sixteen others in a *taxi-brousse*. It was still dark on the waterfront, and the air was velvety and sweet. No one said much. Ahead of us lay the mountains and the bends, 560 kilometres of road, and the prospect of robbers. Most of the passengers were *Karana*, or Indians, who were never at ease outside the cities. The man next to me was reading urgently from his

Quran, as if the words on his lips would drown out his fears. He told me he was furious with himself for not having flown. The French were more nonchalant. There were several old expats in the back, including a woman so chemically addled that her hair was bright yellow, and her breath smelt like fire. When I told her I'd already done this journey once, on the way down, she sneered.

'*Putain tu dois être fou.*'

(You must be fucking mad.)

Beyond Majunga, our little convoy of vans was soon in the hills. In the dawn light, the long ridges of grass looked coppery and endless. I felt braver now, and forgot all the stories. It was surprising how busy the wilderness could be. Way out in the glowing straw, I could see porters and little villages of mud brick and tin. Sometimes, we'd have to slow for a crowd of farmers, in all their trilbies and swords. Even out on the savannah the Sakalava would wear brilliantly patterned shirts, as if all they ever wanted was just to be noticed. The nothingness of it all was compelling, like a world in draft. Occasionally we'd reach a gully and a small iron bridge, where the farmers would gather with their produce. But most of the time we were too much for them, and they'd forget their peanuts and merely stand and stare.

About 20 kilometres south-east of Majunga, we passed a sign for Fort Ambohitrombikely. Even at this stage, the expeditionary force of 1895 had found itself in trouble, and the problem was sludge.

The French plan had looked beautiful on paper. I once found an old army map of the west, dated 1894. Every village was marked, and all the hills in spidery detail. Much of the data had come from explorers and missionaries, and the map-makers had even added in the routes of Grandidier and the Rev. Pickersgill. Amid all this beautiful copperplate, the route to Tana had seemed almost scenic. There would be nothing complicated about it, according to the French commander, General Duchesne. The fleet of barges would carry his army the first 200 kilometres up the Betsiboka, and then they'd unload into carts, and would proceed to Tana by road (which his engineers would build).

But Duchesne hadn't reckoned with the silt or the rain. The barges got nowhere in the shallows, and so the sappers had to start building their cart track in through the swamps, and up through the gullies.

It would be Madagascar's very first road, and would kill almost everyone involved. 'Every blow of the pick brings another bout of fever', wrote Capitaine Roulet of *la Deuxième Brigade*. To make matters worse, the rainy season had gone on and on. Even the advance guard of legionnaires was getting bogged down. Usually they created smart white camps wherever they went, with canvas streets and an immaculate flagstaff. But this time they were mired in red goo, and running out of wine.

As for the carts, they were never a good idea. The army had ordered 5,000 of them from Maison Lefebvre. They were supposed to be handcarts, readily dismantled and easily assembled. As far as I know, only one has survived (out in Moramanga). It looks like a ship's boiler fitted with old iron water-wheels. No sane person would drag a *wagon Lefebvre* anywhere, let alone across Madagascar. One soldier described them as 'more murderous than Malagasy bullets', and ironically they were often used as hearses. Everyone hated them, and as the death rate rose they'd become known as *les voitures la fièvre*. Years later, the British general Lord Roberts was asked what he'd have done with the carts. Dumped them, he said, and made a rush for Tana.

In the capital, the press waited as the expedition slowly ground forward, killing off its men. The British estimated that if the French carried on like this, they'd lose three-quarters of their troops. Edward Knight, *The Times'* war correspondent, described Duchesne's strategy as 'an act of extraordinary incompetence'. Meanwhile, the Merina thought the French were doomed, and that they'd never survive without cattle and crops. All that was needed was to burn the grass, and nature would do the rest. When the French attacked Fort Ambohitrombikely, the Malagasies fell back after only six shots, and didn't stop running for 20 miles. For Duchesne, it was a much needed victory, but the Merina knew better. The French, they said, will never survive our greatest generals: Tazo and Hazo, or fever and forest.

TWENTY MILES ON, WE REACHED crocodile country. The road had now wriggled out of the ridges and was swooping out across a watery plain. For what seemed like hours we saw nothing but rice and channels and Earth's gentle curve. Sometimes, we could even see the Betsiboka itself, running like a platinum thread along the horizon.

Everyone here lived an aquatic existence, sloshing through life with no need for shoes, and a house made of reeds. I began to wonder what it was like, living only within the smooth rim of our world, with no concept of contour or falling or what's underground.

There were still crocodiles out there, although not like before. Handbags and hunger had left them scarce. But in Victorian times, any traveller on the Betsiboka could expect to see several thousand in the course of a week. By the Second World War there were fewer, but the commandos still had to scatter the river with hand grenades before they could cross. The reptiles had even had a town named after them, Marovoay (or 'Crocville'), and still had a taste for human beings. In 2000, they'd found themselves a zoologist, and he'd learnt that although the fauna of Madagascar doesn't often bite, when it does there's nothing left.

It was there in Marovoay that the queen's warriors had made their stand, on 2 May 1895. But they still had no idea how the French would fight; how they'd come unannounced, and how they'd sneak up in gunboats, and rake the shore with rapid fire. In response, many of the Merina did what they'd always done, and threw off their *lamba*, rushing into battle completely naked. It was left to the Algerians and the *auxiliaires sakalaves* to finish them off with bayonets. With that, the rest of the warriors fled the fort, leaving behind twenty-five cannons and several tons of ammunition. Among the first to leave was their general, Ramasombazaha, whose reputation for fleeing had earned him the nickname Ramasse-ton-bazar (or 'Grab your stuff'). Back in Tana, it was ordered that he be burnt at the stake, but then, when he bought his pardon, the matter was dropped.

Meanwhile, in Marovoay, the crocodiles cleaned up. It's said that as the battle ended, hundreds of them crept out of the swamp and dragged off the spoils, both dying and dead.

Lefebvre handcart,
Moramanga

EVENTUALLY, THE ROAD BEGAN TO RISE AGAIN, almost imperceptibly at first. But soon we were back among boulders and picking our way through the gullies of dust and quartz. Most of the time, the landscape felt like some great dry riverbed, as wide as the sky, and tumbling down from the highlands ahead. But there were also little pockets of life, out in the run-off. Whenever I saw anything organic or moving, I'd note it down. We passed a village of lemon trees; some naked men, panning for gold in a trickle of orange; a small market, selling only beans and old suits and then the *gendarmes*, looking magnificent with their rusty guns. At some point, we stopped for a while, in a tiny forest of teak. There, beneath the gigantic, clattering leaves, it was almost possible to forget the heat and the miles and the beautiful, burning world all around.

After a few hours, the riverbed sprang into life as the Betsiboka reappeared. It still looked red and furious after its fall from the hills. But now, wherever there was space, it sprawled out and filled the plains. At this time of year, there was nothing on the water, but back in April a little gunboat would have still found a channel. Further up, the Betsiboka was joined by the Ikopa, and beyond the confluence it was nothing but a torrent, frothing angrily through the rocks. We were treated to one last sight of it – from way above – as we crossed an ancient girder bridge. Even here, the river was almost half a kilometre wide and had a roar like a storm. Next to me, I could hear my Islamic companion shifting uncomfortably as we trundled over the rapids. It seems that, in his terror, he'd become fleetingly existentialist.

'Why am I here?' he gasped. 'What are we doing?'

Beyond the bridge, the grandeur was restored, with hills of silvery grass. Soon we were swinging through the ravines again, and soaring up over savannah. In places, great hunks of the mountain had been torn away like meat, scattering crimson across the slopes below.

The French would remember this stage as particularly deadly. By early June 1895, almost half their soldiers were *hors de combat*. I tried to imagine the engineers chipping out the road beneath us, and the army shuffling forward a few feet at a time. 'It is pitiful to see these unfortunate soldiers,' wrote Capitaine Roulet, 'who began the campaign so full of spirits, now dying without a murmur of complaint, pick in hand, of the fever or heatstroke, which carries a man off in three to four hours…'

The suddenness of death in the tropics was a source of constant surprise. It wasn't uncommon to find a corpse with a cigarette still clenched in its teeth. The blood wagons could never keep up, and often the dead were left where they fell. Even two years later, travellers along this road were finding cadavers, still lounging around in their grubby white drill. If the *corps expéditionnaire* had carried on like this, it would eventually have vanished. But then, one day, a great scarlet buttress appeared in the hills ahead, and the army came to a halt.

I'd also decided this is where I'd stop, at least for a couple of days. In this long-forgotten march, there are few places where one can say with certainty 'This is where men fought' and 'This is where history was made'. But Maevatanana is one of them. If I was ever to stand in the bootprints of the *tirailleurs* and the *chasseurs d'Afrique*, it would be here. So I said my *salaams*, and disembarked.

IT TOOK ME A WHILE TO FIND MY WAY up the buttress. No one I spoke to had ever been there, and they weren't even sure what it was called. To most people, it was just *les pylônes*, thanks to some aerials up on the summit. But I had an idea it was more than that. The French reports had described a redoubt, perfect for artillery, on a commanding promontory, overlooking the road. There was only one place that matched this description: the scarlet buttress.

That first afternoon, I headed straight for it, and set out through the town and into the hills. On the way, I passed the old French hospital, now missing its roof. Despite the mould and the creepers, everything was still in place, including a rack of test tubes, halted mid-test. Perhaps it was all too mystical to plunder. But the cemetery wasn't. It was now a place to shit, and all the graves had been smashed and stripped. I was glad to be out in the corn. After another mile or two, I passed a shack made of reeds, and the farmer came out with a long, crude knife. When he saw me, he dropped the knife and fetched a girl. '*Elle n'a que douze ans!*' he kept shouting. 'She's only twelve!' I wasn't sure how to react to this but thought gratitude would do, and hurried on.

Despite the heat, it was an easy climb. The hills were terracotta-pink and studded with quartz. Across the lower slopes there was a scattering

of tombs, looking just like the little white bunkers I'd seen around Tana. But higher up there was nothing but laterite, all gnawed by the wind into chimneys and columns. I was almost at the aerials when the trail suddenly stopped and a ravine appeared, 50 feet deep. Knowing I'd have to go all the way back, I sat down in the dust. I then noticed that next to me was part of a human arm. It was either a radius or an ulna, now woody and brittle. I was on the right track, if not the right path.

The next day, at dawn, I tried again. This time, I scrambled up the hills to the west, overlooking the Ikopa River. If anything, the laterite was even redder up here, and the trees were a delicate purple. Finally, after about an hour of climbing, I reached the aerials and the top of the buttress. It wasn't what I'd been expecting. From the road, I'd hardly noticed the trees. Now, under the great mangoes, the grass was lush and cool. It was like being on some tiny green island that had somehow detached itself from the desiccation below, and was now safely floating over the plain.

From here, the French would have been visible for weeks, as they shovelled their way up from the coast. I could almost imagine them out there – a line of drill by day, and lamps at night – and I needn't have worried whether this was the place where the Merina had waited. There was debris everywhere: thick shards of glass, broken plates, scraps of metal, a belt buckle, and some slabs of colourful pottery (it was the pottery that gave it away – I recognised it from Mantasoa, as the work of Jean Laborde). Perhaps the bombardiers had been here for months, with their guns and fancy salvers.

But, as usual, the French didn't play by Malagasy rules. This time, a tiny flat-bottomed *cannonière* called *Brave* chugged up the Ikopa and peppered the sleeping warriors. Then, on 9 June 1895, after a blast of

The Ikopa River, navigable by small gunboats up to Maevatanana.

artillery, the French released a wave of legionnaires. Wading out of the river, they clambered over the hills and up to the summit. By this stage, they were in no mood for mercy. The months of heat and *mokafohy*, or bugs, had left them floridly psychotic. At one point, they'd tried to steal a local pig, and some Maevatanana women had unwisely resisted. 'They are beaten in a magisterial fashion,' recalled one of the veterans later, 'and nothing is more comical than their desperate cries, their terrified shrieks.' But mostly the legionnaires would remember Madagascar for its human skin. A woman's breast, they discovered, makes a very fine tobacco pouch.

I hate to think what they did on the summit. Perhaps the ulna had been lost in the fallout.

MAEVATANANA SEEMS TO HAVE FORGIVEN the French for coming here to die. Or maybe it's simply forgotten the great wheeled city that once rumbled off the plain and parked on the town.

Everything here is only passing through, and Maevatanana is still a truck stop. The smart kids all have a trolley, and are selling water by the bucket. My hotel, which was Chinese, could feed fifty people at a moment's notice. But at night, the RN4 fell silent and it was just me and the geckos. Guests weren't encouraged to linger. Although I had a bathroom, it had no running water, and I had to wash in a barrel. It was hard to sleep. The heat even managed to work its way into my dreams, as did the frogs. Several times a night I'd wake up, drenched, and from out in the paddy came a sound like the final *canzoni* of some great froggy opera.

Unsurprisingly, the town square now had a forecourt and was covered in petrol pumps. Lolling in the litter, among the cardboard and oil cans, was a stubby cannon, stamped '1812'. It was probably booty, from the battle on the buttress. Beyond it lay the captors themselves, or at least some of them. What looked like a large iced cake with balustrades turned out to be a tomb for over three hundred soldiers. '*À la memoire des soldats*,' read the plaque, '*morts pendant la campagne de 1895.*' They were lucky to have their Garage of Rest. Elsewhere, the *expédition-naires* had gone to their graves, and then the graves had gone. Back in Maravoay, 1,400 tombs had vanished, along with another 1,200 in

Ankaboka. Until a few years ago, there was a fifty-man ossuary out at Ambato-Boeny, but then it was hit by a truck and the bones dispersed.

Traffic still comes here to die. All along the main road, there were rusty carcasses and wrecks. Some of them were inhabited, or used as stalls. On my last morning, I had breakfast in an old minibus with no windows or wheels. The girl doing the cooking told me her little eatery or *hotely* wouldn't last forever. One day, she said, they'll cut it up, and make it into knives.

The French had done most of their dying up on the hill where the governor lived. Although his little fort had gone, there was still a soldier on duty, dressed in flip-flops and toying a rifle. This was where General Duchesne had set up his new headquarters, soon to be surrounded by thousands of tents. I now found myself scuffing the quartz for some sign of his wandering city, but there was nothing: just the gritty outline of military ditches. Officially, the expedition was going well. Duchesne was only waiting for the rest of his army to catch up. Another 250 tonnes of *matériel* still had to make it up the line.

But everyone knew his soldiers were dying. A Réunion newspaper reported that the new arrivals looked like 'worn-out, bloodless old men'. One field hospital was filling up graves at the rate of thirty a day. 'We heard that they were dying like rotten sheep,' wrote Edward Knight in his report for *The Times*. If it wasn't malaria or blackwater fever that carried them off, it was a touch of madness. The first legionnaire to commit suicide was in early June. Filling his rifle with water, he pulled the trigger. 'His entire head was blown to pieces,' remembered one of his comrades, 'and scattered around the rocky soil.' Others soon followed, or blew off legs and hands. By the end, the Foreign Legion reported eleven suicides, although many others were logged as '*mort naturelle*'. The *expédition* now hardly needed an enemy: it was far too busy killing itself.

For almost three months, Duchesne sweated it out at Maevatanana. To the press, waiting in Tana, the delay was 'incomprehensible'. How could an army simply cease to function? To the Merina, it meant only one thing: they'd almost won. Across the capital, the bands played, and there were great displays of muskets and spears. Suddenly, the women were singing again, and everyone was marching. 'The Merina,' wrote Knight, 'are admirable humbugs.'

T HERE'D BE MORE BONES ON THE ROAD ahead, this time Merina. Their last view of the world was probably as lovely as any. Although there were occasional tamarinds and mango trees, mostly there was nothing. But the emptiness was different here to that on the coastal plain: it was rounder and more golden, and tended to fill up the sky. It was still another 300 kilometres to Tana, almost all uphill. My friend Aro, however, was right about the road, this great grassy wilderness and its infinite, vertiginous beauty. Even now, when I think of Madagascar, it's always here my thoughts end up.

I left Maevatanana on the midday van, and before long I could see the rest of my day spread out ahead. The Ikopa was still there, off to the west, but it looked like a mirror now, spilling down through the straw-coloured hills. Beyond it, way off on the horizon, was the long blue wall of the western escarpment. This was the beginning of the highlands, and the only way in or out was through a vast portal of rock, up at Andriba.

In a moment of exuberance, the Merina had come pouring out of the highlands and across the savannah. It was always a scrappy venture. Although there were 5,000 warriors involved, many were almost naked. Even those who had rifles had been allocated only four bullets each. The prime minister, Rainilaiarivony, was also keeping back the best guns for the defence of Tana. But nobody really knows quite what was happening. None of the journalists were allowed to leave town, and anyone reporting on the war could expect to be shot. Every day, the palace announced magnificent victories. It had become the battle of Lalaland.

It's anyone's guess how many Merina died along this road. The French war artist Louis Bombled has left us with a Dantean image of bodies, heaped up like firewood. They're all now lost in the subsoil. A few bones, however, would make it home to the family tombs (despite all, there were still officers running a lively trade in mortal remains). But not even the great could dodge the bullets and the sweeping fire of *la mitrailleuse*. Among those who died out here was the queen's nephew, Henri Razafinkarefo. His son, Andriamanantena, would settle in the United States, where he'd call himself 'Andy Razaf'. These days, he's best remembered for the song he wrote, 'Ain't Misbehavin'.

A FTER AN HOUR AND A HALF, WE REACHED Andriba, or 'Where There's a Wall'. I'd watched it coming for miles, as we wound our way up through the foothills. It was still the rampart it was in 1895, rising over 3,000 feet out of the plain. In the lower flanks, I could make out tiny paddy fields, but, higher up, great cirques of reddish-black rock had collapsed, leaving the mountain looking scorched and bloody.

The expedition should not have got past. Andriba was a defender's dream, as the Merina well knew. They'd even asked for a European to come and finesse its defences. But most of the British officers had already resigned, including Colonel Shervington. By July 1895, the only one left was Major Graves, a whiskery veteran of the Royal Artillery. He was immediately promoted to general and sent to the front, along with another 5,000 soldiers and a train of porters carrying ammunition. For the next month he'd covered the mountain in trenches and forts. He'd now got 12,000 men at his disposal, along with twenty artillery pieces, including the latest Hotchkiss. This gun had a range of almost 2 miles, and ought to have scattered the French before they'd even arrived.

But the *vazaha* had magic on their side, or so the Merina thought. They simply couldn't understand how the French kept coming even after their comrades were killed. Why didn't they just run away, like everyone else? For weeks, the Malagasies had seen almost nothing of the *expédition*, but then, on 22 August, it hobbled into place, and started blasting away. The noise and the shrapnel was too much for the thready, undernourished Merina. When they saw their gunners chunked and burnt, they began to lose heart. The next day, the very toughest *expéditionnaires* – the Senegalese – were sent up the mountain to finish the fight. To their surprise, they found the trenches empty, and everyone gone.

At last, Duchesne had good news for Paris. '*JE SUIS À ANDRIBE*' ran his telegram, '*MAÎTRE DE TOUTE LA PLAINE.*'

Master he may have been, but he also knew he couldn't carry on lurching through the wilderness at tortoise pace. It was now four months since he'd left Majunga, and there were still a hundred miles to go.

Overleaf: Andriba, a supposedly impregnable Malagasy redoubt. Rising 3,000 feet from the plain, it would be defended by a network of trenches and bunkers.

Beyond Andriba, the path was only 60 cm wide in places, and the first mules toppled over the edge.

Sixty per cent of his army was sick, or, as one soldier put it, '*plus mort que vivant*' (more dead than alive). Worse, the rains were on their way. Recognising he had to get going, Duchesne decided on *une colonne légère*, or a flying column. It was always a risky strategy, pitting 4,000 lightly armed troops against a native army ten times the size. But he had little choice. It took three weeks to find enough men to fill the ranks. Many of them were legionnaires, who were always ready with a lumpy motto. *Marche ou crève*, they'd say. March or die.

They left on 21 September with twelve mountain guns, and just enough food for twenty-two days. This time, the equipment would be carried by American mules, specially imported from Missouri. Of these, twenty-five were set aside for the sick, and were known as *les ambulances*. One of doctors with them was Édouard Hocquard, and his account of the dash for Tana makes uneasy reading. He says that for years afterwards it would keep coming back to him, like a terrible dream. While his prose is bleak and terse, his photographs are oddly surreal. Here are the officers in their pith helmets and laundered whites, sporting canes and gorgeous boots. They look somehow calm and leisurely, as if it's all just croquet or they're out for a stroll.

Beyond Andriba, the mountain path was often no more than a few feet wide. On the first day, the three leading mules lost their footing. Dr Hocquard says he remembers watching them, as they spun through the air, before disappearing into the chasm below.

F OR THE REST OF THE AFTERNOON, we trundled upwards, and out along a great whale of grass. It was no longer so hot. There was even a hint of green in the seething bronze, and the mountains below us looked cool and pale. Sometimes, the land fell away on each side, as if we were picking our way up the leviathan's spine. Everything was grander here: the views, the drops, the muddy ravines and the great clumps of reeds, as tall as a house. Man had only an apologetic presence: villages scattered minutely across the flanks, or his fruit trees, tucked away in deep ravines.

For two weeks, the flying column had marched through here, scrambling over the crests and skirting the slopes. They walked in single file, mostly in silence. Although Hocquard calls it the *grande route*, it was only a trail. In the gullies, the mules would have to wade through thick crimson muck, up to the girth. Soon the column would be too far forward to send the sick back, so it left a trail of invalids, hobbling behind. The Merina had set fire to everything as they'd retreated, including the villages, leaving the air itchy with ash. To Hocquard, this landscape was 'savage and empty', and the troops hated the way the enemy was everywhere but could never be seen. At night, the French bivouacs 'looked like stars, spread out across the hills'. Then, at dawn, they'd be off again, running a repeat of yesterday and all the days before.

To begin with, the Merina remained elusive. It was like a long, hard game of cat and mouse, except they were the cat, being hunted by mice. Major Graves was still in charge, and as determined as ever to make a stand. But each time he did so, it was like Andriba all over again: an exchange of shells, a rush of bayonets and then the empty trenches. The queen's soldiers simply wouldn't engage. At the Battle of Sheep's Gut, or Tsinainondry, over fifty Merina were killed, while only one of their bullets found a mark. 'A poor devil in the legion got a bullet in the head,' noted Hocquard, 'and probably won't survive the night.'

There was much talk of an elite royal guard, known as 'The Eagles', or *voromahery*. On the third day, the column passed a sign at the top of the Kiangara valley: 'YOU WILL GET NO FURTHER. THE EAGLES WILL STOP YOU.' But if they were near, it wasn't obvious. Hocquard only ever saw stragglers, but they still fascinated him. They were 'small, tanned, and slender-limbed', with 'intelligent faces' and a 'miserable countenance'. Most of them wore only a ragged *lamba*, draped about them, Roman-style. Their camps were even more miserable. Throbbing with flies, the little straw shelters smelt of rotting meat and mouldy rice. Realising there was nothing salvageable, the column's commander, General Metzinger, ordered that everything be burnt. Once again, the hills were speckled with fire.

After this, the column split for a while. Some of the colonial troops – the Haoussas and the Sakalava – carried on along what's now the RN4. The rest filed down into the Kiangara valley. They looked 'like a long procession of termites,' wrote Hocquard, 'descending from an anthill'. Along the valley floor were a series of bunkers, perhaps forty in all. Every time the legionnaires got close, the Merina pulled back. Why had they spent so much time building, wondered Hocquard, only then to run away? He also remembered a great spur of rock, shaped like an elephant's head. It would watch them for days, as they plodded along and the landscape emptied.

From the ridge, the old battlefields now looked washed out and blue. Way below, I could make out wisps of smoke, and tiny chips of river like shards of glass among the long pale ribs of savannah. I could see the elephant too, as reproachful as ever (but now marked on the map as Mount Angave). At one point we stopped, and all the passengers got out and wandered off into the straw. It was cold now, and the air was sharp and dry. A short distance away, some herders appeared, but they stopped when they saw us. They were dressed in thick felt hats and *lamba*, which were worn loosely, as if they were dust sheets. I asked the driver why the men didn't come closer.

'*Ici*,' he replied, '*personne ne fait confiance à personne.*'

(Up here, no one trusts anyone.)

Eventually, we began to descend, steeply at first, and then through eucalyptus. In places, the herders had burnt away the hillside, so it looked as it had when the battle passed through. Then, towards the end of the afternoon, we reached a river and Ankazobe, still 50 miles short of Tana. It was a circular village, all gathered up within a ditch. Hocquard had described it as the 'Frontier of Imerina', and in his photographs it looks stumpy and charred. But Ankazobe had long since recovered from its moment of glory, and was now once again crumbling away. As we slowed for the cobbles, I found myself peering down into the stalls. Here was everything a herder could ever need, including trilbies and gun belts and knives made of scrap. I even spotted a cow, ready for despatch, and all trussed up in a parcel of grunts.

After months of marching overland, the French were in poor shape. Nearly 6,000 Europeans perished on the march, and yet only 25 died in combat.

But soon we were out in the rice again, and forests of pine. After the spontaneity of the coast and its searing reds, I felt I'd arrived back in Umbria, circa 1450. Everything seemed suddenly old and deliberate: the ox-carts, the tombs, the brickworks and the little thatched villages, arranged on shelves high in the hills. None of these had been torched in the war. Unable to burn their own kingdom, the Merina had merely plundered the houses, beaten the owners and driven them off into Tana. Thanks to their thuggery, an enchanting world has somehow survived.

Even Dr Hocquard had felt a pang of joy as he crossed the plateau. Wednesday 25 September 1885 had begun, he wrote, 'like a Spring morning in France'. That afternoon, he camped at Babay, under a mountain the shape of a sugar loaf. These days, if you get this far, you're almost in Tana. The old French camp is probably now buried in suburbs or a Chinese factory.

Unbeknown to Hocquard, the Merina were only 4,000 yards away. As soon as it got dark, Major Graves ordered them forward. But this wasn't their kind of fighting, and so after 200 yards, they lay down and slept. The next morning they returned to their lines, and ran away. There were now only 2,200 Malagasies up at the front. Major Graves began to despair. At this rate, he'd be the only one left defending the path. Two days later, he threw it all in and ran for the coast. Trackers were sent to bring him back, but they never found him. His wife made an even more audacious escape, two days later. It's said they eventually made it back to England, a little poorer but largely intact.

From now on, the French strategy was simple. All they had to do was keep on plodding. There were only a few ridges left between them and the capital. One by one they took them, laying down first a carpet of shells, and then moving forward, and finding nothing. They also brought up an 'electric searchlight', so they could carry on flushing and harrying even at night. By 27 September, the column was only 10 miles from Tana, and had to pause at Ambohidratrimo to let its tail catch up. As soon as it stopped, a little town formed. The West Africans started building grass huts, just like home, and the Merina appeared, selling chickens and ducks. Dr Hocquard even managed to set up his operating theatre, and busied himself digging out bullets and teeth.

The Malagasy had never seen war like this, fought with such awful precision. There were moments of spectacular courage, but mostly they fled. On one occasion, the Royal Guard laid down a spirited ambush, but it was soon swept away in the withering response. Another time, they managed to hide guns under their *lamba*, and got right in among the convoy before opening fire. But it didn't change history. By 28 September, the Flying Column was in sight of Tana.

For Hocquard, it was an unforgettable moment. Rising up out of the rice was the strangest place he'd ever seen, topped with a palace and the prime minister's house with its great glass breast. Despite the dead and the stink, he made a note in his diary, '*très pittoresque*'. Meanwhile, the Merina had hoped that, in their excitement, the French would charge straight through the paddy, to be shot down like ducks. But Metzinger wasn't tempted. Instead, the column wheeled north, and vanished from sight.

I SUPPOSE ALL WARS ARE LIKE THIS, with everyone thinking the best bit is to come. The Merina had never doubted they'd win. Either disease would finish off the French or perhaps the rice. Across Tana, there'd been no panic as the *vazaha* came plodding over the plateau. The poor had their magic amulets, and there'd soon be a lively market in bulletproof grease, sold by the pot. Some were so sure of providence that they'd taken to gambling, losing everything in the throw of a dice. Meanwhile, in the upper town, the rich seemed completely untroubled by the thought of war, as if someone else – the slaves, perhaps – would sort it out. Even as the French closed in, the nobility were prettifying their houses and arranging weddings. At one of these great feasts, all the menus were printed in French, and there were thirty-six courses, taking all day to eat.

But, as so often with Tana, there was even less going on under the surface. The government was no longer obvious, or couldn't be found in the usual places. One minister had even opened a salon and was billing himself as the country's 'most fashionable' *coiffeur*. As for the prime minister, Rainilaiarivony, he didn't dare go anywhere, for fear the sorcerers would seize control. He also kept all his soldiers close and all the best guns. On one occasion he sent out a relief force of 500 troops, but with only seventeen rifles between them. Most of the time, people heard nothing from the palace except its crazy news. The *expédition* has been defeated! Britain declares war on France! Six hundred Algerians killed! To hide what was really going on, Rainilaiarivony ordered a ban on funerals. The dead now had to be buried secretly, at night.

His wife, the queen, was also quietly going to pieces. Terrified of assassination, she'd eat only chocolate, served in its wrapper. She may have been right to be worried. There was much talk of spies and plots, and a group of traitors, called 'the French Party'. Every night, they put up posters, urging revolt. Once, they even launched an attack on the queen's uncle, but got no further than blasting a hole in his garden wall. The accused were tried in the street, before a congregation of hundreds and a priestly judge, all dressed all black. The guilty were usually shot there and then. But for traitors of rank, the treatment was different. In a great charade of royal pleasure, they'd be promoted to the provinces. They'd even have a lavish palanquin and a cheering crowd to see them off, and then, down the road, they'd be quietly strangled.

The queen was never at ease in military matters. Often, she'd leave the detail to her favourite nurse. But she did rally when the French appeared at the edge of the city, and called a *kabary*, or public meeting. The speech she made is strangely reminiscent of Elizabeth I's on the eve of the Spanish Armada. 'Are there no men among you who will fight? As for me, I am but a woman, but I would rather *die* in my palace than yield to the French!'

At this, the crowd rumbled with pleasure.

'We will fight,' came the reply, 'until we are killed!'

The last of the British had watched all this from Faravohitra hill. It's still the quietest part of the city, out on a promontory all of its own. I'd often walk up here for breakfast. There was no better place to watch the city wake up, coughing itself back to life. In the lower slopes, there were still a few farms, embedded in the rock. But higher up, it was all the work of missionaries: a village of brick and piety and children's homes. Even my breakfast felt wholesome and prim: cinnamon tea with rice cakes and honey.

If I was really lucky, there'd be a carillon too, from the belfry next door. Sitting out on its own little spur, Faravohitra church always seemed somehow out of place. Everything about it was absurdly English (except for the giant poinsettias and the lattice of rice spread out below). Around the churchyard, there was even a cluster of cottages, looking homely and solid and unmistakably Sussex. At the end of the nineteenth century, this was where the British vice-consul, Mr Porter, had lived. According to the official French, he was nothing but a 'pirate', in cahoots with the queen.

If I'd been here in September 1895, I'd have easily recognised Mr Porter's house, covered in sandbags. He was taking no chances. Since the fall of Maevatanana, Europeans had become deeply unpopular. There were only 160 left, mostly Norwegians and Anglicans. 'Why are they allowed to stay?' people muttered. 'Why don't we cut their heads off?' But no one dared attack the *vazaha* directly, so it was often their servants who took the brunt. Still the missionaries refused to leave. The reporter from the *Daily Telegraph* thought they were mad, staying on and refusing all guns, and told them so in a rousing speech. Porter had no such qualms. He and the *Telegraph* man set about fortifying the cottage. As well as the sandbags, they'd acquired a month's rations, and a formidable stash of rifles and bullets. They'd also found another useful fighter. It was the man from *The Times*, Edward Knight.

The story of Knight's arrival in Madagascar bears retelling: E. F. Knight, as he's known, had never taken no for an answer. His life might best be described as a series of obstacles, keenly surmounted. Like me, he'd started out as a barrister, but his itch was in a different league, and he was soon on the road. For his first adventure, in 1870, he'd signed up with the French, to fight the Prussians. A few years later, he undertook a voyage of over 22,000 miles in a Cornish lugger. Guns were always part of his experience, and he'd even mounted a cannon on the prow of the *Falcon*. Having crossed the South Atlantic, he then sailed up the rivers Plate and Paraná, to Paraguay. There, he acquired a pet puma, and sat out the War of the Triple Alliance. More wars followed, as EFK became a foreign correspondent. It didn't matter where they were – Matabeleland or Hunza-Nagar – he was always there, right in the thick of it.

In January 1895, at the age of forty-two, he was given a new challenge: Madagascar. *The Times* wanted him to cover the impending invasion, but the French were having none of it. They didn't want anyone watching their war, and now had the island under blockade. No one was allowed to land, and every ship would be carefully watched. To EFK, this was too tempting, and smacked of adventure. He booked a return trip to Mauritius, and then, during a brief stopover at Fort Dauphin, jumped ship and crept ashore. That was the easy bit. Tana was still over 400 miles away, the other side of bandit country. Even in peacetime, this would have been a daunting walk. EFK would set out, without maps or roads, just as the country was collapsing in chaos.

His trek took him thirty-two days. Even now, there are adventurers making bold claims about what they've done in Madagascar. But whatever they say, Knight was bolder. His walk would take him through unexplored hill country, and into the territory of warring tribes. Along the way, he'd have to cope with not just robbers and malaria, but also drunken guides, mutinous servants and murderous bearers. As a feat of exploration, this country has seldom seen better.

Even when he got to Tana, EFK was still breaking the rules. This time it was the Merina trying to block his reports. They told him they'd kill him if they ever caught him sending letters. But to Knight, this was just another 'no' to be ignored. Employing a network of spies, disguised as pedlars, he'd send them off to the front, loaded with soap and snuff. His reports were then written out in invisible ink on microscopic sheets of papers, and smuggled away, tucked in a snuffbox. This always annoyed Rainilaiarivony. How was London getting its news? And how come everyone knew more than him?

When the French appeared, on the edge of the rice, it caused a frisson of farce. Suddenly, everyone was running around, trying to look military. For some reason, hundreds of barrels of gunpowder were carried up the hill and stacked in the palace. Then the prisons were emptied and all the convicts were allowed to wander around, half-naked and fettered. Everyone was considered fit to serve, even the children. There was now a regiment of infants, and farmers' force. At one point, a mob of 'drunken savages' appeared, saying they were ready to fight for the queen. Only Knight was suspicious of their loyalty. They were just opportunists, he wrote: here for the losers, to clean up their spoils.

From Faravohitra, the English looked on as a rabble formed. There were 10,000 tribesmen up on the hill, and another 30,000 out in the paddy. It wasn't safe to go down there, so Knight watched through an eye-glass. Deserters were still being burnt alive, and one day an Algerian prisoner appeared, only to be thrown to the troops and colourfully dismembered. At night, naked figures would sometimes clamber out of the rice and scramble up here, to rob the houses. It turned out that this was the work of the nobles, who were hiring gangs to rob their neighbours.

THE END WASN'T LONG IN COMING. By 29 September, the French were in place in the northern hills. Dr Hocquard would remember thousands of lights, along the ridge. To a passing bird, it must have looked like a strip of the cosmos laid out like carpet. That evening, the *expéditionnaires* were given the order they thought they'd never hear: '*Nous attaquerons demain…*'

Just before dawn, there was a flurry of shells. This time it was the Merina, giving it everything they'd got. But they were too late. The first wave of attackers, the *Infanterie de Marine*, had already left, and were blasting their way from valley to valley. The Malagasy gunners put up a courageous fight but their bunkers fell, one by one. Then the shooting suddenly stopped, as the marines disappeared between the ridges. Across Tana it was assumed that the Merina had won, and – for one glorious moment – everyone sang and danced.

Reality, however, soon reasserted itself, as ugly as ever. A second wave of attackers had appeared, much closer, on Observatory Hill. The two sides now faced each other, almost eyeball to eyeball, across a valley, with a telescope on one side and the palace on the other.

There probably isn't a telescope in the world that's lived such a battered life. It was almost not a telescope at all. Built in Paris in 1882, it had arrived in Madagascar six years later, in hundreds of pieces. These were supposed to have been carried up the eastern escarpment by a large team of *borizano*, or porters. But halfway up, the porters had become suspicious. Somehow they'd decided there was *gris-gris* at work, and had dumped the pieces in the jungle. But the island's astronomer was made of sturdy stuff. Père Colin was a Jesuit, with a bird's-nest beard and a stare like a wintry Sunday. By the end of the year, the porters had gathered up the bits, and the observatory was ready.

For a long time, I'd assumed it hadn't survived the French invasion. Dr Hocquard describes a proper pasting. First it was shelled, and then came the *tirailleurs*, to polish off the gunners. In Bombled's picture of that day, the telescope is back where it began, in little pieces. Surely that was it, I thought: the end of cosmology in this lunar land? But then, one day, I got a call from the university. It was my friend in the Jane Austen department. 'It is most fortuitous,' she said, 'but I think we've found your telescope.'

She was right, of course, and a few hours later I was climbing around, among levers and cogs. Everything had been restored: the little brick towers, the retractable canopy and the turnstile, which made a well-tuned whir as it clunked into place. Père Colin had even managed to reassemble the telescope, once again providing us with a Victorian view of Outer Space. I don't think the *technicien* could understand my excitement. 'You're too early,' he kept saying, 'you won't see anything until it gets dark.'

Tana's observatory, scene of fierce fighting. Now restored, it has a retractable dome and a telescope made in Paris in 1882.

His *observatoire* had played a surprising role in the fall of Tana.

Soon after the *tirailleurs* had taken the hill, Dr Hocquard arrived. He describes how the captured guns were turned around and fired across the valley. 'It was a pleasure,' he wrote, 'to send the Hovas the shells that had been destined for us.' On the hill opposite, a battery of Betsileo tribesmen had installed themselves among the poinsettias, in the grounds of Faravohitra church. Knight had been there only the previous day, feeding them sugar and slices of manioc. But they were still too hungry to fight, and, under sustained fire, they abandoned their cannon and ran away.

The French now turned their attention to the Queen's Palace. Their first shell killed eighteen soldiers, and tore off one of the quirky turrets. For a moment, the Malagasy guns were stunned into silence. How could the French be so accurate, over a mile and a half? The answer was Père Colin and his astronomical data. With these, the French bombardiers knew exactly where to land their shells. The second one landed in the queen's courtyard, destroying her reception hall. It was only lucky that it didn't ignite the vast cache of gunpowder. Had it done so, much of Tana would have been showered in rocks.

But it was too much for the queen. At 3.30 p.m., she lowered her banner and hoisted a tablecloth. The Merina empire had come to an end.

I T WAS A TOPSY-TURVY VICTORY. The French would occupy the city as if they'd lost. There were no celebrations, just *Te Deums*. Although the troops had six months' pay to spend, they were in no mood to party. They were 'thoroughly worn out,' wrote Knight, 'blackened by the sun, lean and haggard, ragged and extremely dirty.' Only the Senegalese had retained their health, and were happy to be here. The end hadn't come a moment too soon for the Algerians. It's thought that, if Tana hadn't surrendered when it did, they'd have spared no one. Now, flyblown and exhausted, they set out their bivouacs up near the palace. 'Some,' wrote Knight, 'lay down in the streets to die.'

But for the Merina it was different. In defeat, they were more exuberant than ever. Those first few nights, there was always music wafting out of the palace, usually preceded by *la Marseillaise*. Everyone was out displaying their feathers, and there were still plenty of splendid uniforms around, and maids of honour in their spangly dresses and dainty shoes. On 1 October, the day after Tana fell, thousands turned out to doff their hats as General Duchesne rode into town. For weeks afterwards, the nobles queued up to greet the general, bearing gifts of turkeys and fruit. With them came the city's Temperance Society and a deputation of Sakalava warriors. They'd caused quite a stir, according to Hocquard, with their spears and braided hair. They'd also been walking for the last three days, and had covered almost 200 kilometres. Once they'd paid their respects, they returned the same day.

At first, Queen Ranavalona hardly seemed to notice her conquerors. In mid-November, she held her usual bathing ceremony, the *Fandroana*. Everyone turned up, including all her slaves, the courtiers, the debutantes, the Royal Guard (dressed in English uniforms of red and gold) and all her splendid generals. A few French officers also came, including Dr Hocquard and General Duchesne. They watched, fascinated, as the queen stepped behind a curtain and took her bath as the court looked on. As she ascended from the water, in a red robe, cannons were fired across the city to announce that the bath was over. The bathwater, perfumed with *eau de Cologne*, was then solemnly sprinkled over those around, including Duchesne.

With that, Ranavalona wished her people a happy new year, and urged them to welcome France. 'It is a great nation,' she announced sweetly, 'and it likes the Malagasy people.'

T HE FRENCH HAD CONTINUED TO DIE, long after the fighting had ended. I'd come across several of their cemeteries around the city. One of them, behind the seminary at Ambohipo, had been well and truly plundered. All that remained were thirty-five bare crosses, and a few cannon, embedded in concrete. When I asked the watchman about this, he sighed and scuffed the dust with his big splayed toes. The nameplates were made of lead, he said, so people took them during the crisis.

'A shame…'

He nodded. 'People take everything, even the bones.'

There were more tombs along the ridge at Soavimbahoaka. It was near the house of my friends Lydia and Avana, and so, one evening, we walked up there and sat looking out over the city. The tamarinds threw out long shadows, and the grass looked pink in the fading light. All around us were *chasseurs* and *soldats*, now safely stowed under their great white slabs. They made for a curious community. Perhaps 'LEGIONNAIRE HACKER' had been an Englishman? And why had Sous-Lieutenant Rouille made one last journey to Tana, having died on the coast? Then I noticed that, among the graves, there were several women washing clothes.

'Why are they doing their laundry here?' I asked.

Avana looked puzzled. 'Because it's where they live.'

The *expédition* would leave Madagascar's grave-dwellers with hundreds of homes. If all the dead had been buried together, it would have been a vast necropolis. Between here and Majunga, 5,756 Europeans had perished, together with 3,550 colonial troops. Around three-quarters of

The French military cemetery at Soavimbahoaka. Of the expedition's 18,000 troops, over half died of disease.

them had died of either malaria or blackwater fever. Only twenty-five were killed in action.

There wasn't much joy on the journey home. Those who'd survived would get one last look at the dead, as they marched back to Majunga. Most of the Europeans had been cleared away but the path was still littered with muleteers, picked to the bone. But even the living must have felt like ghosts. They'd spent months communing with death. In some of the Metropolitan regiments, like the 40e Chasseurs, two out of every three men had died. Of the 845 *légionnaires*, only 348 would make it home.

For the sick, it was a long haul back to France. In Tana, General Duchesne had requisitioned the English hospital, immediately filling it with 300 men. For some, the last face they'd ever see would be Queen Victoria's, hanging over the bed. As for the survivors, they'd be carted back to the coast. It would take twelve hospital ships to get them all home. Even then, the *plateaux* continued to kill them, and on one ship alone, 300 died. 'It is little wonder,' wrote Edward Knight, 'that the people of Marseilles, seeing these successive batches of human wrecks, landed in their port, have come to regard Madagascar as the white man's grave.'

He himself would sail on the *Yang-tse*, with a full complement of crocks. EFK still had many wars ahead of him, and would live until 1925 (he's buried a mile or two from where I write, in Putney Vale). But there was one sound he'd never forget. It was the *Yang-tse*'s engines, slowing at night, as the dead were gathered and dropped overboard.

THERE'S LITTLE TALK NOW OF THE DAY Tana fell: 30 September 1895 is probably the most forgotten day in the city's story. It was almost as if the French had come out of nowhere, or had been here forever. My friends knew all their forebears, and who was around back then, but none of them knew what they were doing. The war didn't seem to matter in the ancestral scheme. People tended to focus on what was the same rather than what had changed. The upheavals to come – in everything from art to politics – were merely details in the family story. Perhaps the French had always recognised this, and had stayed well clear of tombs and tradition. For the time being, Queen

Ranavalona III was allowed to continue as she always had, up in her palace, with her great gilt throne and all her flags.

But it niggled me that this bit of history had become so blank. How had the Merina Empire so meekly vanished?

I knew I'd be hopeless, hobnobbing with ancestors, but I did at least try. The old prime minister, Rainilaiarivony, was entombed in some large overgrown gardens, a few minutes' walk from the Sakamanga. I often went there, to soak up the silence. In a city without much public space, it seemed fabulously lush, like a tract of jungle that had somehow been captured and kept in a box. Often it was only me in there, and a sleeping dog. It was so thin it looked like a diagram, tattooed in the dirt. But for the locals there was far too much death in here, radiating malice. The Rainilaiarivony family had walled themselves up in a vast villa, without windows or doors. It was covered in staircases going nowhere, and superfluous pillars, and topping it all, in the Merina tradition, was a great stone phallus. I wish I could say it spoke to me, but it didn't. The ancestors obviously lived in a very different world, separated not just by time and language but also by logic.

I also realised that Rainilaiarivony had become far more splendid in his afterlife. By the time the French arrived in Tana, his Earthly prelude was almost over. During those first few weeks, he was gripped by paranoia, and slept every night in a different bed. At one stage, it was rumoured that a great Merina army was on its way, to rescue the kingdom. But nothing came of it. Eventually, the French wearied of these antics, and had the old man dismissed on the grounds of dementia. The day he left, Dr Hocquard was in a reflective mood. Most *malgaches* had never known any other ruler, and so with his departure went absolute rule.

But Rainilaiarivony wasn't quite finished. He was one of those leaders who got more and more popular the more dead he became. When he went into exile, he was widely missed. But then, when he died the next year, everyone clamoured to have him back. Eventually, in 1900, he was returned to Tana wrapped in a cloth. His funeral was like a durbar. Hundreds lined the streets as the precious parcel made its way up to the phallus. No man has been more loved for his failures, or for losing everything, including his mind.

J UST WHEN IT ALL SEEMED CALM, William Johnson was stabbed in the throat. He was as surprised as anyone to find his life ebbing away. To those who'd known him, he was a good man. Everything about him had seemed so harmless: his Quaker habits, his modest cottage and his tiny ministry west of Tana.

But it was precisely this goodness that angered his killers. They belonged to an older version of Madagascar, powered by magic and administered by the dead. To them, the queen's defeat was a punishment. The ancestors were angry that they'd been neglected. But it wasn't just sorcerers taking up spears. As the kingdom collapsed, they were joined by others: deserters, robbers, men who'd lost everything and even officials of the old regime. Not much united them except the colour of their togas. The uprising would be known as the Revolt of the Red Shawls, or *menalamba*. It would last, on and off, for the next two years.

When they'd finished with Johnson, the rebels cut up his wife and butchered his daughter. These were going to be difficult times. One day, a wave of outrage would see the Johnsons carried back to Tana and buried in Ambatonakanga, in a tomb – which is still there – the size of a family saloon. But for now, their local town, Arivonimamo, was being pulled apart. On the very day of the Royal Bath, 22 November 1895, the rebels closed in and killed the mayor. The queen responded with a troop of soldiers, who were all immediately dismembered.

There were now almost three thousand rebels massed in the town. This time, the French sent out a detachment of Sakalava, and some fiercesome Haoussas. For a while, the rebels believed themselves invincible, and that their magic shawls would protect them from bullets. According to Dr Hocquard, they kept on coming, in frenzied waves. 'Only the sight of bodies, left in the paddy, would cool their ardour.'

Elsewhere, the rebels were spreading out across the plateau. Wherever they went, they set fire to the churches and killed off the Christians. Fire is good, they said, for cleaning out evil. Eventually, they hoped to reach Tana, and burn it down. But before doing so, they turned south, into the hills. One of the churches on their list was Ramainandro. The man who'd created it was already famous. I'd come across him before, during my time in Menabe. He was an explorer at heart, the first European on the Tsiribihina river, and the man who'd brought the world news of the Sakalava: Edward McMahon. In his photographs, he looks solicitous and kind, but he was good with a gun, and didn't mind fighting.

Unlike poor Mr Johnson, he would not be going quietly.

M cMAHON HAS NOW BEEN LARGELY forgotten across the plateau, despite all his maps and books, a dozen schools and a new cathedral. The family now live in Australia, although they still call by from time to time. Edward's great-granddaughter had introduced me to Lydia and Avana, whose forebears had also been part of Ramainandro. At some stage during the 1960s, the two families had been reunited, and had begun to realise that, without each other, they wouldn't be here. Avana once showed me a picture of his great-grandfather, Paul Rajaofetra. They had the same slightly troubled look, as if whatever was happening was about to go wrong.

'Have you ever been out there, to Ramainandro?'

Avana laughed. '*Non, c'est loin*! Far too far!'

'It's only 70 kilometres on the map…'

'Yes, but no roads up there. Just rocks. And bandits.'

The road to Ramainandro. Few Malagasy roads are paved, and the rest are rinsed away in the annual rains.

'Can we look into it?' I asked.

A few weeks later, we had a trip under way. Avana was suddenly excited, to be travelling back into the past. He was no longer worried about robbers. According to his friends in the police, the security situation was now *bien en main*. He'd also managed to find a *quatre-quatre*, and a cousin to drive it. I'd have been happier without Haja Rabakoson, but he was probably indispensable, and knew his way through the rocks. There was something coldly reptilian about him, an aura of contempt. He particularly hated it that whenever he dreamed up expenses – however ridiculous – I always paid. Perhaps he felt I'd got the better deal (even though I was clearly a fool).

Despite Haja, I was glad to be out, soaring through the highlands. Before us, the day unrolled like all the yellowest bits in *Game of Thrones*. Soon after Tana, we began to climb through the straw and family tombs. Then we were out on a great flaxen plain, amid the herds of ponderous *zebu*. In the glare, the farms here looked like little forts, always beautifully perched for no obvious reason. After a couple of hours, we passed Arivonimamo, where the revolt began. It probably hadn't changed much. A long line of ox-carts were creaking their way up out of the brickworks, before filing off into the blonde.

Soon afterwards we passed Ampefy, and a cluster of old volcanoes. In among them was a large body of water, all moody and grey, like a sliver of long-lost sea. One of the cones was completely black, as if newly cast in a furnace. For Malagasies, this was a popular place to come on holiday. Suddenly, there were vendors everywhere, offering us chunks of fresh-cut pumice. Avana was a determined shopper, and soon we were loaded up with dried fish, foot-scrapers and a sack of roots.

After that, we began to climb again. It took us four hours to get through the mountains, spiralling upwards over the pass. Little brown rivers came gnashing down through the boulders, and the rice now looked like pale blue gingham, lining the valleys a mile below. Haja drove faster and faster through the bends. Just for a moment, it seemed he was happy, as if he could fly.

Ramainandro Church and the tomb of the explorer-missionary Edward McMahon.

In Loving Memory
EDWARD OLIVER McMAHON
ARCHDEACON
WORKED 38 YEARS AT
RAMAINANDRO
Born Jan 15 1860
Passed away Dec 3 1918
"THY WILL BE DONE"

Eventually, we turned north again, and the asphalt ended. Here, the valley had been terraced, with every contour picked out in rice, like a map that's come to life. We probably didn't need the Toyota any more, as we hobbled along at walking pace. It took two hours to cover the last 10 kilometres. The path was little more than an old stream, running emptily upwards through the terraces. Everything passed us, including bicycles, old ladies and a gaggle of children off to a cockfight. Just when it seemed things couldn't get more Asian, Ramainandro appeared. Up on the ridge ahead was a village with fruit trees and bungalows and a little stone church, saffron-yellow but unmistakably English.

On the very day the Johnsons died, the *menalamba* appeared here in the valley. They'd already burnt their way through the district, destroying churches. They'd even managed to dip their spears again, finding two French pastors called Escande and Mainault. Now it was the turn of Ramainandro.

But if they were hoping to find McMahons, they'd be disappointed. One of the rebels, horrified by the Johnson murders, had managed to get ahead and warn the family. There wasn't a moment to lose. The children were still in their slippers and nightshirts when they fled through the terraces, and over the mountains. All night they walked. Occasionally, rebels came close, but when they saw the rifle, they shrank away (or, as McMahon puts it, 'came to their senses'). Eventually, the family got to a neighbouring village, and had just eaten when the mob appeared, and they were on the run again. After a second night in the mountains, they arrived in Ambarinomby. This time, it was Avana's great-grandfather, Paul Rajaofetra, who came to the rescue. He felt he owed everything to McMahon, and was happy to help. He even found clothes for the children (actually, clothes they'd donated the year before), and then the next day he had them all spirited away, back to Tana.

Back in Ramainandro, the rebels took out their fury on the Church of All Saints. They ripped up the books, smashed all the windows and stripped it bare. Everything was stolen, even the processional cross. The chalice became a lamp, and the frontals and stoles were ripped for flags. But the *menalamba* still weren't happy, and so they dug up the altar in the search for treasure. Finding nothing, they set fire to the roof. Then, as a final touch, they burnt down the bungalow, grubbed up the fruit trees, and killed all the cattle.

Remarkably, there's still a photograph floating around of Ramain-andro after the rebels. You'd be forgiven for thinking the place had been bombed.

Our impending arrival had not gone unnoticed. For ages, a crowd had been gathered by the church, watching as we picked our way down through the terraces. The women all wore bonnets and flowery blouses, looking, from a distance, like some great herbaceous welcome. But they weren't particularly surprised to see us. When your world is very small, you think everything else revolves around it.

Avana introduced us.

'Our church is English,' they said. 'How's your queen?'

In among the congregation was the latest incumbent, the Reverend Rakotonidina. Although slight and shy, he was an unmissable figure in his charcoal suit, with a dash of purple and starch. Whatever else had changed in the last 123 years, it wasn't the clerical outfit. He was pleased we'd come in search of McMahons but had no idea what they'd been through.

'They ran away in their *slippers*?' he gasped.

'Yes, slippers and nightshirts.'

'And all their books were ripped apart?'

'Yes, and the vestments and stoles…'

'Then,' said the vicar, smiling, 'there's been a little miracle…'

Inside the church, everything was back in place. There was glass where it should be, and a roof up above. It all looked just as it did the day it opened, in 1889. Even the processional cross had been retrieved from the battlefield and returned to its slot. The Reverend Rakotonidina now looked at it with renewed awe, running his fingers over the dents and scratches. 'I'll show you the house,' he said.

The McMahons' bungalow was set among the boulders, a little higher up. It was a long brick building, with a tin roof and a veranda scattered in chickens. According to McMahon, the family were only away a matter of months. Before long, they were back in their house, holding needlecraft classes and vicarage teas. As with the church, everything had been restored, and even now there was lace around the windows and antimacassars on all the upholstery. In one corner was a large fruitwood cot. 'That was *his* bed,' whispered the vicar, as if McMahon was still there, under the covers.

It was also here that he died, in 1918. He'd lived in the wilds over thirty-eight years, recreating an England he'd not seen since his youth. He was buried in the hard red earth next to the church. Nearby are the two unfortunate Frenchman – Escande and Mainault – who'd died the death intended for him. Also with them was a French soldier, called Corporal Garbit. Six months after the sacking of 'All Saints', another great army had ground over *les plateaux*, scooping up rebels, and laying down law.

France had been slow to react to the insurrection. It didn't worry them at first. The Johnson murders were shocking but there was nothing here a little brutality couldn't sort out. Then more towns were burnt, and the *menalamba* were everywhere. But before anything could be done, the rains came.

The highlands became a slick of greens and sticky reds. Movement was impossible. Without roads, it would be like marching through glue. Meanwhile, in Tana, the streets had turned to rivers, sluicing everything in sewage. 'It's quite a thought,' wrote Dr Hocquard, 'but how many millions of microbes do people eat with every meal?' That December, there was a lively outbreak of typhus. The French hadn't reckoned on this. It was all they could do to hole up in the better parts of town, posting a ring of sentries to keep the locals out. Just before Christmas, the first reinforcements arrived. It took them a month to claw their way up the escarpment. Two-thirds of them never made it, and were left with *les ambulances*, out in the forest.

As the rains receded, the revolt restarted. The *menalamba* now seemed unstoppable, swelling out across the plateau. They would burn down over 750 churches, attacking the Christians with whatever they could: spears, implements and home-made clubs. By mid-1896, they controlled much of Imerina, and Tana was under siege. At night, there was an orange glow along the horizon, as the surrounding villages burnt. The rebels even managed to close in on the royal necropolis at Ambohimanga, seizing handfuls of holy soil. It was at this point that the French gathered up all the dead monarchs and brought them to Tana, where they couldn't cause trouble.

When France finally rallied, people expected revenge. The first response was predictably fierce. A couple of nobles were paraded in front of a firing squad, *pour encourager les autres*. The new governor even had them photographed, as they vanished in the smoke. He then had the queen seized and sent into exile, to live out her days in fusty Algiers (her bones were only finally returned to Madagascar in 1938, to be loved and worshipped all over again). That done, the French sent out their troops, 7,000 in all. It's hard to say how many perished during *la pacification* (among the dead were the great-grandparents of my friend Aro, both shot in their village). Gradually, the threadbare revolt began to falter.

But, surprisingly, it wasn't killing that the governor wanted. He'd asked for *taches d'huile*, or 'spots of oil'. These would be safe havens, little forts radiating calm and civilised values. Eventually, people would be drawn to them and would become dependent on French protection. 'Make sure,' he told his officers, 'that those you rule tremble only at the thought of you leaving.' Back then, this was a novel response to guerrilla warfare, but it seemed to work. By February 1897, the *menalamba* were finished. Within a few years, the rest of the island had submitted to France.

For the first time ever, Madagascar was united under one rule.

T HE NEW GOVERNOR WAS AN UNLIKELY moderniser. When he first stepped from his palanquin, Tana hadn't expected much: another soldier, more uniforms, the waxed moustache and a flash of pebbled glasses. On paper, Joseph-Simon Galliéni was a seasoned plodder. He'd spent much of the Franco-Prussian War in captivity, and since then he'd endured Senegal, Martinique and Tonkin. If he survived Tana, that would be good enough. No one was expecting brilliance. But then Galliéni never did anything people expected. For a start, he was teetotal, vegetarian and unfashionably modest. He also had administration running through his blood. Brought up in the Pyrenees, he was the son of a village mayor. Somehow, the pragmatism of parish politics never left him. He was always the big mayor, stopping at nothing, and would run Madagascar as if it was small. Even now, there are people here who regard him as the greatest leader they've ever had.

His idea was simple: Madagascar would become another France, in spirit if not in miniature. It would be for everyone's benefit to 'Frenchify' – *pour franciser* – the island. Madagascar would know what it was like to be civilised at last, with everything from roads and sewers to a medical school. He'd even create an *Académie Malagache*. But, obviously, he'd have to 'pacify' the country first, and that might mean violence ('I want a hundred legionnaires,' he once said, 'so that, should the occasion arise, I can die decently.'). It wasn't long, however, before his 'spots of oil' were spreading out. With that, his Frenchification could begin in earnest.

The new century was soon sounding different. English was banned in schools, and *frantsay* (français) got everywhere, even into the home. Malagasies now cooked in *lakozina* (la cuisine) and ate at *latabatra* (la table). Modernisation brought new gadgets too. People would hang their clothes in *lalimoara* (l'armoire) and would ride around on *bisikilety*. Even the diet began to change. Suddenly there were exotic new things

The colonial medical school, built in 1897. It proclaimed a new civilisation, magnificently French.

to eat and drink, like *dibera* (du buerre), *pitipoa* (petit pois), *lafarina* (la farine) and of course, *divay* (or du vin). Naturally, none of this was good for the Protestants, and the Sabbath was never enforced again (and became a day for buying and selling). By 1905, a new *république* was well under way. Ten per cent of the country were now enjoying a French education, and there were ever more roads, sweeping off into the hills.

These days, Tana is only French in its little details. The tiny garden city that Galliéni envisaged has now been swamped. Although you can still see bits of the outline occasionally – parks, canals, cobbled streets and tunnels – more than two million people have since poured in on top. Only rarely do you get snatches of the grandeur that was once so common: an old façade, perhaps ('Magasin au Printemps'), or a fancy hat shop that's somehow slipped through the years almost unnoticed.

Occasionally, you might even find an entire mansion struggling on in defiance of the present. One of these is Villa Vanille, which has become something of a city institution (if not entirely a joy). These days, *la propriétaire* is slightly humped and bristly, like a well-coiffed badger, but the food she serves is as French as ever. It's all there, everything from *crème brûlée* to *magret de canard au gingembre*. In a city that sometimes runs out of the simplest vaccines – such as tetanus – it's a remarkable feat of supply and demand.

Of all these colonial knick-knacks, easily the most exotic is the medical school. Known as the *Institut National de Santé Publique et Communautaire*, it's a fabulous confection of Frenchness. There are Doric columns, cascading granite staircases, colonnaded courtyards, latticed sun-screens and clocks with wings. Built only two years after the arrival of the French, it seems to proclaim that anything's possible and that they'd be here forever. Neither, of course, would prove true. These days, the school's students struggle more than ever to prove their worth. Their qualifications no longer have any value abroad, and even in Tana they'll worry their patients. I once met a diplomat who told me that foreigners never used Malagasy doctors, and that, at the very first sniffle, they were off to Mauritius. Here, she explained, there's only one CT scanner in the entire country, and only one diagnosis.

'*Paludisme*,' she said, 'they always tell you you've got malaria.'

Only in their habits are *les Tananariviens* still fleetingly French. Across the city, every day begins with baguettes, bought from a three-wheeled van. People still love their *boules* too, and their handbags and heels, and matching outfits. The most opulent shops are always *les pharmacies*, and all the mannequins are still pink and blonde. Even now, books are sold out in the open, from mouldy stalls run by *les bouquinistes*. You can get anything here, from Victor Hugo to a smelly old copy of *Le Deuxième Sexe*.

Nothing gets thrown away, especially things that are French. Each morning, thousands of *deux-chevaux* and Renault *quatre-Ls*, some almost half a century old, come pouring through the city in a great, wheezy torrent. Sometimes, it looks like a giant stock-car race that began almost a lifetime ago, on the other side of the world, and has never quite finished. Everywhere, the colony lives on in little bits of rust: hydrants, sentry boxes, drain covers, enamelled names and *les téléphones publiques*. The people who made all these things, and hammered them into place, must have thought that this was it, and that everything would change: the law, the language and the land. It must have seemed so permanent once, so reassuringly French, and yet it was only ever a thin veneer.

T HERE ARE STILL A FEW POCKETS where the empire thrives. One of these, I was told, was the Hôtel Colbert. I'd often been there. It was a rambling archipelago of buildings up near the presidential palace. From the outside, it looked like a street of nothing in particular, but, once inside, all the bits were linked. There was always much more to it than first met the eye. It also had a vast subterranean swimming pool, and a restaurant that dangled scenically over a cliff. Every time the front doors slid open, there was a perceptible hiss, as if there'd been some tiny adjustment of atmospheric pressure. In every sense, it was a world apart.

My Malagasy friends loved it, and we'd often meet up in the *salon de thé*. The milkshakes would arrive in great glass buckets, and the croissants were heavy and dense, like a whole week of pastries rolled into one. It was also a good place to watch politics, in all its comings and goings. People often told me this is where the real business of government was done, here in the hotel lobby. Every teatime was a diorama of suits and ministers and NGOs, always borne in on a fleet of gleaming *quatre-quatres*. But they weren't here for the croissants. Avana once told me a story about a politician who'd been mugged leaving the lobby. This would have been an unremarkable event but for his briefcase.

'They found out he was carrying over a *billion* francs…'

I soon realised how much there was I didn't understand.

'Why *here*?' I'd ask. 'Haven't they got anywhere else to go?'

Everyone, it seemed, had a different answer.

'It's more private,' said Manitra. 'Away from all the *fonctionnaires*.'

Others disagreed.

'No,' they'd say, 'it's because the Ministry's lights no longer work.'

Once, after one of my trips upcountry, I rang and booked a room, and ended up staying the week. The Colbert was always less impressive in close-up. The corridors had been artlessly redecorated, mostly in varnish, and my room was completely bare except for a blotchy abstract of a couple of *zebu*. The writer Gerald Durrell says that when he stayed here in 1990, he'd stored his wild animals in his suite, and had allowed the lemurs to climb the curtains. When I saw my room, this suddenly seemed a bit less thoughtless.

By night, it was all eerily French. There was nothing on television except old reruns of *le futbol*, with Troyes and St-Germain. But the bars were full, mostly with *ingénieurs* and *hommes d'affaires*. Occasionally, however, girls would appear, all in black, and squashed into blouses and tiny skirts. At first, I thought they were prostitutes, but then I re-alised they were the croupiers from the casino in the cellars. This was a notorious institution. It was said to be run by the Corsican mafia, who'd made it their home after a clean-up in Nice.

Everyone was doing deals, on the phone, over dinner, or with their drinks. In the old days, this is where Madagascar was carved up before the digging began. They were all here, from 'La Vache qui Rit' to the Michelin men. Perhaps little has changed. France still absorbs almost a quarter of everything exported. Her people have spent almost sixty years enjoying their last days but never quite going. Even now there are 25,000 Frenchmen on the island, running over six hundred businesses. It wasn't so much this that worried my friends as the short walk from the bars to the lobby, and all those ministers. 'The French still run this country,' said Mireille Rabenoro, at the human rights commission. 'They top up the budgets, provide all the aid and choose all our presidents.'

Across Tana, everyone believed this, even my drunken guide up at the *Rova*.

'We're still a tool,' he sloshed, 'a tool of France.'

IT WAS TIME TO TACKLE THE eastern escarpment. Across Tana, it was still thought of as *le faille* or 'the Fault'. For many, the idea of tottering over the edge, or spiralling downwards through the jungle, was just too much. The Merina, it seems, had always felt like this. The escarpment was more than a drop, and had become a sort of mental abyss. If I ever mentioned it, there'd be a perceptible shudder, as if I'd just brought on the rains or an outbreak of yaws. Even now, people would rather go anywhere but east.

The French had tackled the problem differently, by building an enormous ornamental gateway. It's still there, the Soarano Station, at the end of Avenue d'Indépendance. Dervla Murphy once described it as 'the sort of thing that might happen if a Moghul Mosque mated with a Venetian palace'. But, out at the back, there were marshalling yards and warehouses and a little club for *les cheminots*. Galliéni had obviously thought of everything, and had clearly envisaged that, one day, this place would be spouting trains and sending them everywhere, all over the island. His first railway would head straight for the coast. It was a bold idea. By the time the station was finished, there wasn't even a road down the escarpment.

Not much moves now, out of Soarano. But I did find a man in a railway cap.

'Any chance of a ride?' I asked. 'Even a freight train?'

He shook his head. Bits of the line had been washed away.

'Then the road it is,' I said, 'and a *taxi-brousse*…'

If that's the case, said the *cheminot*, I could forget about breakfast.

I wasn't sure what he meant.

'*Tout le monde vomit, jusqu'au bout.*'

(Everyone vomits, all the way the down.)

CHAPTER 8

How to Build a Little France

*The French colonisation of Madagascar reminds
me of a good, loving mother.*

ARKADY FIEDLER
The Madagascar I Love, 1946

*It is accepted that in the colonies, especially
Madagascar, everyone has fever, and that
no one escapes.*

GENERAL GALLIÉNI, GOVERNOR
1896–1905

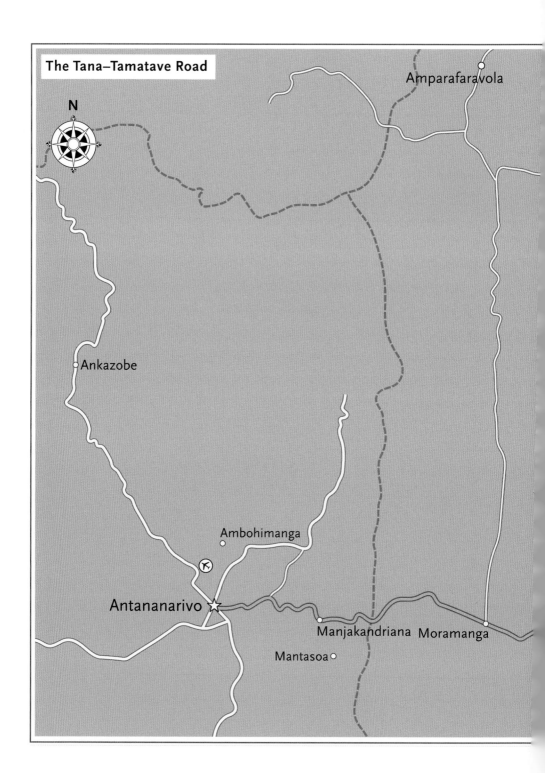

The Tana–Tamatave Road

N

Amparafaravola

Ankazobe

Ambohimanga

Antananarivo

Manjakandriana Moramanga

Mantasoa

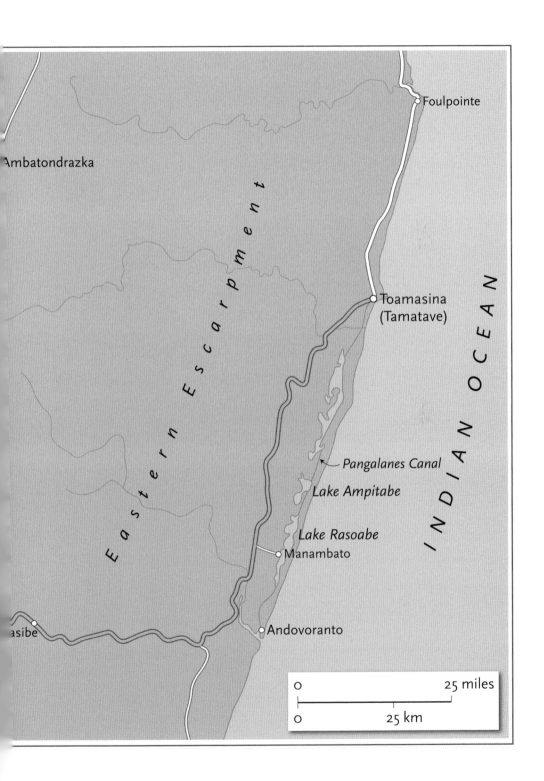

N<small>O ONE MUCH LIKES AN EMPIRE NOW</small> but, without the French, East Madagascar would look very different. Antananarivo would still be all alone, up on its shelf. The coastal plain would be almost another country, and its main city, Toamasina, would still be a village. There'd be no roads, no railways and no canals, and half the names

General Galliéni (seated), a teetotaller and a vegetarian, and, some say, the greatest administrator Madagascar has ever had.

would disappear. You'd also have to rub out a couple of airports, and a scattering of lakes. You might even lose a national park. Suddenly, the east would begin to look very wild and empty, just like everywhere else.

In centuries to come, historians will look at all this, and wonder what the lines were for. My map is covered in public works and big ideas. But the records in Paris will tell a different story, and will reveal that people hated all this: the cost, the waste and the loss of life. But this didn't deter men like Galliéni. France had a duty to give of itself, and to bring a little brilliance to the rest of the world. Given the right technology, people everywhere can be as fulfilled and noble as they are in France. It's hard to say whether tomorrow's Gibbons and Galbraiths will understand all this. The work on the eastern escarpment will look very derelict and grand. They might even see it as one of those little moments of European madness, a bit like the Inquisition, ruffed collars, plastic bags, and the Thirty Years War.

O UT ON THE ESCARPMENT, THERE ARE little disasters every day. The road is always disappearing, and cars and trucks often take to the air. This is not a world designed for wheels. In one section, the land drops almost 5,000 feet in under 30 miles, turning all the rivers into waterfalls. Along the way, there are traces of catastrophe everywhere: a crumpled chassis, perhaps, or an outline in rust. We'd barely reached the lip before we were in the carnage. Two sixteen-wheelers had met head-on. I was surprised how much of them was no longer there. A crowd had gathered, and their faces looked pale and moonlike against the tufts of twisted metal.

We had our own little problems, aboard the *taxi-brousse*. I didn't vomit, as people had predicted, but my neighbour did, and so did the people in the rows behind. I was soon mottled in baby-sick. With each switchback came another gurgle of chyme. But at least we weren't dying, like the man in the front. His lungs sounded boggy and full, and every time we stopped he'd fumble for the door and suck on a cigarette as if it were air. Only our driver seemed untroubled. He'd turned up in gold chains and purple, and obviously thought of himself as the enter-tainment. He had an odd repertoire of videos. We'd have gangsta rap up on the plateau, and then a blast of hymns as we began our descent.

It was mesmerising, the things that fell past the window: hay carts and tiny orange villages at first, then pine and bracken and a tangle of forest with thick, wet beards of dripping lichen. Then, after descending another thousand feet, we were in darkness, plunging through raffia and palms, and great vaults of bamboo. Occasionally, whisky bottles – filled with wild honey – were pressed against the glass, and I once saw a handcart ridden by a pig. But there weren't many people up here. This dank, perpendicular jungle has never suited humankind. For the moment, it's some of the richest montane forest in the country. But almost everyone we saw was up to no good, slicked in charcoal, or hacking out trees.

Slithering down through the cliffs, this has never been an easy road. In its early days, as a path, it barely functioned. The Merina had taken at least a fortnight to reach the coast, a distance of only 100 miles. When the French arrived, they started a mule service, to speed things up. 'Messrs Porter, Aitken and Co' were soon hauling tinned beef and biscuits up to the troops. But it still wasn't enough. The French were trying to build a new Tana, and would need more than 63,000 porters to service their city. Everything was carried up through the rocks, from the palace railings to the governor's bed.

When the new road began, most of the *borizano* were told to be navvies. But they hated the work, and drifted away. For a while Galliéni tried forced labour, and brought out a raft of new rules directed at natives and known as the *indigénat*. It often produced more outlaws than work. Out in the forest, everyone became a shirker or a dodger or an illegal *charbonnier*. In desperation, Galliéni sent his officials east, in search of labour. Before long, Madagascar would get its second wave of Asians, this time 300 Chinese from northern Tonkin.

Eventually, the road was finished. On 1 January 1901, it was declared open to traffic. One of the first up here was Lucy Broad of the British Women's Temperance Society, riding a Sunbeam bicycle. It took her two weeks to reach the top, with all her servants walking behind carrying her luggage, suspended from poles. The foresters had never seen a

The path from Tana to the coast, circa 1880. It could take a fortnight to cover the 100 miles.

bicycle before, and called it 'a horse that feeds on wind'. More strange contraptions would follow, including carts and engines. By 1904, Tana even had its first 'automobile messenger service'. Whether they liked it or not, the Merina people had rejoined the world.

A FTER THREE AND A HALF HOURS, a little China appeared. By now, we'd descended the first step of about 2,000 feet, and ahead lay another of about the same. But between the two lay a narrow plain covered in rivers and rice and washed-out hills. In among the paddy was a small market town, called Moramanga or 'Cheap Mangoes'. It had always been a handy stopover for travellers, but when the Chinese appeared with their strange road, it took on a new lease of life. I'd already decided to break my journey here, and explore the town for a couple of days.

Moramanga still smells of drains and spices, and has its own distinct clatter. I always sensed something else too: indelicacy and precision, somehow merged. I remember stalls strung with offal, and a watch re-pairer with a tiny strand of wire, thoughtfully excavating a set of cogs. Although I've never been there, I've always imagined that China is just like this. At times, the streets were packed tight with old rickshaws, like a traffic jam in wood. In among the bustle there were shop-houses too, selling everything from paper lanterns and fireworks to old Red Army kitbags, now stiff and mouldy after weeks at sea. Moramanga even had two pagodas, both splashed in calligraphy and trimmed in red pantiles. One was on the main street, and was painted a dazzling imperial yellow. The other was on the edge of town, a monument to those who'd died building the road.

The Chinese themselves were harder to find. Over the last century, they've been swamped with foresters and mountain people. But there were still a few Hoa and Cantonese lending money and working the tills. They also ran several restaurants, including the *Coq d'Or* and the *Sirène Dorée*. I loved these places, in all their lanterns and tinsel. It was like being on a journey within a journey. There was a bottle of fish sauce on each table, and every meal began with *soupe chinoise*. Even the television was chattering away in Cantonese. It occurred to me that the original road builders would have been happy here. Only one dish was new, and might have puzzled them: *poulet au Coca-Cola*.

My first evening, I had crispy frogs' legs at the *Flore de l'Orient*. It was owned by Monsieur Fok, who cut a serene figure among all his varnished monkeys and jolly, fat gods. He told me there were still 9,000 Chinese across the east coast, and that they even had their own school, down in Tamatave. Even better, most of them were from the same part of southern China, in the Shunde district.

'Just three villages!' he beamed. 'Fosuan, Saltu and Sakiu!'

'Then you must all know each other?' I said, half-joking.

'Exactly, we're like a bit of China that got away.'

A few weeks later, I'd meet another descendant of the first Chinese. Alain Ah Hu Carron Daso was about seventy, and lived in Tamatave. Although his family tree had acquired a Frenchman along the way, he was still Asian at heart. He also had that Chinese way of understating things, and of underdressing, and when we met for lunch he turned up in shorts and an ancient T-shirt. But I was soon attuned to his optimism and the idea that, for him, life was a series of opportunities, and that all we needed was to find our way through. Perhaps that's what comes of being a geologist all your life, finding profit where everyone else sees only dirt.

Or perhaps it was a congenital outlook. For Alain, there was nothing unnatural about the Moses-like journey his forebears had done. The French had come to the Shunde and offered something better, and that was all that mattered. At the time, southern China was under threat from the Japanese, and so leaving was easy.

'My grandfather was coolie,' he said, 'and arrived in 1900...'

It was a long and difficult tale that took us through fish and rice and two pots of coffee. Alain sometimes laughed at the absurdity of it all, and shrugged off the cruelty of an earlier age. The French had promised *les coolies* they'd buy them tickets home but they never did. Once the road was under way, they started building the railway. As a feat of labour, it was truly pharaonic. By 1909, trains were clanking up the escarpment, through Moramanga, and on to the plateau. Often the coolies were attacked as they worked, by the *fahavalo* (or rebels) who still lived in the forest. 'And that,' said Alain, 'is why so many stations still look like forts.'

'And what about the family? Have you become Malagasy?'
'Yes, I suppose so, although we still speak Cantonese.'
'And, of course, you've prospered here?'
Alain thought about this, and smiled modestly.
'Maybe. We used to break rocks. Now we study them.'

The longer I stayed in Moramanga, the more I realised it was seizing up. My hotel, the Bezanozano, occupied a large industrial space between the main drag and the railway. That first night, I listened out for trains but all I heard was the trilling of frogs. The hotel had obviously been built to receive thousands of passengers, and hundreds of trucks. It even had a swimming pool with a concrete island and a 'willow pattern' bridge. But the boom had never happened, and – in the absence of brides – I was given the honeymoon suite. My bed looked like a Cadillac, with white upholstery and big chrome lights built into the headboard. But the lights didn't work, and nor did the air conditioning or the bathroom taps.

'Must be the power,' said the maid.
'Must be the damp,' said the girl on reception.
Without risking breakfast, I went off in search of the station. At first it looked impressive: a large concrete building, and, beyond it, a great silvery estuary of rails. But then I noticed that the booking hall was empty, and all the *guichets* were shut. Perhaps someone down the line had stolen the track? People often talked about the theft of rails. The thieves, it was said, would steal anything, and even risked their lives stripping out cables. At one point, the government had tried to save the railways by banning the export of all scrap metal. I remember asking the *cheminot* about this, in Tana. That's right, he'd said, you can't even cut up a wreck and send it abroad.

I walked round to the track. It was all quiet out there, except for a little shunter rumbling along with a *pétrolière*. As I watched them pass, I was spotted by some men dressed in beanies and black. One of them broke away and came over, slashed with scars and quivering with menace.

What do you want, he asked.
'*Un train*,' I said, '*jusqu'à la côte.*'
He told me there was nothing running, and they were all on strike.
I said I'd take anything, even the shunter.

'*Écoute, mon pote, rien ne bouge. Alors va te la mettre.*'
(Listen, chum, nothing's moving. So fuck off.)
After almost a century, the *fahavalo*, it seemed, had finally won.

I DESCENDED THE ESCARPMENT's second step with a wedding party. For a moment, I thought there'd be only three of us in the *taxi-brousse* but then, at the last minute, the revellers appeared. The wedding, they said, was in Tamatave in two days' time, and they had with them a generator, a sound-deck, two sacks of charcoal, 60 litres of cooking oil and the groom. It took an hour to load up their gear and tie it in place. By the time we'd finished, I found myself next to the groom.

'*Félicitations*,' I said.

He thanked me, and was soon chatting away in Frenchified English.

He told me he loved the girl, but not the coast.

'Too hot?' I suggested. 'Too many bugs?'

'*Non, trop violent!* Everything there gets very smashed...'

I didn't really understand this until we began our descent. We were soon in the cliffs again, curling downwards through the clouds and black granite. If you're marrying into this world, it may not fill you with hope. But if you're only flirting and passing through, it's deliciously brutal. The rivers here would froth and boil and grind up trees, and then turn to vapour as they found the void. In places, whole mountainsides had unzipped themselves, and you could almost see the flora rushing in to fill the earth: ferns, banana trees and crown bamboo. Surprisingly, there were now lots of people around, living vertical lives and working in gangs. They all carried long curved knives mounted on staves, and looked like extras from an old French film, ambling off to storm their Bastille.

There was more violence down on the coastal plain. Humankind has already done its worst, dragging out the big trees and leaving only *savoka*, or stunted forest. But, despite the robbery, it was still magnificent: a vast, undulating salad of colour, cut with dunes and great, sleepy rivers. Then, as we reached the ocean, we turned north, through a system of sandbars. Everything here had been torn apart. Most of the houses had been prised open, and one of the warehouses had its roof peeled back like a tin of fish. Nothing had been spared, even the old coconut forests. In places, they looked as though they'd been trampled by giant feet, and then everything scattered as if it was straw.

'*Vous voyez?* You see?' said the groom. 'Who can live here?'

Everyone agreed the latest cyclone had been particularly vicious.

'The trees were like planes, flying around!'

The ocean, it seems, was always doing this, brewing up trouble. All year round, clouds form over the water, and then come barrelling ashore. Sometimes, the east coast gets 15 inches of rain in an hour. While the rest of Madagascar is shrivelling in the heat, this long, thin plain is being repeatedly sluiced. Between January and March, the rains visit with particular fury, and it's known as the *fahavaratra* or 'thunder-time'. Rivers turn into lakes and come pouring through the hills; bridges dissolve; roads are flushed into the gullies, and whole villages are sucked away in torrents of mud. In a single cyclone in January 2018, fifty-one people were killed, and over 20,000 people were left with nothing but foundations and the clothes they'd been wearing.

The groom winced at the thought.

'*Le bruit,*' he said, 'the noise was very… *particulier.*'

Everyone remembered the sounds of that night: first, the screaming wind, and then the whistle of metal and trees overhead. The groom said that there are only two moments in your life when you truly pray: one is with toothache, and the other's in the cyclone.

THE FRENCH HAD ALWAYS LOVED TAMATAVE. Perhaps more than anywhere else, it reminded them of home. Even before the conquest, they were fitting it out with cafés and bungalows and a frilly hotel. By 1895, it was considered '*charmante*', with a little society enjoying balls and gymkhanas, as if it were Deauville. To Dr Hocquard, making his way wearily home, it was like a foretaste, or an '*avant-goût de France*'. It was also the only place that celebrated Duchesne's victory. There was a ball at the residency, dinners aboard the men-of-war, and a glorious *retraite au flambeau*. It was almost as though Madagascar was somewhere else, and everyone had forgotten that this wasn't France.

Life had continued like this for the next sixty-five years. It didn't matter what happened to Tamatave, it always came up French. Twice there were epidemics of bubonic plague – in 1898 and 1900 – and every year the town was pounded by storms. The cyclone of 1927 destroyed nearly nine-tenths of the city, but the French merely picked up the pieces and rebuilt it all, just like before. By now it even had its own esplanade, a hippodrome, several sumptuous banks, and a large – and rather surly – beachfront hotel. It was once noted that this was 'the worst hotel in the world'. That was high praise for a place that, only a few years earlier, had barely existed.

Even now, there's a lingering Frenchness about Tamatave. I'd expected to hate it – as the Merina do – but I soon found myself settling down, as happy here as anywhere else. Life still revolved around the esplanade, and every evening people would come down to ride the dodgems and eat their *frites*. '*VIN BORDEAUX*', said the signs, '*EN VENTE ICI.*' The currents were too strong for swimming, but every now and then a very fat lady would appear on a white stallion and ride into the waves to cool her feet.

I imagined that Deauville would be just like this if you stripped off the paint and dug up the streets. On second thoughts, you might also need to flood it with paupers, and cancel the bin men, and let everything grow to twice the height. Tamatave had become a little foresty over the years, and most of the banks had now shed their roofs and were pushing out trees. Of all these little jungles, one was particularly crepuscular: La Place Bien Aimé. The banyans in here looked like molten wax pouring down from the darkness above. I had hoped to find some old gardens beneath the tendrils. Sadly, however, it was now a shortcut for trucks, and they'd churned it all up, leaving only a sticky bog.

But despite these details, all the old furniture was still in place: the arc lights, the cannons, the hippodrome (now a large roundabout), the villas, the war memorials, a gigantic port and a grisly prison. I even found a 10-foot version of the 'Queen of the Southern Seas', her shift as diaphanous and skimpy as the day she was cast. Sometimes, it seemed that nothing was new, and that this was the Miss Haversham of cities, somehow surviving on whatever was left of its grandiose past. It was said that, with every great hurricane, the promenade got shorter and shorter, and was never repaired. It was the same with the mansions whenever

Overleaf: Tamatave was the first town to get Protestant missionaries and a chapel, all Welsh of course.

they collapsed, people would huddle together in whatever remained.

Only the port was getting bigger. Sometimes, the oil tankers came so close to the beach I could see the crew having their tea up on the bridge. France had always envisaged Tamatave as an engine of wealth, beaming her culture across the Indian Ocean. In those days it was coffee, but now it was dirt and minerals and a bright-red slurry of nickel and sulphates. Some of this was pumped all the way down from Moramanga, and the money was huge. When the Canadians opened their first pipeline, the economy leapt almost 10 per cent overnight. For a moment, Tamatave had boomed. Over five thousand contractors had appeared, and even the whores grew fleetingly rich. But despite the jobs, not everyone was happy. My friends in the wedding party told me that the Canadians were thieves, and that it wasn't nickel in the pipes.

'It's gold,' said the groom, 'they're stealing everything we have.'

This was quite common, I discovered: this idea that everyone else was out to rob you. In all the restaurants, it was always the boss working the till. I had to pay for my room in advance, and receipts were invariably written in longhand, and issued in triplicate. Perhaps this was a colonial anxiety that had somehow survived. Anyway, only a fool didn't watch his money. In the street where I stayed, this had a peculiar effect. The Boulevard Joffre was home to the port officials, the jewellers and the prostitutes. It was also the place where the *gendarmes* hung out, all dressed up in camouflage and guns. The jewellers, apparently, had hired them as guards. To most people, this was logical and sensible, and it didn't seem to matter that there were never any police anywhere else.

I'D ALWAYS ASSUMED I'D NEVER FIND a Frenchman to fill this tableau. Very few '*métros*' had ever settled, and it was almost sixty years since independence. Back in London, I'd spent weeks appealing for contacts. Just when I was about to give up, someone introduced me to Michel Fayd'Herbe de Maudave. I already recognised the name.

There were Fayd'Herbes all over the history of Madagascar. They'd be governors and traders, and it was the Compte de Maudave who, in 1769, had introduced the Mexican cactus. The name would also appear on war graves and race cards. The Fayd'Herbes were determined jockeys, and had founded the country's racing club. But they were also Mauritian, which, in 1958, made them distantly British. 'And that,' said Michel, 'is how the family ended up here, living out in Epsom. I was born ten years later…'

But Epsom wasn't the end of the Fayd'Herbe travels. Work and divorce kept them moving. They were in London for the 1960s, South Africa for the 70s, and then all over the place, from here to Brazil. But eventually, in 2011, Michel took the ancestral route, and went out to Tamatave. By then, he had a construction business, and was just in time to catch the boom. These were happy years, but when it was all over he returned to London, leaving his father behind.

'And he's still there?' I asked.

'Of course. I think he wishes he'd never left.'

I asked how I might find him, if I was ever in Tamatave.

'Just ask for *Le Bateau Ivre*,' said Michel. 'The Drunken Boat.'

Everyone knew the Bateau Ivre, and I was soon immersed in the curious world of Christian Fayd'Herbe. He ran the best place in town, people said, and had known all the presidents, and had been their friend. Even on this description I recognised Christian. Although the Bateau Ivre was a barn of building, open to the beach and domed in thatch, it was all about him. There he was, nudging eighty and dressed in cream

and cashmere, directing the waiters, and finding everyone funny and drawing them in. I soon realised that he was ever the showman, but always stopped short of stealing the show. He also knew just when to listen and soothe, and just when to leave. It was an object lesson on how to survive in Tamatave. 'If you ever have problems,' he once told me, 'just give me a call. I know everyone here.'

Naturally, I was easily drawn in, and spent much of the next three days at Bateau Ivre. It was hard to sit Christian down, but eventually a life emerged in bits and pieces. There were always fragments missing, and it was sometimes difficult to make sense of the whole. He remembered his mother's parents, who were Greeks from the island of Kasos, and who'd owned the pharmacy next to the Colbert. But he'd never really known Tana. His family had moved south when he was only four. His father had run the Renault franchise in Fianarantsoa, and was once in trouble for killing a man out in the forest. There were three other brothers, all dead now. During the London years, he was a fashion buyer, working on Bond Street. He'd had three wives, all English. Once, he brought a hundred racehorses into Madagascar, and they'd arrived on a jet. He was surprised he'd survived all the changes and all the coups. You never forget the day you're trapped in the kitchen, with a drunken mob trying to smash their way in. Life's funny like that. You never know what's coming next.

I asked about France and the colony, and Christian frowned.

'I was nineteen when we left Madagascar. My father couldn't stand the thought of independence, and the idea of the gardener becoming vice-president. So, in 1957, we left. We went to Nice for a while before settling in Epsom. My parents were there for the rest of their lives, and are buried there. But the French Embassy soon found me, and served me with papers. They said if I didn't do my national service, I'd be arrested if I ever set foot in France. So, I went over and signed up, and after my training I was sent to Algeria. When I told them I was from Madagascar, they gave me an Arab section. "They're all coons," they said, "you'll know what to do." I had forty-seven men under my command. They were magnificent soldiers and saved my life. I did two years out there, until 1961. Beyond every hill was another hill. We sometimes used napalm, and it burnt everything except leather. You'd see a corpse all black and charred except his belt and his boots.

'I'm still angry. One family out of three lost a child in these wars. Today, I get a pension of thirty euros a month. If I was in France it would be eight hundred. But I'm only a *colon*. You're not French when they don't need you.'

All sorts of people came and went during those few days at the Bateau Ivre. Some came for the *crevettes* or the *pennes aux coquillages*. But most came for Christian, to bask in his patience, or just to feel special. Each night, a politician would call by, either with family or the latest girl. Despite all their mistresses, they still needed Christian to preen their ego and confirm their importance. They always got the best tables, up with the tourists and the visiting sailors.

Then there were all the contractors and the Russians and the stray Lebanese. Everyone was trying to forget something, or trying to remember why they were here. I was once cornered for hours by a man from Beirut who told me about the Muslims and his wife and all the other horrors back home. There was also an old Macedonian, who displayed almost no sign of life except a swirling nimbus of smoke. Meanwhile, the Mauritians were mostly in nickel, and drank from the end of their shift until the money ran out. One, called Joachim, was in a constant state of overload. 'I have to restrict myself,' he once told me, 'to a lover a week.' But even this didn't seem very likely, because most nights he ended up face down on the table, and the bar staff would have to keep his car keys until he could walk.

The Malagasies were just as intriguing, and equally needy. There were plenty of girls, of course, looking for husbands and drinks. Then sometimes a band appeared, and they'd play everything from gypsy to The Beach Boys, often all at once. There was also an old colonel called Poly Jacques, who was very black and sinewy, like a skein of liquorice. He kept his distance from the others, and liked to show everyone the medals his father had won for fighting the French. Christian treated them all as friends, and no one was ever less important than anyone else. One night, the watchmen found a thief in the kitchen, and attacked him with swords. Even then, Christian was indulgent, and took him to hospital to have him stitched up.

'Poor bugger,' he said, 'they had no anaesthetic.'

I once asked Christian why he came back after all those years.

'I always wanted to. But during the 70s, the French weren't welcome in Madagascar. So, what could I do? I waited, and then 1987, it was OK to return. I'd been away almost exactly thirty years. So, why come back? Well, I'd been thinking about this. Where is home? It's not Epsom or Algeria, and I've never really lived in France. It's here. This is where I grew up, and did all those things – you know, first cigarette, first drink, first kiss. You never forget all that. So, yes, this is it. This is home.'

CHRISTIAN LIVED UP THE COAST in the house of the country's most powerful mistress. Even now, people never used her name, and she was only ever referred to in whispers, as if she were close or in the next-door room. It was said she was an imperious beauty, from a Chinese family. Almost every night during the 1980s, the presidential cavalcade had secretly nosed its way down the shore and through the gates. Some people said there were parties, too, and over the years the myths had sprouted hustlers and generals and had turned into orgies. I soon gave up wondering which bits were true. All anyone could be sure of was that the affair was long over, that the old president was blind, and that the girl had gone mad. She was now in Paris, I was told, living out her life on a psychiatric ward. Even Christian never mentioned her. All he'd say is that, while she was gone, he was renting her house.

'Stories are dangerous here, even the old ones.'

But that wasn't the end of the lovers' house. Christian was still keen that I see it, before heading south. On my last night, I took up his invitation and went to stay. Like its lovers, the house was slowly falling apart. Out in the front, the sea was sucking great chunks out of the lawn, and, inside, hinges were crusting over, and all the old cup-boards were now crumbling away under a surfeit of nature. But a long, marble-floored saloon had survived, as well as the suites at each end, with their enamel baths and lime-green tiles. At first, I thought there was a party still in full swing, but then all the colours swam into focus, and I was surrounded by children and animals, full-sized sculptures, and shimmering bodies of coloured quartz. Amid this carnival of things and creatures, I spotted an old diving helmet and a dinosaur's foot. Christian never tried to explain all this, at least not in a way that made much sense.

'The foot,' he said, 'was a gift from the chief of police.'

Eventually I decided that, like the *Bateau Ivre*, the house was a sort of sanctuary. The children came from the outer edges of Christian's family, and were there with their mothers, who all looked exquisitely lovely and never spoke. There was also a young French woman who wandered in and out, looking perceptibly tragic, and a kitchen boy who was said to be given to terrible rages and who'd been with Christian for twenty-five years. As for the quartz, Christian had been collecting it, bit by bit, over the decades. There were great orbs of blue and purple, scarlet pebbles, gingery crystals, blocks of lilac and little bundles of baby-pink, all snuggled up in crates. It was odd to find a man so attuned to humans so in love with rocks. Perhaps it was his way of gathering together everything he cherished in a single room, a sort of geological ark.

The animals were more straightforward: several dogs, a duck called Donald Trump, some geese and a jet-black parrot. In the morning, they all queued at the dining-room table, and Christian cut up his breakfast, and then – Noah-like – sprinkled the pieces over their upturned mouths. He told me he'd rescued the parrot from one of his neighbours, who was about to eat it.

'They say it's good, just like chicken.'

I asked about the sculptures.

They were the work of an old man, who lived in the garden.

'Every morning, he gets up and carves his dreams.'

The sculptor obviously inhabited a complex world. His women often had extra breasts or fishtails, or they shared heads, and the men looked like locusts. Perhaps the Chinese mistress had had the same dreams, before they took her away. Her family must sometimes have struggled with reality. There she was, the president's girl with a ballroom on the beach, and a lime-green bidet. Only a few years earlier, her grandfather had been a labourer, digging one of the greatest waterways on Earth, called *les pangalanes*.

We often talked about the waterway and its 'coolies'. By linking up a series of lagoons, *les pangalanes* would be eight times the length of the Panama Canal. But, like Sisyphus, the grandfather had never finished his task, which would have run on forever. The canal, said Christian, runs through the sand. 'So as soon as you've dug it, it fills itself in.'

I began planning a trip, and soon found a boatman.

'It's magnificent,' said Christian, 'and maybe a little bit crazy.'

I LOVED THE MADNESS OF *les pangalanes*. The canal would emerge from Tamatave, and go nowhere in particular. There were no great towns along the way, and nothing much at the other end. I remember great works of human endeavour: cantilevered bridges, cuttings, berms and a large basin at the start, now a thick black soup of oil and logs. There were also barges around this basin, like old iron barns scattered on the sand. But mostly I remember the emptiness of it all; the great drifts of orange sand; the little watery forests that closed in around, and the lagoons like molten sky. This is how Venice must have looked before the stone arrived, or the people, or anything at all. Out here, you could scream and scream, and no one would hear you except the eels.

My boatman, Rudolf, was obviously born into the world, and had the quick darting movements of a waterside mammal. Although he wore several crucifixes, he didn't like to talk. All I ever discovered was that he was twenty-four and Betsimisaraka, that he had five children, and that it was dangerous to eat pork before going out on the water

The basin, or Port Fluvial, in Tamatave. A useless gift from the USSR.

because it attracted crocodiles. His boat was fast and pencil-shaped, and would slash through the water in bold white curves. He'd always sit up on the gunwale, gripping the tiller between his toes. For some reason, his hood had long floppy ears, so that once under way he looked slightly unhinged, like a high-speed rabbit.

Occasionally, we'd pass through an outcrop of rock – or a *pangalane* – and I'd see the marks made by thousands of Chinese chisels. It had taken them years to peck their way through, to dig out the sand between lagoons, and then to dredge it again and again. The project was started by Governor Galliéni in 1896, and after that it became an obsession. The French were still digging deep into the 1950s, and pouring millions of francs into the sand. By the end, they'd gouged out 80 kilometres of dirt and had created a canal that – if transposed onto Europe – would have wriggled out of Amsterdam, across Belgium, and off to Paris. At its high point, in 1957, a 30-ton barge could have got about halfway, easing itself into the middle of nowhere. But then came independence, and it all silted up. Few public works have ever been quite so persistent, or quite so daft.

Rudolf covered about 60 kilometres that morning, before skimming to a halt on Lake Ampitabe. We'd hardly seen anyone out on the water. Occasionally, little cargo boats, or *boutres*, had wobbled into view, laden with charcoal, or wheezing along under a cushion of fish. The French had always hoped this would be a highway of food, attracting settlement and towns, and churning out profits. But all we ever saw was the odd string of eels, or a great wet field of fish traps, looking like stitches out in the blue. These days, the birds were back in control: the ducks and herons, and the kingfishers, now flitting around like sparks of blue static. It was impossible not to be charmed, and I was as sure as I could be that, against the roar of the outboard, Rudolf was singing.

There was more life on Ampitabe. From now on, a long, thin drool of sand ran off down the coast, separating the lakes from the Indian Ocean. But within the lagoon there was always an air of expectancy, as if this was a stage, several miles wide and turquoise-grey. Around the rim, huts and stalls had appeared on a tiny arc of sugar-white sand, and behind us there was nothing but forest and the escarpment, now looking smoky and jagged. All day, people here watched the water as if something momentous was about to happen. But there was no sound except the distant murmur of surf. The cyclones had already been and gone, stripping the village, and leaving snippets of jetty out in the shallows. Rudolf dropped me by a grand old fig tree, covered in offerings and *zebu* skulls. He then took one last, full-throttled spin out through the seagrass before disappearing off into the wings. I wouldn't see him again until the following day.

I rented a hut from a man called Mobylette, or Moped, who had a keen sense of drama all of his own. Outside his kitchen, there was a pit in which he kept a 10-foot snake. He also allowed the lemurs to wander out of the forest and over the table, climbing the thatch and swigging the sauce. That night, we all sat around watching old reruns of *Downton Abbey*, dubbed in French. I don't think Moped or his family understood any of it, but they did have an old sepia photo of some Downton types. In it, the *vazaha* are all sporting cork helmets and Winchesters, and an enormous crocodile lies at their feet. Moped explained that, during the French period, this was a favourite place for hunting *mamba*.

'Oh,' I said, 'and what's it like for swimming now?'

The family laughed. There weren't many crocs any more.

'And anyway,' said Moped, 'they prefer to eat dogs.'

As if *LES PANGALANES* weren't mad enough, there was also a railway. It had begun long before the canal, and had survived long after. Moped told me that he sometimes heard trains twice a week, as they made their way along the drool. Occasionally, there were freight trains too, although he hadn't seen any for several months. Of course, it wasn't like the old days, when there were four passenger trains a day. Back then, you could be in Tamatave in a couple of hours, without all the bother, and without getting your feet wet. This was a curious thought. It seems that even as the French were busily gouging out their channel, the journey they wanted was already there, mounted on wheels.

That last morning, I found a dugout, and a little old lady to row me across. She got bolder and bolder as she paddled along, and by the time we arrived her price was a pound. But the railway hadn't changed, and now looked like a spine running along the sandy ridge. That day, it was covered in laundry and people, picking their teeth and gutting fish. One of the fishermen offered to show me around. He said his name was Leonard, and he had a tiny baby asleep in the crook of his arm. Not even the breakers woke her, or the disco house, or the girls playing bingo under the palms. Leonard said that Andranokoditra was used to noise. Every February it was blown away, and every March the villagers rebuilt it, with bamboo and leaves. These days, he explained, they had to make everything themselves, from shrimp traps to aphrodisiacs. They even brewed up their own cures, including *Moringa* for headaches, and *Calophyllum* for AIDS.

Only the station was still in ruins. The great storm of 2004 had sucked out the windows and whipped off the roof. All that remained of its glory days was a little sign written in Malagasy: *Please do not urinate in this station.*

That afternoon, Rudolf reappeared, and we headed off to our last lagoon. It didn't take long to cover the next 15 miles. Rudolf was soon skimming over the seagrass, down the narrows, out through the mangrove, and into Lake Rasoabe. Being only about 8 miles from the road, the lagoon had once tempted visitors, and there were signs of a little resort, called Manambato. But then came the cyclones, and it was now a village again. I had a feeling people preferred it that way. Each morning began with the women out on the beach, scouring their pans with handfuls of sand. By the afternoon, they were brimming with gossip, and would wade into the sea to spread out their nets. Nowhere in Madagascar did I ever feel quite so excluded, or so clumpy and white.

But I did at least meet up with my 'Chinese' friend, Alain Daso.

'Come and see my new house,' he said.

I soon realised that there was no limit to Alain's ambition. The house wasn't new but was the old headquarters of the *Compagnie Général de*

Overleaf: Taking a dugout across the canal at Amdranokoditra.

Madagascar. For much of the twentieth century it had stood on the Boulevard Joffre, in Tamatave. But over the last few years Alain had been ferrying it, plank by plank, through the canals. Even the doorknobs had come, and all the cast iron. Now his project was almost finished, and that afternoon he led me up through the rooms, throwing open doors and singing the virtues of all things French. 'They weren't afraid to fail, and that made them great!'

I still wonder about this, and the idea of great projects. Perhaps Alain was right, and France was exceptional? Even now, we're often in awe of her public works, pieces that were once mocked and are still as outlandish as ever. But even her whitest elephants – like the Pompidou Centre and the Eiffel Tower – have ended up loved, or at least admired. Only occasionally have there been catastrophes, like the Maginot Line. But perhaps failure is just a mark of ambition, and it was the same in Madagascar. This was never going to be a Little France without a grand scheme. That probably explains the canal. It would always be either utterly brilliant – the nucleus of economic prosperity – or a home for the herons.

I FOLLOWED THE RAILWAY BACK UP the escarpment. Having found my way through to the road, I'd caught a *taxi-brousse*. This time, no one was sick, although we did have the chicken seller with us. From the roof, I could hear his merchandise cheeping with terror as we climbed through the clouds. I also met a man from Tana, who said he was Jewish. There were only about two hundred Jews in Madagascar, he told me, and they argued a lot. How long should a skirt be? Can a woman wear red? Is Israel legal? But he didn't think it odd that, in their tiny world, there were so many schisms. '*Deux juifs*' – he grinned – '*trois synagogues.*'

Again I broke my journey, this time in a little village of railway stations. Andasibe (or Périnet, as the French called it) had been lots of things in its time, including a logging camp, a wayside halt, a mining centre and a weekend retreat. With each new age came a new station. The loggers had enjoyed gingerbread booking halls and waiting rooms, all frilled and pink. These were now packed with old armchairs and squatters, and the frets were falling away in soft brown tufts. Opposite was the next station, erected in a more industrial age out of bricks and straight lines. Best of all was the station beyond, built for the trippers,

Lake Rasoabe, once a favoured resort of crocodile hunters.

and only completed in 1938. It looked like lots of holidays, all mixed up: a giant chalet, a tent made of bricks, a touch of *Jugendstil* and a roof like a sail.

I picked my way across the tracks and peered through the windows. I could still make out touches of grandeur: varnished pillars, a panelled bar and a monumental fireplace. In its day, the *Buffet de la Gare* was thought of as the Ritz of the eastern escarpment. That may not have been saying much, but people would never forget the 'spotless linen' and 'sparkling glasses', and the Royal Suite. Everyone had been here. Sir David Attenborough once called by on a collecting trip, and would remember Jeanine, the glamorous barmaid, who'd had to leave Tana after '*une grande scandale*', and who 'regarded her exile with the deepest despair' (no doubt it did nothing for her mood when Attenborough's millipedes escaped, a hundred in all, rapidly dispersing through the upper floors).

Everything now was furry with dust and droppings. All the furniture had gone, and there was a sheet of tin nailed over the door.

The Buffet had probably been failing since its earliest days. By the 1980s it was almost over, according to Dervla Murphy, and there were 'huge fearless rats' coming out of the loos. One of its last *maîtres d'hôtel* was an animal smuggler, who was paying the locals to bring him snakes and frogs. In 1997, *The New York Times* provided one final description of the Buffet, now like a runaway zoo. It closed a few years later.

The original station at Andasibe, built around 1900, and now a gingerbread slum.

Like the Buffet, a great plan had faltered. France's ideas for Madagascar never quite came to fruition. Although she'd start a road network, and would lay over 875 kilometres of track, it was never enough. Few settled, and there were seldom more than 50,000 Frenchmen on the island at once. Even then, most were *Réunionais*, and were poor and unskilled. People no longer talked of a little France. Everything seemed to defeat them: the scale, the gradient, the distrust, and the rains. Although there'd be more public works after Galliéni's departure in 1905, there was never the same ambition. Paris still toyed with the idea of a *mission civilisatrice*, but what really mattered was the bottom line. They may not be able to transform Madagascar, but they could at least own it.

D EFIANCE WAS EVERYWHERE, in the hills around Andasibe. This time, however, it wasn't topography or humans but a kind of lemur. The indri would rather die than change. Although it's the largest of the lemurs – and looks like a child in fluffy pyjamas – it lives only in this eastern forest. It never goes anywhere, never adapts, and never eats anything but leaves. Even though it's completely defenceless, it has a call like an air-raid siren, piquing appetites for miles around. But it resists all attempts to move it or hold it, and, whenever it's caged, it stubbornly dies. No one has ever owned an indri for more than a month. The last attempt to get them to Europe was in 1939, when ten appeared in Paris, and immediately perished.

At dawn, I got up to listen to the daily challenge. All around, the forest wailed and hooted as the indris rebuilt their boundaries out of noise. Andasibe and its little stations were easily overwhelmed by this deluge of sound. But indris weren't just sopranos, they were also ancestors. You had to be careful, said one of the station's old watchmen. If you ever attacked them with spears, they'd throw them back with deadly force. 'And that' – he smiled – 'is why the French never touched them.'

I walked back to the village, in search of a bus. One day, all this might change, the songs might stop, and the forest might shrink away. But, for now, things are as they've always been, and here's Madagascar at its obstinate best.

CHAPTER 9

The Outer Edges of *La Mission Civilisatrice*

The custom of the land has it that an unmarried white man should always have a Malagasy girl for company. Everybody should have a vadi or Malagasy wife.

ARKADY FIEDLER
The Madagascar I Love, 1946

Nosy-Bé is a South Sea island small enough to fit into the imagination.

ARTHUR STRATTON
The Great Red Island, 1965

The French treated [the Malagasies] like dirt and often thrashed them during the day and slept with them after dark, and were loved…

PATRICK MEDD
Taking in Sail, 1996

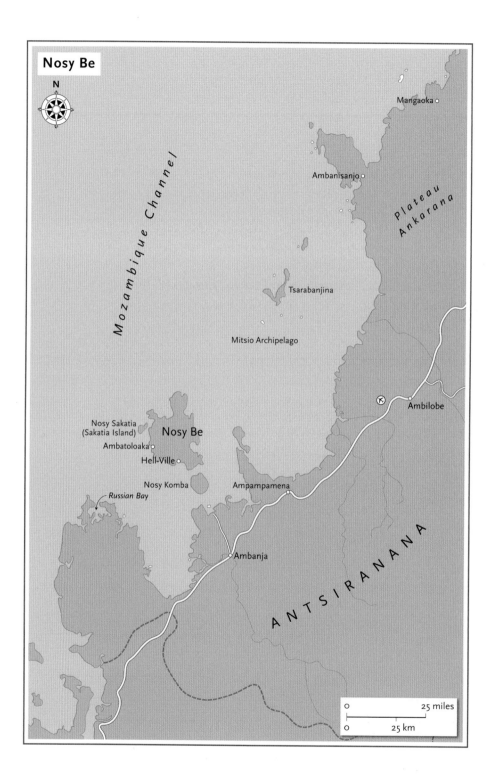

Nosy Be

N

Mozambique Channel

Mangaoka

Ambanisanjo

Plateau
Ankarana

Tsarabanjina

Mitsio Archipelago

Ambilobe

Nosy Sakatia
(Sakatia Island)   Nosy Be

Ambatoloaka

Hell-Ville

Nosy Komba   Ampampamena

Russian Bay

Ambanja

A N T S I R A N A N A

0   25 miles

0   25 km

I F ANYONE EVER WANTED TO REDESIGN Madagascar, they'd probably come up with Nosy Be. It's often been thought of as almost perfect: like the real thing, but smaller and more manageable; a celestial spice garden, or Zanzibar, perhaps, but with some of the world's biggest bamboos and its smallest frogs (*Stumpffia pygmaea*). It's hard to imagine a more ornamental island, only 12 miles across and covered in hills and streams, and clumps of vanilla and cloves. In 1839, the French had reached a deal with the Sakalava, and had been there ever since. Maybe it misled them. Maybe they thought it would all be like this: a gorgeous, abundant land, readily tamed and rich in pickings. Perhaps they'd forgotten that it was only a blueprint, and that if something's perfect, you should leave it at that.

Because it was way off in a world apart, I took the plane, flying from Tana. This was no preparation for what was to come. For almost two hours we rumbled over the north, the land below the texture of bricks, and shot with dark-green veins and dried-up rivers. But then suddenly the sea appeared, swimming-pool blue and pebbled with islands. Far off to the north, I could make out the Mitsio Archipelago, like the outer rim of some ancient explosion, and then – closer in – Nosy Be and tiny Komba Island, which was so green and symmetrical it looked like a conifer growing out of the depths.

Then, as the plane turned towards Nosy Be, it seemed to hesitate, as if unsure where to land among all the craters and coves. I could also see palms now, and thatch, and great bouquets of orange and red, and canoes on the sand. I think everyone falls in love at this stage. The French would call this place *l'île du paradis*, and unsurprisingly the name has stuck. But like all Edens, it had its tempting fruits, and, here, innocence itself would soon seem rare and exotic.

F ORTUNATELY, I DIDN'T HAVE TO TACKLE paradise alone. For the next two weeks, I'd be joined by my wife, Jayne, and our daughter, Lucy. They flew in via Addis Ababa, and I met them at the island airstrip

Overleaf: A desert island off Nosy Be. The French thought they'd found paradise, and that all Madagascar would be like this.

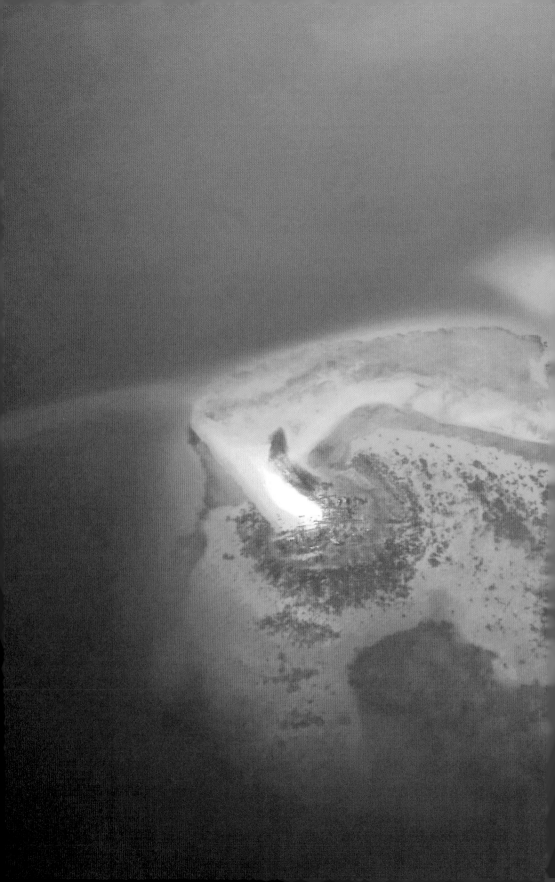

looking luminously pale. We'd been here before, fourteen years earlier. Back then, Jayne and I had stayed on Komba, with two Frenchmen and all their Parisian cats. In my memory, it was pure Gauguin. Everything was made of driftwood and flowers, and our shower erupted from a large wooden crocodile. In a way, Lucy had been with us too, although – at that stage – she was still floating around in the amniotic dark. I've always wondered what it does to you, absorbing a place before you're born. The Frenchmen told us that they now had nothing left but Madagascar. 'Our first hotel was burnt down,' they said, 'and we lost everything – except the cats.'

Sakalava herdsmen washing their cattle in the sea, Nosy Be.

I enjoyed seeing everything again, through teenage eyes. It made me realise how much I'd become accustomed to Madagascar. Now, everything was strange all over again: the baby-sized papayas, the shoelessness, the nakedness, the infinite garden, the wild purples, the great orange shipwrecks and the oil-drum houses with lace in the windows. That first morning, we took an old taxi across the island, and Lucy absorbed it all in silence, as if she was wondering where it was leading. At one point, our driver had to hand over a bundle of banknotes to a policeman in a square blue hat. Another time we came across some knobbly old fishermen, glossy with sweat, and singing as they worked. They'd collected a basket of tiny fish, like chips of glass. Then we passed some men in a stream, each cupping his balls with one hand as he waved with the other. Later a crowd appeared, and among them were two furious cocks, fighting it out in a squall of feathers. To a child, paradise is a much more uncertain place than it is to adults.

By the time we got to our hotel, time seemed alarmingly elastic. Only the petrol stations seemed to belong to our age, and looked like visiting spaceships moored in the woods. But eventually the present shrank into shape. Our hotel, the Nosy Lodge, was made of caramel-coloured cement, and was run by a French woman who had a large bunch of keys and was everywhere at once. I could also see speedboats out in the bay, and a scattering of restaurants under the palms. In each of these places, it was always the same story: a Frenchman, settling down with his Sakalava girl, enjoying a life of flotsam and booze. Only occasionally did time begin to stretch again, reaching out into the past. Usually, it was the herders, leading their cattle out to the reef for a salty bath. But we also had visits from the Antandroy, who'd travelled hundreds of miles to sell us their swords and spears. They told me they made them from bits of old railway track.

Lucy watched as they ambled off, clanking with weapons.

'Makes a change,' she whispered, 'from buckets and spades.'

To the French, all this meant one thing: money. Although a *mission civilisatrice* was always there in the background, what really mattered was the spices. France had always recognised this, and in 1841 Admiral Anne Chrétien Louis de Hell had set up a trading post in his own unfortunate name. Now, Hell-Ville was as exuberant as ever, a town of cannons and fruit-coloured mansions. Hell's little palace was still there, and so was his corniche, and his avenues – speckled with sunlight – and an open-air tailors' quarter that whirred and chattered like a colony of jays. Although the port had largely seized up with rust, there was still a lively exchange of containers, and every now and then a prawn fleet would call by, or a schooner full of bricks.

'*Vazaha!*' people hissed. '*Donnez-moi bonbon!*'

Everyone was either a porter, a barker, a hustler or a tout. In the market hall, which was the colour of mango, there was every cure a quack could ever dream of, together with sparkly jeans, old rum bottles full of chilli, baskets of muddy crabs and some special medicinal necklaces used for treating jealousy and coughs. Someone had even set up a bar in a shipping container, and another little café had rushed into English, calling itself SNACK MY FEELING. But the Oasis *pâtisserie* was still the place to meet, its louvred doors and fluted columns as stately as ever. A few doors down at the *brasserie*, L'Agora, it was the same old French boys picking over their smoked fish and *tartare de pomme*, and only their girls got younger and younger.

'They look hardly older than me,' said Lucy.

'Must be all that crab oil,' said Jayne.

We also found a theatre offering plays in French, and a tiny outpost of the Académie française. Even the town lock-up looked as though it had hardly changed in over 150 years, and was still a miserable hulk known as the *maison d'arrêt*. But although Hell-Ville wasn't quite like anywhere in France, it wasn't Malagasy either. It was more like a holding area between the two, a sort of colonial purgatory. But that didn't mean it wasn't a good place to die, and for those that succumbed there was

Established in 1841, Hell-Ville was France's first successful settlement, heralding the beginning of *la présence française*.

a great French cemetery, complete with 8-foot angels and a herd of goats. The locals had added only one refinement, adorning the graves with shoes and hats.

'Funny,' said Lucy, 'like they're only here for a little nap.'

Naturally, a bit of this Frenchness had spilled into the country beyond. Little churches would nose up out of the sugar cane, and there were mills and *manoirs*, and even a sprinkling of schools. The French had introduced cloves, peppers, sugar, eucalyptus and lemon grass, and in 1903 they'd built a little railway to haul it away. We could still see bits of the track running through the pepper, and once we even came across an old wagon, now covered in creepers and children. One day, I suppose, it will all be cut up, and turned into spears.

But the old plantations had survived, in all their grandeur. They always had their own mansion and a civilising sprawl of roads leading off through the hills. Some of these places were now open to visitors, and they'd have cages of animals to draw people in. One of these *domaines*, which now called itself 'Lemuria Land', even had a giant tortoise that was born in 1810, and was known as Napoleon. He'd been lucky to see his two-hundredth birthday. A few years earlier there'd been a riot in Hell-Ville, and a stray bullet had buried itself in his carapace. But his life had been full of surprises. At the age of eighty, a plantation had appeared on his patch, followed, in 1904, by a factory, fitted out with its own little jungle of copper pipes and condensers. Over a century on, they were still coughing up *ylang-ylang* in big yellow droplets.

One day, said the foreman, this oil would be shipped off to Grasse, and the great *parfumeries*. But, for now, it sat around in old Fanta bottles. It seemed such a tawdry start for something that would one day sell as Chanel No 5.

But the crop worth killing for was still vanilla. Although Nosy Be isn't the most productive area, it still has its guards and its brokers and its vanilla thieves. As a creeper, vanilla may not look much, but it's one of the few orchids that are edible. It also absorbs the scents all around, and can be ruined by perfume or mosquito repellent. '*C'est comme s'occuper d'enfants*', one of the growers once told me. It's like looking after children.

By 1896, the world was hooked, and Madagascar was producing 80 per cent of the planet's vanilla (a share of the market that has fallen since then). But the best times were still to come. Vanilla would feed the Coca-Cola habit, and would appear in all sorts of concoctions, from cures for jellyfish stings to Dune by Dior. In America, it would even be sprayed around hospitals, to calm the patients. But, best of all, it was in ice cream. These days, in the USA, the ice-cream industry is worth $20 billion a year, and Americans eat 22 litres a head. Easily the most popular flavour is vanilla (and it's the same in Britain – nine out of ten ice creams are orchid-flavoured). It's often felt as though vanilla alone has kept Madagascar going, and even now it accounts for a third of her export income. For Nosy Be too, the money's been welcome, and there are plenty of mansions built on ice cream.

By the time we arrived, vanilla – pound for pound – was worth more than silver. Around Madagascar, it still sparks wars. The papers were always carrying stories about crops disappearing overnight, or villages burnt to the ground. In one of these tales, an entire family was mown down as they set off for market with their pods. Somehow, vanilla always seemed to find Madagascar's gangsters at their most Mexican. So, as these things go, it's the sweetest child, if a little delinquent.

EVERY DAY, NEW COLONIES FORM around the island. This time, it's us, the tourists. We may only be passing through but we're in our own world, and live our lives as if we're far away but still at home. Everything comes with us, from the Wi-Fi and the Kardashians down to the whisky.

We think we're better than the *colons* before, but we're just as alien and just as detached. We still need our grand buildings and barbed wire, and we obsess about hygiene and the state of the roads. We often need to possess places, too, and are always belting off to 'pristine beaches' and 'undiscovered coves', just to own them for a couple of hours. Among us, there are still lots of Frenchmen. Every year, across Madagascar, around 250,000 tourists appear, of whom half are French. But there have also been up to 30,000 Italians (all so desperate for sand they fly here direct). The British, Chinese and Americans lag way behind, at only a few thousand each. If colonialism has changed at all, it's just more multilingual.

On Nosy Be, we think we like the natives but they're hard to gauge. Although we've only just arrived, we all seem to know where they're going wrong. They're often too noisy, too inquisitive, too pushy and too close, but we're never sure why. Some of us don't even see them at all, and are only here to bob around in the turquoise haze, communing with giant clams and octopus and that great carnival of fish that we never hear. But if the locals do interest us, it's only ever in their most primal state. The boat operators know this, and are always running little tours out to the islands – like Sakatia – where the rainforest grows. Here, the villagers have long since learnt how to turn their lives into coins. 'When a child's born,' they say, 'we bury the placenta under the mat.'

'And, for the first month of his life, the baby's hidden away.'

At dusk, we all speed back to our colonies, happy we're here, and glad it's not home.

To the Sakalava, we foreigners were equally perplexing, and there were always two things at work: sex and terror. The sex was easy to understand, or at least to envisage. Along the beach, and around the headland, was a little town called Ambatoloaka. Every afternoon at five, it became a market for girls.

We once went down there, to watch the sunset. By day, Ambatoloaka had its charms. There was a long, breezy curve of sand, fringed with villas and little hotels. This is where the tour boats gathered, and all day an old ox-cart creaked up and down the beach, gathering seaweed and rubbish. That afternoon, a funeral cortège came tootling through the town, with the body all wrapped in white, and bobbing along above the crowd. But then, as the light faded, the bars began to fill up, as the old boys gathered. They all looked much the same: joyless, worn, mushroom-skinned and middle-aged. One of them had sores all down his legs, like a modern-day Lazarus after years on the juice. It was obviously a hectic cyclical life: drink, girl, drink, repeat.

On cue, the prostitutes appeared along the beach. It was impossible to totter in the sand, but each was a spectacle of Afros and handbags

One of the girls on the beach at Ambatoloaka, and the day's catch.

and lacy shorts. Some had woven cords of blonde into their hair, and they all looked rangy and listless, as though just being alive was too much effort. Anywhere else, they'd have been beautiful girls, but here, in this grisly charade, they were the Sakalava at their most yielding, giving up everything for the price of a fish. Lucy had never seen such disinhibition, and averted her gaze as if she might somehow be noticed and drawn into their madness. I suppose they were all adults, although it wasn't a look they were after. I suddenly realised that this was all about childhood – the skinny limbs and the tiny shorts – and the younger you looked, the better you sold.

People still argue about where things went wrong. For the Sakalava, sex has always been a commodity, to be traded for favours. This was the same all around the coast. Traditionally, no self-respecting woman would ever give herself up without a new *lamba* or a ride in a taxi. So did *les côtiers* corrupt the French? Or did the settlers bring a new kind of deviancy all of their own? It was probably both: the perfect sexual storm.

To begin with, the mingling of races was a matter of diplomacy and need. The first settlers, like Pronis, were happy to take local wives, often several at once. These early *colons* were often surprised to find women sent to them as gifts, but they soon got the idea. The eagerness of the French amused the Malagasies, and a new song appeared around the coast:

> 'The *vazaha* does not love like other men, aa!
> When he makes love,
> He slavers and bites like a dog'

But everything got more serious after the conquest. France's frazzled soldiery often regarded their new subjects as a little less than human. Out of sight, and perhaps out of mind, the rules changed. In his memoirs, Lieutenant (later General) Paul-Frédéric Rollet talked openly of the *ramatoa*, or 'wife', he took in about 1903, described as 'a small girl of twelve or thirteen years' (she's said to have infuriated his staff with her refusal to wash her feet before climbing into his bed).

It wasn't just soldiers acquiring children. By the 1930s, it was normal for petty officials to have a *vadi*, or local girl. Arkady Fiedler, the Polish writer, would describe how it all worked in *The Madagascar I Love*, which was based on his travels in 1937. Nowadays, this book wouldn't find a publisher, and yet it's a remarkable record of the perversion in play. Not only would Fiedler include pictures of the girls he abused (usually naked), he also revels in the opportunities an empire provided. 'White men in these parts,' he writes, 'are expected to collect nasty taxes, to pass unjust sentences, to have astonishing whims and to rape Malagasy girls – all this belongs to their established privilege.'

The Polish writer, Arkady Fiedler, and one of his local girls, circa 1937.

Fiedler himself didn't hold back. His first girl, who was sixteen, he called 'the Coquette', until she ran away. His second was easier to keep, and he bedded her on the first night. 'This flower was fragrant indeed,' he boasts, 'hardly developed from the bud, it had the intoxication of ripe womanhood.' This was as compassionate as Fiedler ever got, and he reserves his tenderest words for his two pet lemurs.

As the father of a child the age of these *vadi*, I found all this hard to compute.

Even worse was the thought that the menace unleashed was still at large. Madagascar now suffers child exploitation at an epidemic rate, much of it here in Nosy Be. In a recent survey, 40 per cent of the island's young women were found to have lost their virginity in the context of prostitution, many no more than fourteen. Since then, there'd been a documentary by Journeyman TV, revealing that, in Ambatoloaka, the cost of innocence was $21. The cameras had also found boys, some as young as twelve, earning more in a month than most people made in a year. Even the head of the Sex Workers Collective had been rendered indignant. 'Half the girls are under the age of consent,' shrills Madame Florine, 'and it's destroying the future of our youth.'

I couldn't hope to explore this sinister underworld, but I did know someone who understood the system. Alix Brand – which isn't her real name – had been here with the Peace Corps for several years. Originally from Minnesota, she'd adapted well to the insularity, and had spent her first six months living in an old garage. But nothing had prepared her for the child abuse. 'It's like there's no such thing as under age,' she said. 'Sometimes even the parents encourage it! And they never complain – unless the man doesn't pay...'

We'd met at the Oasis, under one of the posters her people had put there: '*LES ENFANTS NE SONT PAS DES SOUVENIRS TOURISTIQUES.*' Alix explained that the hotels were supposed to police the problem, but they never did. Everyone turned a blind eye, and – even when they didn't – there was a network of bribes to make everything vanish. 'And now the fixers have nice big villas out of town. You know, those high walls and rolls of wire... No one sees *anything* more. This really defeats the Malagasies. They think it's somehow the foreigners' problem, and they want the *vazaha* to come and sort it out. It's like a complete collapse of self-esteem.'

'And what about the police?' I asked.

Alix stopped, and looked at me, as if I'd understood nothing.

'You kidding? They don't even have funds for a tank of gas.'

All this links in with the terror.

Foreigners may now be insatiable, but they've always been ogres. The first Europeans had horrified the Malagasies. It seemed that wherever there was whiteness, there was always death. This was true even when Robert Drury was washed ashore in 1703. But he thought Europeans deserved their reputation as albescent killers. 'Having seen no good ones here, every white man is look'd on by them as a monster, as a cannibal is by us…' The anxiety, however, would persist long after the age of empires, and the French departure. White remains a gruesome colour, rich in ghosts. Across the island, there are still those scared of albinos, and who won't eat pale foods on Sunday. There's even a range of 'white words' to express perfidy and horror. 'Stop crying,' Malagasy mothers tell their children, 'or the *vazaha* will cut your ears off.'

At some stage, however, the mythology had mutated. Somehow, the white killer had become conflated with the slavering, over-eager lover. This may have happened during the revolt of 1897, or in the traumas that followed. But whenever it was, a new spirit had emerged, known as 'the heart-thief'. Nocturnal, blanched and surgically cruel, the *mpakafo* was now seeded deep in the collective psyche. All around the island, there were tales of missing eyes and stolen kidneys. The Antandroy had told me that whites were always digging out brains, as a cure for AIDS. In Tuléar, they said that it was the children who were harvested, for the Indian market. Even the Mercy Ships were accused of organ robbery. Every year, this mission sailed round the island, treating the sick, and every year the rumours grew. I once met a man in Tana who said he knew lots of people who'd lost their innards. 'They take what they like, when you're asleep.'

Most people bore their fears privately, but very occasionally they found courage in numbers and sought revenge. All sorts of people have been killed by the crowds, including four civil servants (1967), a Catholic priest (1975) and a couple of Western scientists, who were thought to be gathering hearts. On 3 October 2013, there was even a little moment of white terror here, on the beach at Ambatoloaka. It happened like this:

The day began with a story that had come from nowhere. It involved the body of a small boy, who'd been found with no tongue and his penis missing. Although nobody ever saw the child, everyone agreed this was the work of the *mpakafo*. The townspeople knew what to do, and soon found culprits. Gianfalla was an Italian cook, and had no idea he was a paedophile until the crowd found him. It was the same for Judalet, who was a bus driver on holiday from France. But Ambatoloaka knew better. Over four thousand people gathered, to see it through.

Almost every moment of this great exorcism would be filmed and posted on the web: the sticks, the pleas and the fires on the beach. When they'd finished with the Europeans, the crowd found the boy's uncle, and burnt him too. They then set fire to eight houses, and spent the rest of the night enjoying the glow. By the morning, Nosy Be had no tourist industry and thirty-seven new defendants. Among them were the town's policemen, and the rubbish collector, who'd used his ox-cart to ferry the dead.

'This is what happens,' said Alix, 'when people feel helpless.'

For a while, Ambatoloaka insisted it had done no wrong. Across Madagascar, many believed them. Even my friends in Morondava, the biologists, thought the victims more guilty than those who'd killed them. 'They found a penis,' they told me, 'in the white guys' *fridge!*'

'And what about now,' I asked Alix, 'since the trial?'

'No one mentions it. *Ever*. It just didn't happen.'

A FTER THAT, WE NEVER WENT BACK to Ambatoloaka, and life assumed a more fairy-tale course. There were no real ogres on our beach, but we did have our giants. The turtles came bobbing in like upturned boats, and further out there was a whale, lolling around with her two-ton calf. Even the showers were gentle, just a sprinkling of scents. In the brilliant light, the *pirogues*, with their crescent sails, looked like a fleet of new moons, setting off for the sky. Beyond the beach, the bougainvillea was piled up in great purple clouds. One of the hawkers told me life was easy.

'We have fish and bananas. We are never hungry.'

Some of the beach boys also sold boat trips. Across the horizon I could make out a long attenuated streak of smoky-grey, broken by a gap. One of the boatmen, called Georges, looked like the actor Omar Epps, and had a skiff with a powerful engine. Where exactly did we want to go?

'*Là-bas*,' I said, pointing at the gap.

He was intrigued. '*La Baie des Russes? Pourquoi?*'

It was hard to explain. Every fairy tale has its moment of farce, and Nosy Be has the Russians.

O N 28 DECEMBER 1904, TWO battleships and three cruisers had appeared in these waters. Over the next few weeks, more would join them, and soon there'd be a fleet of forty-seven ships. The little French settlement had never seen such metalwork before, or such a vast display of smoke. But the story of Russia's Second Pacific Squadron is almost as comical as it is sad. It provides one of those rare moments in colonial history when you're never quite sure whether to laugh or cry. Eleven months earlier, the Japanese had attacked the Russian naval base at Port Arthur, in north-eastern China. The assault was so sudden and ferocious it had left the Tsar's Pacific squadron paralysed, and the port – now called Lüshun – under siege. For weeks, the Russians dithered over how to respond. At the time, conventional wisdom had it that no navy could take on an enemy more than 2,000 miles from a first-rate base. For the Baltic fleet, sailing round Africa, it would be nine times that distance.

Eventually, in May 1904, a decision was made: a new Pacific Squadron ('the Second') would sail out to relieve Port Arthur. Almost anything that could float would be sent, including the old, the coal-guzzlers and the unseaworthy. This fleet was never going to worry anyone. Even the best of its warships were top-heavy and in danger of capsizing. Some had so many different guns that finding the right ammunition was a constant headache. The crews seldom trained, and were notoriously mutinous. In September, only a month before leaving, they did their first gunnery practice. It was disastrous. Two cruisers ran aground, and the battleships nearly collided.

The man put in charge of this ragtag squadron was Vice-Admiral

Zinovy 'Mad Dog' Rozhestvensky. In his photographs, he looks harmless enough, covered in medals and braid, with his well-coiffed beard. But in the flesh he was famously shrill, and was always slapping his staff and making officers cry. But he did at least have a sense of the mission's futility, and at every stage he was there, snapping and snarling as it all went wrong.

On 21 October 1904, the new squadron set out from Libau (now Liepāja) in Latvia. Almost immediately, it ran into trouble. Although the Japanese were over 20,000 miles away, the Russians feared an ambush and slept by their guns. As they entered the North Sea, they encountered a British fishing fleet from Hull and, mistaking them for torpedo boats, opened fire. Fortunately, their gunnery was so poor only one trawler was sunk. The battleship *Oryol* is said to have fired over

Imperial Russia's battleship, *Oslyabya*, en route to Madagascar and the war with Japan. She was sunk at the Battle of Tsushima in May 1905.

five hundred rounds without hitting a thing. The only other casualties were Russian. In the confusion, the cruiser *Aurora* was hit six times, and the chaplain was killed. Worse, the squadron had made a new enemy: the Royal Navy. It would shadow the Russians all the way to Spain, where they promised a full inquiry. Months later, St Petersburg settled all claims, with a generous payment of £66,000.

Meanwhile, in the Strait of Gibraltar, the squadron split up. Rozhestvensky was worried his ships might get trapped in the Suez Canal, so only a few went that way. The rest, under his command, would take the long route, around the Cape of Good Hope. Slowly, they wobbled their way down the African coast. They had no allies along the way, and even the Portuguese moved them on. With the older hulks constantly breaking down, the fleet's engineer, Eugene Politovsky, would have to leap from ship to ship, effecting repairs. In his letters home, he described how the humidity turned everything to rust; how towels wouldn't dry and how the drawers wouldn't shut. Someone had shaved the ship's dog, to make it look like a lion.

With no coaling stations en route, the fleet had to refuel at sea. In this, the German company Hamburg America Line had agreed to supply sixty cargoes. It was dangerous work, transferring the coal. Crews would work for twenty-four hours non-stop, stuffing their mouths with wads of cotton. At one point, Rozhestvensky's ship broke a world record, shovelling 120 tons in an hour. The coal not only filled the bunkers, it was also stacked on the decks. Many of the sailors didn't have boots, making it hard to move around. Politovsky would also describe the dust. Several men were smothered, he says, and died in the coal.

Eventually, on 9 January 1905, Rozhestvensky arrived in Madagascar. There, he was reunited with the Suez group, who'd arrived a fortnight earlier. He'd also learn that Port Arthur had fallen the week before, and that its Pacific fleet had been completely destroyed. Realising there was no sense in pressing on, he offered his resignation. It was refused. To make matters worse, the French – under pressure from Britain – wouldn't let him use their naval base at Diego Suarez. Instead, his squadron would be allocated a remote inlet off Nosy Be. This was no place to spend the next ten weeks, and everyone agrees things got a bit crazy. Once known as Ambaratoby, the inlet will now be remembered forever as 'Russian Bay'.

It took us an hour to get across the bay and through the gap. Inside, it was like a turquoise room, several miles across. The water wasn't deep, and so the Russians must have anchored out in the channel. We saw only one other boat moored in the shallows, a Danish yacht. It was funny to think that it too had begun in the Baltic and had undergone a similar voyage, perhaps a little more gently and without the dust.

Russian Bay today. The Tsar's fleet was here for 10 gruelling weeks.

Around the edge was mangrove, and beyond it the jungle, packed tight like a wall of broccoli. Near the mouth of the inlet was a short beach, scattered with clam shells the size of helmets. In among them, some nomadic fishermen were drying their nets and cutting up rays. One of them was also carving out a new canoe – a nick at a time – in the ruins of an old Victorian warehouse. These days, the only permanent resident was an Austrian called Andreas, who'd set up a camp in the trees. His hair was so wild and sandy he looked like part of the beach. He didn't seem to mind that no one ever stayed.

'I love the silence. Sometimes I don't see anyone for weeks.'

Georges the boatman bought some barracuda and cooked it under the palms. At that point, a band of lemurs appeared, and started dancing around in the hope of bread. They were all charcoal-black with orange eyes and pom-pom ears. The Russians had thought they were 'monkeys' and had gathered them up and taken them back to their ships. This had appalled Politovsky. 'Wherever you look now,' he wrote, 'you see birds, beasts and vermin.'

A surfeit of pets wasn't the only problem. Below decks, the air was hot and foul. Rats and coal dust seemed to get in everything. Across the fleet, the crews sank into depression, relieved only by bouts of hard drinking. Oxen were slaughtered on the decks, and men were now wandering around half-naked, asking if death itself was the easy way out. The crews received mail only once, and it turned out to be the letters they'd sent out a month before. At the same time, a supply ship arrived from St Petersburg, bringing fur-lined boots and matching coats. Perhaps it was true, they really had been forgotten.

Hell-Ville wanted nothing to do with this stinking, half-mad rabble, and only the officers were allowed ashore. But even they proved a handful. Not only did they drink heavily, they were also merciless gamblers. Several *fonctionnaires* were left penniless, and eventually the governor had to order his staff to disengage. After that, the officers took comfort in opium, and emptied the town of its last narcotics. As dissipation set in, so the ships began to fail. Across their hulls, they were all now sprouting luxuriant tropical growths, big enough to slow them down. It didn't bode well for the battle ahead.

Everyone was tormented by the Japanese spectre. It was said that 40,000 Russians had died in Manchuria. Perhaps the enemy was already here, in Madagascar? All night, Rozhestvensky's men patrolled the entrance to the inlet, rolling out the torpedo nets. Meanwhile, the crews' gunnery was as chaotic as ever. During practice, no one ever seemed to hit the target (although they once landed a shell on the ship that was towing it). Perhaps the worst moment was when one of their own torpedoes turned tail and headed straight for the fleet, scattering everyone in panic. Even Politovsky couldn't hide his sense of impending doom. 'It's useless for the fleet to go on,' he wrote in one of his last letters home.

The wait got to everyone, jangling nerves. Some of it was due to Hamburg America, who suddenly took fright and reneged on their contract. But part of the delay was down to folly. The Tsar – who was no great expert in naval strategy – had ordered them to await reinforcements, and had put together a third Pacific squadron. As always, Rozhestvensky didn't hold back. The new squadron, he raged, was 'an archaeological collection', and its ships were 'self-sinkers'. This time, the admiralty relented, but it was too late. Within the inlet, several crews had already mutinied, and order was only restored with a boarding party and a firing squad. Fourteen men were shot, and a few others were dumped ashore, to take their chances with the Malagasies.

A few days later, on 16 March 1905, the squadron sailed.

What happened next is still hard to compass. Rozhestvensky's ships had taken them two months to reach the Sea of Japan, dragging weed and scattering rats. There, the Japanese were waiting, and at the Battle of Tsushima cut them to bits. Over the course of two days – 27 and 28 May 1905 – Imperial Russia lost the best of her navy. Twenty-one ships were sunk, including eight battleships and four cruisers. In addition, 4,380 Russians were killed (including three admirals), and another 6,000 were captured. By contrast, the Japanese lost only 116 men and three torpedo boats.

Rozhestvensky's flagship, *Suvorov*, was savaged on the first day. He himself was hit in the head during the early exchanges, and was taken off and later captured. But his crew fought on. It's said that the *Suvorov* was still blasting away as it disappeared beneath the waves. With it went the diligent Politovsky, a complement of iguanas, the black lemurs and over 900 men. There were no survivors.

Of the remaining Russian ships, few escaped capture. Several made it to Shanghai and Manila, but only three got through to Vladivostok. One of the cruisers, the *Dimitri Donskoi*, was supposed to have been

Vice Admiral Zinovy 'Mad Dog' Rozhestvensky, commander of Russia's Second Pacific Squadron. In Madagascar, he was given to bouts of rage and despair.

carrying gold bullion, and limped off down the Korean coast before being scuttled (coincidentally, in the week of our visit to Nosy Be, it reappeared in 1,400 feet of water, and was immediately embroiled in lawyers and writs). Only one vessel got back to Madagascar, a British-built steamer called *Anadyr*. Having picked up over three hundred survivors, she didn't linger. Ahead lay an eventful life, but bombs got her in the end, and she was sunk off Svalbard in 1942.

Around Nosy Be, the visitors from Russia had left little behind. It was said they'd scuttled one of their old rotten transports in the Baie des Russes, but Andreas had never seen it, and it wasn't on the charts. I did, however, find several Russian tombs in the Hell-Ville cemetery, each dating from Rozhestvensky's time and mounted with a big rusty cross. In 1994, the Soviet navy had added a monument of their own, made of bits of old chain and brown bathroom tiles. I couldn't imagine which bit of this story they thought worth remembering. As for the mutineers, there was no trace of them but there were plenty of rumours. Georges told me the last of the Russians had died in 1936. Other versions of this story were less specific but always involved lots of blonde hair and buried gold.

'It's true,' said Georges, 'we're all a bit Russian.'

T HE WORLD ENDS SOMEWHERE OUT IN the edges of this great archipelago, or so it has sometimes seemed. I remembered these islands from the plane, like the eyes in a peacock's tail, scattered on the sea. Most of them were uninhabited, and the Sakalava had used the outer ones for burying their kings. Perhaps they'd realised that the further you are from the Earth you know, the nearer you are to your gods. The French had made no impression out here, and, even now, the islanders had little concept of electricity or Christ or Taylor Swift. Here, the empire had ended and the coral began.

After Russian Bay, we didn't wander far. But years earlier, during our first trip, Jayne and I had gone out to Tsarabanjina. Although this islet was only the size of a few cricket pitches, it was improbably perfect. Nature had obviously put her gardeners to work, and chocolatiers to set up the rocks. By then, Tsarabanjina also had a hotel, which was similarly perfect. For two days, we pottered about, swimming with a giant turtle and communing with the boobies that came to the bar.

Back in 1994, the BBC had made a programme here, called *Girl Friday*. The island was still truly deserted then, and the idea was simple: a winsome actress, Joanna Lumley, would be marooned here with nothing but a TV crew, a few tins and a swimsuit. Nowadays, for this to be considered entertaining, she'd have to go mad or have six different lovers. But back then, audiences still enjoyed the idea that people (just like them) could go to the ends of the Earth, and, by their wits alone, somehow triumph. Lumley proved a noble contender, and was soon writing poetry and making shoes. Only paradise, with its sandflies and its clammy caves, was less than perfect.

O N OUR LAST DAY, WE WENT SNORKELLING off Sakatia Island. For hours, we bobbed around, happily suspended over the coral. But I've always found it hard to relate to the submarine landscape, with its bubbly silence and its cyanic light. It's like a garden without air, or a gallery of freaks. That morning we saw ox-blood roses, fish with beaks, purple stars, and little Picassos with fins and tails.

It was a fitting end to Lucy's holiday. Soon, she and Jayne would fly back home. Even for a teenager, busily absorbing experiences, Nosy Be must have seemed fabulously odd: the swords on the beach, the girls for sale and swimming with cows. Like the seabed, everything was conspicuous enough but didn't really make sense. Perhaps it's no different for adults, and we all understand much less than we think? Even Arkady Fiedler, the wandering Pole, had recognised this, back in the 1930s. 'The abundance of contrast stunned me,' he wrote. 'It seemed as if some madman was dizzily spinning a kaleidoscope.' Maybe that's how Lucy would feel, as she flew away: a little enchanted, and slightly bedazzled.

Meanwhile, I had a long road ahead, up through the north. Just before leaving, I met Georges on the beach, and he wished me luck.

'*Il y a juste eu un cyclone, et maintenant il n'y a plus de ponts.*'

(They've just had a cyclone, and now there aren't any bridges.)

CHAPTER 10

The Diego Interlude

*Madagascar reminded me of Robinson Crusoe's island
and I could not persuade myself that this was war.*

REGINALD COLBY, CHIEF INFORMATION OFFICER
Madagascar, 1942–43

*It is safe to say that Diego is the worst place in
Madagascar. And why limit it? It is one of the worst
places in the world.*

ARTHUR STRATTON
The Great Red Island, 1965

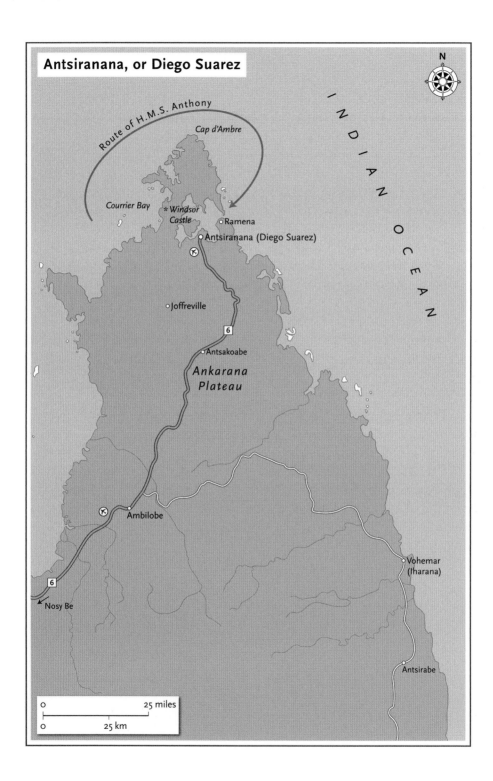

Antsiranana, or Diego Suarez

Route of H.M.S. Anthony

Cap d'Ambre

INDIAN OCEAN

Courrier Bay

* Windsor Castle

o Ramena

o Antsiranana (Diego Suarez)

o Joffreville

6

o Antsakoabe

Ankarana Plateau

o Ambilobe

o Vohemar (Iharana)

6

Nosy Be

o Antsirabe

0   25 miles

0   25 km

N

I N THE MIDDLE OF THE TWENTIETH CENTURY, Madagascar's history took a northerly turn. Diego Suarez is one of the greatest natural harbours in the world, and – just for a moment – it was also import-ant. The French had always predicted this, and for decades they'd been covering it in forts and guns and anti-tank trenches. But it didn't work out as they'd expected. First, they squabbled with each other, and in the summer of 1940 the island was closed down completely. Apart from bootleg whisky, almost nothing got through and nothing left. But then, eighteen months later, Diego Suarez had its big moment, and forty years of fortification and preparation were undone in two days. With that, Madagascar was captured by its oldest friend, and the BBC rang out across Tana. It wasn't the most spectacular war, but it was unforgettable in close-up, and had all the trimmings of make-believe, including mini-subs and knock-out drops, and a plane called the Walrus.

Most Malagasies ignore all this. They had no say in the events up north, and only ever appear in the footnotes. Besides, nobody cared much for Diego Suarez. To many it was like another country, distant and famously degenerate. Civil servants only ever went there if they'd done something wrong (or were about to). Even on Nosy Be, which was only 150 miles to the south, it was seen as foreign. People had heard of the road – the RN6 – but they'd never been up it. And why would they, said Georges, unless they liked holes?

Despite this, I was still keen to rummage around in this lost bit of history. Eventually, I found a driver. Although he was only forty, he'd already lost all his teeth. He also had a moustache like Stalin's. He told me he was descended from the kings of Ankarana, and that his name was Prince Henri.

A S PREDICTED, MOST OF THE BRIDGES were down. Only the big ones had survived, and those in the gullies had been sluiced away. We often had to take to the riverbed, bouncing through laundry, and then grinding our way back up the banks. It still surprises me, the things a cyclone will carry off: parapets, trucks and lengths of asphalt. At one point, the bridge had been replaced by a line of shipping containers, and we had to edge along the top before rejoining the crumbled road. If I hadn't been forewarned, I'd have assumed that another war had

been this way, even more vicious than the one before.

But however mangled it was, this was a beautiful road. First, it wriggled through dry forest, and then we began a golden climb into the grass. Eventually we got to Ambilobe, or 'the Place of the Big Orchard'. It was the last stop before the Ankarana plateau, and this was where the villagers came to stock up on crabs and skinned frogs and bundles of ducks. I bought a ladle made out of melted-down hubcaps. Prince Henri told me children here believe that if they're beaten with a spoon, they'll turn into a lemur. Because it was now late, we decided to stay. I took a room at the National Hotel, and overnight the ants found my rucksack and made a nest.

The next morning, we were up on the plateau. Prince Henri seemed to know everyone here: the rock-breakers, the washerwomen and the miners, digging for sand. As we passed, he'd slow down and wave. This time, it wasn't the Emperor wearing New Clothes but his subjects, and

in the pools below they'd strut around, splendidly naked. Once, however, we saw some Antankarana selling haunches of purple meat, still with its tusks and sprigs of hair, and Prince Henri scowled.

'*Sangliers*,' he tutted. 'They kill them with spears.'

We stopped only once, a few hours short of Diego. Ankarana's *Réserve Spéciale* sits on the edge of a much drier world, and offers one last blaze of greenery. That afternoon felt like a gathering of all the island's weirdest creatures. In my notes there are drongos, giant snails, crowned lemurs (with their punky orange highlights) and panther chameleons as blue as old copper. But Ankarana is also a fortified forest, and nothing

Above: The road north. 'They've just had a cyclone,' I was warned, 'and now there aren't any bridges.'

Overleaf: Diego Suarez Bay, looking towards Sugarloaf Island and the city.

gets through it without a struggle. In places, huge sinkholes, the size of theatres, had appeared among the trees. There was another *tsingy* here too, a vast expanse of hillside, bristling with gigantic stone spikes, and completely impenetrable. Prince Henri also found me millipedes, each weighing half a pound, and a velvety bean that, if touched, would trigger a maddening itch, lasting for weeks. Then, as we were leaving, we passed a waterfall where some Indian tourists had drowned, and Prince Henri left a tiny offering of honey.

'The ancestors,' he said, 'are often angry. Especially here.'

U NLIKE THE ANCESTORS, THE FRENCH had scattered their fury across the Cap d'Ambre. At first, we couldn't see their bunkers and all their old guns. From the mountains, the cape's great inlet, almost 10 miles deep and 10 miles wide, looked fabulously empty. Although it's the second biggest harbour in the world (after Rio), there was no sign of ships or prosperity or anything at all. I could make out nothing but a small island, improbably conical, and then – way off to the east – a narrow opening onto the ocean, known as *la Passe*. This is how the moon would look, if it had water. But then, as we got nearer, I could see the outline of a promontory, shaped like a gauntlet, and, sprinkled across it, the tiny city of Diego Suarez or Antsiranana.

At this point, a fort appeared high above us on the Montagne des Français. From up there, in that speck of masonry, the French would have seen everything – or, rather, nothing. They were the only people who'd ever wanted this void. The Portuguese had named it, in 1543, but had never settled. France took it on in 1885, during her early spats with the Merina queens, and almost immediately began building forts. Some colossal weapons had appeared. Even now, deep in their bunkers, they're like great iron monsters. Out in Number Five battery, I'd find four of these things, each stamped '1884' and the size of a railway truck mounted with a battleship gun. France, it seems, was taking no chances, and perhaps she was right. The Germans were still scrambling for Africa, and the British had yet to prove themselves *cordiale*.

All this puzzled Prince Henri.

'It's everywhere! You should see the stuff around *la Passe*.'

We agreed that, before heading south again, he'd take me out there.

The next morning, we drove round the bay, picking our way along its lunar rim. Towards the mouth, casuarina trees grew in abundance, and there was no sound but their sigh and the scrape of surf. Eventually we got to a checkpoint, where a soldier appeared, crumpled with sleep. A notice announced *la 7ème Batterie d'Artillerie Anti-Aérienne*, but there wasn't much left of their barracks. A great Victorian army camp was now quietly shedding itself of roofs and balconies and settling down in the sand.

Suddenly – *boom!* – the hills shuddered, sending up a ball of dust. 'Old bombs,' said Prince Henri. 'They're destroying them.'

With ordnance now bursting every few minutes, we headed out to the batteries. They'd fared better than the barracks. The great guns of Number Five were still levelled at *la Passe*, and – despite the bats and broken bottles – it still felt as if here was something for the dreadnoughts to dread. There were even more bunkers up on the headland, Orangea, and along the shore on the ocean side. It was like an armoured Riviera,

Number 5 Battery. The guns date from 1884, and were installed to deter the British.

or suburbia with trenches. The man behind much of this is known to posterity as Field Marshal Joffre but, back in 1897, he was only a colonel and an engineer. The cape, however, has never forgotten him, and even now there's a Joffreville, a Place Joffre, a Joffre monument, Joffre Barracks and a long, deadly ditch known as the Joffre Line.

Boom! Another puff of orange rose from the hills.

Up on the headland, there were still plenty of guns. Some were strewn through the scrub, while others were lolling in their huge concrete nests. I also found the old searchlight station, like a box at the theatre, overlooking *la Passe*. During the Great War, a few of the guns had been prised up and shipped to Europe, along with 40,000 Malagasy troops. The soldiers had had a busy war, and by the time it was over, one in ten would leave their bones in French soil. But, here, the guns had stood in silence. Orangea would be the greatest battlefield in the world, lacking nothing except a battle.

This time, I stayed on the edge of the bay, in a hotel called the Suarez. Years earlier, Jayne and I had lodged in an old manor house, up in the mountains. The French had always liked it up there: it was cooler and there was still some water. The *domaine* had been built at about the time of Joffre's defences, and with all the same pride and swagger. The forest had been trimmed into submission, and an entire hilltop tamed. Even the stables had fancy half-moon windows, and there was also a giant marble bath, a 'gun room', and a fireplace said to have been designed by Eiffel & Co.

At first, all had seemed well. In the mornings, we had visits from the fishman and Mother Superior. A lemur would also drop by, and would sit for hours with his friend, the toy camel. He would also catch millipedes, pee on them, and then rub the toxins into his fur. But, despite all this, things weren't happy. The owners, who were French, were deeply immersed in their own little war. At night, we'd lie in bed and listen to them fighting. Sometimes they had nothing left to fight about, and they'd just absorb the anger that seemed somehow to stalk them. I'd often wondered how their lives turned out. Just before Prince Henri headed off, I remembered to ask him.

'She ran away. He found a local girl, and then he died. The French never stay. Maybe they find this place unlucky.'

Perhaps he was right, and perhaps Diego Suarez is truly unlucky. Conquered but not settled, owned but misnamed, famous but ignored, it's never felt like a home. Even now, the city's a mishmash of architectural bits and pieces, with everything from pseudo-Classical to neo-rust. Half the town is covered in barracks, and every afternoon it shuts up tight and goes to sleep. There are still a few who remember the legionnaires, slugging it out in the local bars. The great French base only finally closed in 1973. These days, all sorts of people live in their old concrete blocks: Comorians, Indians, Chinese, Sakalava, Antankarana and Arabs. One day, perhaps, they'll feel they belong here, and that this is their city.

Diego has often horrified outsiders, particularly writers. The worst time was in the last few years of the colony. 'A dirty armpit of a town,' declared Arthur Stratton in 1958. 'It is far off, exotic, sordid, and as dull as can be.' The novelist Rupert Croft-Cooke thought much the same ('that fly-blown port'). Even the ever tactful Attenborough couldn't disguise his disdain. 'An indefinable air of idleness,' he wrote, 'envelops the town.'

But these days, things are different. The curious are creeping back, and there's now a trickle of visitors and a hint of paint. Perhaps we no longer worry about being exotic or even sordid. Everyone likes a little Havana. Parts of Diego look gorgeously rotten, and most of the cars are wheezy antiques. The worst of the drinking holes may have gone but there are still plenty of sots and salts who've washed up here on the ocean currents. It's not unusual to find the New Diegans dripping in bling, or working through lunch with a bottle of Scotch. As ever, noise compensates for style, and wherever I went there was always a blast of something, usually a funfair or gospel choir.

Diego still has its poxes and its insatiable itch. According to official figures, 10 per cent of all medical consultations are for gonorrhoea. But the sex trade is quieter now, or just less flamboyant. In Stratton's time, there was 'a stock exchange for whores', and they all wore belling skirts to be like Marilyn Monroe. All that's gone now – although I did once see a girl on a quad bike, cruising around dressed only in baby-pink spandex.

Of all the ruins, one stands out: the Hôtel de la Marine. It's said that, as they departed, the sailors had smashed it up. Now, there was nothing to stop me wandering through its weedy ballrooms and over-

The Hôtel de la Marine. It is said that the French sailors wrecked it when they finally departed in 1973.

grown halls. Everything had been plundered – including the roof and all the sills – and yet here it was, still gloriously foreign. At the heart of the building was a little *palmeraie* and, up in the walls, some gruesome plumbing. Once, I suppose, Diego was all like this, defiantly French. They say it was almost a miniature of home, complete with a guillotine and a powerful union. During the early 1940s, the city had even had its own fascists, its own armistice, and its own Vichy regime.

It was the Vichy that had worried Churchill.

By the autumn of 1940, the regime was well established in Madagascar. With the fall of France, Vichy had taken over most of her colonies, meekly running them at the behest of the Nazis. They'd had little difficulty winning over Tana. The *colons* had no time for General de Gaulle (and when the British sank the French fleet at Mers-el-Kébir, they weren't popular either). A new governor, Armand Annet, was installed at the Palais d'Ambohitsorohitra. As a dictator's stooge he was perfect: insecure and honourable, and never one to question orders. For the rest of his life he'd insist that he was the patriot, and that everyone else had got it wrong. Surprisingly, he'd meet little resistance. Apart from a shady broadcaster (called 'Free Tananarive'), there was only ever a short-lived spate of graffiti. 'DEATH TO VICHY!' read the daubs. 'ANNET TO THE EXECUTION!' When the perpetrators were finally caught, they turned out to be children, none of them older than seventeen.

Madagascar's pipsqueak regime was not in itself a threat to the British. The island had already been stripped of soldiers: since 1939, some 34,000 Malagasies had been shipped off to defend France (and would spend most of the war cooped up in camps). Although there were still another 8,000 left, they weren't going anywhere soon. All that was needed was a light blockade. Not for the first time, Madagascar was sealed off from the world. Across the island, there are still those who remember the scarcity: no cloth, no flour, no butter and no wine. Soap became a treasure, and all the hinges rusted. To lose a needle, as one man put it, was a family disaster.

But, for the British, there was real danger here. The threat was not so much from Vichy but from its new-found friends, the Japanese. They'd already collaborated over in Indochina, and then, in February 1942, Vichy had announced that it wouldn't hesitate to involve its allies in Madagascar. Worse, the codebreakers at Bletchley had picked up a message from the Germans, offering lukewarm support for a Japanese base. If this were ever to become a reality, it would be a disaster (or, as Churchill put it, 'one of Britain's greatest dangers'). Close to Madagascar ran vital shipping lanes to India, to North Africa and to the oilfields of Persia. Already, Japanese submarines were sinking ships in the Mozambique Channel. If they had a base in Diego, that would extend their reach by another 10,000 miles.

Churchill hesitated for months. As the architect of Gallipoli, he couldn't bear the prospect of another amphibious failure. But then, as the Japanese intensified their assault on the Indian Ocean, the options narrowed. On 12 March 1942, he ordered the capture of Madagascar.

BRITAIN'S PLANS FOR THE BATTLE ahead still beggar belief. If they'd been presented as a novel, they'd have been laughed off the shelves. Warfare isn't like this, or so people thought.

Even now, the ideas sound absurd. First, a task force would be cobbled together. Half of it (the 29th Brigade) would train in Scotland, and Loch Fyne would become a little Madagascar for a couple of days. The other half (the 17th Brigade) would have no amphibious training at all, and would have to learn the drill as they sailed south. Ahead lay a 9,000-mile voyage around Africa and through the U-boats, and they'd be going to a country no one really knew. The admiralty had some charts for Diego Suarez, but the only street map came from a guidebook. It would be Britain's first seaborne invasion since the disasters of the Dardanelles, and it was also urgent. The expedition had to be in Madagascar within two months.

Only the secrecy was sensible. For this, there really was a novelist involved. The thriller writer Dennis Wheatley was put in charge of deception, and would concoct an entirely fictitious landing way off in Burma. When the troops set out, they'd have no real idea where they were going, and all their crates would be stamped 'Rangoon'. The great adventure now had a code name too, the slightly clunky 'Operation Ironclad'.

In the strange way of warfare, these ridiculous plans were soon taking shape. On 23 March, a little army of 5,000 men set out, and as they sailed past Gibraltar they were joined by the navy. The ships of 'Force H' were supposed to be on convoy duty but the Americans secretly agreed to do their job for them. Although some of the ships were old, like the battleship *Ramillies*, they'd been at war for years, and were up for a fight. On the way round Africa, they sank a U-boat and called in at Durban. There, everything was unpacked, and the guns were fired and the batteries checked. All the trucks and tanks had to be sealed too (and, by the time this was done, South Africa was out of Bostik and waterproof tape). But then, on 25 April, everything was ready, and it was time to leave.

Churchill desperately needed a victory, and sent the force one last message: 'IRONCLAD MAY BE THE FIRST STAR IN WHAT WE ALL FEEL ASSURED TO BE A GLITTERING FIRMAMENT.' But privately he was worried. 'I felt a shiver of anxiety,' he later wrote, 'every time I saw the word Madagascar...'

Eleven days later, the fleet was off the west cape, threading its way through the minefields and shoals. Ahead lay the beaches of Courrier Bay and an uncertain reception.

THE ROAD TO THE BAIE DU COURRIER still disappears from time to time. During the rains, the track is washed away, and for the rest of the year it's powdered in sand. The French hadn't expected trouble from the west, and I could now see why. Courrier Bay is a good 20 miles from the city, and on the map there's not much in between: dunes, crags, salt pans and a great expanse of yellowy-brown. As for the west coast itself, it's almost completely bare. Spattered through its bays there are rocks and reefs, but little else. It was hardly the place to land a fleet.

For days, I couldn't find a driver ready to risk his axles. But then, one morning, Jeannot appeared with an ancient yellow taxi. He said he'd heard there was an adventure afoot, and wanted to come. It turned out that this was typical of Jeannot. Nothing was ever too much trouble, and he loved the idea of a day in the wilds. But there was also a touch of brilliance, and – with his prickly silver hair and his homespun English – he seemed somehow wired up to the mains. We laughed a lot that day, mostly about his car. It was a *quatrelle*, or Renault 4L, over forty years old.

'Will it make it?' I asked.

'Maybe' – he shrugged – 'and, if it doesn't, we die.'

It took us almost two hours to reach the coast. The *quatrelle* coughed its way out through the sugar cane and up through the ridges, and then made a noise like a bomber as it flew over the flats. There was still plenty of life out in the dust. At one point, a great yellow prairie appeared, speckled with cattle. Then came Anamakia, a village made entirely of tin, and famous for mangoes. But after that, everything slowed to a trudge, and we saw nothing but scavengers and salt-diggers and a few weary oxen. Way off on the coast, however, there was a new mountain, the shape of a witch's finger. I recognised it immediately from the military records.

'That,' said Jeannot, 'is Windsor Castle.'

He was surprised to discover the name was English, and had never heard of the battle out here. It felt like a lot to explain but I thought I'd begin with the curious story of Percy Mayer.

The Vichy didn't usually trust foreigners, but they'd always liked Mayer. Although he was Mauritian, he knew how to hold a knife and fork, and everyone loved his boozy parties. He was also useful, the best man they had at beating the blockade. He was always finding new places to land flour and petrol (or a bit of Scotch). You never knew where he'd pop up next. That's why no one was surprised to find him here, out in the sand, on 4 May 1942.

But there was another side to Percy, better known as DZ6. For years, he'd been working for the British. At one point he'd even sailed to South Africa to pick up a radio, which he'd then set up in his bathroom in Tana. As well as his shipping reports, he'd also recruited a fabulously colourful cast of agents (which included a zoologist, a prospector, an Anglican bishop and a good-time girl, known as 'Natalie'). For someone who'd never been trained, it was impressive tradecraft. DZ6 would be one of the most productive spies of the Second World War.

Of course, the real test came with Operation Ironclad. For this, his people gathered up a wealth of detail (although most of it was lost, en route through Nairobi). Then, as Force H set off for the Cape, Mayer hurried north and organised a party. It would coincide with the landings and all the top brass would be invited. He'd also acquired a large consignment of knock-out drops but, as things turned out, the booze was enough. With the party in full swing, he slipped away, and drove out here to Courrier Bay. As he ploughed over the ridges, he made one last note of the French positions. Then, in a final flourish, he climbed a telephone pole, and cut all the lines.

It was only then that his luck ran out. Arrested and searched, his notes were discovered. Immediately, he was taken to the Naval Headquarters, where he was told he'd be shot. But as they led him away, off to the cells, the French must have wondered: what was the party for, and why all the grog?

U NDETECTED, THE BRITISH SLIPPED in through the shoals. Even in daylight, it would have been a memorable feat of navigation.

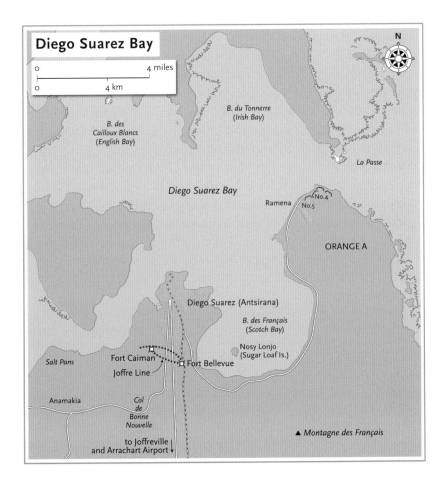

Diego Suarez Bay

0 ————————————— 4 miles
0 ———————— 4 km

B. du Tonnerre
(Irish Bay)

B. des
Cailloux Blancs
(English Bay)

La Passe

Diego Suarez Bay

Ramena   No.4
         No.5

ORANGE A

Diego Suarez (Antsirana)

B. des Français
(Scotch Bay)

Nosy Lonjo
(Sugar Loaf Is.)

Salt Pans   Fort Caiman   Fort Bellevue

Joffre Line

Anamakia   Col
             de
             Bonne
             Nouvelle

to Joffreville
and Arrachart Airport

▲ Montagne des Français

Only one ship was lost, a corvette called HMS *Auricula*. She struck a
mine and broke in two.

Despite the explosion, the French slept on. They'd always imagined
that if the British attacked, it would be way off to the east, in Orangea.
In their battle plan, the Royal Navy would come steaming through *la
Passe*, to be blown away by the giant guns. The British did nothing to
discourage this idea. That night, they attacked the guns with smoke
grenades and dummies dangling from parachutes. It wasn't a sophisticated ruse, but it sent the French in the wrong direction. Meanwhile,
out on Courrier Bay, the defenders knew nothing of this because, of
course, all the phones were dead.

In the early hours, the first commandos crept ashore. They only had one big battery to capture ('Number Seven'). It wasn't difficult. When the raiders burst through the door, there was the crew, still tucked up in bed.

One day, this glorious stretch of coast will be covered in hotels and Seaworlds, and there'll be a cable car up Windsor Castle. But, for now, it's just as it was that day, 5 May 1942. For a while, Jeannot and I stood right on the very tip of Basse Point, enjoying the sands and the distant mountains and the abundance of nothing.

Behind us, sweeping off to the south, was the long white stretch of Ampasindava. Here, the first soldiers ashore were northerners – 'the East Lancs' – most of whom had never been anywhere before. 'Blue Beach' (as they'd known it) had offered a strange introduction to the world beyond, with its tree-trunk boats and its enormous mussels, the size of

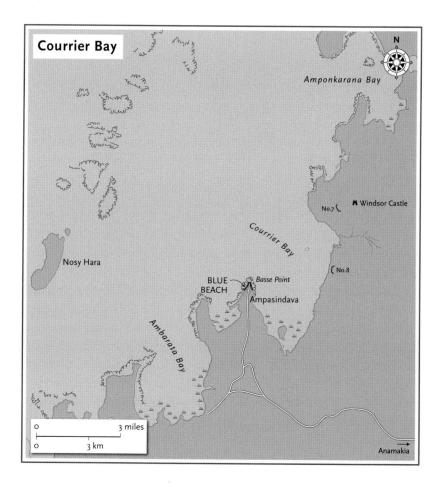

marrows. It must have seemed they'd travelled to the ends of the Earth, only to find themselves deep in the Stone Age. After a brief exchange of gunfire, they'd taken fifty prisoners, who, they were surprised to find, were Senegalese. The Africans were happy to be captured. They didn't care who won the war, as long as they were fed.

Turning the other way, the sea opened out into Courrier Bay. Here the water was as dark as ink but delicately fringed with mountains, rinsed in red. Across the bay, I could also make out other landing beaches, and a tiny bush fire flickering its way up Windsor Castle. I could now see the small fort too, perched on the summit. Throughout that first day, it had spattered the beaches with gunfire. That's when the Walrus came in, flying low and trickling bombs. But still the French held out. At this point the navy appeared, and, eventually, after sixty-five shells, the castle fell silent.

Among the soldiers now advancing inland, there were writers and pianists and several future judges. Rupert Croft-Cooke was already well known, and was now out front on his motorbike. In later years, he'd remember the war as a sort of khaki holiday – but not this bit. The heat was suffocating. Most of the troops had only handcarts to haul their kit through the dust. As he reached the salt pans, Croft-Cooke met three French prisoners, who said they'd been fishing. It was an odd encounter: only a few months earlier, they'd all been allies. No one could quite believe the French were serious and that they'd fight. Eventually, the three prisoners were packed off to Diego with terms of surrender. It was an unforgivable error: now everyone knew where the British were.

After that, life acquired a new fragility along the sandy road. The French were adept in defence, and at using the straw. Quickly and quietly, their ox teams dragged some big guns out to the ridges and hid them deep in the cane. They then sent their snipers forward to the little tin village. Croft-Cooke would never forget how his war began, and the look on the face of the man beside him. 'The bullet got him between the eyes and he died instantly, his limbs scarcely moving as he sat with the rest of us.' After that, everything slowed as the snipers pulled back, setting fire to the grass. For hours, the British were pinned down on the prairie, and so they called in their tanks, the Valentines and Tetrarchs.

Gradually, the battlefield began to move again, rolling upwards into the ridges. Near the top, there's a little gap called le Col de Bonne Nouvelle. These days it's the city dump, and the only people up here are sifters, wreathed in vapours and breathing soot. Back then, it was the perfect trap for British tanks, and the 75s were soon chopping through them. Before long, there was a pile of Tetrarchs, all bent and burnt.

At that point, another unforgettable character appeared. Jack Simon had been in charge of a Valentine, coming up from behind. As the tank reached the col, it was hit. In the chaos, one of the crew, Trooper Bond, baled out and fell under the moving wheels. He'd die begging his commander to finish him off. All this time, the French were out in the sugar cane, firing away. Unable to move, Simon ordered 'a dismounted action', which meant firing back with whatever they had, including revolvers. Eventually, however, there were no more bullets, and the tankers surrendered.

For most of us, that day alone would have filled our life. But Simon remained unstoppable. In the years to come, he'd become an MP, the solicitor-general, and – as Baron Simon of Glaisdale – one of the greatest judges of his generation. I remember seeing him once, around the courts. Everything about him was formidable: the intellect, the bearing and the black silk eyepatch. It's now a few years since he died, at the age of ninety-six. But I often wonder how he'd remembered that day, and whether, in his mind, he was ever back on the col. Or perhaps – like so many soldiers before him – he'd only survived Madagascar by trying to forget it.

Towards Cap D'Ambre

Windsor Castle.

View from Basse Point.

B EYOND THE COL, THE BRITISH advance hit The Wall.
Chunks of masonry still litter the outer slums of Diego Suarez.
Some of the bunkers have now grown upper storeys and have become
workshops and farms. One of them is a mango store, and another is
where the sifters live. In places, a strange metal hedge has also survived,
covered in 3-inch spikes. There are a couple of forts too, called 'Caimans'
and 'Bellevue', both looking pecked and dimpled but as gigantic as ever.
Between them, and running the width of the peninsula, are the remains
of a ditch, 7 feet deep and lined with bricks. It was a murderous design;
men could get in, but they couldn't get out. Nowadays it's full of orchards and old cars, and people grub out the bricks for making homes.

Oddly, all of this came as a complete surprise to the British. There
was nothing on their maps about *la Ligne Joffre*, and nothing in the
plan. Even though it was forty years old (and the ditch alone was 3
miles long), it had somehow vanished. The first to rediscover it were
the Royal Scots Fusiliers. They'd just marched 18 miles from the beach,
and were beginning to think that war was a picnic. The French waited
until they were close before flicking off the catches. Perhaps a dozen
were caught in the hail. Only a few got through, in among the bunkers.
One of them was a young subaltern called Peter Reynier. People were
so sure he'd perished that, a few days later, prayers were said for him at
Westminster Abbey. But somehow he'd survived, and later that week
he reappeared, in a field hospital. At that point, it was the French
themselves who put him up for a medal.

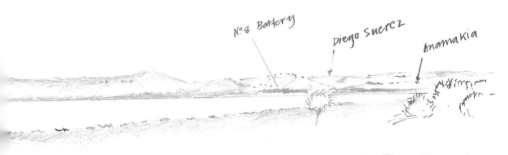

Courrier Bay, Diego Suarez

The Scots spent all the next day pecking away at the concrete line. General Sturges, the British commander, also sent in the Lancashires (both 'East' and 'South'), urging them on as if they were archers, off to Crécy. 'SPEED AND SAVAGE HEARTS IN THE ATTACK', read his message, 'TOLERANCE IN VICTORY.' For the South Lancs, the day went well enough. They managed to get round the back of the line, where they caused a donkey stampede, and took 200 prisoners.

But this still wasn't enough for Sturges. He was a veteran of Gallipoli, and knew what it looked like, a failing campaign. The line wasn't

Fort Bellevue today. With its spiked fences and brick-lined moats, it was Madagascar's Maginot Line.

moving, and the navy was almost out of shells, and running low on water. A new plan was needed. It would have to be something so sudden and bold the French wouldn't know quite what had hit them.

A S VON MOLTKE ONCE SAID, 'No battle plan ever survives contact with the enemy'. If Sturges had ever thought about this, he'd have realised that the enemy didn't really feature in his scheme, and that there wasn't much planning at all. His men would have no proper maps, no backup, no obvious objective and no Plan B. But he would at least surprise the French, by doing what they'd always expected: he'd put a ship through *la Passe*, and land his raiders in the heart of the city. The navy were easily persuaded to go with the scheme. Sturges told their commander, Rear-Admiral Syfret, that his sortie would 'take the Frenchman's eye off the ball'. Absurd though it sounded, Syfret agreed it was better than nothing.

Once again, there's a sense of fiction taking over. Fifty commandos were selected for the raid, and, with a smutty song, they were piped aboard the destroyer *Anthony*. There are still a few pictures of them, looking deceptively harmless in their macaroon helmets and baggy shorts. But they were brawny men – 'leathernecks' – who thought nothing of 'getting stuck in' and 'taking things out'. As the *Anthony* set off, they were already priming grenades and loading guns. It's 120 miles around the cape, and everyone was seasick. Along the way, the captain made a sketch of the harbour, marking the wrecks he had to avoid. Then, just before eight that evening, they reached *la Passe*, and, with all guns blazing, charged the gap.

Orangea's gunners were so surprised they barely had time to loose off a shot. For a second, there was a bright beam of light from the little balcony up in the cliffs. But then, from way offshore, came a squall

HMS *Anthony* draws up against the battleship *Ramillies*, to pick up the 50 commandos.

of shells, and out it went. Now everyone was firing, and not hitting much. From the mountains came delicate filigrees of tracer, but none of it found the *Anthony*. She did the last 8 miles in a blaze of sparks, but arrived at the wharf without a scratch. Finding no obvious berth, the skipper backed her up against the quay, and – with the engines still running – the marines scrambled over the depth charges and down the back. Their orders were to 'attack everything', and men like Ray Tebble would never forget that moment, as they leapt ashore. 'We fixed bayonets, and doubled forward.'

It's still possible to follow the trail of destruction through Diego. Just before he died, in 2015, Tebble had left detailed notes with a friend of mine. They make rugged reading, and are rich in salty terms and good-natured killing. But it's all there: the buildings they captured, the guardhouse they'd bombed, and the path they took. After silencing the port, the commandos had set off for the barracks. If I wanted to follow, all I needed was Jeannot, a map, and the old *quatrelle*.

'And while we're there,' said Jeannot, 'we can buy some chickens.'

This made more sense, as we got closer. The great naval base was no longer so naval, and had all the makings of a little village. That morning, there were strays all down the *Rue Militaire*, cockerels in the plasterwork, goats on the commandant's terrace, and strings of washing across his gates. The gardens now looked like little boxes of jungle, and a crowd had gathered at the navy's last tap. At the end of the road were some old brick barns, which turned out to be barracks for the native troops. Luckily for the marines, they'd arrived from the other direction. Completely lost, they'd scrambled up through some ox pens and onto the hill. Reaching a high white wall, they climbed over.

Jeannot looked at the wall, and whistled. 'It's the artillery base.'

That night, it had been all quiet, so on they went to the naval depot.

Jeannot never got his chickens, but we did find the depot. It was a large Victorian building, vaguely Palladian and splashed in whitewash. There were still guards outside but they no longer wore uniforms, and waved us away in their jeans and flip-flops. Their predecessors had been easily dispersed with a few grenades. Inside, Tebble and his companions were surprised to find fifty-six Allied prisoners, including Jack Simon and Percy Mayer (who was about to be shot). The captives were freed and armed, and joined the raid. Mayer would carry on spying for the rest of the war, and finished up in Limoges with the rank of major.

The raid ended at the commandant's house. Assuming that an enormous force had landed among them, he and his staff immediately surrendered. When this news reached *la ligne*, resistance wilted. The last few hours had been the fiercest of all. It's said the highlanders had charged forward with a roar of Gaelic. In the blur of bayonets a head came loose, and one of the Scots had his arm bitten off by a Senegalese. But then, suddenly, the fighting stopped, and the British poured through into the city.

'The noise of engines grew louder,' recalled Tebble, 'and out of the dust emerged the Squaddies. We handed over the prisoners to their tender care, and received cans of bully and biscuits in exchange.' In the small hours of the morning, on 7 May, the Vichy forces gave in. As the marines returned to their ship, their captain sent a message to Syfret: 'OPERATION SUCCESSFULLY COMPLETED. COAST DEFENCE GUNNERS REQUIRE FURTHER PRACTICE.'

O N MY LAST EVENING, I WALKED DOWN to the bay, and sat on the shore. The day put up a beautiful fight as it burst into flames before turning purple. Out on the water, Sugarloaf Island – or Nosy Lonja – seemed to float on the embers.

The great harbour had seen its fair share of fighting. British planes, Swordfishes, had taken a heavy toll of Vichy ships, sinking several merchantmen, a sloop and two submarines. Jeannot insisted that one of them, the *Bévéziers*, was still there, in the port, but all I could see were a few knobs of rust. Nothing is more unforgiving than war, except perhaps the weather.

As the battle ended, the bay reopened. For a while, the batteries at Orangea had held out. But when an officer called Colonel Stockwell drove out there with a bugler and two bottles of gin, a truce was soon agreed. With that, the *Ramillies* made her grand entry through *la Passe*. She'd only fired a few shells, but to powerful effect (each one was the weight of small car, and could plunge through concrete). These days, all that remains of her is a gun barrel. It sits outside the Imperial War Museum, worrying Lambeth.

That ought to have been the end of the fighting here but, three weeks later, the Japanese appeared. They'd always promised to do their bit. At first, it may not have seemed like much. Three weeks after the surrender, two mini-subs came bubbling into the harbour. Their first torpedo hit the *Ramillies* (putting her out of action for the next six months). The second sank the *British Loyalty*, a tanker. Too late, the navy put up a furious response. One of the mini-subs, M-20b, escaped the depth charges and made it out to some offshore islands. The crew – Lt Saburo Akieda and Petty Officer Masami Takemoto – might have got away if they hadn't been spotted by fishermen. Both died in the firefight that followed. As for the other sub, it's probably still out there, wreathed in coral, and a blaze of blues.

Before leaving, I paid a visit to the dead in the Commonwealth ceme-tery. It always amazes me, the way the British can make a foreign field feel like home. It was months since I'd seen lawns like this, or Portland stone. Altogether, about a hundred Britons had perished in the battle for Diego. Among the graves were a few names I recognised. Captain Palmer had been killed on the Joffre Line, and Trooper Bond had been crushed to death. One of the 'South Lancs', Private Dale, was only twenty-three when he died. His family's epitaph was impeccably stoical: *A life nobly given that we might live.*

But in the weeks to come, the survivors would often wonder about this, and whether Diego was worth it. Croft-Cooke didn't think so, angrily denouncing it as 'one of the most superfluous battles of the war'. Like others, he thought the Japanese would never have invaded, being far too preoccupied with China. Besides, a month after the battle, their fleet was completely obliterated at the Battle of Midway. If only the British had waited, none of this would have been needed. But he reserved special contempt for the French: they'd fought with 'pig-headedness', knowing they were bound to lose, rejecting an offer of honourable peace, and ignoring the fact they had 'a common enemy', the Axis powers.

The French, however, had also suffered. They'd lost 700 men, and all their naval vessels had either been crippled or sunk. In Diego alone, 8,000 servicemen were taken prisoner and marched down the Avenue de France, and off to the barracks. The best of them would change sides (including the commanders, Claerbout and Maerten, who fought with distinction during the liberation of France). As for the Senegalese, they all signed up to join the Free French. The rest, the hardcore Vichy sympathisers, were shipped to South Africa and kept in camps.

Croft-Cooke was right about their 'pig-headedness'. The island's governor, Annet, still refused to surrender. With his last 6,000 men, he vowed to fight on. It was about pride and bluster more than anything else ('*le drapeau français sera défendu jusqu'au bout!*'). But Churchill didn't rise to the challenge: they weren't worth the trouble. 'Madagascar,' he said, 'must be a security, not a burden.' For the next four months, nothing would happen. British rule would begin in Diego Suarez and peter out a few hours south, on the Ankarana plateau.

Those leaving were glad to go. 'I must admit we had no regrets in seeing Madagascar receding into the distance,' wrote Jim Stockman of the 17th Brigade. 'It was certainly one of the darkest chapters of our lives…'

From the British graves, I doubled back through the Commonwealth section. Some of the headstones here were inscribed in Arabic, and others in Swahili. But one in particular caught my eye: a Mauritian.

When the Malagasy war eventually restarted, all sorts of Africans had joined the fray. It was often Kenyans and Tanzanians out in the field, South Africans in the air, and Somalis on the boats. Now, here was a continent gathered together. It took me an hour to work my way round the tombs. Among them were gunners and Ugandans, launderers, askaris, a sea captain of sixty-one, and, of course, the boy from Mauritius.

It was really his name that caught my eye: FAYDHERBE. He was a distant cousin of my friend Christian, and in his inscription there was the same voice, playful and laconic: '*Devant ma froide pierre passant, dis une prière, car ici je n'ai pas d'ami*' (As you pass my cold stone, say a prayer, for I've no friend here). I don't know why this makes me smile. Perhaps it's the idea that death is somehow sociable, and that it's only here you're on your own.

M Y JOURNEY NORTH ENDED AS IT had started, in the air. Part of me would like to have followed the Africans south, over the plateau and down through the forest. But road travel hadn't got any easier in the last seven decades. Even without the roadblocks and blown-up bridges, it would've taken almost a week to get to Tana. Instead, I opted for the plane, and rode out to the old airbase at Arrachart.

To my surprise, life out here had evolved only slowly. The *Armée de l'Air Française* still had their insignia over the gate, and whenever a plane landed, all the sirens would sound. I even spotted a few stumps of the old hangar, looking twisted and shredded. On the first day of the battle, Arrachart had lost all its planes and buildings, and hadn't recovered. I once saw a photograph of some British officers – dressed in dazzling whites – inspecting this hangar. They look as though they were here for tennis, amid the wreckage.

Soon after the fall of Arrachart, the South African Air Force had taken over. Cut off for months, they became curiously feral. The men started growing beards, and wearing coloured hats, as if they were now a Flying Circus. They also gambled, traded pin-ups, and stole motorbikes

In Diego alone, the British took 8,000 Vichy French prisoners. Many of them would change sides and fight for the liberation of France.

off the British. But the flying was real enough. Setting out in old Marylands, they prepared Madagascar for new ownership, bombing Majunga and Tana, and some Japanese submarines off Nosy Be.

My plane took much the same flight path, down to Tana. As always, I struggled with the enormity and texture of the world below. For hours, it seemed there was nothing but terracotta, marbled in green. Perhaps Africans see things differently when it comes to scale. They didn't seem to mind the malaria or the months on the road. The East Africans would chase Annet deep into the south, covering a distance of over 630 miles. The French only ever fought on the roads, setting up ambushes and then falling back. But they hadn't reckoned with the Africans' stamina. By the time the Annet was caught, they were as keen as ever, but almost out of fuel.

Eventually, on 6 November 1942, the Vichy forces gave in. The ports had fallen easily (Tamatave was captured after a three-minute bombardment, and Morondava surrendered without a shot being fired). Little by little, the interior had fallen under Allied control. When the end finally came, Tana erupted in joy. The British held a ball at the town hall, and all the French came, as if nothing had happened. The atmosphere was stand-offish at first, but once the generals had left, the party took off. Only the missionaries disapproved. A century of British propriety was undone in a night.

No one was happier than the Malagasies. They thought the French had gone for good, and that never again would they have to pay taxes. These would be happy days under the bumbling British and General Legentilhomme, their obliging puppet. Surely things would never go back to the way they were?

For Madagascar, the greatest disappointment of the Second World War was the fact that it came to an end.

CHAPTER II

Rising

White men are rarely molested in Madagascar.

EDWARD F. KNIGHT
Madagascar in War Time, 1896

The rebellion took everyone by surprise in 1947.
Not even the rebels, let alone the majority of peaceful
Malagasy, knew what to make of it.

ARTHUR STRATTON
The Great Red Island, 1965

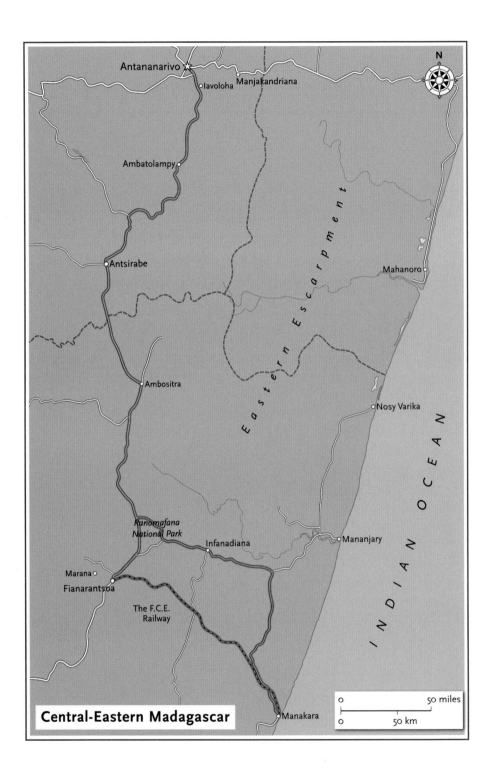

Central-Eastern Madagascar

The F.C.E.
Railway

	50 miles
0	
0	50 km

Antananarivo

Iavoloha Manjakandriana

Ambatolampy

Antsirabe

Ambositra

Ranomafana
National Park

Infanadiana

Marana

Fianarantsoa

Manakara

Mahanoro

Nosy Varika

Mananjary

Eastern Escarpment

INDIAN OCEAN

N

A FEW WEEKS LATER, I WAS WITH some lepers in the central high-lands. Their hospital, or *léproserie*, was out at Marana, deep in the eucalyptus. From the outside, it looked like a great red castle, with enormous steel doors and glass-topped walls. Completed in 1911, it was all the work of a Polish Jesuit. While everyone else was enjoying a golden age, Jan Beyzym was out gathering lepers. There are still a few pictures of him, sitting with his charges. There was no 'multidrug therapy' then, and so they had skin like pebbledash and branches for hands.

These days, the lepers like a few visitors, the director had told me. She was already waiting by the doors when I arrived. Sister Ramasinoro then ushered me in, through a labyrinth of cloisters. Somewhere, way off, I could hear someone chanting, and the rasp of a key in an old iron lock. For *les malades*, she said, it was a constant struggle with isolation. There were seventy in total, including sixteen admissions within the last year. Many of them never got visitors, and couldn't go back to their village. 'So they're probably here for the rest of their life.'

We stopped first at the dispensary. The leprosy itself is easily cured, said *la directrice*. She placed a small package in my hand. That's it, she said: a year of pills, one a day. But the stigma is harder to treat, and so is the damage to tissue. In Madagascar, once you're infected you're always an outcast, even after the drugs. Only that morning, a man of twenty-two had appeared, to begin his life as a leper. 'It takes courage,' said the Sister, 'to hand yourself in. And some of them leave it far too late...'

Beyond the dispensary were the dormitories. There was a courtyard for women, and another for men. The rivalry between the two was clearly intense, and reckoned in marigolds and pansies. I was to meet some of the old boys who'd been here forever. Ten of them shared a long, vaulted hall, laid out with stools and little iron cots. As it was cold now, they were all huddled together, wrapped in children's blankets. But when they saw me, they waved and smiled. What's it like out there, they joked, *quel temps fait-il?*

Soon everyone was talking, all at once.

Was I Polish? Did I have a garden?

Was there still a train to Manakara? And how much was a beer?

The Polish still sent money but they made their own clothes.

No one ever went anywhere.

Did I like Madagascar?

'*Tout le monde ici a peur de nous.*' (Everyone here is scared of us.)
For a moment there was silence, until one of them laughed.
In this country, he said, everyone's frightened of everyone else.

I F THE RN7 WERE EVER TO ADOPT a catchy name, it would probably end up as the 'Road to Revolt'. By the time it reaches Ihosy, in the deep south, it's already in bandit country (and, if you keep going south, the laws peter out, and so do the roads). But long before that – and all down the spine of Madagascar – there are some famously surly towns. Antsirabe has been a rich source of rebels since Merina times, and in 1811 the entire population of Ifandana was considered insufferable and driven over a cliff. Almost all the towns here had been punished with fire or a little bodily pruning. The men of Ambositra had, of course, paid in testicles ('the City of Eunuchs'), but plenty of others had been shorn of noses and ears. Not that this stopped them. By the twentieth century, the highlands were ready to rise again.

But, for all its tantrums, it was a glorious road. I was convinced that, for the next six hours, we were constantly climbing. Perhaps it's because there was now more sky and less of everything else. I remember boulders the size of tower blocks sitting in the rice, and a pine forest so vast it rolled off through the mountains and then faded away into the vapours. But the detail was also intriguing, and sometimes unsettling: the blown-up bridges and the scraps of railway. At some stage, we passed a cattle truck that had missed the corner and overturned. All the animals had been secured by their noses and tails, and I could now see them inside, dangling in mid-air, like angry puppets.

My minibus stopped only a few times. Once, the driver pulled over to buy some strawberries and a string of fish. Another time we stopped at a large concrete eating-house, to be blasted with hymns. The people getting on were now different. They all wore pillbox hats made of straw, and the women had knitted their hair into thick black coils, like rope. The man next to me was a bullfighter, called Hervé, and said he never took his hat off, even in bed. If you do, he explained, you begin to forget things, and eventually you forget everything, including your name.

And what do you call yourselves, I asked.

We're the *Invincibles*, he said: the Betsileo.

I COULDN'T RESIST THE IDEA of Eunuch City, and so I disembarked at Ambositra.

Hervé was also getting off, and insisted on taking me out to his bull-ring. It was only an hour away, he said, up in the hills. After dropping my bag at a hotel, and bolting some rice, we set off. It was a strange walk, both magnificent and quirky, a bit like a hike through Cervantes' Spain. The Betsileo built bigger houses than anyone else: enormous orange mansions, three storeys high and made out of mud. Despite all the space, everyone lived in the roof, with no one downstairs except the cows. Meanwhile, out in the rice, there were obelisks everywhere, great Quixotic structures, 10 feet tall and strangely thuggish. As for the bullring, it was tiny and gouged from the hill. The audience sits around the rim, said Hervé, while he and his bull would be squashed together in the pit below.

It's very dangerous, he said proudly, we're often killed.

On the opposite hill was a castle, or at least its outline. Although no bigger than a couple of tennis courts, it was here the Betsileo had made their last stand, in 1811. Their kings had been impressively despotic. One of them considered himself far too good to waste, and even had a slave to eat his toenail clippings. Another had ordered that, when he died, his favourite wife be trampled to death. But none of this helped much, in the big revolt. The last king was killed on the parapet by a Merina arrow, and then – as we now know – everyone else would lose their balls.

Ambositra had recovered from its losses, and was now as brash as ever. From dawn to dusk, everyone was out making noise. It might be nuns singing, sculptors chipping, *gendarmes* marching, or just the lantern sellers or the rat-trap man. The sound was always ecstatic. It sometimes seemed the whole town was out, trying to make up for the years of lost clamour. With few cars, it was left to the rickshaw-pullers to fill that auditory niche. There were hundreds of them, running around with handbells and the full range of flattery and insults. They'd keep this up for as long as there was sunlight, but then – as soon as it got dark – everything fell silent.

If I still wanted noise, there was always my hotel. Although it was known as 'Le Grand', only the fireplace was large. The rest was a hobbitry, a sort of human honeycomb of lumpy passages and cells.

There was a miniature courtyard too, just the right size for pixies and ponies. But the fireplace was truly enormous, and cut from granite. Every night a band would meet on the hearth and take up the challenge of creating sound. They'd whistle and sing, bang lids, and blow into bottles. Eventually, the audience would engage, and soon the Betsileo were all singing along.

These rooms hadn't always enjoyed such merriment. Back in 1912, they were part of a military stronghouse. Already, the French were beginning to hear strains of dissent among the noise. Although Madagascar was supposed to have been enjoying its own *Belle Époque*, there were now angry voices across the highlands. The following year, the *colons* got wind of a new society called the VVS (or *Vy Vato Sakelika*, 'Iron Stone and Network'). They indulged it for a while, until a rumour emerged of enough gunpowder to blow the colony to kingdom come. Five hundred were arrested, and eight of the dissidents were given hard labour for life. This seemed to work for a while, or so the French thought. Across Ambositra, there wasn't a sound except the whistles and bells.

To understand the anger, I took the road to Manakara. My *taxi-brousse* would only travel in convoy, and so we had to wait for two other vans. It would take four hours to reach the coast, crossing the plateau and then picking our way down the escarpment. Everyone was edgy out on the road. There were also roadblocks every few miles, manned by soldiers. They wore berets, old French uniforms and big black boots. It created an odd sort of anxiety, as if we were off to the Front or, at the very least, the Great Unknown.

It didn't help when the landscape fell away. Once again, the road dropped through the gorges, with little rivers pouring down from above. Near Ranomafana, we came across one of the minibuses that had left before us, now lying on its side with all its luggage scattered over the asphalt. The passengers were huddled in the verge, undecided which was worse, the road or the forest. The Betsileo believe that jungle this dark conceals all sorts of creatures, and they're probably right. Only a few years ago an entirely new primate appeared near here, called the golden bamboo lemur. It may sound cheerfully Chinese, but it's proof of an imponderable world between the plateau and the sea.

Eventually, the forest fell back, and the road levelled out. As always, the coast felt like another country with its thorn and its palm trees and its outsized bananas. The tribes too would be different now. One of them – the Antemoros – even had its own alphabet and had become inexplicably Arabian. But at least they all shared a common enemy with the Betsileo, and that was the road. It wasn't just this road, but all roads. Over the years they'd brought nothing but misery, including Frenchmen, Merina and governments. But worst of all was the curse they brought, otherwise known as work.

In 1926, France began work on the FCE railway. Some 10,000 Malagasies died during its construction.

The tribes' resistance to work had almost defeated the French. People here had been farmers and slave owners, and found the concept of pay faintly disgusting. But the *colons* were desperate for workers. For a while, they'd used the Merina system of forced labour. When that didn't work, they introduced the Chinese. But they still needed native labour to get things done. Another idea, in 1901, was a tax, which could only be paid in government wages. It was bound to fail. The Malagasies despised tax almost as much as pay.

Undeterred, the French persisted. Although there are many reasons they became unpopular – including land grabs and sacrilege – it was always the work that made them hated. In 1926 they came up with their worst idea of all. Even the name was sinister: SMOTIG (or *Service de la Main-d'Œuvre des Travaux Publics d'Intérêt Général*). Under the scheme, young Malagasies would be conscripted into an army of workers, drilled, trained and sent out to the camps for a couple of years. If the French had to do national service, why shouldn't *les malgaches*? But the rest of the world didn't see it like that, and in 1930 SMOTIG would be condemned as 'slavery' by the International Labour Organization. The *colons* were unmoved; the work, they said, had a 'high moral purpose'.

Roads like this were soon edging their way out to the coast. Some say they were more use to France than Madagascar, and that they were merely a means of exporting loot. But they did at least form a focus of revolt. Every inch was built with rage. If the Malagasies were going to be dressed as conscripts, and treated as conscripts, then it was only a matter of time before they'd fight.

MANAKARA HAS ALWAYS BEEN a town of departures. It was built by coffee exporters to despatch their beans. By 1939, Madagascar was the world's greatest producer of robusta and much of it came this way. The town had grown rich, packing up ships and seeing them off. It had even acquired a club, for those passing through, and a large concrete church. But habits had changed. These days, not much coffee leaves from here. Even the money seems to have somehow grown legs and wandered off. One day, perhaps, the only thing leaving will be the people themselves.

I'd honour this great tradition of departure by immediately booking a ticket out. In a town now whiskered in mould and weeds, the one thing still working was a little railway. The train would leave at dawn the next day. It was to be a big event for Manakara. Already the traders were setting up stalls around the station, selling fried bananas and chickens' feet. The booking hall too had clearly been busy. Although it was empty now, and felt like a hangar, I could still make out where the queues had been, slithering around in their muddy bare feet.

I aked the clerk how long it would take to Fianarantsoa.

'*Un jour*,' he said, '*peut-être plus…*'

Meanwhile, I had a night in Manakara. As it wasn't yet dark, I hired a *pousse-pousse*. It was hard to convey the idea that I didn't want to go anywhere in particular, just pedal around. The rickshaw boy wore a dish-dash, and had teeth like a cat. I soon realised that he didn't speak any French, or even Malagasy, and that everything I said just made him stare. If we were to make any progress, we'd need some help from passers-by.

I'm looking for a mosque, I'd say.

Down by the market, said the chicken-feet man.

And what's that, I'd ask.

Une fosse commune, said a woman in a turban. A mass grave.

And who's buried there?

Les fahavalo, she said, but more than that, she didn't know.

It was the rebels, I realised, adding their names to those who'd departed.

THE FCE, OR *Fianarantsoa-Côte Est*, isn't like any other railway. Usually, we take so much for granted, like the time of departure, or the day, or how long things take, and when we'll arrive. That's the joy, or the tyranny, of trains. We even know precisely which route we'll take, or at least within a couple of inches. But the FCE erodes all that certainty. Across Madagascar, most people aren't sure if it still exists, and then – when you get there – no one knows if the trains will leave, or when they'll arrive.

People can't even say which route it'll take. Every year, great swathes of track are washed away and replaced with something else. The worst of the cyclones was in 2000, when there were 300 landslides, almost flushing the railway off the escarpment. On that occasion, it was the

Swiss who'd rebuilt it. They'd even supplied a few old trains, which is why – that morning – I set out on the Sainte-Croix flyer, with a snowplough still fixed to the front.

There were only a few carriages. Up near the engine were the goods waggons, and a couple of trucks deemed second-class. These were so hot and full that some of the passengers would sit out on the steps, or cling to the sides. There were more people riding along on the couplings, and then there was my carriage with big orange seats and jolly Swiss maps. To begin with, it was like a souk, so packed with traders I could hardly move. But then, eventually, there was a distant clank, and as we began to move, the traders fled. That left only me, a few French cyclists and a party of Basques.

Today, an old Swiss ski train services the FCE. Some of the rails are German, confiscated after World War I.

'Amazing,' said the Basques, 'it's like the ski train…'

But the cyclists weren't so sure, and had already decided they felt unwell.

'*Je pense que ce sont les écrevisses,*' said one. '*Je vais mourir.*'

(I think it's the crayfish. I'm going to die).

We were soon clattering along through pale-blue paddy. In the dawn light, the chewed-up bridges and girders looked like monuments, and I couldn't help wondering if the whole thing was jinxed. The mountain people may now love their railway, but this wasn't always so. There was once a time when everyone hated it, especially the men who'd built it. Every year, from 1926 onwards, SMOTIG would find another 5,000 conscripts, who'd then have to cut their way up through the jungle and into the gorges. Over the next decade, they'd perish at the rate of about a hundred a mile, and by 1936, as many as 10,000 had died. They'd have no graves and no memorial, but it's not hard to imagine them out there, riding the storms and unleashing the mud.

After a few hours, we reached Sahasinaka, and began to climb. The slope was gentle at first, but soon the track climbed upwards through the ravines, doubling back, and then catching sight of itself way below. Over the course of our journey, we'd go through forty-eight tunnels and cross sixty-eight bridges, ending up a kilometre higher than when we began. When it was built, this railway would have been incomprehensible to the people up here: the tunnels so long they turned into night; the portals like castles, and the little stations – often works of art deco – perched in the cliffs. But now, for over 100,000 tribesmen, the FCE is their only link with the outside world. Unsurprisingly, wherever we went, crowds appeared, to watch the news come chugging through. At this, the Basques would get up and throw handfuls of sweets out of the window.

'Look!' they'd say. 'They're really hungry!'

At the end of our carriage was a guardroom, where the soldiers sat. They all wore camouflage except the captain, who had an orange rubber coat. Every now and then they'd patrol the aisles with their Kalashnikovs (I often wonder what they expected to find: a new generation

Overleaf: Rice fields on the FCE. The railway negotiates 48 tunnels and 68 bridges.

of rebels perhaps? – or some long-lost *dahalo*, or bandits?). It was also their job to control the crowds whenever we stopped. For the villagers, our visit was a big moment. Some had been waiting for hours with their trays of meatballs and doughnuts, beads, beer, ducks' eggs, spaghetti and pepper. Shivering with cold, they'd press up against the captain's cordon. Occasionally, however, children would get through, and that's when he'd have to give chase, pounding through the train, swatting little heads and slapping legs.

I don't suppose life on the platform had changed much over the years. Freight was still packed in baskets and thrown in with the sugar cane. I suspect that Frenchmen of my great-grandparents' generation would have recognised other things as well: the old coats, the tatty pinstripe jackets and the pillbox hats. There was always a pig, too, on a piece of string, and the higher we got, the less we saw of shoes. It was like a scene that had been shot in sepia and had somehow blossomed and come out in colour. Only the rails themselves seemed out of place, and were even older. Some were stamped 'HOESCH 1888'. It seems they were the spoils of war, plundered in 1918 (and had once been laid out across Alsace).

The arrival of the train is still a big event on the escarpment, with over 100,000 tribesmen depending on the railway.

Higher up, I noticed the hats change again (now square, and tabbed in red). Everyone here was smaller, but with powerful limbs and big splayed feet. I don't think I'd ever seen people with such perfect teeth, or so resplendently muddy. They all wore rags, and yet they had a presence about them as if they were beautifully dressed. The children were bolder too, and we were often raided for scraps and empty bottles. I asked the captain if we'd crossed an invisible border and were now in Tanala country.

Yes, he said. A fine people, maybe a little bit wild.

It's always been like this for the Tanala, or 'the People of the Forest'. In Madagascar's league table of ferocity, they're almost as bad as the Antandroy. But, unlike the southerners, the Tanala were always deep in the undergrowth, and seldom seen. Although they're merely a variant of the Betsileo, they've never been truly owned or ruled or brought to heel. Even as late as the 1860s, the Merina found it impossible to capture their strongholds. They'd get as far as the escarpment, only to find themselves showered with boulders and arrows. Every member of the Tanala tribe would turn up and fight, including the women, who considered warfare a form of sport.

When Edward Knight came this way, on his great trek of 1895, he found the Tanala 'untouched by any form of civilisation'. Their gangs, he wrote, 'are more brutal than any other natives on the island'. They wouldn't let anybody pass through their territory; they wouldn't deal with Europeans, and they had no interest in money. All their transactions were done in salt and beads.

We get one last report of them before the tragedies of 1947. It's from an English zoologist called Cecil Webb, who was here during the Second World War. By that time, the Tanala were deep in coffee country, and now had a railway running through their midst. Beset by sorcery, they lived in a state of 'naturally evolved communism', devoid of ambition or greed or anything modern. It was, wrote Webb, 'a stable existence at the lowest possible level, giving nothing and expecting nothing'. This, he noted with satisfaction, worked well for the lemurs. The Tanala never killed them because they believed them to be ancestors, the spirits of those who, long ago, had been lost in the forest.

But what no one had spotted was the rage. One of the first to die was a policeman, up on the plantations. He would be found by the army with his genitals stuffed in his mouth, and a note pinned to his body. LOOK YOU FRENCH, it read, YOU SEE WHAT OUR LITTLE KNIVES CAN DO.

ALTHOUGH THE TANALA WEREN'T THE only tribe to rise in revolt, they're often at the heart of this story. This is strange, given their rarity and their isolation. Perhaps it's their enthusiasm that marks them out, or the fact that they held out the longest and were the hardest to track. Up here, almost all the plantations were destroyed, and, for months on end, the eastern escarpment was run without rules.

While the details of the uprising are now strangely vague, everyone remembers how it began. There was no forewarning, just a sudden and massive eruption of violence. One of the first places hit was Moramanga, the little 'Chinese' town on the road to Tamatave. On 29 March 1947, a rabble, around two thousand strong, arrived at the barracks, armed with spears and slash-hooks. They had no obvious leader and not much of a plan. But they easily overwhelmed the Senegalese garrison, and a bloodbath followed. The surviving Senegalese then gathered themselves for revenge, and swept through the town killing whoever they found, including women and children. That night would set the tone for the rest of the revolt.

Within days, the east coast was on fire. Barracks were stormed and armouries plundered. Nearly all the small towns were captured, although Manakara held out (and acquired its mass grave). By the third week, the insurgency seemed unstoppable. Almost a million people had joined the fight; the east coast was beyond government control, and there were rebels active across a quarter of the island. The railway lines were under constant attack, and in Fort Dauphin the settlers were once again holed up in the fort and under siege.

The French still had no idea how to stem the rage. Initially, they blamed Moramanga on the independence party, MDRM, despite its condemnation of the 'odious attack'. Among those arrested was my friend Aro's grandfather (who'd spend the next year in jail). Worse, on 6 May, several hundred MDRM activists were herded into cattle wagons, which were then shunted into the sidings at Moramanga (the same place I'd had my encounter with the striking *cheminots*). There, the French opened fire on the trucks with machine guns, killing up to a hundred and sixty of those on board. When the news got out, there was international outrage, and in Paris the atrocity was likened to the deeds of the SS. One report even described it as the 'Oradour malgache', a bitter reference to the massacre of an entire Limousin village, Oradour-sur-Glane. The *colons* were unimpressed by their compatriots' squeamishness.

With all restraint abandoned, the revolt went wild. It was always at its darkest up in the farms. Across Madagascar, over 8,500 plantations were destroyed. The settlers were shown little mercy, and mutilation became a potent psychological weapon. Body parts were hacked off and fed to animals or tied to dogs. Most of the victims were from Réunion (only thirty planters from metropolitan France were killed). One of

A Tanala tribeswoman. Egalitarian and shy, the tribe bore the brunt of the 1947 revolt.

those who died up here was Maxime Dumont, a Mauritian. He was remembered by my friend Christian Fayd'Herbe, whose family was also here at the time. 'Maxime wouldn't hurt a fly,' Christian told me, 'and lived quietly with his Malagasy wife. She was killed first, speared with a *sagai*. They then got Maxime, and stabbed him too, just little cuts, but again and again. And when he lost consciousness, they gave him some kind of injection to bring him round – just so they could carry on tormenting him. It was a terrible way to go… And then, when they'd finished, they put his head on a spear, and left it up in the village.'

For many of the rebels, this revolt wasn't so much about independence as ancestors. Like the *fahavalo* of 1895, they believed in the restoration of magic and the natural order. Christianity, Frenchmen, education, medicine, all these things were offensive to the *razana*, or forebears. It wasn't just colonialism that had to be wiped out, but also every trace of modernity, in all its aberrations. Across the escarpment, anyone with the title 'doctor' or 'teacher' was killed, along with the *chefs de canton* and the *fonctionnaires*. It was easy to find men keen to do this cleansing, and to cut up the 'heart-stealers' so they were properly dead. Particular fury was reserved for the *assimilés* and the *evolvés*, those who'd taken up with Christians and foreigners, and who were seen as traitors to the taboos and the fetishes. They could expect nothing less than to be chunked and displayed.

By mid-1947, the rim of the escarpment had fallen silent. The coffee had been abandoned, and the plantations had emptied. Just for a moment, the Tanala were what they'd always been: simple anarchists, bred on magic, and living up in the cloud. They knew that whatever happened next, they'd have their amulets and their crocodile teeth, and that nothing could hurt them. Besides, the French – or *les Oreilles* ('the Ears'), as they were known – had long since gone, fleeing in glorious disarray westwards, up the line to Fianarantsoa.

Although it was now dark, I could feel the train subtly levelling out and gaining pace. At some point we'd crossed a watershed, and – from here on – the rivers, instead of crashing down into the Indian Ocean, would begin their long meander off across the country to the Mozam- bique Channel. It was also colder, and the cyclists were now nuzzled together in a litter of Gore-Tex. In the colourless glow of the carriage lights, the points sounded louder than ever, like great dysphonic bells, hammering out a tuneless night. I might have dozed off for a while, but it was more like concussion than sleep. At around midnight, I became vaguely aware of more changes, and of a city forming out in the rice. Amid the great glassy rhomboids of moonlight, sparks appeared, and brickworks, and then cement and light bulbs and a jumble of tin.

Eventually the train stopped, and as it lay there, hissing and panting, we all clambered free. It was too dark to see much, except the rain. But I did manage to find an old taxi to take me up the hill. It was another Renault, but this time stripped of almost everything, including the paintwork, the upholstery and all the handles. Running through its pared-down anatomy was a rubber fuel line, connecting the engine to a plastic bottle on the seat beside me. As we began to ascend, the car filled with smoke, so we had to stop and coax a few windows open. We were now little more than a chassis climbing up through the night-time clouds, at the whim of a lawnmower engine. Light-headed, slightly nauseous and numb with cold, I was beginning to wonder what might go wrong next.

Does it ever snow in Fianarantsoa, I asked.

The driver explained that they get a bit of icy stuff called *fanala*.

But no, he said, we don't have a word for snow.

FIANARANTSOA MAY NOT BE AT the heart of the country but it often claims to be the brains. Like Tana, it's a hierarchy based on hills. But unlike Tana, money alone doesn't get you up the slope. Here, it's an ascending scale of brilliance. At the very pinnacle of the city are the academics and the clerics, and then, falling away in ever-increasing rings of ignorance and sloth, there's everyone else. None of this is new: Fianarantsoa (or 'Where Man Learns Virtue') has always been about what you know, not what you own.

I'd spend a couple of days wandering between the tiers, in search of old rebels. Down in the rice, there was no one but the brick makers, the shoeless, the vulcanisers, the charcoal burners, the pickers and the chicken-herds. I had a feeling people down here don't survive seventy winters, and that there'd be nobody around from 1947. But there were a few traces of an earlier age. I remember several discarded railway carriages scattered round the station, and a statue of the Three Graces, now looking slightly less elegant in their nest of waifs and old cardboard boxes.

More promising was the next tier, where the artisans lived. This was the place to buy brushes and horseshoes, or oil lanterns made out of

The chicken-herds of lower Fianarantsoa.

old tomato cans. Although people here had heard of the revolt, they weren't quite sure when it was. But in the next layer were the bankers and the pig merchants, and the purveyors of Chinese Tupperware and fancy goods. I even found a vintner up here ('Côte de Fianar'), and a little business making cars. They didn't know any rebels, but they did show me a 'Karenjy'. It's a brave machine, with all the chunkiness of a Humvee and the whir of a kitchen appliance. In its own way, I suppose, it's ingenious, but still some distance from the top of the hill.

After that, the streets rose steeply to a shelf where the bureaucrats lived. This is where the French had built their clinics and ministries, a town hall, some big frilly barracks and a concert hall. There was also a cluster of war memorials, with everything remembered except 1947. My guest house, the Tsara (or 'Beautiful'), was up here too, and had been part of a convent. When I saw my room full of chintz and old cane furniture, I thought I'd somehow arrived in just the right era. But talk of rebels obviously wasn't good for business and so, when I asked about the insurrection, the manager looked theatrically horrified and changed the subject.

'How about a tour?' he suggested. 'Some lemurs perhaps?'

I carried on upwards. Across the brow of the hill was a forest, and in among the trees I could make out the university: great blocks of theology and law, rendered in cement and stained with a rich, black patina of tropical mildew. Then, up near the top, Oxford itself appeared – smaller and red-brick, but with just the same spires. Although, in close-up, it was more Himalayan than Home Counties, with staircase streets and villas on stilts, there was still something quaintly British about it. The London Missionary Society had found fertile ground up here, for sowing their dissent. Two of Madagascar's greatest thinkers and nationalists – Ravoahangy and Relaimongo – both went to the tiny college perched on the summit.

For a moment, I also thought I'd found a rebel. Mme Ramavamalala sold fish, and had a little house in the ditch around the old Merina fort. She remembered the *tabataba*, or 'the Troubles' as she called it, but was too young to fight. The guerrillas were fine young men, who called themselves *Marosalohy*, or 'the Many Spears'. She also remembered the power cuts and the aeroplanes and all the dead dogs. The *Marosalohy* always killed their dogs when they ran away. If they didn't, 'the Ears' would find them, untie them, and then follow them out to the forest. The dogs, she said, got many people killed.

I began to realise I was too late for the rebels. If there were any alive, they'd have to have been at least ninety, and that was too much in this town of smogs and damp. But I did at least meet a man who'd photographed the last of them. Pierrot Men had been taking pictures for over forty years, beginning with babies and passports, and still had a studio in the lower end of town. His photographs, however, had made him famous around the world, and he now had assistants and wore a quilted tweed jacket. Perhaps being part-Chinese and part-French, he'd somehow gone unnoticed among his subjects, and his pictures always find the Malagasies at their most intimate and unguarded. He was surprised I was here, writing about humans not animals. Me too, he said, my work's about people, and why they are what they are.

His pictures of the rebels, collected together as *Portraits d'Insurgés*, were now over twenty years old. They're all dead now, said Pierrot, as we sat leafing through the pages. In their photographs, the insurgents look defiant and stately, despite their old sticks and their knobbed joints and patched clothes. Some are forest people, Tanala, a little uncertain of the camera and where to look. But others have a surer gaze, and seem wearily urban. There were lots of reasons they joined the *fanafahana*, or liberation movement: tax, brutality, SMOTIG, the humiliation of the French in 1940, their defeat in Diego Suarez, and the promises of the United Nations. Some even assumed that the USA would come and free them. More than once French officers were seen in American fatigues and mistaken for liberators. There's always a hint of disappointment about these portraits.

Some of the rebels still wear the shreds of an old uniform, and had been soldiers themselves. For the thousands of men sent to defend France in 1940, independence couldn't come quick enough. They'd spent the war being shunted around, unwanted. First, they were sent east to prison camps in Prussia, and then they were returned to France as labourers and foresters. Many had joined the Resistance, becoming adept in explosives and sabotage. Then, when it was all over, the French – now looking weak and deadbeat – had taken a year to get them home. The *tirailleurs malgaches* would return furious, and spoiling for trouble.

In early 1948, the last survivors of the revolt emerged from the forest. Perhaps 80,000 had perished.

Pierrot closed the book, and I could sense him searching for words. What did they think of the revolt, I asked, after all these years? *'Ça n'a jamais fini. C'était avec eux tous les jours, jusqu'à leur mort.'* (It never ended. It was with them every day, until they died.)

On 29 March 1947, this ragtag army of old soldiers and tribesmen had emerged from the forest and poured into Fianarantsoa, several thousand strong. A few had muskets or shotguns, but most were armed only with *sagais* and *coup-coups*. They'd already cut off the electricity, and hoped that by now most of the *colons* would be dead, killed by their servants. But the plan had been betrayed, and the French had escaped and were now holed up in the little concert hall. More joined as the *Marosalohy* began running up through the streets, clinking with amulets and metal. Many were now naked, in the great tradition of war, and invoking the blessings of those who'd already died.

AMONG THOSE BARRICADED INSIDE the concert hall was the Fayd'Herbe family, including Christian, then aged eight. 'We used to call it the *Trano-Pokonolona*,' he told me, 'the People's Hall. And we did all kinds of things there… recitals, plays, a bit of Molière perhaps, or some *Comédie-Française* to entertain the troops. Anything really, *tous les trucs français.*'

The hall was still just as he'd described it: a long single-storey building, with slots for windows, and a Norman tower at either end. Along the front was a veranda, with a white balustrade, and then all around was a wide, open space where a market was held. Inside, there was nothing but a great expanse of polished teak, and the little slots, high in the walls. Whether or not the French had ever intended to create a fortified theatre, it was a natural citadel, and the perfect place to make a stand. On 28 March 1947, the entire French community had assembled inside.

'My parents were told to bring nothing except guns,' said Christian, 'and we waited until dark, and then all set off for the concert hall. Once there, we were in one big room, and I remember playing. It was very exciting…'

'Weren't you scared?'

'Not then. We loved it. Later, I looked out of the little windows (even though we weren't supposed to). It was dark outside, and the soldiers had arranged all the cars around the hall, facing outwards. Then, when they heard the rebels, they turned the headlights on, and – there they were! – a great mob with spears. Suddenly everyone was firing, both the soldiers and *les colons*, with their hunting rifles. And I remember the rebels were shouting "*Rano fotaka!* Muddy water!", because they thought their charms would turn the bullets into water.'

'It must have been carnage…?'

'Yes, I remember looking out, and seeing the bodies piling up. They died one on top of another. And then something changed – maybe they realised – and suddenly they pulled back! There were corpses everywhere, all around us. You don't forget these things. As a kid, it made a big impression. And all the people shooting.'

For four months the settlers held out, in the concert hall. 'The soldiers had a heavy machine gun,' said Christian, 'which they kept moving around, to make it seem we had more guns. It was a really big thing, and took three men to move it. I remember them hauling it up to the turrets…'

Slowly, France began to respond. Until then, Paris had never taken the threat seriously, and there were only 6,500 troops in the colony (of whom 1,000 were Senegalese, and 4,000 were Malagasy). But it wasn't easy gearing up for another war. France was already facing a revolt in Indochina, and couldn't afford a second front. So, as Christian put it, 'they had to hit it hard'. All civil aircraft were commandeered, and the settlers were armed and organised into little militias. Then the colony was sent a new general, Pierre Garbay, who'd become known as 'the Butcher of Madagascar'. There'd be more troops too. By July 1947, five North African battalions had arrived, and these would be followed by paratroopers, Senegalese, and *légionnaires*. Eventually, there'd be 30,000 soldiers on the island, and they could begin combing the forests in their search for dissent.

The French were just as brutal as the *insurgés*, but more efficient. While the rebels were intimate in their violence, the French could be detached and remote. Their planes came from nowhere, and scattered the forest with gunfire and deadly ordnance, and then were gone almost before they'd arrived. The troops too seemed somehow aloof, rolling across

Even now, the gendarmes struggle with banditry. In 2018, 18 officers were killed by the *dahalo*.

the landscape with industrial ease and sowing it with terror. It's said that many of the *légionnaires* were German war veterans, desperate for a return to military life. By contrast, the Senegalese were more spontaneous, and would rekindle the idea – still prevalent among many Malagasies – that all Africans are savages. They and the Moroccan *tirailleurs* would be particularly remembered for the way they moved around, burning villages wherever they went, and shooting anyone in a raffia shirt.

There wasn't much justice for those who were captured. In Fianarantsoa, the lucky ones were sent to the city jail, Ankazandrano (which still looks like a Victorian piggery in the middle of town). The rest were sent out to the camps to be shot or forgotten. In Fort Dauphin alone, the tribunal ordered the execution of 120 suspects, including doctors, governors and *chefs de canton* (although, fortunately, even the army recognised that this was madness, and refused to man the firing squad). Pierrot's photographic assistant nearly lost his mother in the clean-up.

She'd been caught with the rebels, and was about to be shot. 'But they spared her,' said Mr Tsangandahy, 'because she had a snapshot of my father, dressed in military uniform, out in Indochina…'

The army's approach to suspects wasn't normally so touching. There was the usual panoply of terror: people dunked in piss and petrol and thrown out of planes. Here, a 'wooden horse' wasn't something remotely equine but a way of tying someone into a human knot. Journalists weren't allowed near any of this, and it was left to Albert Camus to lead the protests in his magazine, *Combat*: 'We did in Madagascar that which we accuse the Germans of doing…'

Eventually, by early 1948, the revolt began to fizzle out. After the best part of a year, life became eerily normal. Gradually, the settlers began to return, including families like the Fayd'Herbes (after the concert hall, they'd fled to Mauritius, where they'd spent the next six months). Soon, they were planting again and selling Renaults and making wine. But it was now a very different landscape. Across the Betsileo plateau, whole villages had disappeared. Tens of thousands had fled to the forest. If it wasn't the army driving them out, it was the rebels, demanding recruits. Of those who fled into the *savoka*, some wouldn't emerge for a year, and many wouldn't return at all. According to the Butcher's own figures, over 80,000 people had perished, most of them dying of starvation out in the jungle. The Tanala, of course, had been decimated, and the tribe would never be quite the same again.

The recriminations went on for years. The colonial authorities registered 558,000 captives, and of these, 5,765 were tried and sentenced. Most of them were given hard labour, although another twenty-four were shot. There were also show trials for the nationalists, under the great glass bosom of Andafiavaratra Palace. They were all convicted, and their lawyers beaten up. Fianarantsoa's own home-grown hero, Ravoahangy, would be shipped off to Corsica, where he'd spend the next ten years in Calvi's oubliette.

Some say that Madagascar has never recovered from 1947. It would certainly never be the same colony again, dreamy and compliant. But what horrifies Malagasies is not so much the savagery of the French but their own ferocity. The revolt had opened up old fractures, and had revealed that, under the slightest pressure, people would still turn on each other. Along the eastern escarpment, thousands had died at the hands of their neighbours, and the middle classes had been all but wiped out.

'You couldn't even find a barber,' said Christian. 'Everyone had gone.'

FOR ANYONE PICKING THROUGH the ashes, only the Merina are missing. *Les Tananariviens* were never keen on the revolt, and took little part. It wasn't that they didn't want independence; it just made them anxious, the thought of *les côtiers* up in arms. Even their big nationalist party, MDRM, was horrified by all the witch doctors and warriors and the fanatics out in the forest. It denounced them as 'cruel reactionaries, savages, dangerous and wild'. It was even worse for the aristocrats, who were naturally uncomfortable with the idea of revolt. For them, the insurrection was like a journey backwards through the last hundred years, and they saw their power beginning to unravel. Another group, PADESM, was more accommodating of the *côtiers* but didn't see the need to upset the French. This was not a view it was wise to express out on the escarpment, and nearly two thousand PADESM people were sliced and killed and sent out with the dogs.

Soon, all the tribes were settling old scores, and the course was set for the rest of the century. These days, every town hall down the spine of this country bears the slogan *MALAGASY DAHOLO, TSY MISY AVAKAVAKA*, or 'We're all Malagasy, there are no more tribes'. But even within these words there's a tiny vestige of anxiety. I sometimes wonder if the old leper was right, and that – at least out here – everyone's frightened of everyone else.

SOMETIMES IN MADAGASCAR YOU wonder whether it's you going mad, or everyone else. I had a moment like this on the journey north, in my *taxi-brousse*. The other passengers wouldn't say much, but whenever they heard Billy Ocean or 'Power of Love', they'd sing their lungs out. Up in the hills, we passed a lorry painted gold, and a pigherd, alone on the savannah, wearing only a shawl and a Father Christmas hat. Then there were the little wooden trolleys, with wheels made out of old brake discs, which the locals would ride straight down the mountain – whooping with joy – and with no obvious cargo except themselves. None of this, I realise, is evidence of insanity, but it was confusing, at least for a while. Just when you expect to find Malagasies at their most miserable, they come up smiling, or announcing that they've been Saved, or that this is the best day ever.

The happiness was catching, and I was soon mumbling along. I loved the enormity of that day, and the tiny villages up on the ridges. Some were so small it was like picking our way through a room full of toys. There was always a watch mender, and a rickshaw full of chickens, and every householder had his vaccination records chalked to the door. How could people live such miniature lives in such a gigantic world? Once out on the savannah we might see no one for miles, and then suddenly, out of nowhere, we'd come across a *famadihana* and a crowd of revellers off to dig up the dead.

France had eventually wearied of this landscape, and of fixing its bridges after the storms and the bombs. She'd never enjoyed Madagascar in quite the same way after 1947. The revolt had cost the lives of 350 soldiers, and over a ten-year period she'd spend the equivalent of $4 billion in crushing resistance and repairing the damage. Although, in 1951, the Minister of Overseas France – a youthful François Mitterrand – had declared that Madagascar would always be French, the public felt differently. 'Of what use is it,' asked *Paris Match* in 1956, 'to pour out huge sums of money into an outdated empire?' Two years later, General de Gaulle was elected with a mandate to dissolve the colonies, and turned up in Tana, telling people that soon Madagascar would all be theirs. By 26 June 1960, the French were gone.

It wasn't the kind of departure where anyone actually left. There were still 68,000 Frenchmen on the island, including an army, a navy, a thousand government advisers, and 250 presidential staff. All that had changed was that the Malagasies got the titles and ministries, and the French no longer paid. France even retained a palace – the old *résidence* – and got to choose the politicians. The new president, Philibert Tsiranana, announced that everything would carry on just as before, and that the *colons* who'd stayed would be regarded as the 'nineteenth tribe'. As he famously put it, 'You can't kick away the canoe that helped you across the river'.

Madagascar would continue like this for the next twelve years. For the settlers, it was like France in draft, with French in the classrooms, the town halls, the constitution, the menus and the maps. In some ways, it was even better than France, because the clock had stopped in 1960. Even in the early 70s, a girl here couldn't wear a miniskirt, and boys with long hair could be forcibly shaved. The French press called it the '*Île heureuse*', always a sign of trouble to come.

The happy days of Little France ended abruptly on 18 May 1972. Along the spine of the country, from Tana to Fianarantsoa, the towns once again rose in protest. It was an odd struggle, known as the *rotaka*, and lasting a week. It began with the arrest of a boy called Modeste Randrianarisoa, down in Ambalavo. One moment he was out on the street, denouncing neo-colonialism, and the next he was lifeless after a relentless battering down in the cells. When they heard this, students everywhere dressed up in cowboy outfits and came out on the streets.

These latest rebels called themselves ZWAM, or the 'Malagasy Western Slave Youth' ('*Zatovo Western Andevo Malagasy*'). Modelling their uprising on the Spaghetti Westerns of the time, they could be casually violent. In Tana, they set fire to several shops and the town hall, and swaggered around as if this was the O.K. Corral. *Something fishy is going on*, announced President Tsiranana, *thousands will die!* As one of my friends put it, he then went 'a bit gaga' and started shooting cowboys. Forty-nine students were killed in the stand-off on 13 May 1972, and another 400 were packed off to a penal colony. But it couldn't last. A few days later, Tsiranana resigned.

With that, the French surrendered their palace, and promised to abandon their bases within two years. Once again, the Malagasies declared their independence, this time for real. It was the end for ZWAM and the cowboy-slaves, and the beginning of 'the Second Republic'. For the first time ever, Madagascar wasn't just united, it was also free to make its own decisions, and to pursue happiness in its own peculiar way.

AFTER 236 KILOMETRES OF BILLY OCEAN and the rolling road, I took a break, at Antsirabe. It's an unlovable city, despite all the foreigners who've tried to cheer it up. The Norwegians were the first here, 150 years ago, with their pine trees and churches. Then came the French, lavishing everything with frets and towers, wrought-iron

balconies, and great tapestries of brick. Their railway station was so elaborate it had ended up looking Chinese, with giant red doors and pagoda roofs, and a tiny clock tower, perched on top. But even the French never truly loved Antsirabe. It was just another version of Lille: worthy, industrious, forgettable, and damp.

Although things have got a bit scuffed and dusty over the years, Ansirabe still has a hint of that northern French city. Across the grid of old warehouses and mansions, there are even a few new factories, all the colour of a rainy day. This is where the beer's made, and all those garments that Europeans will wear only once. I also spotted a *fromagerie artisanale*, and an old brickworks trailing a great black nimbus of smoke, like an ancient steamship. As in all industrial cities, everyone was rushing around, not getting noticeably richer, but keeping things going. The brickworks' carters still didn't have shoes, and across town there were over 5,000 rickshaw boys, each getting by on about a dollar a day. My favourite character was the *chausseur*, who walked around festooned in footwear, as if he was wearing a suit of shoes.

At the top of the town were some hot springs. Around a hundred years ago, the French had come up with the idea of a resort up here, and had branded it *Le Vichy de l'Océan Indien*. Although the pump house was now crumbled in rust, and the water smelt like recycled sweat, a magnificent folly had somehow survived. Built in 1922, the Hôtel des Thermes looks like a wedding cake designed by architects on absinthe. I suppose it was designed to glorify the empire, and – up in the icing – everything's there: art deco, classical balustrades, lacy trimmings, a bit of Chinese, some Merina pillars and a touch of Tiffany.

But these days, it's hard to enjoy this sort of place, and, with the French long gone, Antsirabe is now more sarcophagus than spa. By the mid-1970s, *la Belle Époque* was finally over, and two-thirds of the settlers had left. Some drifted away, others were forced out. *COLONS DEHORS*, read the graffiti, SETTLERS OUT! Many would leave taking nothing with them but their expertise (and whatever they could carry). I once met a Parisian travel agent who remembered all too well the eviction, and her sudden departure at the age of five. Her grandparents

The Hôtel des Thermes, like a wedding cake designed by architects on absinthe.

had lived here for forty years, and would arrive back in France feeling penniless and foreign. The Hôtel des Thermes is all that's left of a great French dream.

Inside, it wasn't even that. As I made my way through the lobby and down the hall, I realised that every trace of Frenchness had been eradicated and replaced with geometry and thick brown varnish. I recognised the style immediately: the ugly frosted lamps, the brutalism, and the politburo curtains. Everything about it seemed to proclaim a new era: welcome, it said, to the Malagasy Soviet Socialist Republic.

M ADAGASCAR WOULD NEVER HAVE its own Stalin or Lenin, but it would get Didier Ratsiraka.

Like all great commissars, he emerged from the gunsmoke. After the fall of the French puppet, Tsiranana, there'd been a period of chaos. First to seize power was an aristocrat called General Ramanantsoa. This pleased no one except a few Merina, and so the rioting continued. Eventually, the general was replaced by a colonel, descended from the *andevo*, or slaves. Colonel Ratsimandrava had lots of enemies, not least the nobility, the French and the southerners. On his fifth day in power, 11 February 1975, he was driving through Tana's Upper Town when he ran into a blast of machine-gun fire. The place where he died is now a roundabout, piled with flowers. No one was ever punished for his murder, but by the time the dust had settled, it was Ratsiraka who'd taken charge.

The 'Red Admiral', as he's known, has now been around over forty years. For many Malagasies, he's the leader they've known all their life, and since 1975 he's always been either in power, in exile, in the wings or in the shadows. To begin with, he seemed full of promise. At only thirty-eight, he'd already risen through the ranks of the navy, and under the French he'd commanded a frigate. He also had his own party, called *Avant-Garde de la Révolution Malgache*, with a startling agenda of reform and change. The aristocracy would no longer run the country, and the Merina would share their power with the other eighteen tribes; women would acquire equal rights on divorce; and Madagascar would stop sounding French, with all the old cities being given new names. This didn't entirely work (and Taolagnaro is still Fort Dauphin), but at least the future would look Malagasy.

Didier Ratsiraka, 'The Red Admiral', starring in his own Little Red Book.

Didier's difficulty is that he always had a touch of *folie de grandeur*. He was the admiral of a fleet that didn't really exist, and the Supreme Revolutionary Council, over which he presided, was usually no more than his family and friends. Although he was a canny survivor, he was never quite as brilliant as he imagined, and his speeches would often get lost in a maze of subjunctives. He seemed to love the idea that he was somehow chosen ('I'm an officer by profession,' he'd say, 'and a politician by accident') and that he was the Mao Tse-Tung of the Indian Ocean. He even had his own 'Little Red Book', or *Boky Mena*, full of diktats and Didi-isms. Soon, there was gobbledegook everywhere, all dressed up as 'Christian-Marxism'. One of Didier's favourite ideas was *tous azimuts*, or 'All Directions'. It implied that every avenue would be explored but – in reality – almost all of them led to Russia.

Over the next fifteen years, the spirit of the USSR would seep deep into the subsoil. Although Madagascar would have other friends – like Libya and North Korea – it always emerged looking like Russia. By the 1980s, Aeroflot was the only airline calling by. The Soviets also sent advisers and teachers, and even now there are remote tribesmen who can still manage a *spasiba* or perhaps a *puzhalsta*. But, mostly, Moscow sent weapons:

thousands of Kalashnikovs and a fleet of jets. At one stage, Didier paid over $300 million (or the equivalent of a year's export earnings) on a consignment of MiG-21s. A few years later, the planes were spotted by the writer Dervla Murphy, standing in the long grass, and looking – as she put it – 'rather under-exercised'.

Despite all this, Didier still had his fans, including my friend at the human rights commission, Mireille Rabenoro. 'Politics was less corrupt,' she insisted, 'and life was easier then.'

Soviet Madagascar: guns but no butter.

It was certainly simpler, during the Russian years. Didier would strip the economy of all complexity, including profits and credit and almost all private ownership. One day, the oil executives arrived at work to find troops in their offices. Nearly everything came under public ownership, from cinemas to cotton. By 1977, 60 per cent of the economy was state run, and it began to grind along at a Soviet pace. During the Didier years, industrial production would shrivel by three-quarters, and even though the population doubled, the average GNP growth was an inglorious 0 per cent. In 1980, the last of the French car plants closed, and the government was reduced to distributing soup. Friends in Tana would often try to explain to me what life in the Malagasy *oblast* was like.

'The shops were empty,' said my fixer, Nivo.

'We had to get up at four,' said Lydia, 'just to buy rice.'

'…same with salt and flour…'

That's when the water failed, people said, and the electricity.

'…and you couldn't even post letters…'

'…and there weren't any doctors…'

Sometimes, it seemed, the only things left in abundance were the guns made in Russia. By the end of the 1980s, Madagascar was one of the poorest countries in the world (ranked at 186 out of 204). Antananarivo, wrote journalist Tim Ecott, was 'a twilight city beset by potholes, power cuts, bubonic plague and cholera… vagabonds and cutthroats stalked the streets.' Despite all the Marxism, only the rich seemed to thrive in the squalor. For some reason, they weren't paying any tax at all. I once met a diplomat who was sent here by the World Bank to find out why. He managed to get an interview with Didier, and put the question directly. The president looked at him as if he was mad. 'You cannot expect the rich to pay tax,' he snapped, and that was that. In Didier's Madagascar, it seems, you were either too poor to pay tax, or so rich that no one could touch you.

By this stage, Didier had worked up a chronic case of paranoia, and began sifting the country in the search for detractors. In Tana, this would spark a curiously feudal struggle. For some time, Didier had been using paramilitaries, made up of *andevo* or 'slaves'. In response, the young aristocrats had started training in martial arts, and prowling around in Kung Fu outfits. For the second time in a decade, the government was facing an uprising in fancy dress. But, this time, Didier was having none of it, and sent in the army to smash up the gyms.

Plenty of others were caught up in the raids, including the Muslims, the Comorians, and the *Karana* or Indians. But the real bogeymen were the South Africans. Didier insisted that Pretoria was about to launch a full-scale invasion, and fortified his palace with anti-aircraft guns. Meanwhile, it was always assumed the South Africans would come pouring ashore at Fort Dauphin. For years, the town was on edge. On one occasion, some children were caught with a bonfire, and were arrested for signalling to enemy submarines. Another time, a Frenchman let off a flare, and at that point all the foreign residents were rounded up and thrown into jail, some of them only emerging five months later. Didier also once sent a TV crew down to film the landings. For days they stood there – Canute-like – watching as the sea did nothing, and a little more reality ebbed away.

ABOUT 10 MILES SHORT OF TANA, we passed an enormous mock-up of the Queen's Palace. My *taxi-brousse* didn't stop but I'd seen Iavoloha several times before. I always thought it looked like a plaster cast of the real thing, or like some strange Cyclopean starship made of styrofoam. But everyone assured me that the concrete was real enough. There was even a rumour that, during construction, Iavoloha had used up so much cement it caused a national shortage. It made everything look small, even the forest. Inside, people said, there were miles of corridors, and the carpets went on forever. The whole thing was a gift, apparently, from Supreme Leader Kim Il-sung. When Madagascar wasn't being Russia's plaything, it was a far-flung outpost of North Korea.

Didier was also enjoying a little mockery here. Although he was married to a Merina, he'd never trusted them. He once told his own people, the Betsimisaraka, that – given power – the Merina would own them again; that they'd reinstall a queen; that everyone would have to mourn her dead dog, and crawl up to Tana with an offering of eggs to build her new palace; that the Merina would become tax collectors again, and that, once again, the *côtiers* would have to carry them round in *palanquins*. Such ideas had wide appeal, and sustained the president through several elections. The palace at Iavoloha was all part of this. What better way was there to humiliate the Merina than by building a *Rova*-rival, just like theirs, except bigger, whiter and bombproof?

By mid-1991, the Merina had had enough. After nine months of strikes, Tana erupted. On 10 August, over four hundred thousand people set off through the rice, bound for Iavoloha. There were no weapons, and no particular plans. They were just there to shout at the concrete. For weeks, I besieged the palace with letters, begging a visit. Eventually, in mid-2018, the presidential secretariat replied, inviting me over. But by the time I got there, Tana was once again bristling with unrest, and Iavoloha was ringed with paratroopers. Beneath their outsized helmets, their faces looked burnt and sunken, and were divotted with scars. I recognised them immediately as Antandroy, here to enjoy a life of guns. '*Pas de visites,*' said their sergeant, '*tout est annulé.*'

What about my letter, I protested.

He shrugged. Not even the Pope gets in today.

I retreated to the other side of the paddy, and sat under a big sign saying LE PETIT PRINCE (a nursery, as it turned out, not a jibe). An ox was working its way, plashy-hoofed, through the mire. When the demonstrators had reached this point, back in 1991, they'd found the rice planted with mines. Both sides had filmed what happened next, and the videos are still occasionally played in bars, set to Jackie Chan music. In some, the presidential guard are opening fire, as people struggle in the mud, and there's a helicopter, sprinkling the crowd with hand grenades. Sometimes you can hear a voice too, and it's Didier himself. '*Hit the black car!*' he screams. '*Shoot them in the legs!*' Officially, eleven died that day, although, given that it was the government counting, it could have been a hundred.

But Didier was never allowed to enjoy his victory. Two months later, he was brought down by a coalition of his enemies. With the end of his seventeen-year rule, the Second Republic fizzled out. Eventually, Didier was evicted from the palace too, and would set off for exile in Paris (where he'd struggle by, with an apartment in Neuilly worth $1.4 million). It's said that, as he left Iavoloha, he stripped it of everything, including the light bulbs.

A FTER THE SOVIETS, MALAGASY DEMOCRACY found new strength, in milk. Dairies began appearing everywhere. I even spotted one near Iavoloha, a great gleaming hulk of sterility and pipes. In the years after Didier, these places began popping up all over Imerina, like a stainless white empire, under the name of Tiko. It had a fleet of liveried tankers too, and over five thousand workers, all rushing around in their corporate whites. Meanwhile, across the billboards were happy faces, smeared in yoghurt. *Tiako I Madagasikara*, ran the slogan, 'I love you Madagascar'. Curds and country had become somehow conflated.

I lost count of the Tiko outlets between here and Tana. There were milk bars and creameries in every shanty, and all the streets had a Tiko shop. The man who owned it all, Marc Ravalomanana, had started out with just a couple of cans and a bicycle. But by the end of the century, he'd got his own jet, and had bought the house of the old governor-general. He was also ready, he said, to run the country. After over fifty years of revolts, the future, it seems, was being crafted from yoghurt.

CHAPTER 12

The Land of Milk and Buckshot

Madagascar – the world's best-kept secret.

Malagasy Tourist Board slogan, c.1990

After a long search, we came across what seemed to be Tana's last packet of envelopes.

DERVLA MURPHY
Muddling through in Madagascar, 1985

This country has minerals, oil and an amazing natural environment. It has a sophisticated population. It is a land of enormous potential. And it always will be.

THE BRITISH AMBASSADOR
quoted by Tim Ecott in Vanilla, 2004

ALTHOUGH I WAS INITIALLY THRILLED to be back in Tana, there'd be a new sound I'll probably never forget: the rattle of gunfire. I can hear it now, each bullet like ice cracking or a steel hatch slammed shut. I still don't know what I feel when I remember that noise: horror, certainly, but also exhilaration, and a flutter of excitement that seems somehow wrong and of which I'm ashamed. People were dying among the clatter.

It's a bit like a dream, this part of my journey. I'm up in the gardens at Antaninarenina, amid a crowd of pedlars. Below us, the lower town is spread out like an amphitheatre, and we can see the market and some burning tyres. We can hear cheering too, as the great rabble swills back and forth through the stalls. Occasionally, we see soldiers in armour, and a *quatre-quatre* with its blue lights flashing, under a drizzle of rocks. Then there's a splatter of gunfire, and the pedlars all look at each other. They know all the sounds.

'*Chevrotine!*' they laugh. Harmless buckshot.

The mob seems to swell and gather itself, whistling and jeering, loudly now. Then there's another crackle, and the market is latticed with fluffy white trails of vapour. '*Bombes lacrymogènes!*' squeal the hawkers. Tear-gas grenades! We can hear the *bombes* fizz as they streak through the crowd. Occasionally, they're fired up the steps towards us, and although they fall well short, we all scatter backwards in panic, stumbling over the stalls and into the flower beds. But immediately we're back on the terrace. Splat! Splat! Below us, there's now a multitude, seething and swarming, and suddenly it bursts, spilling out of the market and down Indépendance.

Instantly, there's a new sound. Crack! CRACK!

'*Balles réelles!*' the vendors gasp. Live bullets!

The clatter is urgent and insistent, and seems to last for minutes. We can no longer see the soldiers, but there's now sound all around us. Sirens come bawling through the hills, and at the height of the firing there's a peal of merry English bells, as the churches ring the hour. CRACK! Crack! The crowd is roaring now, reaching a crescendo of fury as the shots fade away. Then, suddenly, it all falls silent, and the next thing I know I'm running down the steps. There are craters everywhere, where people have prised up masonry, and the great stone staircase is littered with missiles. I'm alone now and I'm terrified, and I keep saying to myself I shouldn't be doing this, but then I think I've come so far and I can't just stop, and I have to know what happens next.

As the Sakamanga was fully booked, I'd found a new place, in the red-light district. The Central Hotel was like an office block, all glass and chrome, sitting among the stalls and bonfires of the lower town. There were always a few thugs in combat gear, hanging round the doors, and, where the garbage ended, the marble began. It was like passing through a time lock, into the Space Age. Nowhere better exemplified the concept of an economy *à deux vitesses,* or a two-speed system.

Inside, it was expensively bland. Everything was either taupe or leatherette or a chocolatey velvet. On reception, I even found some cards for 'Classic Massage', whose girls were not just '*calme et discrète*' but also smiley and blonde. There was also a restaurant on the top floor called Vertigo, a superfluous reminder of one's sensory overload. From up here, I'd catch occasional glimpses of Tana, way below, now looking strangely blue and inert.

Almost all the other guests were wealthy *Karana*, or Indians, up from the coast. I imagine this was the only way they could handle Tana, filtered, sanitised and soundproof. They never seemed to go out, and

Iavoloha Palace

had turned my corridor into a sort of bazaar. No one ever shut their door, and they'd all wander from room to room, dressed in sarongs, sharing tea and doing deals. Some, I discovered, were gem traders, but others were here to sell oil and ores, or to carve up the phone networks, or buy a forest. They didn't often come to breakfast, but I did once sit next to a man who had a chain of wedding halls. He described a stateless existence: work here, schools in France and money in Mauritius. But he seemed to enjoy his life on the road, and on the corridor.

'Things are *booming* here,' he said. 'Anything goes…'

Outside my window, people were working too, but doing all the old jobs, without tea or taupe. Whenever I looked out, they were there, like the extras in a silent film. One woman was at her stall all night, boiling up rice and corn. Then there were the taxi drivers, the carters, the prostitutes, the guards and the bread man with his bucket of baguettes. But mostly they were children. Each evening, they'd build themselves a huge nest of cardboard, and bed down inside. Like two million other urchins across the island, they'd absorb all the little jobs, and spend their day picking and scavenging and living off waste. One day, they'd stumble into adulthood, stunted and illiterate, and barely aware that they'd ever been children.

Only for the girls was business booming. It always surprised me how respectable they looked, as if prostitution was done in the office or involved the in-laws. They never had to wait long for work, and by midnight they'd all been claimed and carried off in taxis. The last two were picked up by a gang of rich Merina boys, all dressed in identical American flying jackets. What was going on? A frat gathering? Or an aviators' orgy? It was odd to think of the Malagasies buying each other again, and sharing people at their parties.

Perhaps the *Karana* was right: perhaps, if the money's right, anything goes. Even here – within a few yards of my bed – you could buy whatever you wanted: a jungle, perhaps, some ships, 20 kilos of sapphires, or a girl from the country. As my friend Mireille Rabenoro once put it, 'Capitalism is in freefall. The market's gone mad.'

Money hadn't been a memorable feature of the Soviet era. When it was all over, people would struggle with the new freedom, and the idea that they could keep what they'd earned and nothing else. The Third

Republic, founded in 1992, had been launched on a surge of greed, as everyone helped themselves. From all over the Indian Ocean came fraudsters and advisers and dodgy princes, to pick over the carcass. The new president, a genial cardiologist called Professor Zafy, hadn't seen any of this coming, and soon his ministers were piling in too. There's a joke from that time about a man who leaves his bicycle against the palace wall. 'You can't do that,' says the guard, 'the government's people come this way, ministers and deputies…' 'Oh, that's all right,' says the cyclist. 'I've got a padlock.'

Just when things couldn't get any worse, Didier reappeared. For some reason, people thought he could save them from themselves, and he was given a standing ovation all the way in from the airport. In terms of probability, it was like the triumphant return of Rumpelstiltskin. But Didier continued to defy the odds, and in 1996 he was once again elected president. This time, he didn't waste his efforts on Marx, but spent the next five years making free with the coffers. Although there are no castles or pots of gold in the Rastsiraka tale, none of his friends or family were allowed to go hungry. By the end of his rule, there were 125 generals, and his daughter, Sophie, was able to make off in a truck filled with booty from the National Bank.

Only someone very rich could take on Didier now. That's where the yoghurt baron comes in. Tana hadn't seen a leader like Marc Ravalomanana for years: someone low-born, Anglophone and devoutly Protestant in the Welsh tradition. There was even something vaguely American about him, with his sharp suits and his friends in Washington. He'd already proved that, like his milk, he was whiter than white. As the city's mayor (1998–2001), he'd flushed the place clean. By the end of his tenure, there was lighting everywhere, and no one dared piss in the street. At that point, he decided to apply his great lactary fortune to national politics, challenging Didier to the fight of his life.

The Ratsirakistes didn't stand a chance. 'Marc', as he was known, would tour the country as if he were running for Capitol Hill, handing out T-shirts and baseball caps and pots of yoghurt. 'Don't be afraid of anything,' he told people. 'Just believe in me.' Big Money, it seemed, had come to the rescue of Madagascar. There was only one problem: Didier now had the support of the French, and was already cooking up a civil war.

AT THIS POINT, *le monstre politique* sprouted a second head. In December 2001, Ratsiraka established a rival government. For a while, there was two of everything: two presidents, two cabinets, two directors of the National Bank and two capital cities. Over the next seven months, the outside world had little idea which head to talk to, as the country thrashed around like a mini-Hydra, mad with rage.

It all began when Didier cried foul, declaring martial law. Ravalomanana's people were 'fascists', he insisted, and the whole election had been a fraud. But Tana wasn't having any of this, and a million people came out on the streets. Marc urged non-violence, and so his supporters besieged Didier with hymns (and then cleaned up the streets wherever they'd been). After two months of singing and dancing, Didier decided he could take no more, and fled to the coast. As he left, he destroyed all the bridges down the escarpment. Tana was finished, he announced, and Tamatave, or Toamasina, would become the new capital.

After that, Didier tried to starve his rival out. All the power lines to Tana were cut, and all the roads barricaded. At each roadblock, the admiral installed a little gang of thugs, known as the *zatovo*. Sometimes, Sophie could be seen among them, in designer camouflage, dishing out money. The *zatovo* would let nothing pass, except on payment of a hefty 'tax', or bribe. During those months, petrol in Tana cost ten times as much as it did on the coast, and would arrive in bottles. Soon there'd be no more aspirins or nappies, and even salt became dangerously scarce. For people, too, it was a dangerous business moving around. Over a hundred were killed on the barricades. One of those trying to get home was my Sakalava friend in the Jane Austen Department. 'One had to exercise the great caution,' said Gladys. 'There were armed men everywhere, demanding to know how we'd voted. One had to choose one's words carefully, or things could get very unpleasant...'

Amid this unpleasantness, the economy collapsed. First, the banks closed and then the embassies emptied. Soon, even the skies fell silent, as all the flights were cancelled. Without any tourists, Air Madagascar simply ran out of everything, and was grounded in Paris. Before long, industry seized up too, along with healthcare and roads and the supply of charcoal. Over those seven months, 150,000 jobs were lost as one of the world's skinniest countries began haemorrhaging money at the rate of $15 million a day. Few other nations have become so poor

Defeated in the 2001 election, Ratsiraka would set up a rival government in a rival capital.

post-independence, without actually fighting a full-scale war.

Eventually, even Didier realised that, once again, he'd been beaten. On 26 June 2002, the USA recognised Ravalomanana's government. Grudgingly, France followed a week later, and Didier fled. According to Christian Fayd'Herbe, the *Ratsirakistes* spent their last night in the *Bateau Ivre*, drinking Black Label. The next day, they took to their boats, and sailed for Mauritius. That left only the *zatovo*, who – because they hadn't been paid – ransacked the *résidence*, helping themselves to the last of the taps. A few hours later, Tamatave was captured by a single tank.

This ought to have been a turning point for Madagascar. The *ancien régime* had been swept away, and this was once again A Tale of One City. Principled and canny, the new president was suddenly the darling of the Western world. Soon, there were investors queueing at the Ambohitsorohitra Palace, and in no time at all GNP had grown by 7 per cent. *Les Tananariviens* could hardly believe their luck as supermarkets started popping up all over town, at the rate of six a year. Ravalomanana promised roads and hospitals too, and, as if to prove it, they began appearing on the banknotes. He'd also abolish the Malagasy franc, as he set the country on a more Anglophone orbit. There was even justice for Didier, who was charged with the theft of $80 million, tried in absentia, and given ten years' hard labour. Although he never served a single day, this felt good at the time. The hydra had been finally tamed – or shorn, at least, of its ugliest head.

But, like all hydra, this one had plenty of heads to replace those lost. Within a few years, Ravalomanana had a new tormentor, called Andry Rajoelina. His background is almost as improbable as that of the Great Milkman himself. Born into the elite, he'd made a fortune as a DJ, and now – at the age of thirty-four – he had a string of nightclubs and a pop channel called Viva. Immaculately groomed and daintily coiffed, he was also slyly ambitious and had a reputation for stopping at nothing. His loathing for Ravalomanana was well known but inexplicable. Some thought it was the French, pulling his strings. Others thought it was Didier himself (now enjoying another break in Paris, courtesy of President Chirac). By January 2009, Rajoelina was cranking up the volume, and urging revolt.

Things were soon in flames. Ravalomanana lost all his TV stations after trying to close down Viva. But easily the biggest fire was on Indépendance. An entire department store was burnt down, and forty-four people – mostly looters – were incinerated as the building imploded. There was always gunfire on occasions like this, and by the end of the month there were nearly two hundred dead. But Rajoelina was by no means finished. First, he ordered his fans to make a *ville mort* (or ghost town) of Tana, clearing the streets and shutting everything down. Then, when that didn't work, they turned their attention to the palaces, and marched on Ambohitsorohitra. This was never a day that was going to end well.

During my last week in Tana, I'd often walk up the mid-levels, and pause at the palace. Pausing was as much as anyone could ever do, without exciting the guards. '*N'approchez pas!*' they'd shout, rising to their feet and rattling their guns. '*Restez à l'écart!*' There was still a red line too, around the walls, defining the frontier between life and death. It all seemed very undignified for a place like Ambohitsorohitra. She'd become the Old Lady of Tana: lacy, fading and wilted. It was now over a hundred and thirty years since she'd been carried, fret by fret, up the escarpment.

I doubt Ravalomanana had ever been comfortable here. It was all too fusty and dark for a man of milk. But a little bit of the grandeur had somehow got to him. In the end, Ravalomanana failed because he broke the first rule of survival, and became too great. In Tana, people told me, no one should ever get above himself, or think he's better than anyone else. The final straw was probably the presidential jet, a Boeing 737, painted up like Air Force One. After this, the mob needed little encouragement. Just a word from Rajoelina – and a tinkle of pop – and there it was, at the palace gates.

Nearby is a monument to those who died. They are remembered as heroic golden figures, coldly martyred by the little stone soldiers. Twenty-eight demonstrators had crossed the *ligne rouge*, to find themselves on the Other Side. Ravalomanana would never be forgiven. One by one, his strongholds were overrun, beginning with the ministries. The army headquarters fell next, and then finally, on 16 March 2009, old Ambohitsorohitra herself. The following day, Ravalomanana resigned at gunpoint, and was put on a plane to Swaziland.

The Yoghurt Years would end in a five-star bathroom, on the other side of town. I've never really understood the attraction of the Carlton; it was built during the Soviet era, and looks like an old tooth, umpteen storeys high. But governments have always loved it, treating it almost as a second home. Over the last half century, it's doubled as a spare treasury, a banqueting house, a harem, a bolthole and a bunker. Upstairs, it even has a casino, and a great wooden army carved into the panels.

In fairness, it's brighter inside, and the floors are so shiny that everywhere you go, you see yourself, walking around upside down. Had I been here on 29 April 2009, I'd have seen Rajoelina's men skidding through the lobby. They were looking for the last of Ravalomanana's ministers, who'd been running Madagascar from an upstairs suite. It took them an hour to find anyone, but eventually the prime minister turned up, hiding in the shower. It was an ignominious end to the Third Republic. Rajoelina's people would be merciless with the dairies, breaking up Tiko and looting the factories. This, I suppose, was only logical: no milk, no threat.

But it wasn't much of a victory. The Western powers were unimpressed by the *coup d'état*, and refused to recognise Rajoelina. Despite

In recent years, *les Tananariviens* have learnt to live with road-blocks and riot police.

this, he had himself sworn in as president, and – at thirty-five – he was the world's youngest head of state. But, once again, the hotels emptied and the investors left. For the next four years, stalemate ensued. With no one truly in charge, the forest was plundered. Everyone was bribed in this chainsaw massacre, including the rangers, the police and the customs. Within a matter of months, over 45,000 rosewood trees had been cut up for furniture and sold to China. Each plant had been more than five hundred years in the making.

The stand-off did, however, end, with the elections of 2013. Although there were over three million voters missing from the register, the outside world had little choice but to accept the result. This time, it seemed, Madagascar had experienced a spasm of righteousness, electing an accountant. But he proved an unremarkable man. Perhaps his only truly distinguishing feature was his name, now the longest of all the world's leaders: Hery Rajaonarimampianina. He also suffered the same old temptations, and was soon bending the rules and dressing his wife as if she were empress. Within eighteen months of his election, he was facing impeachment. By the end of his term, in 2018, he was about as unpopular as it was possible to be.

The search for a new president was well under way by the time I arrived. There were no fewer than forty-six candidates, including all the old faces: the Milkman, the DJ, the Accountant and the Admiral, now aged eighty-two. They were all tainted in some way or other, and everyone believed the result would be rigged. It was almost as if the hydra had taken a new lease of life – more vicious, more exuberant, and with more heads than ever.

M OST OF MY FRIENDS HAD ALREADY left town by the time the riots began. People had known for weeks that things were about to get violent. The election campaign had become bigger and dirtier than ever. Malagasy elections are famously extravagant, and cost twice as much as those held in France. In his last campaign, back in 2013, Hery the Accountant had spent over $43 million dollars (or twice as much per vote as that spent by Donald Trump). Now all the candidates were at it. Everywhere I went, voters were being bussed around, and wooed with free hats and T-shirts and boxes of chicken. It was said

there'd been a spike in kidnapping, to fund all these treats. Even the
old drunk in the ruins of the *Rova* knew that this election wasn't about
policies or looks or kissing babies.

'The winner,' he said, 'will be the man with the money.'

Hery, it seemed, would do anything to hang on to his presidency.
To begin, he was backed by Moscow, whose 'dirty tricks' team had
arrived in Tana on tourist visas. Known as 'the Company', the Russians
had plenty of cash, and would buy the island's biggest paper. But it
was never an easy relationship, and because they couldn't say Hery's
name, they called him 'the Piano'. Eventually, however, they realised
how unpopular he was, and switched their funds to Rajoelina the DJ.

'So now,' friends warned, 'Hery is desperate.'

Every day, there were more rash measures. The president even tried
to amend the constitution to write off his rivals. First, he announced a
residency rule to exclude Marc the Milkman (who he'd sent into exile),
and then he decreed that all candidates should be at least forty-five,

thereby disqualifying Rajoelina (who was only forty-four). It was a particularly cheap shot in his sordid – but lavish – campaign.

Tana reacted angrily. A big demo was planned for 21 April 2018.

'Get out of the city,' warned my friend Avana, 'it's not safe.'

But Mireille at the human rights commission thought I should stay. 'You must write about it,' she said. 'Just be careful.'

Across town, people braced themselves for a bloody Saturday. There were long queues at the cash machines, and everyone did their shopping early, clearing the shelves in the supermarkets. The Peace Corps announced that the centre of the city – Analakely – was a *zone rouge* and that none of its volunteers were to venture down there. Outside each bank, a little private army appeared, all clad in black and wearing masks. Even in the mid-levels, the jewellers, who were mostly Indian,

On the morning of 21 April 2018, the army took up position, closing off Avenue de l'Indépendance.

removed their stock and shuttered their shops. There was no panic about any of this. *Les Tananariviens* know the routine, just as they know the difference between the splat of buckshot and the clatter of bullets.

W HEN THE BIG DAY ARRIVED, Tana was ominously quiet. Soon after sunrise, I crept down through the streets to Analakely. I'd never known the city so serene. The *taxis-be* were refusing to leave the suburbs, and so there was almost no traffic. Without the minibuses and the stalls, the trucks, the snake charmers and the mobile coiffeurs, Tana was almost its old self again: a little French town of leafy boulevards and royal-blue skies. When I heard the soundtrack to *Frozen* warbling through the streets ('Let it go! Let it go!'), I began to wonder if the day hadn't somehow been Disneyfied, plunging its characters into a magical sleep.

But down on Indépendance, *les Forces de l'Ordre* were quietly group-ing. Some of the soldiers carried shields and clubs, and wore thick black plates of plastic armour. Others, packed together crocodile-style, were scuttling off towards the *Zoma*. From 'Le Glacier', the whores looked on sulkily, in their tiny shorts. More armed men arrived. Even the names on their trucks – FIGN and Emmo – sounded like characters in a cartoon that's gone wrong. I tried to get through the cordon but was stopped by a corporal in a helmet and visor. The Perspex was so worn I couldn't see his face, but, through the scratches, his voice was sad.

'*Tout est fermé. Personne ne peut entrer.*'

As the sun began to bleach out the shadows, more people appeared. Most were here to watch, and climbed the lamp posts and onto the walls. Even the statues had their own little mahouts, perched on their shoulders. A lot of them were children, with no shoes and a T-shirt they didn't understand ('DON'T WORRY WE ALL DIE ALONE', read one, while another said simply 'ORPHAN'). The first of the *marchands ambulants* had also reappeared, now selling face masks soaked in vinegar. They knew exactly what the day would bring, and how demand changed with a whiff of gas. I decided I didn't have the courage for a ringside seat, and so I climbed the great stone staircase to Antaninarenina's gardens and took my place at the edge of the terrace. In the TV clips of that day, the *gendarmes* are seen driving the crowds back with buckshot and tear gas. But then *les manifestants* surge out of the *Zoma*'s pavilions, and the soldiers realise they've been outnumbered. They retreat, walking backwards, pumping shotguns as they go. By now the rioters have overturned a skip, and are pushing it before them, like a home-made tank. The soldiers panic, but they find it hard to run in their plastic armour. Lumps of concrete are now landing among them, in a deadly downpour. One of the *gendarmes* crumples, and his comrades drag him clear. They're firing their Kalashnikovs now, causing the crowd to thin out for a moment, where people have fallen. But by this time the surge is unstoppable, and the soldiers scramble away out of the frame. They leave behind a *quatre-quatre* – one of Emmo's trucks – and it's immediately engulfed and stripped and set on fire. Then, suddenly, the street is almost empty, and the way is open into Indépendance.

It was at this point that I crept down the steps, and onto the rubble. In my memory, there's no sound but my heart, flapping around like a bird in my chest. It's very hot too, and the street looks brilliantly white and overexposed. All around me, the road is scattered with rocks and cartridges and little oily black fires. I also remember seeing playing cards everywhere, as if a great game of poker had been interrupted. Just for a moment I hesitated, unsure what to do. To my right was the beginning of the Avenue de l'Indépendance, and to my left, the market. In that instant, there were only a few of us on the road in between, and I felt I'd arrived just as the battle was turning. But then suddenly, from out of the market, came an enormous procession, complete with drummers and trumpets, and a forest of flags.

I don't know who was right that morning, but it felt like the people's day. Most of them were ordinary citizens in their glittery hats or old pinstripe jackets. It surprised me, how much I shared their euphoria. But then, I reasoned, blasting them with guns had been nothing but criminal, and so it felt right when the army fled. As the marchers sang their way – thrumming and tootling – down Indépendance, I tagged along behind. Their mood, a heady mix of jubilation and fear, was highly infectious. Was this what it's like being on the chorus of *Les Misérables*?

Overleaf: As the soldiers fled, *les Tananariviens* appeared with trumpets and drums. Three died in the gunfire.

Perhaps (except without the sweat and the flip-flops and the reek of gas). But it didn't take much to put us to flight, and when a nearby motorbike backfired we all scattered in terror and dived into the side streets.

Outside the town hall, *les manifestants* broke into hymns. Although I was the only white face in the crowd, no one seemed to notice. People were completely absorbed in the moment. They'd driven the army out of the city centre, Analakely, and the government was nowhere to be seen. One man was carrying a great Perspex *bouclier*, or shield, from the fallen *gendarme*. Another had blood all down the front of his trousers. He told me he'd been picking up the wounded, and that at least one of them had died. '*On pouvait voir sa cervelle*,' he said. (You could see his brains.)

I tried another question, but the man just looked at me blankly.

'*Merci d'être venu*,' he kept saying. Thank you for coming.

I THOUGHT IT WOULD TAKE ME DAYS to make sense of what I'd seen. At first, all I wanted to do was talk about it, testing each moment, in case I'd dreamt it. But my friends listened politely, without shock or surprise. They said Malagasies had spent much of the last thirty years out on the streets, begging for leaders. Even the Jane Austen lady said there was nothing new in the world, and that they'd seen it all before. Rubber bullets and gas were, it seems, just part of the tapestry of political life. Everyone had learnt to live with it, finding their own variant of reality, either in God, drink, bones or the English novel. Only Camille the Lebanese had something vicious to say. I ran into him one evening at the Sakamanga.

'You know why these riots are so violent?' he sneered.

No, I admitted, I didn't.

'Because people here are cowards.'

'*Cowards?*'

'Yes, they only find courage in numbers, and then they're unstoppable.'

It was hard, sifting fact from the rumours. In one story, the army had used all their tear gas in a single day. In another, seeded by the president himself, it wasn't the soldiers who'd opened fire but someone else. The newspapers were always last with the news. They couldn't even agree on the numbers killed. Some said two and some said four (with

The day after the riot, the army re-appeared, and the dead were laid out in front of the town hall.

twenty injured). The matter was only finally resolved when three coffins appeared – each draped in the national flag – outside the town hall.

I often went down there, unsure what to expect. The army had quickly recovered the avenue, packing it with soldiers. With all their shields and helmets, they looked like a great, green phalanx of myrmidons. They'd also promised never to shoot people again, and so perhaps – like Troy – the next big battle would be reckoned in blows. But there was no sign of that now. Once again, the vendors were selling old iPhones and chicken feet, and even the commandos looked calm and replete.

The coffins were there for several days. If *les Tananariviens* agreed on one thing, it was how to be dead. A pretty little pergola appeared, together with a bank of flowers, and all along the avenue the speakers crackled with hymns. The government would spare no expense in seeing its detractors off to the afterlife. Aro the palaeontologist once told me that when a man dies, it's the job of all of us to see him safely to his tomb. Anything else, he said, is a bit like killing him all over again.

During those last few weeks, I was often surprised by people's capacity for joy. I began to realise that almost everyone I knew was, deep down, inexplicably content. Of course, it helped that – for some – this life was merely an interlude with the Real Thing to come. But even the faithless were stubbornly happy. Friends like Lydia and Avana seemed to distil pleasure from the tiniest details: a few bars of music, a sliver of moon, or a string of fish. There was never much talk of the things they lacked. Lydia once told me that she loved her life just as it was. It puzzled her, the sadness of foreigners, with all their agony aunts and their introspection. And why were the Americans all taking pills? 'Perhaps,' she concluded, 'they just care too much.'

'And would you live anywhere else?' I asked.

It was an unthinkable idea. Despite the coups and the plagues, Madagascar was perfect. Everyone felt like this. We're in *Tanin'drazana*, they'd say, the Land of the Ancestors, and so we're almost in heaven. And what other country offers the Creator such reverence? And makes a spectacle of poetry, even greater than football? To most Malagasies, nowhere else was so spiritually wired. It was always left to outsiders to wallow in the figures, and to remind everyone this was now one of the poorest nations on Earth, and that most of its people lived on less than $1.90 a day. 'That's probably true,' said Aro, 'but there's more to this place than the things we don't have.'

This strange, unfathomable contentment was everywhere, I realised, even in business. Every day, there were calls for *téléopérateurs*, in page after page of newspaper ads. The employers were always French, and all they wanted was language and '*charme*'. One of the call centres, called Teleperformance, already employed 5,000 Malagasies and was about to increase its workforce by a factor of ten. It was partly about money, but also empathy. The French had spotted a particular talent for calming and soothing; for dishing out refunds and adjusting losses; for sorting out queries (and *les clients mécontents*), and for mopping up anger the other side of the world. It was sometimes hard to compute all this. After centuries of exporting misery and slaves, Madagascar was now selling happiness, smile by smile.

I OFTEN WONDERED WHAT WOULD happen to this country, and its cheery paupers. Of course, no one really knew. In everything I'd read there was a range of opinion from the rosily tinted to the starkly Malthusian. In the most apocalyptic versions, Madagascar would face a fiery end, as the population doubled over the next twenty-five years, and the jungle burnt off. One savant even had the island dissolving, as the erosion wins. But in other predictions, oil would appear, and the natives would become sleek and rich. They'd also be selling off sapphires by the truckload, together with chromite and rare earths, and great girders of gold. There'd be no hunger either because, by then, they'd be eating seaweed and powdered crickets. Naturally, tourists would love it, and the country's coast would be lined with resorts like some gigantic Mauritius. Even poor little Tamatave would be almost unrecognisable, as the new Miami.

But none of this meant much to ordinary Malagasies. The sort of people I encountered didn't fret about locusts for lunch or the flaming forest. For most, the future was either an imponderable luxury or a matter of fate, and nothing they did would make any difference. 'Madagascar,' I was often told, 'is a rich country inhabited by poor people.' There was no sense that the two ideas were somehow linked, and could be reconfigured. But not everyone was without plans. One man I came across was now busily mapping out the road ahead. We'd met when I was looking for a car, and was given the number of Little Johnny.

Like all Little Johnnys, he was amusingly huge, and could easily fill out a Renault without much need for me. 'Sorry, a bit small,' he'd say, as I compressed myself into the remaining inches. We were soon getting on. It turned out Johnny was much more than a driver and could fix up anything from a trip to the telescope to a walk through the slums. Everyone knew him, and wherever we went, he was cuffed and ruffled. It was like going around with a private bear. But I'd also come to think of Johnny as the New Tananarivian (or the Spirit of Our Age, except a bit bigger). He wasn't only an entrepreneur, he also spoke English, worshipped all things American, and voted for Marc. 'I do all this for my boys,' he once told me. 'They have to learn English, if they're going to survive.'

Only his car let him down. It was a typical Tana taxi, painted the regulation sludge. Because it was rented, Johnny never wanted to fill it up, and so we'd drive around on half a litre of fuel. Occasionally, it simply shuddered to a halt, and it would take a dozen strong pushers to get us moving again. Sometimes bits would fall off – like the exhaust and the mirrors – and we'd watch as they bounced along on the road behind. But there were lots of cars like this in Tana, some without paint and some without doors. Even the road signs were becoming scarce, and along the airport road almost all the lamps had been plundered and stripped. 'This is a beautiful city,' said Johnny, 'but things work differently here.'

I asked about his boys, and their future.

'They'll do things we can only dream of.'

'Like what? University?'

Little Johnny laughed and shook his head.

'You ever seen it? We used to call it Beirut.'

That afternoon we drove up to the campus, to survey the damage.

The poorest *Tananariviens* live on about a euro a day. Some 40% of the electricity is abstracted illegally.

France's great parting gift of 1960 – the Université Charles de Gaulle – was almost unrecognisable. Only a few stubs of modernity remained. The rest had been not so much strafed as overrun. During the city's various crises, whole families had moved in, to live with the students. Most of them were farmers with no experience of inhabiting concrete. They'd harvested almost everything to make themselves comfortable: the paving, the drain covers and all the bins. The accommodation blocks now looked dank and bucolic. Most of them were wreathed in old cables, and leaking chickens and effluent. Built for 2,000 students, they now housed three times that number. Occasionally, the government would evict *les squatteurs* but they'd soon come back, as scrawny as ever. No one was paying the bills. From time to time, the electricity company would simply turn off the lights, and the whole university would disappear beneath the trees.

'See what I mean?' said Johnny, 'Our latest slum…'

None of this did much for academic life. My television contact, Rahanta Rakoto, once told me that her daughter was teaching up here but was seldom paid. Most academics spent their careers on strike. Malagasy degrees were now almost worthless, and weren't recognised abroad. Meanwhile, the students were operating at about the level of a twelve-year-old in Europe. But at least they were surfing the internet, unlike their teachers. 'Some of the professors,' said Johnny, 'don't even have email.'

'So, if this isn't the future, what is?'

'Data,' he said. 'Just you watch us.'

This wasn't new, the idea that one day – for the first time ever – Madagascar would be at the centre of something. Until now, the problem for trade had always been one of nerves. In such a *coup*-prone country, nobody wanted to invest in structures, or put down roots. It was said that even the garment factories could be packed up and gone within forty-eight hours. But the internet was changing all that. Fibre optics had brought Madagascar into the chatter, and it now had the fastest speeds in Africa ('Far faster than anything in Wales,' moaned a missionary I once met). There were now nearly two million users, almost all of them signed up to Facebook. That's an intriguing thought in a country where you can still eat a chameleon, killed with a spear.

'So now,' said Johnny, 'my boys are working all over the world.'

The work wasn't immediately obvious. But Little Johnny was soon pointing out logos and offices. There were now more than two hundred companies in town, processing data and employing over 15,000 people. 'We want to become a hub,' said Johnny, 'of the virtual world.' To some extent, this was already happening. According to one business magazine, *Quartz*, Madagascar was now a 'stellar digital player'. Everyone was sending it data, including the Moroccans and the French National Library. There was almost nothing the Malagasies couldn't collate and crunch up, from payrolls and invoices to supermarket coupons. Here in Tana, for example, they were collecting subscriptions for *Marie-Claire*, and running customer services for Deliveroo. With a few words of English, Johnny's boys were even venturing out, beyond the Francophone sphere.

'It must give them a strange impression of life in Europe?'

Johnny paused, torn between curiosity and tact.

'Well, yes. I mean, who are the Bubbledogs? And what's a Dead Hippie?'

I HAD HOPED FOR ONE LAST GULP of greenery before departing. This wouldn't be easy in Tana. It may feel like thousands of villages gathered together but they're packed in so tight not much country survives. Although there are still a few little sprigs of jungle, they're usually up in the cliffs, or walled up in concrete. For most *Tananariviens*, if they want to know what emptiness looks like, or grass or dappled shade, they have to go to the zoo. Tsimbazaza (or 'Children Keep Out') was once a burial ground, and while it may not sound welcoming, it's still a big treat. Everyone dresses up for a visit, and all the children are scrubbed and preened. It will be a day of endless delights and surprises, including peanut brittle, a hand-cranked carousel, and a stall selling kites and little plastic Kalashnikovs. After this, there will be no need to see the rest of the country. It's just like the zoo, except dangerous and dirty.

Only the animals were missing. A delightful network of paths lolloped off through the woods and round the ponds. I remember clumps of super-saturated colour too, and a *Ravenala* – or traveller's palm – like a gigantic quiver of dinosaur feathers. But most of the pens

For all its data processing, Tana is still a city of villages compacted together.

were empty and the cages bare. The zoo's star attraction seemed to be a trio of camels, now looking faintly bemused by the turn life had taken. Hadn't Attenborough and Durrell found tenrecs here, and a gallery of snakes? And where were the lemurs I'd seen, back in 2004?

'Don't know,' said Johnny. 'Maybe somebody stole them.'

Perhaps one day, Madagascar will all be like this: a hard-baked land, speckled with zoos? As humankind settles down on its new-found island, things are bound to get damaged. For those here counting trees, it's a gruelling sight. 'In 2017 alone', wrote Victoria Gill from the BBC, '500,000 hectares were cut down – half a million football pitches of rich, diverse rainforest. Gone.' The fauna, too, has a struggle ahead. Hundreds of species will probably vanish. Many of those that survive the felling will be eaten and squashed and sprayed with chemicals. Others, as Johnny knew all too well, will simply be stolen.

'You know what you get for a little snake? $300!'

Almost anything that moves, he said, now gets stolen: frogs, zoo animals, turtles and bugs. These days, the illegal trade in wildlife is second only to that of narcotics. That makes Madagascar rich in loot. Even as we spoke, creatures were being bundled into speedboats and carried off to the continent. According to *The New York Times*, 'Madagascar is a pirate's paradise'. But like all good piracy, it begins at home. Much of this booty is bound for the USA. Every year, Americans spend over $3 billion on butterflies, potions, exotic pets and skins. If things carry on like this, an entire ecosystem will end up in Chinese bottles, or across the walls of American homes. But to my surprise, Little Johnny hated the idea of conservation. It was like being a colony all over again.

'You can't tell hungry people how to starve.'

But this wasn't the end for the lemurs and tenrecs. We agreed that, one day, a beast on the run would be worth more than one in the bag, and – at that point – the looting would stop. By then, perhaps, Madagascar will be a nation of zoos, each with its own little army and a grand hotel. Johnny seemed to like this idea, and was soon playing along. His zoo-land would be all linked up with buses and trains, and the New Malagasies, now rich on oil and data, would be swooping around, cuddling creatures. 'It'll be great for business,' he laughed, 'everything bigger and better!' Perhaps he was right, but it's hard to picture: the gleaming arcades of peanut brittle, the giant carousels and the new generation of plastic AKs.

C HINA WAS A RECURRING THEME throughout my goodbyes. As always, it took me days to track people down. It still surprised me, how easily Malagasies could disappear, pulling down shutters and cutting off the phones. Some of my friends hadn't been back since the riots. Aro was lying low in Tuléar, and Manitra had returned to his family fort. Rahanta Rakoto, of course, was now more reluctant than ever to leave her TV studios and come into Tana. But I did have tea with my friend from the university – as Austenesque as ever – and a big, fatty lunch with my old host, Avana. 'We're being invaded,' he announced, through a mouthful of beef. 'They're sending us triads and all their convicts.'

It was a popular idea. Although no Chinese were ever seen, people insisted they were being overrun. One night, I went for a last drink at the Sakamanga, and ran into Camille and his latest girl. 'There's going to be trouble,' he said. 'Hery has sold 20,000 passports to the Chinese. How stupid is that? You allow one in, and they bring all their uncles and aunts, and then you're swamped.' His mistress nodded. And they'll steal everything, she added: '*les arbres, l'or, et même les poissons*' (the trees, the gold and even the fish).

Only Mireille, from the human rights commission, felt differently. China was paying for everything, she explained. It was the biggest importer, and the biggest investor. They'd also patched up the roads and the airport, and had established the 'Institut Confucius'. Now they were building railways and a tramline for Tana. They'd already given it the *Palais des Sports*. 'Maybe you've seen it?' she said. 'Out in Mahamasina?'

I had. It looked like origami among the scrunched-up hovels.

'And will you be swamped?'

Mireille smiled. 'Most will leave. A few will stay.'

Her words sound funny now, in the light of what happened. Perhaps the future comes sooner than we think. A few days later, it was announced that, from now on, Madagascar would receive a quarter of a million Chinese tourists every year. Such a gigantic island can probably absorb numbers like this. But it's only a beginning. There are over a billion people out there, now on the lookout for their own Mallorca.

F ROM TIME TO TIME, THERE were reminders of the coming election, as the candidates resurfaced. Only the Admiral – now frail and blind – kept himself to himself. Everyone else was all over the papers. Each day, a different candidate would buy up the columns and fill them with praise. This never cost them more than the price of a good breakfast, and it gave the impression of a saintly contest. No one ever seemed to have any dark secrets, mistresses, slush funds or gigolos. In a town steeped in stories, this was sometimes confusing. Even the grubbiest of crooks could emerge from the Sundays looking laundered and clean. Only one of the candidates – President Rajaonarimampianina – struck a sour note, accusing the others of trying to kill him.

At these times, there was always plenty of money washing around. Demonstrating that he was no ordinary DJ, Rajoelina went everywhere by helicopter, and was often leaping around in beautiful suits.

His supporters were also the first to take up graffiti, stencilling his portrait all over the city: 'The Dandy in Blue'. It was said the Russians were out too, shopping for candidates once again. Several presidential hopefuls were offered bungs of up to $2 million. One of them, Pastor Mailhol, could hardly believe his luck, and gladly accepted. 'It was a *cash* payment!' he told reporters excitedly. 'Just like that!'

Other candidates, like Omer Beriziky, turned down the money.

'That must be hard,' I remarked to my friend Rahanta, the journalist.

'You should meet him,' she said. 'I'll fix it up.'

My morning with the old prime minister was refreshingly humdrum. When I first saw Beriziky's compound, I thought it looked like the Alamo, with its 10-foot walls and a great steel door that rolled away. But in the middle of its *plaza de armas* was a small, yellow, pebbledash house with a carport and a few half-hearted orchids. Just when I was wondering if I had the right place, two balls of snarling white fluff launched themselves off the top step, landing at my feet in a pile of yaps. At that moment, a girl in an apron appeared, gathered up the dogs, and steered us inside.

For a moment, I was taken aback by the sheer modesty of it all. Beriziky had been an ambassador in Belgium at the time of his appointment in 2011. He'd then been brought home, to guide the country out of chaos. Is this all he had to show for his three years in office: some plastic armchairs, a woolly rug, a couple of quartz coasters and one of those ten-second paintings you find in hotels?

The door swung open, and Beriziky appeared, dressed from head to foot in royal blue. I recognised him immediately from his posters. Powerfully built, handsome, hairless and of unspecific race, he always reminded me of Yul Brynner, doing his turn as the Siamese king. But, in the flesh, Beriziky was curiously unceremonious, and we were soon chatting away about his early life. He was half-Sakalava, he said, and had been a teacher of history. It must have seemed strange, I ventured, suddenly to find yourself running the country?

'*Oui, après la Belgique, ce fut un choc.*' (Yes, after Belgium, it was quite a shock.)

Half a million *Tananariviens* now work as pedlars, selling everything from samosas to garden shears.

This might have been an interesting line, but it soon disappeared into a speech. Perhaps the genial Beriziky was thinking of newspaper columns, and needed to fill them. It was all too much for the dogs, which sank into the wool, and slept. It was too much, too, for my tape-recorder, which would recall that morning as a long, low buzz like a bee in a bottle. Although I managed to salvage a few *promesses et visions*, Monsieur Beriziky's alluring words are now lost forever. When it was time to go, he, the dogs and the maid all stood on the steps and waved me off.

'A nice guy,' I said, as Johnny drove away.

'Yes, very popular. A good man.'

'What are his chances?'

'Zero. No money. No family. Wrong tribe.'

EVERY GOOD JOURNEY ENDS IN REGRETS, or perhaps a fanfare. Even on my last day, I was still rushing around, trying to gather up memories. I also suffered an acute attack of shopping, and bought a home-made spoon, a satin flag, two French medals, some magic twigs, several bars of Malagasy chocolate, more beads, another felt hat and a tiny Citroën cut from a can. Of course, I recognised the symptoms; all this stuff was supposed to keep me somehow anchored in the moment because, deep down, I didn't want to leave. Madagascar and its people may often seem impenetrable, but there's no better place to be happily lost.

There was no fanfare as such, but I did find a rally. People had been talking about it for weeks: a great gathering called by Marc the Dairy-King, to boost his campaign. It would take place at the National Stadium, and so I decided to walk. Zigzagging down through the mid-levels, I reached the marshalling yards, and the area where they cut up cars and sell the pieces. With its dirty fires and oily mud, it was one of the more apocalyptic parts of town, but it no longer worried me. I'd often seen women tottering through here, in their heels and twinsets. Everyone was on the move that day, and many of the children had ridden into town, clinging to trucks. Eventually, however, we all reached the lake at Anosy, and worked our way round to Mahamasina.

The stadium was already in the throes of a gigantic party. There were gospel choirs warbling away, acrobats, trumpeters, and several enormous wagons of yoghurt. Although I had only an hour to spare, I followed the crowds up into the stands. As I sat there, with the burnt-out palace overhead, I realised how much of the story had happened here. This is where Radama had assembled his great army; where deserters were roasted; where the Merina had made their big stand, and where General de Gaulle had announced independence. I mentioned the queens to the couple next to me, but they looked puzzled at first. They were up from the country, and spoke only snatches of French.

Yes, they said, there are lots of ghosts.

Despite the sun, everyone danced and sang. Someone gave me a plate of tripe and a cardboard Stetson in party colours. The country couple had a small baby with them, and were appalled to hear I had only one child. Who'll look after your tomb, they asked, and keep it clean? They had eight children, they said, and this was the youngest. I asked what her name was, and the couple laughed. She was too young for that. A nice name only arouses the evil spirits. And this, they said, is why we call her *la cochonne laide*, or Ugly Pig.

That morning never got any simpler, or cooler. By noon, the Great Marc still hadn't appeared, and it was time for me to go. The farmer wished me well in the sky, and I wished him well on the truck ride home. With that, I slipped away, bidding a silent goodbye to the ancestors and the ghosts and Ugly Pig.

Afterword

The bubonic plague returned as always. During *la saison pesteuse* of 2018–19, there were 105 cases (and 19 deaths), with a small rise in 2019–20, to 179 cases.

During the year of my visit, some 7,000 zebu were stolen.

The presidential elections were won by the disc jockey, **Andry Rajoelina**, after a glittering campaign. He continues to deny that the Russians contributed.

The election also saw the end of **Didier Ratsiraka**, 'the Red Admiral'. At eighty-three, he'd dominated Malagasy politics for over four decades, but was finally humiliated with only 0.45 per cent of the votes.

As predicated, **Omer Beriziky** got nowhere in the polls. He has returned to Belgium as the Malagasy Ambassador.

Pope Francis visited in 2019, and a million people turned out for mass.

That year, the **Malagasy National Football Team** reached the quarter-finals of the Africa Cup. Each of the players was made a Knight of the Malagasy National Order.

Corruption has continued to dog the country. During 2019, the head of the Customs Service was jailed for theft, along with ten senior executives from the Malagasy Red Cross.

Madagascar seemed strangely invulnerable to **Coronavirus**, at least to begin with. When the infection first appeared, in March 2020, everything stopped: the shops, the minibuses, the taxi-be, the ports and the airports. At night there was a curfew, and anyone found not wearing a mask was ordered to sweep the street. With fewer jobs and no tourism, more people became street vendors or took to plundering the forest. Many fled the capital seeking out the sea (which they thought was safer) or the family tomb (in case they died). Soldiers were sent out to track the runaways through the jungle. But still there were no reported deaths until early May. There was even a period of déconfinement, or 'unlockdown', until the deaths started mounting. By mid-August, however, only 164 had died, compared to over 46,000 in the UK.

The president attributed the country's deliverance to to **Covid-organics**, a tea made from the sweet wormwood plant. Despite the scepticism of the WHO, Rajoelina even went on television, announcing that he'd found a cure, and that Madagascar would change the history of the world.

My friend the Jane Austen expert is now completing her PhD. Her studies have been interrupted first by endless strikes and then by Covid-19.

Until the pandemic, the palaeontologist **Aro Rakotondrabao** had been creating an outside museum 40 miles to the west of Antananarivo, at Ambatolevy. The site was formerly a Vazimba settlement, and the villagers there continue the tradition of sacrificing lambs.

Christian Fayd'herbe has sold the Bateau Ivre, and Tamatave's favourite restaurant has now closed.

Manitra Andriamialisoa's dreams for a new expedition business, called 'Madagascar Endemics and Resorts', are temporarily on hold.

Work has however resumed on the restoration of the burnt-out Rova, the **Queen's Palace**. President Rajoelina is also adding his own touches, including a Roman-style coliseum, called Masaondro, 'The Sun'.

Selected Reading

General history

For Anglophones, probably the most accessible history is *Madagascar Rediscovered: A History from Early Times to Independence* by Mervyn Brown (Damien Tunnacliffe, 1978, London). Meticulously researched and cross-referenced, this is also a delightful read, both panoramic in its scope and delicious in the detail. The author (himself a former British ambassador to Madagascar) clearly had great affection for the country, and has been scrupulously fair to its heroes and villains.

Another excellent history is provided by Nigel Heseltine in *Madagascar* (Pall Mall Press, 1971, London). Although strictly speaking an economist, Heseltine has a superb grip on the island's history, and seems to have burrowed deep into French sources. As a polymath, he also explores a bewildering array of other matters, from meteorology to geology.

More recently, there have been some interesting histories with a strong anthropological perspective. These make challenging reading, with some obscure jargon and unusual English (with words like 'indexicality' and 'presencing'). However, two stand out. First, *Madagascar: A short history* (Hurst, 2009, London) by Solofo Randrianja and Stephen Ellis, places slavery at the heart of Madagascar's story. Second, Zöe Crossland's *Ancestral Encounters in Highland Madagascar* (Cambridge University Press, 2014, New York) explains the enduring effect of the brutal campaigns of the Imerina kings in the eighteenth and nineteenth centuries.

Also worth a mention is Pierre van den Boogaerde's *Shipwrecks of Madagascar* (Eloquent, 2009, New York). Although intended as a reference for divers, it is exquisitely researched, and is a fascinating document. Among all the rust and wreckage, there are some remarkable tales of greed, ambition, trickery and, of course, calamity.

Madagascar's tribes

Professor John Mack provides a helpful layman's guide to the evolution and cultures of the island's eighteen tribes in *Madagascar: Island of the Ancestors* (British Museum Publications, 1986, London). This short volume is also magnificently illustrated. Rather longer, but equally well illustrated, is *Madagascar: The Red Island* (Winco, 1995, Leiden) by anthropologist Arlette Kouwenhoven.

There are some useful observations on the lives of the Vezo in Professor Rita Astuti's *People of the Sea* (Cambridge University Press, 1995, Cambridge).

Early travellers

In *A Relation of Three Years Sufferings of Robert Everard, upon the Coast of Assada near Madagascar, in a Voyage to India in the Year 1686* (1746), Everard describes an extraordinary ordeal. Only a boy when he left London, he was marooned on Nosy Be, and became a slave of its Sakalava king. His account of his captivity makes harrowing reading but is frustratingly light on names and dates.

Robert Drury, a Londoner, was also taken captive on the island. Shipwrecked on the south coast in 1703, he'd spend fifteen years as a slave of the Antandroy and later the Sakalavas. His account of that time, *Madagascar: or Robert Drury's Journal, During Fifteen Years Captivity on that Island* (W. Meadows, 1729, London) has often been regarded as a hoax, and yet the detail can only have come from someone who was actually there. An extraordinary tale of humiliation and hardship, Drury's account would inform our understanding of the island for the next two centuries.

Particularly enjoyable is *In Search of the Red Slave: Shipwreck and Captivity in Madagascar* (Sutton, 2002, Stroud) by archaeologist Mike Parker Pearson and anthropologist Karen Godden. Revisiting Madagascar several times during the early 2000s, the pair undertook a painstaking search for traces of Robert Drury (above). The authors provide convincing evidence that the events he described are true, and that his book is almost certainly a genuine account.

The Merina Empire and the British

Captain Lewis Locke, RE, was part of a diplomatic mission to the King of the Ovahs (or Merinas) in 1817. His report, 'An Account of the Ovahs, a Race of People residing in the interior of Madagascar' (*The Journal of the Royal Geographical Society of London* Vol. 5, 1835, pp. 230–242), offers a fascinating glimpse of Madagascan royalty at the peak of its power.

Despite its racy cover and title, Dr Keith Laidler's *Female Caligula: Ranavalona, the Mad Queen of Madagascar* (Wiley, 2005, Chichester) is a highly readable account of the despot's reign. While the author tends to focus on the intriguing details, the big picture is daunting enough. During Ranavalona's reign (1828–61), it is conservatively estimated that, thanks to her excesses, a third of the population perished.

Although Captain W. Rooke covered 40 miles of the Pangalenes canal system, his description of the journey is brief and curiously uninformative: 'A Boat-Voyage along the Coast-Lakes of East Madagascar' (*The Journal of the Royal Geographical Society of London*, Vol. 36, 1866, pp. 52–64).

In his introduction to *The Working of Miracles, Photography in Madagascar 1853–1865* (British Council, 1995, London), Simon Peers describes the intriguing world of the missionary-photographer William Ellis.

Madagascar under French rule

Edward F. Knight was sent out by *The Times* to cover the French invasion of 1895, and he would be one of the few journalists present at the capture of Antananarivo. But his account, *Madagascar in War Time* (Longmans, 1896, London), is equally fascinating for its descriptions of his journey. Dodging the French blockade, Knight walked over 500 miles to reach the doomed city, travelling through areas that were rebellious, dangerous and often unexplored.

A full account of the invasion is provided in Henri Galli's *La Guerre à Madagascar* (Garnier Frères, 1897, Paris), which is exquisitely illustrated with 121 engravings by Louis Bombled. The French army's deadly march across the island was also grimly documented by Dr Édouard Hocquard, the physician to the general staff. His journals would later be published as *L'Expédition de Madagascar* (Le Tour de Monde, 1897, Paris).

The French Foreign Legion 1872–1914 by Martin Windrow (Osprey, 2010, Oxford) has a useful section on the equipment and the units involved in the campaign. Some dark tales from the legionnaires themselves appear in Jean-Vincent Blanchard's *At the Edge of the World* (Bloomsbury, 2017, London).

A personal account of the 1895 revolt is given by Archdeacon McMahon in *Christian Missions of Madagascar* (SPG, 1914, London). Although primarily concerned with church matters, McMahon also describes his family's hair-raising escape from the mission station at Ramainandro. His earlier adventures are described in the Rev. George Herbert Smith's *Among the Menabe* (SPCK, 1896, London).

Among those travelling through colonial Madagascar was Miss Lucy Broad, who describes a remarkable bicycle ride in an article, 'A Thousand Miles a Wheel in Madagascar' (*The Wide World Magazine*, 1902). Her beautiful photographs portray a traditional society as yet unaffected by the arrival of the French.

Another intrepid female visitor was Olive Chapman, in 1939. Although this forty-seven-year-old widow undertook a journey of almost 3,000 miles, she was not a particularly effective writer, and *Across Madagascar* (Burrow, 1941, London) is surprisingly bland. Nonetheless, there are intriguing glimpses of French colonialism, which Chapman depicts as a veneer of civilisation on an otherwise simple and uncouth land.

More troubling are the adventures of Polish writer Arkady Fiedler. These days, *The Madagascar I Love* (Orbis, 1946, London) would never find a publisher, being too overtly racist. But it is perhaps a useful document, expressing the detachment and superiority that Europeans felt. Nowhere is this more obvious than in Fiedler's sexual antics, and in his bedding of teenage girls. As a chronicler of exploitation, he proves devious, obsessive and unnervingly honest.

John Grehan provides an exciting and meticulously researched account of the British capture of the island in 1942, in *Churchill's Secret Invasion* (Pen & Sword, 2013, Barnsley). The battle for Diego Suarez is also described in befuddling military detail in *The War in East Africa 1939–1943* (Pen & Sword, 2015, Barnsley), a compilation of reports from the top brass. A very readable précis appears in *Five Ventures* (HMSO, 1977, London) by Christopher Buckley. Another useful, if rather rosy, summary can be found in Sir John Hammerton's *The Second Great War, Volume 6* (Waverly, undated, London). The illustrations are excellent.

As to personal accounts of the war, the best is probably *The Blood-Red Island* (Staples, 1953, London) by the novelist Rupert Croft-Cooke, although by today's standards the tone is uncomfortably chauvinistic. A similar account is provided by K. C. Gandar Dower in *Into Madagascar* (Penguin, 1943, London). In *The Odyssey of an Animal Collector* (Longmans, 1954, London), Cecil Webb describes how he became trapped in Madagascar in 1939, and how a four-month expedition turned into a six-year sojourn. There is also a short section on Madagascar in Patrick Medd's memoir, *Taking in Sail* (Panama Hat, 1996, Harrogate).

There is very little on the revolt of 1947, despite the fact that up to 2 per cent of the country's population perished. Some interesting observations on the long-term effects of the trauma can be found in Jennifer Cole's *Forget Colonialism?* (University of California, 2001, Berkeley).

At the end of the colonial period, in 1958, Arthur Stratton (1911–75) called by. A distinguished war hero (twice awarded the Croix de Guerre), he was working for the CIA when he did his two tours of Madagascar. Travelling with silk shirts and a suit, he laments the departure of the French, and his account of his travels, *The Great Red Island* (Macmillan, 1965, London), is witty, occasionally outrageous and often wildly discursive. As one contemporary reviewer noted, 'The temptation to put in irrelevant facts is not resisted.'

The story of a French colonial family, the de Heaulmes, and their role from 1928 to the present day, is told with great charm by Alison Jolly in *Lords and Lemurs* (Houghton Mifflin, 2004, New York).

Finally, there is a detailed political, demographic and economic assessment of the island at about the time of independence in *The Malagasy Republic* (Stanford UP, 1965, Stanford) by Virginia Thompson and Richard Adloff.

Recent troubles

The upheavals of the 2000s have yet to be fully explored. Cole's *Forget Colonialism?* (above) offers an anthropologist's perspective on the resurrection of old fears and enmities. Tim Ecott, who was a reporter for the BBC, deftly describes the anarchy of Tana in 2001 in *Vanilla: Travels in Search of the Ice Cream Orchid* (Penguin, 2004, London).

Adventure

The last few decades have seen several excellent books describing the ordeal of Malagasy travel. Of all the writers, perhaps the best known is Dervla Murphy, who arrived with her teenage daughter in 1983. Together they ambled into the unknown, and covered vast tracts of wilderness by taxi. The result is *Muddling through in Madagascar* (John Murray, 1985, London), a hugely engaging tale of encounters and minor disasters. Rebellious, indignant and extroverted, Dervla Murphy is not to be ignored.

In *Dancing with the Dead: A Journey through Zanzibar and Madagascar* (Hamish Hamilton, 1991, London), British travel writer Helena Drysdale also takes on some of the remoter parts of the island. To begin with, she and her husband search for traces of her ancestors, who traded here in the nineteenth century. These parts of the book are beautifully researched, and Drysdale is momentarily enchanted. But as the couple head off into the interior, disillusion sets in as they are ground down by exhaustion, illness and disappointment. Although the underlying message is forlorn, this is a curiously engrossing read.

Next came Christina Dodwell. Compared to some of her earlier adventures, the trips she describes in *Madagascar Travels* (Hodder, 1995, London) are relatively tame. She stays with various 'smart friends', acquires a horse and gets into the racing. Nonetheless, there's still time for the odd wild foray, either in a rented stagecoach or with her inflatable canoe.

In around 2000, another Briton, Mark Eveleigh, set off to ride or walk some of the remote regions of western Madagascar, and the result is *Maverick in Madagascar* (Lonely Planet, 2001, Footscray, Australia). He makes an amiable companion as he and his eccentric guides (one wears a bulletproof vest) battle with heat, rain and needle-like seeds. For his first journey, he buys a *zebu* bull, and walks south through the Montagne d'Ambre range. For his second trip, he crosses the vast Bemaraha Valley and the '*zone rouge*', an area infested with dangerous cattle rustlers. Along the way, he absorbs the hopes, stories and superstitions of his Malagasy companions, providing a charming portrait of these remote regions.

Wildlife

Between 1993 and 1997, Peter Tyson visited a number of expatriate and Madagascan scientists around the island. In *Madagascar: The Eighth Continent* (Bradt, 2013, London), he describes their work and findings. The various chapters on how Madagascar acquired its curious population of animals and humans are fascinating, and the complex scientific issues are well predigested. Other sections, particularly those dealing with the politics of conservation, are somewhat specialist, and those who have only a passing interest may find themselves skimming parts of this very long (410-page) book.

Likewise, Jane Wilson's *Lemurs of the Lost World* (Impact, 1990, London) is relatively specialist. Although the tone is light, the author describes in great detail the research she and others undertook during two scientific expeditions in 1981 and 1986. Naturally, there is some fascinating science here. I particularly liked the *scolopendra* centipede ('one of the most ferocious fighting machines ever designed by Nature or Man'), which can not only bite and sting but can also inflict terrible wounds with every leg.

Although now very dated, David Attenbrough's *Zoo Quest to Madagascar* (Lutterworth Press, 1961, London) remains a favourite.

Gerald Durrell was also a regular visitor to the island, collecting specimens for his conservation projects. The attractions of collecting may have paled somewhat over the years, but Durrell remains indomitably jolly. *The Aye-aye and I* (BCA, 1992, London) describes his last Malagasy trip, from which he never recovered. Despite chronic arthritis, an outbreak of cerebral malaria and the death of his brother, nothing ever seemed to get him down.

A somewhat more improbable adventurer was the actress Joanna Lumley. After the success of 'Ab Fab', she spent nine days on the deserted island of Tsarabanjina, with only a TV crew for company. The photographs in her book, *Girl Friday* (BBC, 1994, London), look like swimsuit adverts, but this was no paradise. Life out on the islands, she discovers, is about sandflies, wet feet and hunger.

Guidebooks

Nobody knows Madagascar quite like Hilary Bradt and Daniel Austin, who, between them, have made dozens of trips and expeditions over the last few decades. The twelfth edition of *Madagascar: The Bradt Travel Guide* (Bradt, 2017, Chalfont St Peter) is easily the best guidebook available, and is particularly strong in its scientific sections. A new edition is due out in June 2020.

Madagascar and Comoros (Lonely Planet, 2008, Footscray, Australia) has nothing like the background material but it has some useful sections on the practicalities of travel.

Acknowledgements

Like all journeys, this one depended for its success on the generosity, wisdom and patience of a great number of people. Some, as I've explained, should remain anonymous, but my thanks go out to these individuals nonetheless. At the same time, I'd like to extend my gratitude to the following:

In Imerina and Antananarivo – Lydia and Avana Andrianarivony, who opened up their home to me in Soavimbahoaka, and who were endlessly generous with their hospitality and support; my palaeontology friend, Aro Ilon'aina Rakotondrabao; Hanta Randrianarimalala, who runs the girls' care home, Akany Avoko Faravohitra; Zohasina Razafinjatovo, formerly with the office of the *Secrétaire Général de la Présidence*; Simon Peers, the creator of the magnificent golden orb spiders' shawl, and his wife, Ange; Peter and Ros Metcalf, both veterans of Madagascar, and kind and fascinating hosts; Manitra Andriamialisoa; the ever efficient and charming Helen Fayd'Herbe of Domaine de l'Hermitage, Mantasoa; John and Catherine Butlin; Herizo Andrianandrasana, who is one of the country's most energetic conservationists; Lanto Robivelo of Famille d'Accueil de Madagascar; the Reverend Stéphane Rakotoniaina, the vicar of Ramainandro; former prime minister Jean Omer Beriziky, who kindly agreed to an interview, and his assistant, Onja Rasamimanana; Andry Ravelomanantsoa, city guide; Nivo Malala Ravelojaona of Za Tours; Gladys Zanafy; Philippe Rakotson, the 'heretical' pastor of Ambohimalaza; Viviane Rajaonarisoa, who runs delightful accommodation near the airport, called Amy House; the staff at the Sakamanga Hotel; Geoffrey Gorrie; Professor Michel Razafiarivony, rector at la Faculté de Théologie Anglicane at Ambatoharanana; Mireille Ranenoro, to whom this book is dedicated, and whose work for the Malagasy human rights commission, la Commission Nationale Indépendante des Droits de l'Homme (CNIDH), is both important and potentially dangerous.

On the east coast – Christian Fayd'Herbe de Maudave, who not only provided me with some remarkable insights into the island over the last eighty years but was also a generous and highly entertaining host; Louis Aubert Dieudonné Raholiniaina, in the port of Tamatave (or Toamasina); Fidelys Raharimandimby, *Président Conseil d'Administration* at Tamatave's tourist office; the historian Solofo Ranrianja; the Hotel Acacias in Manambato, and my Malagasy-Chinese friend, Alain Ah Hu Carron Daso; Solofo Razafimahazo, my guide to the Perinet reserve in 2004; Elianne Marie Blanc of Elidolysmada, who arranged my travel through the Pangalanes canal.

In the north – Jeannet Trazanamiarana, my driver in Diego Suarez, for whom nothing was too much trouble; Rudy Larcher of Nosy Be; Philippe Barratier of Le Suarez Hotel.

In the west and Isalo – Mme Laurence Ink, who runs the wonderful Hôtel Entremer in Belo sur Mer; 'Coco' the guide, on the Isalo Massif, and the kind and thoughtful staff at the Hôtel le Relais de la Reine, one of my favourite roosts in the country.

In Fianarantsoa – Sister Sabine Rahasinoro of the Leprosy Treatment Centre at Marana.

In Australia – Sigrid McMahon and Allison Cameron, who provided help with the story of Edward McMahon , and for their kind introductions.

In Japan – Professor Taku Iida of the National Museum of Ethnology, for his help and advice in relation to the Vezo people.

In Holland – Dr Ben Appelmelk of the Vrije Universiteit, Amsterdam, who provided me with some invaluable materials on the bubonic plague in Madagascar.

In the USA – Craig Handfinger; Stephanie Sang, a Peace Corps volunteer, who kindly introduced me to her colleague in Nosy Be.

In England – The committee and members of the Anglo-Malagasy Society and – in particular – Julian Cook, Chris Brown and Daniel Austin, who have provided invaluable support and advice on all aspects of my journey; Ben Morison of Far and Wild; Camilla Swift at *The Spectator*; Andrew Purvis at the *Daily Telegraph*; John Hall for his introductions to the wonderful Fayd'Herbe family; Michel Fayd'Herbe; Dr David Mann and Dr Tamsin Booth, both of whom have served at the Good News Hospital, Mandritsara; Dr Gavin Bowd of St Andrew's University; Nigel Richardson; Joel Louis; Bob Dewar; Sydney Chawatama; Rob Lane of the Royal Navy, who was indefatigable in helping me try to track down veterans of the Battle of Madagascar (1942); Mike Pinchen of the Royal Marines Association (and the biographer of veteran Ray Tebble); Anthony Wynn; Ken Elam; Nick Syfret QC; Tim Butcher; Steph Allen of Eland Books; Tim Ecott, author of a fascinating Madagascar-related tale, *Vanilla*; Al Harris of Blue Ventures; Guy Outhwaite; Colin Cunliffe of Ribchester; the author and naturalist Gehan de Silva Wijeyeratne; Mark and Lee Taylor; Irenee Rajaona-Horne of Money for Madagascar; my sister, Philippa Gimlette, and my brothers, Edward and Matthew.

I'm also hugely grateful to Rainbow Tours (www.rainbowtours.co.uk), and their indefatigable Derek Schuurman. They provided highly effective and generous support for parts of these travels. Some of the episodes in this book first appeared – in a rather different form – in *The Spectator* and the *Daily Telegraph*.

As to the writing and production of this book, I'm also indebted to Daniel Austin for fact-checking the draft manuscript; there is probably no one in the UK who knows Madagascar better. Thanks too to Gaëlle Richards for her comments on the text; to Yvonne Bunn for logistical support, to my agent Georgina Capel, to Richard Milbank at Head of Zeus and to his assistant, Anna Nightingale. I also extend my special thanks to my father, Dr T. M. D. Gimlette, for all his help and encouragement, and for his invaluable suggestions on the draft manuscript. I am only sorry that my mother, Ruth Gimlette, did not live to see this book published, having been so supportive and enthusiastic during its early stages.

Finally, there's my wife, Jayne, and daughter, Lucy. As usual, they've borne with great patience my long periods of absence (both in Madagascar and the attic). I couldn't have done any of this without Jayne, who, once again, has been a tireless source of inspiration and encouragement. I was delighted when she and Lucy agreed to join me for a few weeks in Nosy Be, and I know I repaid them miserably with some very un-holiday-like activities (such as investigating the issue of child abuse). To their credit, however, they've shared and nurtured my enthusiasm for this remarkable country. To both, my gratitude therefore comes, as always, with all my love.

Index

prostitution 26, 31, 45, 46, 95, 203, 235, 236, 285, 302, 330, *331*, 332, 334, 357, 419, 420, 430
Protestants 24, 39, 138, 283, 421
pygmy hippo 63, 64

Quakers 202, 212, 274
Queen's House, Mantasoa ('The Black Versailles') 216–17, *216*
Queen's Palace (*Rova d'Antananarivo*), Antananarivo 19, 27, *28–9*, 32, *189*, *196*, 197–203, 198, 206, 207, 210, 218, 220, 222, 223, 224, 237, 239, 269, 286, 414, 415, 428, 449

Rabenoro, Mireille 5, 36–7, 117, 285–6, 412, 420, 429
Radama I, King 198, *199*, 200–3, 204, 206, 207, 214, 447
Radama II, Ling 217, 219, 220, 223–5, 226
railways 286, 295, 296, 310–11, 314–15, *316–17*, 328, *378*, 380, *383*, 385–6, 385–91, *386*,*388–9*, *390*, *391*, 395–6, 409, 443
Rainilaiarivony, Prime Minister *224*, 225–6, 228–9, 254, 263–4, 266, 273
Rajaofetra, Paul 275, 278
Rajaonarimampianina, Hery 427–8, 443
Rajoelina, Andry 424, 425, 426–7, 428, 429, 443–4, 448, 449
Raketa 146
Rakontondrabao, Aro 37, 38, 39, 40, 41, 55, 56, 92, 191, 232, 241, 254, 281, 435, 436, 442, 449
Rakoto, Rahanta 9, 36, 439, 442
Ramainandro *234*, *274*, 275–6, *277*, 278, 279
Ramillies 360, *370*, 372, 373, 375
Ranavalona I, Queen 206–7, 209, 211, 212, 213–22, 224, 227
Ranavalona II, Queen 226
Ranavalona III, Queen 209, 226, 227, *227*, 264, 269, 270, 272–3, 274–5
Randrianarimalala, Hanta 212–13
Randrianja, Solofo 13–14, 47, 187, 212
Ranohira *101*, 122
Ranomafana *378*, 382

Ratsiraka, Didier 410, *411*, 412, 413–15, 421, 422, *423*, 424, 448
Ratsiraka, Sophie 421
Ravalomanana, Marc 416, 421, 422, 424–5, 426–7, 428, 446, 447
Ravoahangy 398, 404
Razafinkarefo, Andriamanantena (Andy Razaf) 254
Relais de la Reine *101*, 120
Réunion 93, 110, 138, 195, 253, 394
revolts: Revolt of the Red Shawls (*menalamba*) (1897) 274–81, 335; (1947) 377, 392–5, 396, 398–9, *400*, 401–5, 406
rickshaw (*pousse-pousses*) 97, 381, 385, 406, 409
Rollet, Lieutenant (later, General) Paul-Frédéric 332
rotaka (1972) 407
Rozhestvensky, Vice-Admiral Zinovy 'Mad Dog' 337–45, *344*
Rudolf (boatman) 308–9, 310, 311
Russia 219, 343, 345, 412, 413, 428, 444
see also Soviet Union

Sakalava 35, 46, 47, 52, 57–98, 104, 108, 109, 110, 112, 113, 114, 120, 121, 124, 130, 168–9, 211, 241, 245, 260, 270, 275, 321, *324–5*, 326, 330, 332, 345, 357, 422, 444
Sakamanga ('Blue Cat') hotel, Antananarivo 26–7, 31, 32, 37, 41, 42, 443
Sakatia Island *320*, 346
Samuel, Abraham 140, 160, 165–6
sapphires 125, 128, 129, 420, 437
savannah 52–3, *52*, *53*, 61, 68, 73, 77, 80, 84, 112, 114, 117, 120, 121, 125, 129, 130, 185, 202, 206, 211, 232, 245, 248, 254, 260, 405, 406
savoka (scrawny woodland) 61, 297, 404
schooners 90, 93, 94, 95, 96, 105, 235, *236*, 326
Second Pacific Squadron, Russian 337
Second World War (1939–45) 358–9, 392; Operation Ironclad 358–76, *375*
sex 13, 88, 90, 92, 109, 113, 139, 178, 179, 204, 214–16, 330, *331*, 332, *333*, 334, 357